Idea and Ontology

Idea and Ontology

AN ESSAY IN EARLY MODERN METAPHYSICS OF IDEAS

MARC A. HIGHT

THE PENNSYLVANIA STATE UNIVERSITY PRESS
UNIVERSITY PARK, PENNSYLVANIA

Library of Congress Cataloging-in-Publication Data

Hight, Marc A., 1969–
Idea and ontology : an essay in early modern metaphysics of ideas / Marc A. Hight.
p. cm.
Summary: "Provides an interpretation of the development of the ontology of ideas from Descartes to Hume that reaffirms the vital role metaphysical concerns played in early modern thinking"—Provided by publisher.
Includes bibliographical references and index.
ISBN 978-0-271-05877-1 (pbk : alk. paper)
1. Ontology.
2. Idea (Philosophy).
3. Metaphysics.
I. Title.

BD301.H54   2008
110.9—dc22
2008002466

Copyright © 2008 The Pennsylvania State University
All rights reserved
Printed in the United States of America
Published by The Pennsylvania State University Press,
University Park, PA 16802–1003

The Pennsylvania State University Press is a member of the
Association of American University Presses.

It is the policy of The Pennsylvania State University Press to use
acid-free paper. This book is printed on stock that
meets the minimum requirements of American National Standard for
Information Sciences—Permanence of Paper for Printed
Library Material, ANSI Z39.48–1992.

For ICT and SNJ
and
IN MEMORY OF RENÈE ELIZABETH HIGHT
(1968–2006)

CONTENTS

Acknowledgments xi

List of Abbreviations xiii

Introduction:

Idea Ontology and the Early Modern Tale 1

1 THE TRADITIONAL ONTOLOGY 11

1.1 Substance 12

1.2 Modes 20

1.3 What Is an Idea? 22

1.4 Stretching Idea Ontologies 34

2 DESCARTES 37

2.1 Representation 38

2.2 Perception, Ideas, and Images 41

2.3 Innate Ideas, Dispositions, and Causes 47

2.4 The Complications of the *Passions* 51

3 THE CARTESIANS: MALEBRANCHE AND ARNAULD 55

3.1 Malebranche's Theory of Ideas 56

3.2 Substantializing Ideas 61

3.3 Attacking Modes 66

3.4 A New Ontology? 70

3.5 Arnauld's Theory of Ideas 72

3.6 Critique of Malebranche 75

3.7 The Cartesian Debate 78

4 LOCKE 79

4.1 Locke "Deontologized" 81
4.2 Lennon's Locke 88
4.3 Locke's Contemporaries 94
4.4 Locke's Implicit Ontology 99

5 LEIBNIZ 116

5.1 Resolving a "Tension" 117
5.2 Ideas as Dispositions 120
5.3 Reading Leibniz 121
5.4 Ideas: Being One vs. Having One 124
5.5 Innate Ideas 126
5.6 Difficulties with Dispositions 129
5.7 Ideas as Modes 136

6 BERKELEY 138

6.1 Minds and Ideas 139
6.2 Ideas as Objects 141
6.3 Ideas as Modes 148
6.4 Qualities 155
6.5 Unperceived Existence 159
6.6 Phenomenalism 161
6.7 Berkeley and the Early Modern Tale 172

7 DIVINE IDEAS 177

7.1 Divine Ideas and Archetypes 178
7.2 "In" the Mind of God 181
7.3 Permutations 189

7.4 Defending Berkeley's Theory of Divine Ideas   193

7.5 Fleeting Ideas   209

8   ABSTRACTION AND HETEROGENEITY   218

8.1 Abstract Ideas   218

8.2 Kinds of Abstraction   219

8.3 Berkeley's Attack   223

8.4 Berkeley's Solution: General Ideas   231

8.5 Perceptual Heterogeneity   233

8.6 The Molyneux Thought Experiment   236

8.7 The Argument from Difference in Content   237

8.8 Adding Visible and Tangible Lines   238

8.9 Heterogeneity and the Nature of Ideas   240

8.10 Ontology to Heterogeneity   241

9   HUME AND IDEA ONTOLOGY   246

9.1 Perceptions as Substances   248

9.2 Dependent Perceptions   258

9.3 Concluding Remarks: The Demise of the Early Modern Tale   265

References   269

Index   275

ACKNOWLEDGMENTS

Work on this book was generously supported by a Mednick Memorial Fellowship through the Virginia Foundation for Independent Colleges and several Summer Faculty Research Grants from Hampden-Sydney College. During the course of writing the book I incurred many debts to colleagues and scholars. I am grateful in particular to Robert Muehlmann, Daniel Flage, Tom Stoneham, Michael LeBuffe, Tom Lennon, and several anonymous referees whose comments and discussions have improved the quality of this endeavor. I owe a special debt of gratitude to Ian and Diana Tipton, who in the summer of 2004 provided me with a place to stay, excellent food, and days of stimulating discussion about matters early modern.

Some parts of the book are based on earlier publications of mine. Parts of chapter 4 are based on "Locke's Implicit Ontology of Ideas," *The British Journal of the History of Philosophy* 9, no. 1 (2001): 17–42. Section 6.6.1 is based on "The New Berkeley," with Walter Ott, *Canadian Journal of Philosophy* 34, no. 1 (2004): 1–24. Portions of chapter 7 draw on my "Defending Berkeley's Divine Ideas," *Philosophia* 33, nos. 1–4 (2005): 97–128. Sections 8.5–8.10 are based on "Why We Do Not See What We Feel," *Pacific Philosophical Quarterly* 83, no. 2 (2002): 148–62. All of these materials are used with the gracious permission of the journals, and I express my gratitude to them for their use.

ABBREVIATIONS

Full bibliographic information may be found in the reference list. References to works that employ paragraph or section numbers (e.g., most of Berkeley's works) are to those paragraph and section numbers; otherwise, they are given by volume and page number. Thus "*PHK* 49" refers to Berkeley's *Principles of Human Knowledge*, par. 49, and "*CSM* II:120" refers to *The Philosophical Writings of Descartes*, vol. II, p. 120. The following abbreviations have been used for various primary source texts cited in the book, sorted by author. (Note: Because the Nidditch edition of Hume's *Treatise* has been replaced by the newer Norton edition, I also provide references to the Norton for the convenience of readers.)

Arnauld
    TF   *On True and False Ideas*

Berkeley
    IPHK   *Introduction to the Principles of Human Knowledge* (vol. 2 of *The Works of George Berkeley*)
    MI   *George Berkeley's Manuscript Introduction*
    NTV   *An Essay Towards a New Theory of Vision* (vol. 1 of *The Works of George Berkeley*)
    PC   *Philosophical Commentaries* (vol. 1 of *The Works of George Berkeley*)
    PHK   *The Principles of Human Knowledge* (vol. 2 of *The Works of George Berkeley*)
    S   *Siris* (vol. 5 of *The Works of George Berkeley*)
    TVV   *The Theory of Vision Vindicated and Explained* (vol. 1 of *The Works of George Berkeley*)
    3D   *Three Dialogues Between Hylas and Philonous* (vol. 2 of *The Works of George Berkeley*)

Descartes
    CSM   *The Philosophical Writings of Descartes*, vols. I and II
    CSM/K *The Philosophical Writings of Descartes*, vol. III

Hume
- N   *A Treatise of Human Nature*, ed. David F. and Mary J. Norton
- T   *A Treatise of Human Nature*, ed. L. A. Selby-Bigge, revised by P. H. Nidditch

Leibniz
- G   *Die philosophischen Schriften von G. W. Leibniz*
- L   *Philosophical Papers and Letters*
- NE   *New Essays on Human Understanding*
- PE   *Philosophical Essays*
- SSB   *Samtliche Schriften und Briefen*

Locke
- ECHU   *An Essay Concerning Human Understanding*
- EM   "An Examination of P. Malebranche's Opinion of Seeing All Things in God" (vol. 2 of *Locke's Philosophical Works*)

Malebranche
- DMR   *Dialogues on Metaphysics and Religion*
- LO   *The Search After Truth*, with *Elucidations of the Search After Truth*
- OC   *Oeuvres complètes de Malebranche*

Spinoza
- CWS   *Collected Works of Spinoza*

INTRODUCTION:
IDEA ONTOLOGY AND THE EARLY MODERN TALE

Traditional metaphysics has not fared well since its glory days in the early modern period. Gone is the fascination with developing an ontology that can account for our experiences in the world. Cartesian dualism, Leibnizian monads, Berkeleian immaterialism, and similar metaphysical investigations have been replaced by discussions of language, confident assertions that epistemology alone is first philosophy, and pronouncements that ontology is dead. Hilary Putnam has even delivered a talk in a distinguished lecture series entitled "Ontology: An Obituary" (2004, 71–88). It is not that metaphysics is no longer studied or held in *historical* esteem; rather the guiding assumption today seems to be that we have advanced far enough to recognize that ontology is an exhausted—perhaps useless—enterprise. It seems we have nothing left to learn from ontological speculation and metaphysical system building.

Whence this antimetaphysical attitude? John Heil argues that an implicit adherence to a Wittgensteinian picture theory is to blame, but I suspect the roots are spread more broadly and deeply.[1] The dominant view is that ontology has relatively little to offer contemporary philosophers. The early moderns generally had robust, rich ontologies, but this robustness became an embarrassment when it was discovered that no ontology appeared to fit well with the powerful new theory of ideas. Here we find a historical pedigree for contemporary antimetaphysical views. If one wants to undercut the importance of metaphysics and ontology, then pointing to historical developments that support this attitude can be a potent tool. This is, in fact, precisely what has been happening. Early modern scholarship (often unconsciously

---

1. "My contention is that metaphysics as it has been conceived at least since Kant has been influenced by an implicit adherence to a Picture Theory of representation" (Heil 2003, 5).

influenced by contemporary thinking) had, so the argument goes, developed strains of thought bent on establishing the primacy of epistemology by the time philosophers like Berkeley became active. Thus one lesson that history is supposed to teach us is that, between the time of Descartes and Berkeley, the early moderns learned that ontology could not provide the answers we seek about the world. The point is made by targeting the concept most vital to all of these discussions: that of an idea. If the early moderns abandoned ontology with respect to ideas (so that we need not ask ontological questions about them because they are idle or do not apply), then today we are on firmer ground setting aside metaphysics and ontology generally. A story has thus been developed and told so often that it is now routinely thought of as the traditional view of what transpired in the early modern period. I call this *the early modern tale*.

The tale told about seventeenth- and eighteenth-century philosophy runs roughly as follows. Descartes broke free of the fetters of Scholasticism by simultaneously advancing a new mechanistic theory of the physical world and a new concept of the mental that relegated many of the features of ordinary experience to the mind. To facilitate the latter move, he reached up and brought ideas down from the heavens—historically, ideas had been understood to be purely divine entities—and applied them to finite creatures in the mundane world. Ideas thus spread in meaning to cover thoughts, images, concepts, and sensations. Ideas played *the* crucial role in early modern epistemology; to discover how they functioned and represented the world was to discover the mechanism by which everything could be known. The new way of ideas promised scientific access to a universe the old Aristotelian system could not imagine, much less explain. But alas, as the story goes, the new system did not work. The way of ideas was a poor fit with the traditional ontological categories of substance and mode. Descartes and his earliest followers did not completely grasp this fact. There were good reasons both for denying that ideas could be modes of the mind and for denying that ideas could be substances. In light of this, subsequent thinkers, though following Descartes' lead, slowly eroded the Cartesian metaphysical framework. The promise of idea philosophy was too strong to be fettered by ontological chains. At its core, Descartes' philosophy still adhered to the traditional substance/property ontology of its predecessors.[2]

---

2. On my account, "traditional ontology" includes both the ancient substance/property distinction *and* the narrower "Cartesian" substance/modification division that developed from it. I see the Cartesian ontology as a natural outgrowth of Aristotle's own ontology and therefore regard it as "traditional."

Thus when the Cartesian system began to break down, its ontology did as well. Yet perhaps its most crucial element, its theory of ideas, flourished, and it dominated the philosophical scene long after the heyday of Cartesianism.

Why did idea philosophy flourish when its ontology was allegedly faltering? Our early modern tale tells us that advances in the philosophy of ideas led the moderns not only to reject the old ontology *but also to abandon ontology altogether with respect to ideas.* This is not to say that ontology in general was abandoned. Yet ideas in particular were not deemed susceptible to ontic analysis because they had no ontological status at all. Thus scholars like Richard Watson and John Yolton argue that the main figures of the early modern period undermined the exclusive and exhaustive nature of substance and mode.[3] Here is one representative example of the tale in action, as told by Yolton:

> *The point of this last remark* [made by Locke in reply to Norris] *is that Locke did not consider ideas to have an ontological status;* he wanted to concentrate upon their role in perception and knowledge. Having Malebranche's theory as an example of a theory that gave to ideas an ontological status, Locke had a twofold reaction: he rejected Norris's attempts to fit ideas into the standard ontological categories of substance or mode, and he stressed the cognitive, awareness features of ideas. The language of "having ideas" is identified with being aware, with perceiving.[4] (1984, 94, emphasis in the original)

What it *means* to deny that ideas have an ontological status is a matter open for discussion and analysis. What matters for the present is that this tale is being told at all. Locke allegedly starts the assault on substance by attacking our conception of it. Perhaps the problem with characterizing the nature of ideas lies with the very notions we have about ontological categories. Substance is, in Locke's famous phrase, an "I know not what." Locke is not merely setting aside a discussion of ontology in the *Essay Concerning Human Understanding;* according to the early modern tale, when it comes to ideas, he is *abandoning* it. Most scholars, of course, do not jump immediately to this radical conclusion. But its basic thrust pervades a lot of the work done

---

3. Some moderns use the term "accident" instead of "mode." I will use "mode" or "modification" exclusively for clarity and consistency. See Yolton 1975, Yolton 1984, Yolton 1985, Yolton 1996a, and Watson 1987.

4. For Locke's comments on John Norris, see Acworth 1971.

on the early moderns. If Locke does not abandon ontology for ideas, he is at least pointing us in that direction. Thus D. J. O'Connor writes: "In Berkeley's words, he [Locke] 'bantered [i.e., challenged] the idea of substance' and though he himself did no more than point the way to his successors, the traditional theory never recovered from the attack which he led" (1967, 73). O'Connor himself does *not* take the step of alleging that Locke abandoned ontology with respect to ideas. Yet even in accounts that deal squarely with the ontologies of various early modern philosophers, there is an undercurrent that pushes one to think either that the ontology is of historical interest only or that it is being scrutinized solely for the purposes of revising its emphases to give it more contemporary relevance. This undercurrent may be felt more keenly with respect to the nature of ideas. Thus even where the presence of the early modern tale is not explicit, its influence often lurks nearby.

The famous immaterialist George Berkeley is the key to the early modern tale. He denies that we can have any reasonable conception of material substance and his own ontology of ideas allegedly reveals either that the way of ideas reduces to epistemology alone or that the modern penchant for ontology is sadly, if imaginatively, misguided. Some ascribe roles to other philosophers (most notably Hume), but once Berkeley is folded into the tale the story is essentially complete. Hume's primary contribution in this context is that he continues the story already implicit in Berkeley's system. To use Yolton's expression, ideas in the early modern period are "deontologized" by the time we reach Berkeley.

The problem, however, is that the early modern tale is actually a *fairy* tale. The early moderns did *not* abandon ontology when it came to their reasoning about the nature of ideas. They preserved an idea ontology. Asserting that there must be an ontology of ideas does not imply, however, that there were no tensions between the way of ideas and the traditional substance/mode ontology. The friction between the epistemological roles of ideas and their ontic status is one of the key elements driving developments in metaphysics in the modern period. A core traditional ontology was never abandoned but instead occasionally "stretched" owing to the new pressures that the introduction of ideas brought to bear on it. This work aims to establish that the early moderns remained committed to a more or less traditional ontology with respect to ideas and that reading the early moderns as idea ontologists results in better philosophy and more accurate history.

What, then, was the early modern conception of ideas that our key figures—philosophers such as Descartes, Arnauld, Malebranche, Locke, Leibniz, Berkeley, and Hume—inherited, and how did it contribute to the destabilization of the substance/property (mode) ontology without leading to its abandonment? What were the effects of this interplay between ideas and the traditional ontology? These questions frame this project and lead to its conclusion. I discuss this "breakdown," first by exploring the nature of the traditional ontology and then by examining how select philosophers, emphasizing Berkeley, struggled to place ideas within it. In the end, I conclude that the moderns did not abandon the substance/mode ontology for ideas. The radicalization of early modern metaphysical systems (the adoption of more unusual metaphysical positions, like immaterialism and Humean skepticism) is attributable primarily to the poor fit between the epistemological roles played by ideas and the substance/mode ontology. This radicalization, however, is evidence of how the moderns sought to *retain* the traditional ontological categories, even if their attempts were not always successful. Hume's work demonstrates the point, since he embraced much of Berkeley's thinking about the nature of ideas but could not avail himself of Berkeley's unusual solution. The moral is clear: insofar as one wants to understand early modern thinking, especially about ideas, one *needs* to use the traditional ontological distinctions as a framework. The lesson is especially true for Berkeley, who will correspondingly take center stage in this study; it is also true, to a lesser extent, for Hume, with whom this study will conclude.

In order for this endeavor to make sense, we first need to explore the basic concepts and categories I employ. I start with an analysis of substance and mode as used by the moderns.[5] Created substances (God is a special case) have to satisfy two key requirements: *endurance* and *independence*. Any entity that endures and underlies change without requiring any other kind of thing to exist is itself a substance. Modes are dependent modifications of substances. The analysis in the first chapter is important not only because it frames the discussion of subsequent chapters but also because it helps identify clues that will reveal whether a given philosopher treats ideas as substances or as modes. The issue is not always clear. Many historians of philosophy have sought to replace the language of substance and mode with talk about reification. Although the concept of reification is perhaps useful for some contemporary discussions, I argue that it is not when one is seek-

---

5. One might wonder about a potential third category, relations. Locke, for instance, talks about three kinds of complex ideas: modes, substances, and relations (*ECHU* II.12.3). Relations, however, do not constitute a fundamental *ontological* category for the early moderns. Relations are a kind of *complex* idea reducible ultimately to substance(s) and mode(s).

ing to determine the ontological commitments of early modern philosophers.

The main part of the book offers a careful discussion of a select history of the ontology of ideas in the early modern period. This select history in turn is divided into two large sections. The first, mainly exegetical, part engages the perceptual theories and theories of ideas of Descartes and the early Cartesians. They are foundational figures in the development of the ontology of ideas and are not generally alleged to have abandoned ontology with respect to them; instead, they did important work in this area, work with which later philosophers were familiar. The inconclusive confrontation between Malebranche and Arnauld over the ontology of ideas led Locke and even contemporary commentators today to take the unusual step of sidestepping questions about ontology with respect to ideas. My task in these chapters is only to be clear about what these theories of ideas were and what sorts of problems confronted them; the aim is to provide a context for our more pressing analyses of later theories of ideas. Therefore it is not my intention to give a systematic history of the philosophy of ideas but only a history relevant to the development of the ontology of ideas.

Our first important early modern figure is of course Descartes, whose philosophy of ideas I engage in the second chapter. Descartes is important not only because he introduces the concept of idea that most of the moderns will essentially adopt but also because he has a rather difficult time fitting this concept of idea into his ontology. Descartes initially flirts with views that make ideas rather like corporeal substances. The problems with this early position are sufficiently obvious that he later adopts the familiar theory that makes ideas modes of the mind. Ultimately he endorses the interesting position that all ideas must be innate to the mind. The tangle of problems he leaves is inherited by the first generation of Cartesians, especially Malebranche and Arnauld, whose views I examine in the third chapter. The famous dispute between Malebranche and Arnauld over the status of ideas is all the more intriguing because both of them otherwise claim to be good Cartesians. The nature and quality of their arguments occupy my attention for most of the chapter, although I am forced to conclude that neither achieves a clear victory in their dispute.

The discussion through Arnauld sets the stage for the second part of the historical investigation, where I really begin to make my case for an ontological reading of the early moderns. Starting with the fourth chapter, which concerns Locke, I argue that key early modern figures remained committed to a traditional substance/mode ontology with respect to ideas. To this end,

I employ both textual and philosophical arguments, since I also hold that, ceteris paribus, readings that make the early moderns both historically plausible *and* philosophically stronger are to be preferred.

Locke is our first central figure in the early modern tale, for it is with him that many advocates of the early modern tale believe that we can see the start of the "abandonment" of ontology with respect to ideas. In particular, I engage such scholars as Thomas Lennon and John Yolton, who argue that Locke has an exclusively epistemological understanding of ideas. In the fourth chapter I argue that although Locke did want to set aside certain questions of ontology, he nonetheless had an underlying implicit ontology of ideas. There are formidable textual and philosophical reasons for thinking that Locke reasoned within the confines of a substance/mode ontology even as he consciously preferred to explore issues more connected with epistemology than ontology. My analysis places considerable emphasis on the much-neglected "An Examination of P. Malebranche's Opinion of Seeing All Things in God," where Locke engages Malebranche and John Norris. I conclude that Locke does not abandon ontology with respect to ideas and thus cannot play the role allotted to him in the early modern tale.

I have elected not to include a chapter on Spinoza, primarily because he is not considered a vital figure in our fairy tale. Spinoza's striking metaphysics dominates the rest of his philosophy and leaves little doubt that ideas—whatever their roles—are ultimately grounded in the ontology of substance and mode. In *Ethics* II-D3 Spinoza tells us, "By idea I understand a concept of the Mind that the Mind forms because it is a thinking thing."[6] In the explanation he goes on to point out that all ideas involve mental activity (which is why he says "concept" instead of "perception"). Spinoza also distinguishes the idea from its object (*ideatum*), preserving the Cartesian distinction between objective and formal reality. Ideas are a particular kind of mode of the one substance, God. The distinction between an idea and its object (and other uses to which Spinoza puts the term "object") makes the analysis cloudy and difficult, but for my purposes here the core claim is not controversial: Spinoza does not contribute to the early modern tale nor am I aware of anyone who has attempted to make a case for his inclusion in it (*CWS* 1:447).

Like Spinoza, Leibniz generally has not been considered a vital figure in the development of the way of ideas. Recent work on Leibniz, however, has introduced novel understandings of his theory. Benson Mates and Nicholas

---

6. See Kashap 1978 and Wilson 1996, esp. 89–96.

Jolley in particular have each argued on separate grounds that Leibniz thinks of ideas as mere dispositions.[7] Although their analyses (rightly) do not push them to argue that Leibniz's theory of ideas lies outside of the traditional ontology, the possibility remains that one *might* so argue. Therefore I engage in some preventative analysis in the fifth chapter by examining Leibniz's theory, demonstrating that his innovations with respect to ideas remain within the traditional ontology.

The most important of the early moderns for this study is Berkeley, and thus his philosophy takes center stage. Trumpeted by several scholars as representing the final break from the traditional ontology of ideas, Berkeley is often said to be the key philosopher who completes the transition to epistemology as first philosophy. Such scholars do not assert that Berkeley lacks a metaphysical system; instead, the claim is that Berkeley's theory *of ideas* liberates them (ideas) from the confines of ontology entirely. Consequently it is particularly important to resist the trend in contemporary scholarship toward the early modern tale with respect to Berkeley.

In the sixth chapter I seek to establish that although Berkeley did stretch the traditional ontology of substance and mode by introducing a new category for ideas, he did so as part of an attempt to *preserve* that basic ontology. Careful investigation of Berkeley's texts reveals that he thinks that ideas are *like* modes in that they are essentially dependent beings but that they are also like substances insofar as they are distinct from the minds on which they depend without being modifications of them. They thus have characteristics of *both* substances and modes, requiring the positing of a new hybrid ontological category I call quasi substance. Mine is, of course, a controversial reading of Berkeley that has important consequences for the rest of his philosophical system. Nonetheless, I argue that there is significant textual and philosophical evidence that pushes the careful reader of Berkeley to this conclusion.

In order to more thoroughly defend this reading of Berkeley's theory of ideas, I explore some of its consequences. In the seventh chapter I apply this understanding of ideas to his much-maligned theory of divine ideas, demonstrating that there is a plausible and textually consistent reading of the theory. Divine ideas, like ideas generally, are quasi substances in that they depend on the mind of God for their existence but also are nonetheless distinct from (i.e., not a part of) God's mind. This move allows Berkeley to employ the theory of divine ideas to solve a wide range of problems, espe-

---

7. See Jolley 1990, esp. 132–35, and Mates 1986, esp. 171, 246.

cially those concerning our perception of a continuous and unfragmented world, without it producing disastrous conflicts with the rest of his metaphysics. Given the demands of philosophical charity and the benefits that emerge from my reading, I conclude that we have excellent evidence to read Berkeley in this way.

The eighth chapter takes up two additional important features of Berkeley's metaphysics and applies my new interpretation of his ideas to them. First, I seek to reconcile his theory of ideas with his rejection of abstract ideas. When we understand that Berkeley considers ideas to be distinct from minds but also dependent on them, we discover a new and more compelling reason for him to dislike abstraction. Abstract ideas, again like ideas generally, must be entities that exist in a two-place relation with the mind. Thus, in one important sense, ideas are "external" to the mind. They are neither modes of the mind nor parts of it. As such, abstract ideas are particular entities. Berkeley holds the not unreasonable view that *all* particulars must be fully determinate. That is, for every property, a particular existing thing must either have that property or its complement. There are no such things as particular objects that are indeterminate with respect to their properties. As a result there can be no such things as abstract ideas, which are described by Locke and others as ideas (things) that are indeterminate with respect to at least one property. Thus my reading of Berkeley has the additional virtue of providing a more charitable understanding of Berkeley's resistance to the existence of abstract ideas.

Second, and still in the eighth chapter on Berkeley, I engage his controversial heterogeneity thesis. Berkeley alleges that we do not see the very same objects we feel. More generally, the objects of any one particular sense modality are different in kind from those of every other sense modality. The moderns, however, inherited the concept of common sensibles from Aristotle, where one particular object is perceived by multiple sense modalities. Berkeley accordingly denies what was a commonly held and intuitive position about sensible objects. The main oddity surrounding the heterogeneity thesis is not the veracity of the claim itself but instead why Berkeley came to be such an apparently passionate advocate of it. Here I provide an explanation that again relies on the (ontological) nature of ideas developed in chapters 6 and 7. After considering and rejecting the main rival accounts, I argue that Berkeley's overidentification of the content of ideas with their ontological status explains the depth and certainty of his conviction that ideas are heterogeneous.

The ninth and final chapter examines Hume's ontology of perceptions.

Frequently read as abandoning the concept of substance, or as at least relegating the concept to the bin of meaningless terms, Hume is often placed alongside Berkeley as a philosopher who "deontologized" ideas. Like Locke, Hume was not specifically interested in many ontological themes; nonetheless, that his focus was elsewhere does not entail that he thought ideas lacked an ontological foundation. Contrary to the anti-ontological tradition, I argue that Hume fairly straightforwardly thought of perceptions as traditional substances. That said, he also believed that the notion of substance was conceptually thin. That is, learning that perceptions are substances does not do much work in any philosophical system. I maintain that Hume was driven by the same sorts of concerns as Berkeley and demonstrate that he never abandoned the traditional ontological categories with respect to perceptions. Reading Hume as a philosopher minimally sensitive to certain metaphysical concerns actually helps us make better sense of his recantation in the appendix of the *Treatise* and helps us resolve other textual difficulties in his philosophy. My engagement of Hume is admittedly controversial but arguably provides him with a more consistent and plausible system.

The lesson from our extended engagement with Berkeley and Hume is twofold. First, neither Berkeley nor Hume can properly be understood outside the constraints of their ontological commitments. And because of their ontological commitments neither can play their assigned role in the early modern tale. Each is a philosopher thoroughly in the grips of the early modern ontology. Berkeley is most clearly a traditional idea metaphysician, despite developing an unusual hybrid ontological category. Second, an unreflective adherence to the early modern tale may blind us to some of the insights of the early moderns, obscuring these thinkers' philosophical power. In particular, accepting the tale makes it more difficult to be charitable to them, especially Berkeley, in a historically sensitive way. The early moderns are of both historically antiquarian *and* genuinely philosophical interest. Diligently pursuing the moderns charitably reveals in a particularly clear way the poverty of the early modern tale.

I

THE TRADITIONAL ONTOLOGY

Philosophers in the seventeenth and eighteenth centuries operated within a substance/property ontology, narrowed to a substance/mode distinction, inherited from Aristotle via the Scholastics. Thus to ask after the ontological status of ideas among the early moderns is, at least initially, to ask where ideas fall within this traditional classification. Unfortunately, the issue is not as easy as asking whether particular individuals treated ideas as substances or as modes. The substance/mode ontology was "breaking down" in the early modern period under the stress of difficulties generated by theorizing about the nature of ideas, and this makes it hard to delineate conceptual categories easily. Nonetheless, I argue that the early moderns adhered to a *core* conception of substance (and modification) that remained essentially consistent over time. Motivating this claim is a principal aim of this chapter. I am not arguing that there was only one conception of substance *in general*; there were, in fact, substantial variations. Yet all these variations were supported by two core features. When I refer to the "traditional" conception of substance I intend *only* these minimal criteria.

Initially, the substance/mode distinction employed by the early moderns was rigid, exhaustive, and exclusive.[1] According to that model, whatever is not a substance is a mode, and vice versa. Leibniz is particularly clear on this point, taking as an obvious premise in an argument concerning transubstantiation that "[w]hatever is not substance is accident or appearance" (*L*, 116). Apparently the premise is so self-evident as not to require any justification at all. Descartes likewise deftly reduces the universe to substances and modes, arguing that universals and numbers fit the model (*CSM* I:210–12;

---

1. As I subsequently argue in chapter 6, Berkeley stretches the ontology such that it becomes decidedly less rigid and exclusive, although it remains identifiably traditional.

Principles I:52–58, esp. 58; *Principles* I:58). Spinoza, using the Euclidean geometrical method, even makes the exhaustive nature of the distinction an axiom. "Whatever is, is either in itself [i.e., a substance] or in another [i.e., a mode]" (*CWS* 1:410, I-A1).[2] We should expect, then, that ideas are either substances or modes. What it actually means, however, for an idea to be a substance or a mode is not obvious; this necessitates my laying out the conceptual geography of substance and mode before engaging some of the issues that surround the question of what ideas actually are.

1.1 Substance

Aristotle writes in the *Categories,* "A *substance*—that which is called a substance most strictly, primarily, and most of all—is that which is neither said of a subject nor in a subject, e.g. the individual man or the individual horse" (2a12–13). The essential thought behind this definition is the notion of substance as a *thing.* Here he means "thing" in the sense that a horse and a table are things, whereas wisdom and irritability are not. The key feature Aristotle highlights is *endurance:* that which survives and underlies change without itself changing or is able to have contrary properties at different times without sacrificing its identity. A wise but irritable man is still a man, even if he becomes less sagacious and more pleasant. "It seems most distinctive of substance that what is numerically one and the same is able to receive contraries. In no other case could one bring forward anything, numerically one, which is able to receive contraries" (4a10–12). Substances are also importantly the subjects of predication, the "this" that receives and supports qualities and in which change is registered. In a basic sense, Aristotle's notion of substance is equivalent to that of particular "thingness," where substances ultimately underlie everything. This *Categories* conception of substance is the one adopted by the early moderns, even though Aristotle did attempt to clarify his understanding of substance in the *Metaphysics* by introducing the notion of substantial forms (Frede 1987, 73–80). The early moderns, however, did not typically follow the later complications of the *Metaphysics* (one might think Leibniz a partial exception). The changes introduced by Aristotle need not concern us, for even if Aristotle did change his mind about what he had originally thought were clear cases of sub-

---

2. For my parenthetical insertions, see *CWS* I-D3 (why "in itself" means a substance) and *CWS* I-D5 (why "in another" means a mode).

stances, his essential conception of substance did not undergo significant revision (Frede 1987, 78–79).

Substances, as particulars, are "thises." Universals, on the other hand, are "suches." Things are said of substances, or are "in" them, and Aristotle most often uses this conception to classify things as substances. Immediately, however, a complication arises. A genus frequently can be predicated or said of its species. For instance, we can say of dogs that they are animals, thus making the kind "dog" technically a substance. Aristotle calls these substances "secondary." "The species in which the things primarily called substances are, are called *secondary substances*, as also are the genera of these species. For instance, the individual man belongs in a species, man, and animal is a genus of the species; so these—both man and animal—are called secondary substances" (2a15–18). Secondary substances are those of which other things are predicated (making them substances) but are also themselves predicable of other things. The key difference between primary and secondary substance, then, is that only primary substances are not predicable of anything. This distinction allows things to be substances so long as something is predicated of them and underscores the point that Aristotle's main concept for substance is the "thing-thought." Nonetheless, when the moderns referred to substance simpliciter, they nearly always meant primary substance only, and thus, despite Aristotle's distinction, qualifications were added to the core notion of substance that ultimately excluded secondary substances from being genuine substances.

In particular, it was thought that the notion of substance was meant to capture more than mere thingness. Aristotle can sometimes be read as confirming this as well. I believe that part of the problem arises from an intrinsic ambiguity in how the word "thing" is used. We use the word, as it were, on different "levels." Consider the following example I borrow from William Kneale (1939, 105). The Athenian state is a thing in colloquial usage. But it is also a substance given Aristotle's definition. The state is not predicable of anything else nor present in anything else. (This analysis assumes, plausibly, that states are not *identical* with their organizations or their citizens. The nonidentity prevents one from arguing that a state is predicable of an aggregate of persons, although as we will quickly see, states might be otherwise dependent on them. Leibniz might be seen as denying this nonidentity when he argues that armies are simply aggregates of soldiers, but the point is preserved since Leibniz does not think armies are substances.)[3] Nonetheless,

---

3. See Leibniz's letter to Arnauld of 30 April 1687 (*PE*, 86).

I suspect Aristotle might not have been comfortable with this result. Certainly those who followed him were not. The problem is that "thing" in Aristotle's most basic sense implies nothing more than that which endures through change.[4] Since change can occur on many levels of analysis, there will be many different levels of things. One might want to deny that the Athenian state is a substance because, although it is a thing, it is not a *basic* thing. Arguably, states depend on their citizens and perhaps their laws for their existence. Thus the concept of "state" can be further analyzed. In a real sense, therefore, it is not ultimately "thingy," as changes occur "underneath" it. The citizens, on which the existence of the state depends, change, both as a collection and individually, thus casting doubt on the supposition that states are substances. Aristotle himself seems to support this analysis with one brief remark: "It is because the primary substances are subjects for everything else that they are called substances most strictly" (2b38–3a1). The moderns took this problem seriously and in effect were seeking to deny that secondary substances are genuine substances at all.

A second element is therefore crucial to a proper understanding of substance. In addition to *endurance,* one needs *independence.* The nature of the independence of substances may be expressed in several ways. Some early moderns used simplicity while others relied on a causal notion of independence. The most common move, however, was to attach the notion of ontological independence to substance. All of these variants are trying to capture that feature that separates primary from secondary substances. Thus we should not be surprised to see some philosophers endorsing more than one expression of the independence thought. Leibniz, for instance, tries to articulate the independence thought both in terms of simplicity (aggregates cannot be substances) and causality (substances are causally independent of all other things). Typically these views are not mutually exclusive.

Consider first the most typical understanding of independence as ontological independence. If x is ontologically dependent on y, then it is necessary that y exists at all times that x exists. If an idea is a modification of a substantial mind, then that particular idea is ontologically dependent on that mind. Mental modes do not exist without the minds they modify. A child, however, is not *ontologically* dependent on its parents for its existence, even though the child may be *causally* dependent on them (more on causal dependence shortly). Something is ontologically independent when it

---

4. Some might insist it implies nonpredicability as well, but that is true only of primary substance. Part of the reason for allowing secondary substances to be substances at all is to account for the intuition that there are "levels" of thinghood, an intuition I engage shortly.

requires nothing other than itself in order to exist (at a time). By extension, a substance is a thing that requires nothing else for its existence. When we turn to examine Descartes' descriptions of substance, one can detect both the "thing-thought" and the independence criterion in play. "By *substance* we can understand nothing other than a thing which exists in such a way as to require nothing else to exist."[5] Substances are *things* that are ontologically independent. What he means is made clearer when he argues that the word "substance" applies multivocally to God and created substances. Technically, the only genuinely independent substance is God, but since created substances depend only on God, for human purposes they are otherwise independent in the requisite sense. Even Locke, who emphasizes the thingness of substance more than most, weds a notion of independence to substance as well. The following are typical of his descriptions of substance:

> Because, as I have said, not imagining how these simple *Ideas* can subsist by themselves, we accustom ourselves, to suppose some *Substratum,* wherein they do subsist, and from which they do result, which therefore we call *Substance.*

> The *Idea* then we have, to which we give the general name Substance, being nothing, but the supposed, but unknown support of those Qualities, we find existing, which we imagine cannot subsist, *sine re substante,* without something to support them, we call that Support *Substantia;* which, according to the true import of the Word, is in plain *English, standing under,* or *upholding.* (*ECHU* II.23.1, 2; II.23.2)

Locke's conception of substance is clearly one that is closely tied to that of a substratum; substances are the unknown *supports* for qualities. Such a conception is one of endurance—there must be some *thing* that persists to underlie, support, and unify the qualities we perceive. Locke stresses this understanding of substance, yet when he describes the nature of these supports about which we do not know much, all he says is that they satisfy the independence criterion: "The *Ideas of Substances* are such combinations of simple *Ideas,* as are taken to represent distinct particular things subsisting by

---

5. I read "require" instead of Cottingham's "depends on" for "*indigeat*" (*CSM* I:210, *Principles* 51).

themselves" (*ECHU* II.12.6).⁶ Thus, even though I grant that Locke concerns himself primarily with the thingness of substance (substratum account), he recognizes the necessity of independence. At least created substances are independent supports of qualities.

As hinted earlier, simplicity is often used to capture independence, since ultimate simplicity guarantees that the "thing" being considered will be of the lowest level. Generally, this version of independence is thought of in terms of part-whole relations. Thus Leibniz writes:

> It also seems that what constitutes the essence of a being by aggregation is only a mode of the things of which it is composed. For example, what constitutes the essence of an army is only a mode of the men who compose it. This mode therefore presupposes a substance whose essence is not a mode of a substance. Every machine also presupposes some substance in the pieces of which it is made, and there is no plurality without true unities. To put it briefly, I hold this identical proposition, differentiated only by the emphasis, to be an axiom, namely, *that what is not truly* one *being is not truly one* being *either*. (*PE*, 86, emphasis in original)

Substances must be unities, or ultimate simples, to truly exist. Independence here is garnered through irreducible simplicity. The thing-thought remains, but only simple things are genuine substances.

Descartes would seem to challenge the idea that only simple things are bona fide substances since he takes matter to be a substance yet attributes infinite divisibility to it. But since it is matter "all the way down," we actually never reach a lower (logical) *level* for the parts. Recall that in his definition of a substance, matter qualifies because it requires nothing *other than itself* to exist. For matter, parts are parts, and all parts are essentially homogeneous in their properties except for those associated with size and motion, and those are only accidental. In the synopsis to the *Meditations*, Descartes suggests that matter is a substance but only when considered as a whole (when "taken in a general sense" [*CSM* II:10]). I submit that the main issue for Descartes was not simplicity per se but rather the need for a continuant. Matter underlies change as a whole, regardless of how far down one needs to go to get an appropriate explanation. The need for ultimate simplicity in

---

6. See *ECHU* II.12.4, where he distinguishes modes from substances in virtue of the fact that the former cannot subsist by themselves.

the notion of substance grew out of inadequacies in the Cartesian program. So, returning to our analysis, if a substance is not a unity, then it is not a thing of the lowest level, and it depends in some sense on its constituent parts. Now I say "in some sense" as ontological dependence is not the only one invoked by the moderns. At least one philosopher prefers to marry the narrower conception of causal independence to the notion of substance instead of the broader notion of ontological independence. Causal dependence concerns the *nature* of being rather than the brute fact of existence itself. A stone I placed on a table might be causally dependent on me for its current state even though it is not ontologically dependent on me (for its existence per se). Thus philosophers who emphasize causal dependence are imposing additional restrictions on the nature of substance, restrictions that specify the nature of the (in)dependence of the item in question.

Leibniz, as we have seen, defends the view that substances are partless unities but denies that mere *ontological* independence is sufficient to capture independence on the grounds that such a view drives one to Spinozism. God is the only substance that can be thought of as truly ontologically independent (despite Descartes' protests that this still leaves room for created substances). This recognition in turn might lead one to conclude that God is the only substance and humans are but modifications of Him. On the other hand, Leibniz protests, if we accept Descartes' suggestion and restrict substance to created things, then we might have to admit that other things that seem ontologically independent yet ought not to be considered substances are in fact substances.

> For example, active force, life, and antitypy [the resistance of matter to penetration, associated with solidity] are something essential and at the same time primitive, and one can conceive of them independently of other concepts, even of their subjects, by means of abstractions. Subjects, on the contrary, are conceived by means of such attributes. Yet these attributes are different from the substances of which they are attributes. So there is something which is not at all substance, yet which cannot be conceived as any more dependent than substance itself. Hence this independence on the part of its concept is not at all the mark of substance, since it must apply also to what is essential to substance. (*L*, 620)

Leibniz's replacement is causal independence. He defines substance as "being which subsists in itself" but explains that by "subsists in itself" he means "that which has a principle of action within itself" (*L*, 115). That is, substances are those things that determine their own states of being. Hence if a thing is such that it requires no external cause for its being, then it is a substance.[7] Interestingly, Leibniz has a precedent for this view, namely Aristotle's doctrine of the unmoved mover (which is a substance for Aristotle, though not the only one). Substances are uncaused generators of activity, and this eventually gets translated into causal independence.

Note that, according to Leibniz's analysis, there are no material substances (recall our earlier problem of classifying Descartes' conception of matter). Since matter is essentially divisible, there can be no lowest level of thingness for bodies. This claim happens to correspond with the equally telling point that no particular body can be causally independent, bodies being nothing more than aggregates dependent on their smaller parts for their properties. The analysis here underscores the fact that some believed that ultimate simplicity captured the independence thought. Every substance is indivisible and simple. For Leibniz, this means that genuine substances lack parts, that is, they are the *most* simple things (*L*, 526; see also *L*, 344). Although Leibniz's description of the requirements for substancehood stands out as among the most clear, virtually every philosopher in the seventeenth and eighteenth centuries shared the conviction that *endurance* (thingness) and *independence* complete the minimal concept of created substance. Hume, at the end of the early modern period, reveals the persistence of the conception when he describes what he takes the common understanding of a substance to be in his own era: "My conclusion from both is, that since all our perceptions are different from each other, and from every thing else in the universe, they are also distinct and separable, and may be consider'd as separately existent, and may exist separately, and have no need of any thing else to support their existence. They are, therefore, substances, as far as this definition explains a substance" (T, 233 / N, 153 [1.4.5]). Perceptions are independent and endure.[8] In light of these features, Hume tells us that, according to the understanding of his contemporaries, perceptions (which for Hume includes ideas and impressions) are therefore substances. The *core* traditional conception of a substance remains remarkably consistent.

An important caveat must be inserted at this juncture. As I have noted

---

7. If we are being careful, that there is no external cause for being might perhaps only be a necessary condition for substancehood. Leibniz, however, apparently thinks it sufficient as well.

8. One might worry that Hume's conception of perceptions makes them fleeting and hence *nonenduring* beings. Such a concern is unfounded. I address the point explicitly with respect to Hume in section 9.1.3.

without emphasis above, the traditional conception of a substance in fact primarily applies to *created* substances. There are two obvious possibilities for complication. First, one might object that endurance is a temporal notion. God, a per se substance, typically does *not* satisfy the endurance criterion. God is an eternal, atemporal being and hence does not persist through change in the requisite manner. Endurance, however, can be construed more broadly as simply some kind of continuant underlying change. Even if we stipulate a "God time," such that the entirety of human existence occurs within an instant of God time, there remains a sense in which God endures relative to our judgments. Independently, as Descartes notes, God is thought of as a special case separate from considerations that apply to created substances. Since the issue concerns the ontology of ideas and ideas are created things, we can restrict our analysis to the created world without doing violence to early modern understandings of ontology. Second, some early moderns have conceptions of even created substances that might make them atemporal as well. Berkeley, for instance, defines time in terms of a succession of ideas, placing even created substances like minds outside the human temporal order. Again, in these cases the endurance criterion arguably nonetheless applies, given that there is still something that underlies the changes that take place with respect to the substance (the mind). Even if time is identified with the changes in ideas a mind perceives, there is nonetheless some continuing thing that "remains." Such cases are difficult primarily because little careful attention is paid to these kinds of complications by our historical authors. Berkeley's theory of time, for instance, is not well developed with respect to the rest of his philosophical system. What is important to keep in mind here is that the endurance criterion is not strictly a *human* temporal requirement, even if some sense of temporality is otherwise necessary.

If in fact most early moderns share this minimal *core* conception of substance, this is not to say no one ever sought to narrow or enrich this understanding. Two additional points are worth mentioning here. First, philosophers in the Platonic tradition emphasize immutability over (or in addition to) endurance. For instance, Malebranche characterizes ideas as immutable archetypes in God, following Augustine. Yet despite the perceptible shift in emphasis, the underlying *core* conceptions of substance are roughly the same. Some form of endurance and independence must be preserved. A second consideration is what I call "epistemic priority." Some argue that our knowledge, or understanding, of substance is epistemically prior to our understanding everything else. Descartes explicitly endorses this view, arguing that modes cannot be understood without adequate knowledge of the substance in which they inhere (*CSM* I:213–14). Modal distinctions are unintelligible until we have knowledge of the substance that underlies the modes in question.

1.2 Modes

From Descartes onward, philosophers narrowed the substance/property distinction until it became a substance/mode distinction. In terms of the ontological status of existents, everything is either a substance or a modification of a substance. Later this dichotomy would not be strictly exhaustive, but it consistently frames modern discussions of ontology. As a result I am going to restrict my analysis here to modes as counterparts to substances. Now that we have a more detailed characterization of substance, we can define a mode both negatively and positively. An entity is a mode if it is not a substance. More helpfully, we usually find mode defined as a state or modification of a substance. Descartes writes in *Principles* I:56: "But we employ the term mode when we are thinking of a substance as being affected or modified" (*CSM* I:211). He does not seem to explicitly recognize here the possibility that modes can affect or modify other modes. Since substances are only *independent* things, it follows that modes can be things as well, just not independent ones. Thus we ought not to think of modes in opposition to substances qua things but in opposition to substances qua *independent* (often simple) things. In *Principles* I:64, Descartes continues: "If, on the other hand, we attempted to consider them [modes] apart from the substances in which they inhere, we would be regarding them as things which subsisted in their own right, and would thus be confusing the ideas of a mode and a substance" (*CSM* I:216). Confusing a mode with a substance produces the Scholastic concept of a real quality, an impossibility to Descartes since there is nothing (i.e., no substance) through which one can conceive such an entity (see *CSM/K* III:216–17).[9] The independence criterion is paramount in separating modes from substances.

An immediate point of clarification is required. The moderns differentiated between modes and attributes. Descartes tells us that we ought to think of modes as qualities that inhere in substances. Attributes are special kinds of qualities that are often identified as essential modes. Not all attributes are

---

9. For the separation between the Cartesian and Suarezian theories of mode, see Glauser 2002, esp. 427–40.

modes, but when they are, they are *essential* modes. Extension is an attribute of matter since every bit of matter must have extension.[10] It is unintelligible to think of matter as not being extended, that is, as not being modified in that manner. Whereas most qualities are thought of as contingent (a bit of matter might be red or not), attributes are essential. Descartes rightly tells us in *Principles* I:56 that God does not have qualities but rather only attributes, emphasizing that none of God's modes is contingent or accidental (*CSM* I:211). Spinoza even explicitly links essence with attribute. "By attribute I understand what the intellect perceives about a substance, as constituting its essence" (*CWS* 1:408, I-D4).[11] Despite the special nature of attributes, they nonetheless are subject to the same conceptual limits as modes. They depend on substances for their being, even if their dependence is perhaps less striking than modes generally. Attributes are more *inter*dependent with their substances, since they are essential to them. Hence one cannot find a substance without its attribute. Modes, by contrast, are utterly and asymmetrically dependent on the substances in which they inhere.

In general, the moderns thought of mental modes along the lines of physical modes. Authors frequently spoke of inclinations and sensations as modes of the mind because such things were thought of as activities where the mind is in a certain state. Hence motion is a mode of physical objects, and particular instances of sensing might be called modes of the mind or soul (see, e.g., *LO*, 2–3 [1.1]).

Yet this analogy, even if appropriate, does not tell us much about what modes actually are. There are two competing understandings of modes among the moderns, but I am interested here in preserving a core sense that is neutral between the two. First, drawing from the Platonic tradition, one might think of a mode transcendentally; on this approach, a mode is like a kind of universal. A red ball participates in the universal red, but the red "in" the ball is not a separate particular thing. Nonetheless, the mode is

---

10. Some might think this confusion, but the moderns are fairly clear and frequently use the terms "mode" and "attribute" in the same breath. This is true even of the empiricists. Consider Berkeley at *PHK* 49: "[S]ince extension is a mode or attribute, which . . . is predicated of the subject in which it exists." Attributes are conceived as special kinds of modes here. Descartes is more straightforward about the relation between mode and attribute, even seeking to disambiguate them because they are frequently used together. "We must take care here not to understand the word 'attribute' to mean simply 'mode,' for we term an 'attribute' whatever we recognize as being naturally ascribable to something, whether it be a mode which is susceptible to change, or the absolutely immutable essence of the thing in question" (*CSM* I:297).

11. The translation is mine, adapted from Curley's. Spinoza's conception of attribute is the one least identifiable (directly) with modes but nonetheless preserves the important distinction between them (attributes are essential, modes are not).

dependent on the ball for its particular being. Redness is a thing, but redness itself is not a mode; it is a substance. Only *instances* of redness are modes. Second, one might think of modes immanently as more like particular individuals. This latter view is certainly the dominant one for the moderns. The red in the ball is like a quality instance and is also utterly dependent on the substance for its being. On either interpretation modes are dependent beings, even if they are things.

Assuming we have a solid conception of what substances and modes are, we can now ask after the status of ideas. We are fortunate in one important respect when it comes to determining whether ideas are substances or modes; there are a few indicators. Naturally the most obvious one is how inclined an author is to treat ideas as mind independent. The more independent ideas are, the more substance-like they are. Additionally, we can look to see whether a given philosopher takes perception to be a monadic property or dyadic relation. In dyadic relations the relata are distinct and usually (but not always) thought of as independent of one another. Hence the relata are thought of as substances. When taken to be monadic properties, ideas are treated as modes. How one speaks of perception thus often reveals what one thinks about the status of ideas. When coupled with the issue of dependence, the conceptual territory surrounding the nature of ideas is familiar and well trodden. We also know one pitfall to avoid: using thing talk as an indication of a particular ontology. Simply because an author speaks of ideas as or like things is a poor guide to his metaphysical views, for both modes and substances can properly be called things. Substances are *independent* things; modes are *dependent* things.

1.3 What Is an Idea?

When determining the ontological commitments of a philosopher in the seventeenth and eighteenth centuries the first question one should ask is where ideas fall within the substance/mode spectrum. Since everyone purported to believe in the generally exclusive and exhaustive nature of the ontology, at first glance one ought to *expect* that ideas will be either modes or substances. Although the early moderns had a reasonably stable core conception of substance and mode, difficulties persistently arise when philosophers attempt to fit ideas into this ontology—the obstacles that bar our understanding are serious enough that many scholars have sought to impose different conceptual distinctions on the early moderns in an attempt to clear up some of the confusions. One distinction in particular warrants close inspection. We might ask the deceptively straightforward question of whether a given philosopher reifies ideas. Another question, related to this one, is whether and to what extent the philosopher treats ideas as objects, either of the understanding or of perception. Here the analysis focuses on the nature of the perceptual relation posited by the philosopher, from which conclusions about his understanding of ideas are derived. We must be wary, however, since both questions, whatever their clarity in a contemporary context, often cannot be directly applied to the early moderns with the aim of trying to determine the ontological status of ideas in their philosophical systems. Let me be clear: it is often fruitful to ask these questions, but their value has been overestimated in application to the early modern period, occasionally resulting in muddied analyses. Accordingly we antecedently need to be clear about what these distinctions are and what we might be able to expect from their use.

1.3.1 Reifying Ideas

The temptation to divide the early moderns into reifiers and nonreifiers is particularly powerful.[12] Developments in twentieth-century theories of perception, especially sense-data theories, make the distinction intuitive and compelling. To reify an entity is to treat it as a *res*, a thing. The term is generally applied to mental or abstract entities. Thus one reifies numbers or appearances (sense data) by treating them like material things.[13] Common sense, we are frequently told, instructs us that chairs, cherries, and children are things while wisdom and irritability are not. To treat wisdom or moods like chairs or cherries or children is to reify them.

Contemporary philosophers tend to have a sharper conception of what constitutes a thing than did the moderns. Ever since W. V. O. Quine's influential paper "On What There Is" (1980, 1–19), philosophers have typically defined a "thing" as that over which one quantifies. This characterization is neat and clean. If one can quantify over something, on some level it exists. Quine's criterion for thinghood is flexible, allowing for the domain of things to be tiered and to take into account that there can be "levels" of things.

---

12. To provide just one example relevant to the context of this book and the early modern tale, consider Thomas Lennon's observation that "This [inferring factual thing-claims from appearance claims] seems to me precisely the reification, or ontologizing of ideas, that Yolton has tried to preserve Locke from" (2004a, 327).

13. See the *Compact Oxford English Dictionary*, 2nd ed. (1994), s.v. "reify" and "reification."

The domain of "things" remains the same and the variables keep the same meanings even as the predicates change. We can quantify over modes or states of being as well as over individual substances and call them all things in a perfectly clear sense. Unfortunately, that sense is not shared by the early moderns, and so discovering that someone reifies ideas is often patently unhelpful. Knowing that an idea is a thing in this minimal sense does little to fix its ontological status and role in the larger theory. In particular, it does not distinguish between substance and mode, since both were routinely taken to be things.[14] Nor does it reveal what level of thing an idea happens to be. Even if we grant that the Athenian state is not a substance but a thing, nevertheless the state is importantly distinct from bricks and atoms, even though we can quantify over all of them.

Perhaps most tellingly, the distinction between reifying and not reifying ideas lacks *genuine* clarity when applied to the early moderns. We might be clear about those who reify ideas, but what would be the status of ideas for those who do not reify them? No suitable contrast class exists.[15] If ideas are not things in the sense that we cannot quantify over them, then their status is decidedly murky. Sometimes those who employ this distinction claim that the alternative is to treat ideas as modes. Yet we have already seen that this is *not* a proper contrast class. Modes are things too. We quantify over thoughts and colors as well as buildings and bricks. What about the initial and admittedly intuitive distinction with which we started? We treat children and cherries as things but not wisdom or irritability. Given our powerful sense that something is wrong with reifying moods, there must be *some* kernel of a genuine distinction here. And indeed there is, though the issue is not one of thinghood. Consider Jonathan Bennett's enlightening discussion of why it is wrong to reify moods and sense data (1971, 31–35).[16] First, one ought to note that Bennett starts out with the same sort of intuition that I do. He says, "Of course there are moods. I was in a bad mood this morning, and my mood changed around noon. Still, one hesitates to say that there are such *things* as moods—it seems wrong to reify moods" (32). Bennett offers two justifications for his claim. First, statements about moods

---

14. Consider Leibniz, who in his commentary on Descartes' *Principles* takes Descartes to be treating ideas (qua modes) as things (L, 390).

15. I am ignoring attempts to apply a Meinongian distinction between existence and subsistence, first because it is obviously foreign to the early moderns, and second because Meinong's distinction is not between things and nonthings, but between existing things and nonexisting things.

16. Bennett modifies this analysis but preserves the relevant point for this discussion in *Learning from Six Philosophers* (2001), 2:8–12, secs. 158–59.

are statements about being *in* moods. Thus there is no sense of moods *being* things. Second, statements about moods are equivalent to nonrelational statements about persons. He gives the example that "He is in a good mood" is equivalent to "He is cheerful and friendly." The contrast is thus between existence and nonexistence. When we reify, we are claiming that something exists. Therefore we ought not to reify moods because they can be reduced to other things that do exist, and there is no need to posit a new entity, a "mood." The analysis here is good, but perhaps less than compelling. Bennett presents a straightforward case, but not all statements are like these. Consider the statement, "Those two are in the same good mood." This is not reducible to "He is cheerful and friendly, and the other fellow is cheerful and friendly." It is unclear that being in a "good mood" entails the same properties for everyone. I might be in a good mood when not friendly because I am not generally friendly. Of course there are possible responses to this and similar concerns, but I am only concerned to note that the issue is not one easily decided. I am not interested here in dwelling on Bennett's reductionist contention, which even if mistaken is nevertheless interesting and does seem to capture an important point about how we talk about moods. Still, even granting that we can reduce statements about moods to nonrelational claims, I submit that Bennett has not quite put his finger on the underlying issue. Consider his first justification. Why does Bennett believe it is important to say that statements of moods are statements about being *in* moods? I suggest that what is worrying Bennett (and others) is that moods do not exist apart from people. We say "in" to express the *dependence* of moods.[17] The problem is not in treating moods as things but as *independent* things. Moods do not satisfy the independence criterion for substancehood. It is difficult to separate thing talk from substance talk and I speculate that our hesitancy about reifying moods stems from our conflating substantiality with mere thingness. Bennett's second justification buttresses my case. One feature of nonrelational states (as indeed of all states) is that they do not exist without a subject. Again, the issue here is one of substantiality and not thingness. Moods for Bennett are states, and since states, like modes, are dependent things, they are not things simpliciter. He helpfully notes, "Does it follow that we cannot say about moods anything of the sort we can say about things? It does not. Moods are states; and states, like things, can be owned and clocked and compared with one another" (32). I

---

17. This point will become especially important when we discuss Berkeley (see section 7.2), who uses "in" to express the ontological dependence of ideas on minds without implying that ideas are modifications of the mind.

agree. Yet a better approach is to admit that moods and states *are* things, just not primary substances (i.e., simple things), which would explain the parallels. Moods and states do persist through change and we can quantify over them. Thus they are things. In short, Bennett's reasoning is absolutely sound, but he fails to draw a deep enough lesson. My point is that we often *think* asking the reifying question draws clear lines when in fact it does not. The issue here is one of substantiality (the distinction between substances and nonsubstantial beings) and not mere thinghood.

One might object that good scholars do not anachronistically apply Quine's criterion for thinghood to past theories. But even if we were to resist the temptation to read the moderns as Quinians—using instead the traditional endurance conception of thinghood when trying to understand their conception of ideas—we would still not yet be free of problems. Precisely because the term "thing" ranges over levels of dependence on other entities, it is often difficult to separate the traditional thing-thought (the notion of endurance underlying change) from that of independence (including simplicity). Even today when we accuse someone of reifying we most often conjoin the two. Thus Plato reifies forms (ideas), and we are especially confident in this case since the forms have both endurance and independence. In other words, if someone treats ideas as substances, then he or she clearly may be said to reify them. But the rest of spectrum is less transparent. We can have modes as well as modes of modes. Hence a color might have hue or brilliance. Certain modes thus underlie change and are reified while others do not and thus are not reified. Yet what are we to say about the philosopher who treats ideas like modes in both senses (such that some modes are reified and others are not) or who does not see that he needs to distinguish between the two? The category simply does not allow for clear conceptual divisions.

More to the point, on this accounting, philosophers who do not reify ideas apparently commit themselves to the position that ideas do not underlie change. We might attribute this view to some early modern philosophers (perhaps Berkeley) but certainly not all. Descartes' official position treats ideas as modifications of minds. Does this mean that he thinks that his idea of red cannot underlie changes of hue or brilliance? Such a claim appears dubious. Once one is clear about the two contrast classes, the thing-nonthing distinction loses its appeal. Only when we can blur the lines by adding the independence criterion does the use of reification as a conceptual tool seem promising.

Another compelling worry emerges when we try to find someone attempting to provide criteria for determining when a philosopher does in fact reify ideas. Suspiciously, this task has proven rather difficult. Aside from someone generously telling us that he or she is reifying ideas (in a sense that does not amount to substantializing them), there are no conclusive indicators that a person reifies. In most cases, philosophers who use this distinction do not even bother to list the characteristics they take to be indicative of reifiers. Ian Tipton attempts to provide a definitive list, but his commitment to his own criteria does not inspire confidence (1986, 577). He provides three signs that someone *might* be reifying. First is the tendency to construe the notion of "presence to mind" spatially. Secondly, there might be an inclination to push hard the mirror model (camera obscura) of perception. Finally, we might expect reifiers of ideas to use imagistic talk in describing ideas. None of these, however, is a dependable indicator, and the last Tipton himself describes as "rather unreliable." We ought to be on our guard when asked to classify theories and philosophers without any clear set of criteria. In this case, I doubt that any such illuminating set exists.

1.3.2 *The End of Ontology?*

I have, up until this point, ignored one possible interpretation of the distinction between those who reify and those who do not. Some have argued, most notably John Yolton and Richard Watson, that the distinction ought not to be thought of within ontological or metaphysical bounds at all.[18] One might think instead that to reify ideas is to commit oneself to the notion that ideas have an ontic status and to avoid reifying ideas is to *deny* that ideas have ontic status.[19] I question, however, whether we can conclude anything about the ontological status of ideas for an early modern philosopher simply on the basis of an absence of reifying talk. Something minimally has an ontic status provided that one can quantify over it. We require this broader contemporary understanding in order to follow possible moves that the early moderns might make when thinking about the traditional ontological categories of substance and mode. Trying to deny that ideas have an ontic status, however, is both conceptually confusing and simply mistaken.

I nonetheless suspect that many will find the motivation for denying that ideas have an ontic status compelling. Trying to join ideas, theories of representation, and the traditional substance/mode ontology is painful at best.

---

18. See Yolton 1996a, esp. 1–19; Yolton 1984, 100–103; and Watson 1987, 109.
19. See Lennon's remark cited in n. 12 of this chapter.

Despairing of finding a way to reconcile their theories of ideas with this ontology, philosophers like Watson make the interesting argument that several early moderns rejected the notion that ideas have any ontic status at all. Others, like Yolton, are less clear about embracing this alternative, but careful analysis reveals that they do in fact endorse a similar view. Yolton originally argues for this thesis primarily with Locke in mind,[20] but in later work he extends it to Berkeley as well (1984, 132–44, 181–201). His analysis starts with an attempt to free Locke from the charge of representationalism. For Locke, an idea is not some tertium quid in perception. Instead, Yolton emphasizes that ideas are not "entities" at all: "[B]ut on the Locke-Arnauld concept of ideas those problems do not involve ideas as entities standing between us and external objects" (102). Yolton has a tendency to shift back and forth between speaking about ideas as "things" and as "entities." One might suppose they are synonyms; they are not. That he does not treat them as synonyms is made eminently clear in a reply of his to an article by Ian Tipton. Yolton writes: "Berkeley tells us that he has not turned things into ideas, but just the reverse. Thus ideas *are* things. Does this mean they are entities?" (1986, 584). If the question is meaningful, there must be *some* kind of distinction between things and entities. At first one might be tempted to read the difference as between things and substances (independent things) but that turns out not to be what Yolton has in mind. In his exposition of Berkeley's theory of ideas, Yolton makes it clear that ideas are neither modes nor substances (1996a, esp. 148). Yolton's language here mirrors his treatments of Locke. The distinction he is trying to employ operates on a level outside of a particular ontology. Thus when he tells us that the answer to the question of whether for Berkeley ideas are entities is "no," I suggest that he means that ideas *have no ontic status at all.* I confess that Yolton is not always perfectly clear on this point, but I can construct no other consistent position to attribute to him. At the very least he is not alone in endorsing a position like the one I am ascribing to him here.

Yolton presents a similar case for Locke. His argument is straightforward. Locke does not reify ideas, nor does he treat them as intermediate objects of any sort. And so he must have rejected the substance/mode ontology altogether.

> We might then distinguish kinds of indirectness. One kind involves another ontology, an ontology where "object in the mind" is taken

---

20. "The substance-accident ontology was applied to Locke's empirical epistemology, an ontology which Locke rejected as far as ideas were concerned" (Yolton 1996b, 95).

> as "immaterial substance" (special things) and where "exists in" also has an ontic meaning. Another kind of indirectness rejects this ontology, preferring to read "ideas" not as things but simply as "conscious mental contents," and it translates "exist in" as "understood." On this second kind of indirectness, perceiving an object is having or receiving ideas. On this point, Locke and Malebranche agree. The difference is in the nature of ideas. For Malebranche, an idea is God-given and thing-like. For Locke, ideas are the result of a physical process and of a psychological process, but they are not thing-like. (1984, 102)

Ideas for Locke are not things but "conscious mental contents." The claim that ideas "exist in" the mind does not have an ontic meaning but merely an epistemological one. The contrast is clear. To speak of ideas as things is to speak within an ontology. But when one asks whether ideas are entities, one is asking if ontic categories apply to them *at all*. For the moment let's set aside the exegetical issues and focus on the philosophical merits of this position. I engage and argue against this thesis on textual grounds in the subsequent chapters on Locke, Berkeley, and Hume.

If ideas have no ontic status—if they are not "entities"—then what alternative remains? A natural inclination might be to invoke the Cartesian formal/objective distinction. Perhaps Yolton intends ideas to be modes yet focuses on their objective aspect as representing content. But this is not his claim. Instead, he radicalizes the distinction by shearing off the formal reality altogether. Ideas are "conscious mental contents," we are told. They are representations, objects of awareness and "epistemological beings" only. I confess I do not really know what an "epistemological being" is. Vere Chappell tries to put a good face on Yolton's point, arguing that all he means is that ideas are necessarily dependent beings. Hence, despite the confusing terminology, ideas *are* entities, just dependent mental ones best described as "intentional objects" (1994, 32–33). If so, then whether such intentional objects are mental substances or modes (or some kind of third substance) remains to be determined. Yet it is difficult to accept Chappell's reading. Yolton argues that after Descartes the moderns abandoned the ontological model as a framework for their theories of ideas. The following is typical of Yolton's analysis: "For Descartes, this kind of existence in a mind had the same meaning as it later did for Berkeley: the object is known by the mind. This is what the objective reality of ideas is: at one and the same time, representative of and also the reality of the object.... The ontological flavor of Descartes's talk of the *being* of objects existing in the mind is missing from Berkeley's formulation; only the cognitive translation remains" (1996a, 148). We have left ontology behind altogether. In essence, Yolton rejects as meaningless the question "What is an idea?" He grounds the argument in a careful exposition of the development of the "way of ideas" among the moderns. The problem, as he sees it, is straightforward. The shift away from ontology to "pure" epistemology is a result of the inability of the moderns to reconcile two important principles. They held both that there is no cognition at a distance and that knowing requires presence to the mind. Yet as long as presence to the mind was interpreted along the lines of a spatial metaphor, no progress could be made in eliminating the conflict between the two principles. It was simply not possible to explain representation and cognition inside an ontological model of ideas. As a result the metaphor and its ontological assumptions were jettisoned. Richard Watson sums up the conclusions of this view nicely in an article on Malebranche:

> Neither Malebranche nor Foucher saw that the modern way out was to be an utter denial of the meaningfulness of the question "What is an idea?" taken as a demand to provide an ontological model that explains how representation can and does take place, and that the modern answer to how causal interaction takes place was to be the rejection or at the very least the ignoring of the demand for an ontological explanatory model . . . but instead . . . a description—not an explanation on metaphysical or ontological grounds, but a mere *description* of the course or sequence of events. (1991, 31–32)

One might think that we have here an account of reifying that perhaps not only makes sense but reveals an important truth about the development of the concept of an idea. Those who reify ideas, in the most basic sense, accept an ontological model. Those who do not, such as Locke and Berkeley (according to these interpreters), deny the appropriateness of such a model, favoring a "purely epistemological" approach.

I find it odd that neither Watson nor Yolton consider an obvious alternative. If the traditional ontology is demonstrably inadequate, why not generate a new ontology? Perhaps the ground needs to revised, not abolished. The logic seems to be that because *this* ontology fails to account for ideas and representation, we must abandon ontology altogether as grounding our understanding of ideas and their roles. In questioning this logic, I am not claiming there was no focus on the epistemological aspect of ideas but rather that this focus did not come as result of rejecting the notion that ideas need to have an ontological ground. The mere fact that some have argued that Locke and Leibniz (among others) thought of ideas as tropes should give us reason to pause.[21] This point notwithstanding, I think that the anti-ontological project suffers from serious conceptual difficulties.

There are philosophical reasons for rejecting the thesis that ideas are "purely" epistemological beings. The first problem stems from another misleading characterization of ideas. Perhaps one of the most ubiquitous descriptions one finds of ideas is that they are the objects of perception. Locke says so, as does Berkeley, Descartes, Malebranche, and others. Contemporary commentators are particularly fond of latching on to this point due to the close connection this particular definition has with issues in representation. This characterization of ideas initially accords with the anti-ontological thesis, which proposes that ideas should be thought of as "objects of awareness." Saying that an idea is an object could mean several things, however, depending on what one takes an object to be.[22] The two main readings are: (1) an object is a thing, and (2) an object is the referent of a particular act of perception. (1) and (2) are not identical. The former collapses into straightforward reifying talk, and the latter invokes ideas as relata in perceptual relations.

Object talk and thing talk run dangerously parallel, so one might reasonably substitute "thing" for "object" without any loss of meaning. This kind of substitution usually happens in analyses of perception. Is there a distinction between act and object in perception? The analysis usually runs as follows. If not, then ideas (as the immediate objects of perception) are not things but something else. If so, then ideas must be things that are in some sense (this sense varies by commentator) distinct from perceiving minds. Some therefore want to move from "an idea is an object" to "an idea is a thing" on the basis of a philosopher endorsing an act/object distinction.[23] As I have been arguing, this effort is all well and good but does not reveal much about the nature of ideas. Even if one *denies* the act/object distinction ideas might still be things. Only if endorsing the distinction compels one to treat ideas as substances can we credit ourselves with progress. Yet, as often

---

21. Unfortunately, the best example of the argument for a trope reading has not been published (Alston 1976).
22. Yolton also recognizes this point (1996a, 140).
23. See Winkler 1989, 4–6, 290–309. Winkler adduces other reasons for thinking that ideas are "entities," but the main move rests on dividing acts from their objects.

as not, scholars do not want to make that leap.[24] Those who do often find their analyses of perception falling into incoherence, but that is, after all, exactly what one should expect when operating within an ontology that cannot properly accommodate ideas.

Most often scholars want to endorse something like the anti-ontological thesis and adopt (2), avoiding the ontological issues altogether. Ideas are here characterized as ungrounded intentional objects. They are "intentional" since the act of perception (or cognition) is "about" the object. It was generally accepted among the moderns that all acts of cognition and perception are intentional; every thought has an object, what the thought is *about*. That object is an idea. In this light, Malebranche and Locke, they say, mark a decisive break simply because they consider ideas only as *epistemological* entities, ignoring or resisting the ontological issues altogether.

A closely related move is to treat ideas as phenomenal individuals that have phenomenal properties. To say that my idea has color and shape is only to attribute *phenomenal* color and shape to the idea. Reifying an idea is to attribute actual shape and color properties to ideas, which turns them into robust entities. The alternative to reifying is then to treat ideas not as things but in purely phenomenological terms. I want to be clear about this point. I have no principled objection to phenomenological accounts that provide an ontological ground for the phenomena; I am only resisting any possible accounts that treat phenomena as *purely* "epistemological entities." Whether one wants a phenomenological account or one that treats ideas as intentional objects, the difficulties these views engender are considerable.

First, the notion of an ungrounded intentional or phenomenological object, one without any ontological foundation, is mysterious. Consider an appropriate parallel: dispositional properties. Dispositions in contemporary discourse are thought of either as grounded or not. Ungrounded dispositions are brute-fact regularities we discover in the world. Nothing else about the world explains the tendency. Most often, however, we are inclined to think of dispositional properties as grounded in other nondispositional properties. What would we say about someone who argues that the color red is an ungrounded dispositional property? Many now think of colors as dispositional properties. Red just is the power of objects to cause certain phenomenological states in appropriate perceivers. Even here, however, the dispositional view is credible because it is grounded in the reflective proper-

---

24. Winkler, for instance, only maintains that Berkeleian ideas, as objects, are "weakly" distinct from minds. Hence, they are some form of mental "entity" but are not substances. I can make no clear sense of what he takes the ontological status of ideas to be for Berkeley.

ties of the surfaces of objects. To say that seeing red just happens when we see red things (under standard lighting conditions) provides a description but no explanation. Similarly, solubility would be mighty mysterious were it not for the fact that we ground the property in a chemical theory about molecules and their interrelations. Where we think of ideas as dispositions, we need to worry about whether and how such theories provide us the opportunity to explain important features within the realm of ideas. I am not arguing that dispositional theories of ideas are impossible; I am arguing that such theories require special care to make them plausible. To abandon an ontic grounding *without good cause* undermines the intellectual and scientific enterprise of genuinely explaining the phenomena we encounter. To attribute such a view to the moderns with their heightened sense of the burdens of the new scientific enterprise is prima facie suspect.

Even if one could somehow accept the consequences of ungrounded intentional objects, however, additional problems for the anti-ontologist remain. To hold that ideas are "purely" epistemological entities still portrays ideas (as objects) as relata in perceptual or cognitive relations. Relations, however, fall underneath the umbrella of ontological entities. Relata *have* to be minimally "thingy" creatures, for they fall within the domain of that over which we can quantify. In short, it does not make sense to say, of polyadic relations or even monadic properties, that a relatum has no ontic status. To endorse this odd view is to say that one cannot ask *what* is being related. To complicate matters further, perceivers (minds) have a clear ontic status (at least insofar as they are substances and *things*). Thus on the view that the status of ideas is purely epistemological, perception and cognition involve relations between that which has an ontic status (the mind) and that which does not (ideas). I have no difficulty conceptualizing relations between different kinds of beings (say substances and modes), but I must confess ignorance about what it *means* to relate something that has an ontic status to a "being" that does not. To deny ideas an ontic status leads to incoherence.

Perhaps the early moderns simply ignored the ontological implications of their theorizing. Even if this was their intent, the ontological questions do not simply vanish. Convinced of Locke's epistemological conclusions, one does not then merrily go on one's way, unmindful of the underlying ontology his system requires. Although Locke does explicitly set aside metaphysical questions in the *Essay*, he does not suggest that they ought to be entirely ignored. A convinced Lockean would have to, at some point, tease out and reconcile the ontological commitments with the epistemological superstructure.

Aside from the complications raised by the problem of relations, a third philosophical difficulty emerges for the Watson/Yolton thesis. Insofar as they want ideas to be "purely" epistemological entities, we ought to expect that they can deliver results on certain important questions. In particular, we should expect our opponent to be able to explain representation. Consider an example. Assume that we want to know *how* a particular idea represents its particular content. Thus we want to know how an idea of a dog is an idea of a *dog* and not something else. In order for this question to be meaningful, we need to be able to conceptualize an idea separately from what it is "of." If ideas have no being other than as intentional or epistemological "entities," then there is nothing of which we can ask what makes *it* an idea of a dog.[25] I am not saying that occasionally bracketing off ontological questions cannot be fruitful. Ignoring them, however, courts disaster. Even though Descartes, for instance, separates the formal from the objective aspects of ideas, there is no hint that he thinks ideas can exist objectively (i.e., merely as representing content) in whatever sense without having some formal (i.e., ontic, as a mode) existence. Even those moderns who embrace the view that ideas are modes of the mind all recognize that an idea is something that represents, independently of what they think constitutes the "thingness" of the idea.

In short, there is no profit in ignoring ontology. If ideas are intentional objects or phenomenological, then we must assume they have some ontological ground if there is to be any rational discourse or understanding about them at all. And if not, then our efforts are idle. The exasperation many have encountered when trying to untangle the ontology of ideas is understandable and probably unavoidable, but that does not license our ignoring it. I thus reject attempts to deal with the present difficulties by trying to sweep them away.

1.4 Stretching Idea Ontologies

Although the main thesis of this work is that the early moderns preserved a common *core* of the traditional substance/modification ontology, I also admit that under various pressures the early moderns stretched the borders of that ontology. In one sense my claim is obvious. A careful survey of the

---

25. The same holds true generally for images. Images must have *some* ontological status, else we cannot analogously ask what makes *it* (the image) an image of something (this point is made in Alston 1976, 2–3).

major philosophers of the period reveals that they understood the details of the concept of substance differently from one another. I have addressed some of those differences above. Yet for all of these differences, a central adherence to a notion of substances as enduring, independent things remains. If that claim is plausible, then what might it mean to say that the traditional ontology was "stretched" by the likes of Berkeley?

I contend that pressures arising from the epistemological roles that ideas play helped radicalize the metaphysics of ideas, especially for Berkeley. While recognizing that ideas played epistemological roles such as representing content, forming belief and knowledge claims, and so on, Berkeley simultaneously recognized that these epistemological vehicles had to have some ontological foundation. From an examination of the history of the way of ideas starting with Descartes, however, we discover that ideas never quite fit either the category of substance *or* modification. Depending on what features one chooses to emphasize, ideas can look like both. Berkeley was familiar with Cartesianism and the debates that exercised its adherents. He was also familiar with the moves Locke made and the central role he accorded to ideas when it came to human understanding. In light of this history, Berkeley provides us with an ontological innovation. He crafts a hybrid ontological category I call "quasi substance." Ideas formally possess one feature usually reserved for substances, namely a kind of separation from other entities such that they are neither modes nor proper parts of other substances. Yet they also possess the one feature most distinctive of modes: they are ontologically dependent on these distinct substances. What emerges is a theory of ideas that makes them volitionally independent of finite minds, such that we have the appearance of an independent, external world, yet also recognizes that the world is nonetheless ontologically dependent on something else. Providing the background and then argument for this account constitutes a large measure of my challenge to the early modern tale. Blending the category of substance and mode is not a rejection of the *concepts* of substance and modification; it is a new application. How this pointedly ontological account of the development of the way ideas in the early modern period arises unfolds in the remainder of this book.

For any particular philosopher, the most appropriate question to ask with regard to the status of ideas is the one with which we started. Are they substances? If not, are they modes? And if neither, then what are they, and in what relation do they stand to the traditional ontological categories? To repeat for emphasis, I argue that despite superficial indications to the contrary, the moderns did not abandon the *core* of the traditional ontology.

They stretched it, they fought with it, *but their thinking did not genuinely extend beyond it*. Early modern metaphysics became increasingly radicalized as philosophers became aware of the problems of reconciling idea philosophy with ontology. Yet a radicalization of metaphysics is not a rejection of it. I argue here that, suitably understood, the substance/mode distinction is not only conceptually meaningful but in fact preferable when it comes to making ontological judgments, at least among and about the early moderns. They understood the issues themselves through the core substance/mode ontology. To stretch or even test the categories is not to deny the categories themselves. Additionally, I argue that trying to avoid issues of ontology when it comes to ideas invites incoherence. We have sober philosophical reasons for thinking that the early moderns *ought* to have kept an eye on ontic issues. What remains is to show that in fact they did.

2

DESCARTES

Conventional wisdom, like the early modern tale, holds René Descartes responsible for effecting a revolutionary break from the Scholastic tradition, particularly in the theory of ideas. Although he applied the term "idea" in a new way and built an innovative mechanistic theory of perception that capitalizes on this new use, it is not at all obvious that Descartes advanced a new and clear theory of the ontological status of ideas. We are, in the main, still in familiar conceptual territory. He tells Hobbes in the Third Replies that "I used the word 'idea' because it was the standard philosophical term used to refer to the forms of perception belonging to the divine mind, even though we recognize that God does not possess any corporeal imagination. And besides, there was not any more appropriate term at my disposal" (*CSM* I:127–28). Perhaps the main innovation accorded Descartes is that of shifting the application of the word "idea" from the contents of the divine mind to the *human* mind. It is worth noting that Descartes indicates he is using the word not in spite of its traditional use but because of it. Nicholas Jolley suggests that this is a clue that Descartes is ascribing some properties to the human mind that were formerly reserved for God (1990, 12). This move makes Descartes' use of the word "idea" no less innovative but perhaps less unexpected. His Jesuit education at Le Flèche emphasized the Thomistic tradition, but he was exposed to a variety of important Scholastic luminaries including Ockham and Duns Scotus (Gaukroger 1995, esp. ch. 2). As a result, although he was to push a new theory of perception and was the first to use the word "idea" in the modern sense, Descartes' musings are in many important respects Scholastic.

Descartes' official final view is that ideas are properly modes, but the details of this position turn out to be rather complex. Descartes gives us what many take to be the official definition of an idea in the Second Replies.

"I understand this term [idea] to mean the form of any given thought, immediate perception of which makes me aware of the thought" (*CSM* II:113). Importantly, however, he distinguishes between kinds (or rather *aspects*) of ideas, and it has frequently been remarked that these divisions are crucial to understanding his general theory, since he often employs the different senses of idea without signaling that he is doing so (Chappell 1986, 177–78). Descartes appears to discuss not one but rather several distinctions that apply among ideas. He distinguishes between taking ideas formally and objectively, materially and formally, and finally materially and objectively (*CSM* II:27–28, 162–63, 7). The first is the main distinction, the second refers to an additional distinction within the context of material and formal *falsity*, and the last is simply a variant of the first. Nonetheless, Descartes' use of terms makes his discussion in the Third Meditation occasionally difficult to unravel, as he fails to use the same language to describe the distinctions being invoked (*CSM* II:27–28). To further complicate matters, he uses the word "idea" to apply to corporeal images in his early works on perception. Despite the varying usages, the underlying distinction is a familiar one. Ideas taken materially (or often, formally) are modes of the mind, and this generally refers to the ontic status of ideas. Ideas taken objectively (or more rarely, formally) indicates their representative content. In accordance with standard use, I shall refer to ideas taken materially as ideas$_m$, and ideas taken objectively as ideas$_o$.

The material/objective distinction, because not a "real" distinction in the Cartesian world, makes this bit of philosophy more difficult to penetrate. Descartes tells us that the material and objective aspects differ only by a distinction of reason. Thus when talking about an idea (the form of a thought) materially and objectively, there are not two entities. Rather there is but one thing, about which we speak in two different ways. Descartes is notoriously vague on this point (see, e.g., Chappell 1986, 193–94). As a rule, he treats ideas$_o$ as the contents of ideas$_m$. Most scholars are tempted to hold that ideas, strictly speaking, are modes, but Descartes sometimes confusedly speaks (as do the rest of us) of the content represented by those modes as ideas.

2.1 Representation

Ideas are modes that express content, and when speaking of that representative content we speak of ideas objectively. Of course, this does not tell us much about the *nature* of representation, only that it occurs and can be conceptually separated from the ontic status of ideas. It is an odd but perhaps understandable feature of seventeenth- and even eighteenth-century philosophy that everyone talks about representation, but no one actually tells us what it is. There is no shortage of examples of what it is not (Arnauld tells us it is not like a painting nor is it like a reflection in a still pond), but unsurprisingly such insights are rarely helpful. Many philosophers operated with some sort of resemblance theory. An idea represents an object x if it resembles x in *some* respect.[1] Simon Foucher even argued that either ideas represent by likeness or they do not represent at all (1995, 35). Resemblance theories are, of course, puzzling for any adherent of a form of substance dualism. There can be no resemblance between mind and matter, and this tenet seems to kill a resemblance theory for any serious nonmonist.[2] None of the major Cartesian figures enthusiastically and unequivocally endorsed a resemblance theory, and probably for just this reason. Descartes himself can be difficult to fix on this point. On the one hand he seems to explicitly deny that representation must be by resemblance. As he notes in the first chapter of *The World*, "For although everyone is commonly convinced that the ideas we have in our mind are wholly similar to the objects from which they proceed, nevertheless I cannot see any reason which assures us that this is so. On the contrary, I note many observations which should make us doubt it" (*CSM* I:81; compare *CSM* I:165). On the other hand, he certainly seems to allow that representation frequently does involve resemblance, especially in those passages where he speaks of ideas as properly being images.[3] How ought we to resolve this incongruity? When Descartes discusses resemblance, he usually does so only in the context of the veridicality of ideas (i.e., their correspondence with reality). That is, he equates resembling with veridicality, as in the following:

> But there was something else which I used to assert, and which through habitual belief I thought I perceived clearly, although I did

---

1. As Descartes notes, it is best if the idea does *not* resemble the object *too* much. If it did, then we would not be able to distinguish the idea from its object. See *CSM* I:165.

2. Although this principle is clearly held by most early moderns, one wonders about such similarities as number (we can count both physical objects and minds) and other abstract relations.

3. For example, in the Third Meditation he claims that "Some of my thoughts are as it were the images of things, and it is only in these cases that the term 'idea' is strictly appropriate" (*CSM* I:25). This kind of passage is not infrequent. See also *CSM* I:165 in the *Optics*, where he discusses images in the brain clearly in terms of resemblance. Where ideas are images, resemblance is not far away.

> not in fact do so. This was that there were things outside me which were the sources of my ideas and which resembled them in all respects.
>
> But the chief question at this point concerns the ideas which I take to be derived from things existing outside me: what is my reason for thinking that they resemble these things? Nature has apparently taught me to think this. (*CSM* II:25, 26)

So when he denies that representation requires resemblance, he more properly should be said to be addressing a point about veridicality. Seen in this light, the best we can conclude is that Descartes has no clear theory of the veridicality of ideas. We have ideas that do not in fact resemble their objects, and assuming they do resemble them is often a source of error, but neither of those claims in and of themselves constitutes strong evidence that Descartes rejected representation by resemblance. We might conclude that he has no considered view, but the issue is complicated, and the literature on the topic is substantial.[4] Nonetheless, I take it that Descartes, if pressed, would recognize that representation by literal similarity cannot be the whole story. If that supposition is right—because he saw the complications arising from mind-body interaction—then at least his claims fit more broadly with his remarks on the veridicality of ideas. We thus have the following conjunction of positions to which I wish to draw attention: Cartesians broadly tended to emphasize the distinction between formal and objective reality (in ideas) while maintaining that resemblance was not the entire picture in representation. One obvious element responsible for these views was the increasing "mentalization" of ideas (treating ideas as in the category of the mental, either as mental substances or modes of the mind). The further separated ideas become from the physical, the greater the strain on the epistemological (particularly representative) functions of ideas. As we shall see, Descartes is a transitional figure here, finally recognizing the difficulties with physicalistic conceptions of ideas, although whether he completely frees himself from a mechanical understanding of perception (and hence ideas) is not at all clear.

Returning to the main issue, most early modern philosophers talk about "signs" when discussing representation. An idea can be a sign of an external object in the way that a few letters strung together can be the sign of a

---

4. See Wilson 1994, 209–28, who thinks that Descartes has no considered view. For sophisticated engagements of the issue, see Simmons 1999 and Hoffman 1996.

concept. Such a move is used to circumvent the objections to imagist theories of ideas. Ideas represent not by providing us with pictures of things but by serving as signs of things more generally. Malebranche tells us that to represent is to make present that which is absent (see Nadler 1992, 49). Signs fulfill this role. The book on the table in the next room is not present to my mind, but the idea I have of that book is.

This understanding of signs highlights an interesting feature of many early modern philosophies of mind. Just as Descartes railed against action at a distance in the material world, so too he and other philosophers rejected the idea of perception (broadly construed) at a mental distance. Knowledge cannot be had without something being immediately present, or joined, to the mind. Malebranche argues that "my soul must be united in some manner to whatever it perceives" (*OC* 6:212, also quoted in Nadler 1992, 67). As we will see in the next chapter, Arnauld objected that this principle did not entail local presence, as suggested by the principle's spatial cousin, but he nonetheless accepted the basic spirit of the claim. Mental representation thus posed a particularly difficult problem for the early moderns, including Descartes. On the one hand, material nonmental objects were to be represented, but on the other, such representation had to include some sort of intimate contact between the mind and the *representans*. It is small wonder that such a perplexing problem began to generate increasingly unusual ontologies.

Ultimately most early moderns simply avoided the issue. Arnauld and Pierre Nicole take a characteristic approach and say it best in the beginning of the *Logic, or; The Art of Thinking* (known as the *Port-Royal Logic*): "The word 'idea' is one of those that are so clear that they cannot be explained by others, because none is more clear and simple" (Arnauld and Nicole 1996, 25). From this we may conclude that the representative power of ideas is basic and not subject to further explanation. During the period immediately following Descartes, the difficulties representation presents constitute the focal point of the debate around the ontological status of ideas. For the moment I am content to claim merely that difficulties in the representative function of ideas were held to be closely connected to their ontological status.

2.2 Perception, Ideas, and Images

Descartes' works on perception sometimes seem a world away from the later *Principles* and the *Meditations*, at least with respect to his understanding of ideas. We must first understand the outlines of his theory of perception; only then can we turn to examine the changes his conception of ideas underwent. Descartes saw himself as opposing a long and venerable Aristotelian Scholastic tradition. His principal move was to shift perception out of the mysterious spiritual realm of "flying species" and into the more accessible and newly flowering mechanistic world. These deviations from Scholastic theories quickly became points accepted among the early moderns as obvious truths. Descartes took ideas to be the immediate objects of perception and argued that secondary qualities, such as color, are not external to the mind (Wolf-Devine 1993, 1). Locke took over this position and Berkeley simply assumes these points, proceeding from there.

Despite Descartes' break with the Aristotelian conceptual apparatus, much of his theory of perception is nonetheless reminiscent of Aristotle. Of particular interest is that Descartes' early thinking about ideas mirrors that of Aristotle inasmuch as they are not deemed exclusively mental entities. Descartes argues that the sense organs are the passive receptors of corporeal images, using the same analogy of a wax impression Aristotle used in *De Anima*. In Rule 12 in *Rules for the Direction of the Mind,* Descartes writes:

> [S]ense perception, strictly speaking, is purely passive, even though our application of the senses to objects involves action, viz. local motion; sense-perception occurs in the same way in which wax takes on an impression from a seal. It should not be thought that I have a mere analogy in mind here: we must think of the external shape of the sentient body as being really changed by the object in exactly the same way as the shape of the surface of the wax is altered by the seal. (*CSM* I:40; compare Aristotle 424a18–23)

Descartes makes good on his warning that he wants to take the example literally. All forms of sensory perception reduce to touch—pushes and pulls. Vision, for instance, involves the impression of shapes on the outer part of the eye, audition involves a change in the shape of the eardrum, taste involves physical changes on the tongue, and so forth (*CSM* I:40). We perceive only through a mechanics of contact.[5] The so-called secondary qualities likewise have shape and are extended. "Whatever you may suppose color to be, you will not deny that it is extended and consequently has shape" (*CSM*

---

5. This is implicit throughout his works on perception, but he does explicitly endorse this characterization as well. See, for example, *CSM* II:174, where he notes that "we have sensory awareness of something only by contact."

I:41). No matter the modality, sensory perception involves the passive reception of change in the appropriate sense organ.

The passivity Descartes describes ought not to be thought of in terms of an act/potency distinction. Rather he has the more mundane concept of mechanical passivity in mind. The sense organs do not, strictly speaking, act during perception. They are acted on. Likewise, Scholastic "forms" are abandoned in favor of physical shape. Whereas Aristotle treats secondary qualities as basic and robust entities, Descartes does not. Color perception supervenes on the reception of the geometrical properties of objects. Qualities are thus all fundamentally alike. That is, they are all ultimately geometrical and reduce to shape, number, and motion.

Although Descartes abandons much of the Scholastic conceptual framework, he retains the old contagion theory of causation (see Adams 1975, 73–75). He speaks of causes "giving" to their effects, as in the Third Meditation: "For where, I ask, could the effect get its reality from, if not from the cause? And how could the cause give it to the effect unless it possessed it?" (*CSM* II:28). Therefore instead of vision being caused by the transmission of forms, we now have vision caused by the transmission of shape and motion. Perception is accordingly *more* of a physical process (still not entirely so), but the story remains fundamentally causal. External objects impress on our sense organs. The images or impressions are conveyed to the corporeal imagination and thence, somewhat mysteriously, to the incorporeal understanding. In his early works, especially the *Rules,* Descartes holds that mind and body do interact. "The intellect can either be stimulated by the imagination or act upon it" (*CSM* I:43, Rule 12).[6] It is this interaction between the imagination and the understanding on which we must focus our attention.

Earlier I mentioned the definition usually taken to be Descartes' "official" one for ideas (which appears much later chronologically). A few pages later (still in the Second Replies), however, he provides another equally important characterization. "But I make it quite clear in several places throughout the book, and in this passage in particular, that I am taking the word 'idea' to refer to whatever is immediately perceived by the mind" (*CSM* II:127). This version leaves open *what* might be immediately perceived by the mind. In particular, if the corporeal imagination interacts directly with the understanding, why might we not suppose that things in the imagination are ideas

---

6. The imagination for Descartes is corporeal, as the rest of the paragraph (not reproduced) confirms. For additional evidence that the mind and body must causally interact, see *CSM/K* III:149, letter to Mersenne, July 1640: "for it is certain that the soul must be joined to some part of the body."

as well? In fact, this is exactly what Descartes does. Throughout his early works Descartes uses the term "idea" to refer to not merely images but corporeal images as well. Some of the passages are explicit, others are merely suggestive, but the overall picture is hard to miss. For example, he argues in the *Discourse on Method* that

> I also indicated what changes must occur in the brain in order to cause waking, sleep and dreams; how light, sounds, smells, tastes, heat and other qualities of external objects can imprint various ideas on the brain through the mediation of the senses; and how hunger, thirst, and the other internal passions can also send their ideas there. And I explained which part of the brain must be taken to be the "common" sense, where these ideas are received; the memory, which preserves them; and the corporeal imagination [*phantasia*], which can change them in various ways, form them into new ideas. (*CSM* I:139)

Passages like this one indicate that Descartes uses the term "idea" rather widely to include corporeal images (see *CSM* I:355, 370, 376, and *CSM* II:25). In more careful moments, however, he clarifies this position. Not just any image impressed on the brain will count as an idea. When he says "brain" in these cases, he means specifically that part of the brain responsible for the transmission of images to the understanding: the infamous "gland H," otherwise known as the pineal gland. Thus in the *Treatise on Man*, he states:

> Now among these figures, it is not those imprinted on the external sense organs, or on the internal surface of the brain, which should be taken to be ideas—but only those which are traced in the spirits on the surface of the gland H (*where the seat of the imagination and the "common" sense is located*). That is to say, it is only the latter figures which should be taken to be the forms or images which the rational soul united to this machine will consider directly when it imagines some object or perceives it by the senses. (*CSM* I:106, emphasis in the original)

Read carefully, *all* the passages normally taken to imply that corporeal images are ideas cohere with this sharper explanation. Not any corporeal image will do but only those imprinted on that special organ responsible for the specifics of mind-body interaction. Despite the unusual nature of gland H,

Descartes' description of it nonetheless implies that the ideas imprinted on it are corporeal. The gland has a surface and a physical location. Images impressed on this gland must be corporeal.

What, then, are these images? One might argue that Descartes can extend his theory of the nature of ideas to include images. Images thus would be modes. In this case, they are states of the gland H, and the impressions on the pineal gland are analogous to modes of mind. He wants to employ the wax example literally, so strictly speaking there is nothing substantial present other than the wax formed in a particular way. He later confirms this story in a 2 May 1644 letter to Mesland:

> I regard the difference between the soul and its ideas as the same as that between a piece of wax and the various shapes it can take. Just as it is not an activity but a passivity in the wax to take various shapes, so, it seems to me, it is a passivity in the soul to receive one or other idea, and only its volitions are activities. It receives its ideas partly from objects which come into contact with the senses, partly from impressions in the brain, and partly from prior dispositions in the soul and from movements of the will. Similarly, the wax owes its shapes partly to the pressure of other bodies, partly to the shapes or other qualities which it already possesses, such as heaviness or softness, and partly also to its own movement, in so far as it has in itself the power to continue moving when it has once been set in motion. (*CSM/K* III:232–33)

One needs to be careful when considering Descartes' letters to the Jesuit Mesland, since political considerations might well have influenced his particular choice of words. The relevant point here, however, is appropriately present elsewhere. The wax analogy is repeatedly used by Descartes in just this form (see *CSM* I:40 and the Second Meditation). It would seem that corporeal images, being so like ideas in the mind, are modes as well. Note that Descartes here also indicates that the soul receives ideas from the brain, a corporeal organ. So if the mind receives ideas, which are corporeal modes, from the brain, *what is it* that the mind receives? The interaction is causal and thus falls under his stricture that causation involves giving. Descartes needs some account of how the physical image alters the mind. The best we get is an unsatisfactory appeal to "animal spirits" in gland H.[7] In this discus-

---

7. See *CSM/K* III:62, letter to Mersenne, 24 December 1640; *CSM/K* III:190, letter to Hyperaspistes, August 1641; and *CSM* I:100–104, *Treatise on Man*.

sion the causal interaction appears entirely corporeal. The spirits are able to literally move muscles as they are forced through substances, yet the mind, despite its power to move bodies, is entirely incorporeal.

Now it is routine to say that Descartes' early discussions of ideas as (corporeal) images can be set aside since he later abandoned that particular usage of the term "idea" (Chappell 1986, 179).[8] Although corporeal images still play an important role in perception, they are no longer strictly counted as ideas. That is right to a certain degree, but it seems to ignore the problems still facing Descartes in his theory of perception. He does *not* abandon the more general claim that images are ideas.[9] Rather he reinforces that view. "For by 'idea,'" he notes in a July 1641 letter to Mersenne, "I do not just mean the images depicted in the imagination; indeed, in so far as these images are in the corporeal imagination, I do not use that term for them at all. Instead, by the term 'idea' I mean in general everything which is in our mind when we conceive something, no matter how we conceive it" (*CSM/K* III:185). Ideas are not *just* images, suggesting that at least some ideas *are* images. In the Third Meditation Descartes maintains the same view: "Some of my thoughts are as it were the images of things, and it is only in these cases that the term 'idea' is strictly appropriate—for example, when I think of a man, or a chimera, or the sky, or an angel, or God. Other thoughts have various additional forms: thus when I will, or am afraid, or affirm, or deny, there is always a particular thing which I take as the object of my thought, but my thought includes something more than the likeness of that thing" (*CSM* II:25–26). The "as it were" qualifier in this passage might give some pause, but in general Descartes consistently denies that corporeal images are ideas while simultaneously asserting that images, broadly conceived as mental entities, are. As a result, although not all ideas are images, all *mental* images appear to be ideas. But corporeal images, as nonmental entities, do not qualify as ideas. Descartes' strategy throughout the *Replies* is to deflect criticism of his theory of ideas by arguing that his opponents wrongly take him to think that corporeal images are ideas. Even after that denial, however, the relation between the mind and its objects remains a murky affair.

Ultimately his final position is that although there is causal interaction between the material world and the soul, sensory ideas in the mind are nonetheless innate. This theory, which supplants his early one, also has significant problems; I explore these issues in the next section. I want to em-

8. See *CSM* II:113, 251.
9. See section 2.4.

phasize before moving on that Descartes never abandoned his *basic* theory of the mechanics of perception. Even the mature Descartes held that corporeal images are impressed on gland H.

2.3 Innate Ideas, Dispositions, and Causes

Descartes lists yet another set of categories for ideas. He posits an additional distinction among adventitious, innate, and invented (or fictitious) ideas (*CSM* II:26). Adventitious ideas are those caused or generated from without, innate ideas are caused from within but not by the mind (they are "derived from my own nature"), and invented ideas are both internal and generated by an act of the will. Confronting his earlier problems explaining how sensory experience gives rise to understanding, Descartes deftly employs this distinction to reason that all sensory ideas must be innate, deftly noting in *Comments on a Certain Broadsheet* that

> [n]othing reaches our mind from external objects through the sense organs except certain corporeal motions, as our author himself [Henricus Regius] asserts in article nineteen, in accordance with my own principles. But neither the motions themselves nor the figures arising from them are conceived by us exactly as they occur in the sense organs, as I have explained at length in my *Optics*. Hence it follows that the very ideas of the motions themselves and of the figures are innate in us. The ideas of pain, colors, sounds, and the like must be all the more innate if, on the occasion of certain corporeal motions, our mind is to be capable of representing them to itself, for there is no similarity between these ideas and the corporeal motions. (*CSM* I:304)

Recall Descartes' problem. If perceived qualities are all physical and geometrical in nature and perception is basically causal, then how do we represent them to ourselves in our immaterial minds? The inadequacy of the original view was obvious to everyone. Accordingly Malebranche writes: "Since ideas are spiritual, they cannot be produced from material images in the brain, with which they are incommensurable" (*LO,* 223 [3.2.3]). Causation is by contagion, so corporeal images cannot transfer anything to the understanding. Thus Descartes concludes there can be no interaction and the ideas we have of external objects must be innate. Ideas not only can not be caused by corporeal images but also generally do not resemble them either. Sensory ideas are adventitious only in the sense that external objects provide the occasion for the mind's forming a particular idea.[10]

Although Descartes does not adopt the contagion theory of causation exactly as the Scholastics endorsed it, the underlying principle is the same. "Now it is manifest by the natural light that there must be at least as much reality in the efficient and total cause as in the effect of that cause" (*CSM* II:28, Third Meditation). His formulation suggests that it is not necessary that the (numerically) *same* form be transferred in causation (as the Scholastics would have it) but only that at least as much reality exist in the cause as in the effect. Descartes nonetheless operates with a theory of causation that requires "contact," implying that whatever is transferred is of the same order of being (e.g., both parties involved must be physical). In an August 1641 letter to Hyperaspistes, he invokes this principle and explains that he cannot fathom an instance of causation without contact (*CSM/K* III:192–93). We do not cognize or conceive the external material world by entertaining extension, motion, and shape. Corporeal ideas have nothing else to "give" the understanding, and hence they cannot causally give rise *directly* to ideas in the understanding.

Sensory ideas, then, are innate. Because they are innate, when they are not occurrent, they exist within us only potentially. Hence every possible sensory idea we might have exists within us already in some sense. As Descartes argues in *Comments on a Certain Broadsheet,*

> [I]t is surely obvious to everyone that, strictly speaking, sight in itself presents nothing but pictures, and hearing nothing but utterances and sounds. So everything over and above these utterances and pictures which we think of as being signified by them is represented to us by means of ideas which come to us from no other source than our own faculty of thinking. Consequently these ideas, along with that faculty, are innate in us, i.e. they always exist within us potentially, for to exist in some faculty is not to exist actually, but merely potentially, since the term "faculty" denotes nothing but a potentiality. (*CSM* I:305)

One consequence of this view is that we can have an (innate) idea of something without thinking of that something. It is tempting to read this as indi-

---

10. Thus we should read passages like those in the Sixth Meditation (e.g., *CSM* II:55) as being somewhat elliptical. External objects are not strictly the cause of our ideas of them.

cating that ideas are *simply* dispositions, but given that faculties are clearly dispositions for Descartes, ideas would then be dispositions of dispositions. I find no evidence that he endorsed that view, and it seems dubious. More charitably, we have innate ideas in the sense that we have the corresponding disposition, whether or not that disposition is activated. These can still loosely be interpreted as modes, especially since he insists that the mind need not have ideas that are strongly distinct from the mind's faculty of thinking (*CSM* I:303). Only now ideas are occurrent thoughts. When a disposition is activated, an idea is actualized as the object of thought.

A natural question arises. If all sensory ideas are innate, do external stimuli play any role in the formation of our ideas? Descartes is already committed to the claim that they play no direct causal role. His reply to this sort of question is surprising. External stimuli, he tells us, are remote causes while our mental faculties are the primary or proximate causes. Descartes, as we have just seen, tells us that our faculty of thinking is the "source" of our ideas. In his explanation leading up to this conclusion, he assures us that only our mental dispositions are proximate causes (*CSM* I:305).[11]

The difficulty now is how to reconcile this account with Descartes' already established commitment to a theory of causation as contagion. Consider two ways of understanding dispositions. In the first, dispositions supervene on grounding nondispositional properties. We generally do not think of dispositions as possessing causal powers; rather we think of the underlying properties as possessing them (Ryle 1984, 118ff.). Thus salt is soluble because it (and water) possesses certain nondispositional chemical properties. We can account for dispositional properties on this view with counterfactual conditionals. To say that some salt is soluble is to indicate that were someone to place the salt in water, then a particular result would obtain (it would dissolve). Descartes, however, has no theory of counterfactual conditionals and appears to treat dispositions as ungrounded entities. In that case, we may legitimately inquire what mental dispositions "have" to give to other mental states. For salt, one might appeal to its basic chemical properties for an answer, but there is no correlate for ungrounded dispositions. Perhaps we need a more charitable understanding of dispositions. A second understanding denies that dispositions possess causal powers on the grounds that dispositions *are* causal powers. That is, they are simply discovered regularities in the world. For Descartes to claim that innate ideas are dispositions is only to assert that if there is a particular stimulus of a certain

---

11. See Jolley 1990, 36–37.

sort, then there will be a response of a certain kind. This view, however, also runs afoul of his larger theory of causation, since he is antecedently committed to there being something that is transferred in an instance of causation. He cannot, recall, imagine causation without some form of presence ("there can be nothing in an effect which was not previously present in the cause" [CSM/K III:192]). More generally, Descartes owes us a theory of mental-mental causation that makes room for his theory of innate ideas.

Descartes does not discuss mental causation as much as one would like, but it is at least clear that he retains his adherence to the principle that causes must have at least as much reality as their effects. Hence, the cause of an idea must have at least as much reality as the idea itself. When speaking of ideas$_m$ this principle seems innocent enough. Any mode might reasonably be supposed to have as much reality as another qua mode. But Descartes does not discuss instances of causation *between* ideas. All of his examples involve external causes of our (internal) ideas. Consider the following typical passage, from the Second Replies:

> It follows from this that the objective reality of our ideas needs a cause which contains this reality not merely objectively but formally or eminently. It should be noted that this axiom is one which we must necessarily accept, since on it depends our knowledge of all things, whether they are perceivable through the senses or not. How do we know, for example, that the sky exists? Because we see it? But this "seeing" does not affect the mind except in so far as it is an idea—I mean an idea which resides in the mind itself, not an image depicted in the corporeal imagination. Now the only reason why we can use this idea as a basis for the judgment that the sky exists is that every idea must have a really existing cause of its objective reality; and in this case we judge that the cause is the sky itself. And we make similar judgments in other cases. (*CSM* II:116–17)

For any idea$_o$ we represent to ourselves, there must be a really existing cause of its content. The same must hold of ideas generated by other means, such as via mental operations, but he provides no hint of a theory in this regard. At this point Descartes simply has nothing else to offer. His theory of the status of ideas evolves in response to criticism, but he never manages to produce a view free from pressing and obvious difficulties. What matters for our purposes is that he and his contemporaries were aware of the problems driving his developing analysis.

2.4 The Complications of the *Passions*

Despite the ample textual evidence that Descartes shifted to a view where all ideas are innate, an understandable move on his part given the philosophical pressures that had been brought to bear on his thinking, one might object to my analysis on the grounds that Descartes returns to his older position of ideas as corporeal images in his late work *The Passions of the Soul*. The *Passions* was published in late 1649, although there is evidence that initial versions of the piece were written as early as 1646. The important *Comments on a Certain Broadsheet* where Descartes lays out his occasionalist understanding of ideas was written in December 1647 and published in 1648.[12] What makes the *Passions* troubling, at least initially, is that in it Descartes straightforwardly defends a naive version of interactive dualism. The soul receives some of its ideas externally through the famous pineal gland, suggesting that Descartes might have been less than sincere in his claim that sensory ideas are actually innate. "Apart from this gland," he writes, "there cannot be any other place in the whole body where the soul directly exercises its functions" (*CSM* I:340). The mind and body interact through the medium of animal spirits.

> Let us therefore take it that the soul has its principal seat in the small gland located in the middle of the brain. From there it radiates through the rest of the body by means of the animal spirits, the nerves, and even the blood, which can take on the impressions of the spirits and carry them through the arteries to all the limbs. . . . To this we may now add that the small gland which is the principal seat of the soul is suspended within the cavities containing these spirits, so that it can be moved by them in as many different ways as there are perceptible differences in the objects. But it can also be moved in various different ways by the soul, whose nature is such that it receives as many different impressions—that is, it has as many different perceptions as there occur different movements in this gland. (*CSM* I:341)

Why would Descartes return to this account after having apparently abandoned it? The question is all the more pressing because nothing in the *Passions* provides even a hint of an answer to the problems raised and engaged

---

12. See the translators' comments in *CSM* I:293, 325.

in the *Comments*. The philosophical pressures that led Descartes to court occasionalism are nowhere in evidence in the *Passions*. Two possible reasons for his return to interactionism suggest themselves. First, it might be that Descartes did indeed write the *Passions* before the *Comments*, in which his more careful thinking manifests itself, and simply did not revise it. He says in a 23 April 1649 letter to Clerselier that he has been "indolent in revising it and adding the things you thought lacking" (*CSM/K* III:376). I find this explanation unsatisfying, however, since Descartes appears to have been seeking to publish the work for some time.[13] If he had been unhappy with his claims in the work, it is unlikely that he would have been so enthused about having the piece published.

More probably, Descartes simply had not resolved all of the difficulties and tensions within his own philosophical system. I do not think that Descartes believed that the two accounts were in conflict at all. He holds that there are two kinds of objects when it comes to perception: one sensory (corporeal images) and one mental (ideas). This division must be the case since our sensory images do not always exactly resemble the ideas we form in thinking. The prick of a pin does not resemble the idea of pain it putatively causes. Furthermore there is still the familiar causal picture in place. Corporeal motions cause the soul to have the (mental) ideas it does, but the ideas in the soul are not the sensory items intromitted through the corporeal imagination. As he notes in *Comments on a Certain Broadsheet*,

> if we bear well in mind the scope of our senses and what it is exactly that reaches our faculty of thinking by way of them, we must admit that in no case are the ideas of things presented to us by the senses just as we form them in our thinking. So much so that there is nothing in our ideas which is not innate to the mind or the faculty of thinking, with the sole exception of those circumstances which relate to experience, such as the fact that we judge that this or that idea which we now have immediately before our mind refers to a certain thing situated outside us. We make such a judgement not because these things transmit the ideas to our mind through the sense organs, but because they transmit something which, at exactly that moment, gives the mind occasion to form these ideas by means

---

13. In a letter to Freinshemius in June 1649, Descartes talks about publishing the *Passions*, but he notes that he only did so after securing permission from Queen Christina, to whom the work was presented privately. His willingness to have the work published as it was suggests that he had not seriously changed his mind about the nature of ideas and mind-body interaction.

of the faculty innate to it. Nothing reaches our mind from external objects through the sense organs except certain corporeal motions, as our author himself asserts in article nineteen, in accordance with my own principles. (*CSM* I:304)

We can perhaps forgive Descartes for using the phrase "ideas of things presented to us by the senses," given that in the Second Replies he ardently claims that strictly speaking nothing in the senses is an idea, but only an image.[14] But the picture is otherwise the same as in the *Passions*. In a sense, the story is at once both interactionist *and* occasionalist. The senses cause alteration in the soul through the pineal gland, but the change is not direct. The corporeal motions that influence the gland H—and hence the soul—provide an "occasion" (Descartes' word) for the soul to activate its own dispositions to have otherwise purely mental ideas, which presumably would be modes of the mind.

This account has all of the defects of both theories and no special advantages. The sort of causal connection present between the animal spirits and any particular mental idea is still left mysterious. What explains the occasional connections is equally unclear. Yet the view, despite its defects, is also testament to the profundity of Descartes' thinking. For although Descartes is too deeply committed to the interactionist thesis to let go of it at this point, he is at least vaguely cognizant of the problems it engenders and tries to introduce a modified occasionalism to smooth out some of the kinks in his system. It is small wonder that such diverse philosophers as Malebranche and Arnauld would both claim to be genuine Cartesians.

Some have argued that it is vain to pursue a unified, coherent Cartesian theory of the mind. Descartes worked diligently to fashion a new and radical mechanical theory of the world and then simply dumped everything that did not fit into that model into the "dustbin" of the mind. In particular, secondary qualities (proper sensibles) were relegated to the mind because they could not be fully explained by his physical theory.[15] I find this understanding of Descartes unsatisfying but nonetheless largely correct. He tried to integrate ideas and qualities into his new mechanistic philosophy but ultimately failed. More importantly, in this failure he refused to squarely confront the problems generated by making ideas purely mental entities. We

---

14. This thesis is supported, for example, by his claim concerning the distinction that separates brutes from humans. Brutes have images in the senses; it is not until the mind regards the images that they become ideas (*CSM* II:161; see also *CSM* II:97).

15. See Shoemaker 1990, 109–31, and Cook 1996, 17–33.

have no theory of mental-mental causation and little more than hand waving about the interaction between mind and body.

We at least know the following: Descartes never officially abandoned his core commitment to ideas as modes. The problems generated by trying to explain how external stimuli cause adventitious ideas led Descartes to separate corporeal images from mental ideas and introduce an odd version of occasionalism in which bodies do affect the soul despite the fact that the soul's ideas are nonetheless proximately caused only within the mind. The unsatisfying nature of this theory and the unclarities within it provide a fertile ground for debate and illustrate the fundamental incongruity between idea philosophy and the traditional ontological categories. Descartes, as it were, sets the stage for the drama concerning the debate over the ontology of ideas. He is nonetheless firmly entrenched within the confines of substance and mode. He passed this metaphysical constraint on to his intellectual audience, who would continue to wrestle with the nature of the ideas.

3

THE CARTESIANS: MALEBRANCHE AND ARNAULD

Nicolas Malebranche, although he considered himself a devoted Cartesian, was a potent critic of Descartes' theory of ideas. In particular he denied that ideas could be modes, claiming that Descartes was simply unclear about their exact nature (*OC* 6:172, Réponse 24.)[1] In this way, he hoped to enlist Cartesians in his cause without endorsing a particular claim he was convinced was in error. His hope was short-lived, however, as most Cartesians either ignored Malebranche or else rejected his theory of ideas. Antoine Arnauld, a renowned Port-Royalist, entered into a lengthy debate with Malebranche not only about the nature of ideas but also about which view should be properly attributed to Descartes. The starting point is the familiar early modern one initiated by Descartes. Malebranche, for instance, characterizes an idea as "the immediate object, or the object closest to mind, when it perceives something, i.e. that which affects and modifies the mind with the perception it has of an object" (*LO,* 217 [3.2.1]). Arnauld does not quarrel with this definition per se; he only questions whether the perception of ideas requires a representation distinct from the mind (*TF,* 35).

Malebranche alleges that treating ideas as modes engenders skepticism and confuses the psychological with the logical. Thinking of x is different from the concept of x. The former is a mode of the mind, the latter is an abstract entity. To conflate them, he argues, is a gross error. Both of these larger concerns stem from his conviction that modes cannot properly fulfill the representative role accorded them by Arnauld and other supporters of that view. In other words, on Malebranche's view, the functional roles ideas are supposed to play in the new idea philosophy launched by Descartes cannot be accomplished by modes but only by substance(s). Malebranche

---

1. See Nadler 1992, 38.

therefore proposes instead a theory that divides Cartesian ideas into ideas proper, which are *substantival* abstract objects (substance-like but not necessarily substances per se) that represent the external world, and sensations (*sentiment*), which are modes of the soul and cannot represent anything external to it.

3.1 Malebranche's Theory of Ideas

Malebranche accepts Descartes' distinction between ideas taken materially and those taken objectively. Malebranche, as I mentioned above, wants to distinguish between (1) thinking of x and (2) the concept of x. The former involves an activity and is a mode of thinking substance (mind) whereas the latter is an abstract entity. To conflate the two is a significant error in Malebranche's view, and he aims to demonstrate the mistake by arguing that modes cannot genuinely represent things or events external to that which is being modified. Hence modes cannot represent the external world. Ideas, insofar as they are the *objects* of the mind representing an *external* reality, must be independent of the mind.

> Everything the soul perceives belongs to either one of two sorts: either it is in the soul, or outside the soul. The things that are in the soul are its own thoughts, i.e., all its various modifications—for by the words *thought, mode of thinking,* or *modification of the soul,* I generally understand all those things that cannot be in the soul without the soul being aware of them through the inner sensation it has of itself—such as its sensations, imaginings, pure intellections, or simply conceptions, as well as its passions and natural inclinations. . . . But as for things outside the soul, we can perceive them only by means of ideas, given that these things cannot be intimately joined to the soul. (*LO,* 218 [3.2.1])

Part of his conviction on this point stems from the Platonic/Augustinian influences that dominated his intellectual development. Platonic conceptions emphasize the immutability and eternality of ideas. Such conceptions, when coupled with Malebranche's belief in the transparency of the soul (no idea is present in the soul of which the soul is not aware), makes ideas ontologically distinct from minds.

To start, Malebranche tells us that the mind gains knowledge of the world in three ways: through pure understanding (or conception), imagination, and sensation. Only the first strictly involves ideas exclusively. Although early on Malebranche briefly held that ideas are particular entities, he quickly corrected his position, arguing that they are all abstract and general. "[F]or the mind never sees clearly what is not universal" (*LO*, 5 [1.1.2]). Knowledge of individual external objects requires that the perceived ideas be "particularized" by sensations, which are modes of the soul. In sensory perception, sensation is added to the idea to produce a particular perceptual experience (see *LO*, 234 [3.2.6]). It should be emphasized, however, that for Malebranche the pure perception of an idea *is* the perception of an external entity. Sensations, such as color, tone, or temperature only individuate ideas.

> However, in order to satisfy partially the desire you have to know how the mind can discover all kinds of figures and see the sensible world in intelligible extension, note the three ways you perceive a circle, for example. You conceive it, you imagine it, you sense or see it. When you conceive it, intelligible extension is applied to your mind with indeterminate limits in respect of size, but equally distant from a determinate point, and all on a single plane; and then you conceive a circle in general. When you imagine it, a determinate part of this extension, the limits of which are equally distant from a point, lightly touches your mind. And when you sense or see it, a determinate part of this extension sensibly touches your soul and modifies it by the sensation of some color. (*DMR*, 17, Dialogue I.10)

What Malebranche labels "imagination" is in no-man's-land, not quite pure intellection and not sensation, involving only the idea "touching" the mind. Not much good use is made of imagination, and I largely ignore it in what follows. Of most importance is the play between sensation and conception. The state of the mind (its mode) particularizes the universal idea it perceives.

It is tempting to argue that Malebranche holds an adverbial theory of sensation (but not of ideas). When, for example, we perceive a particular red line we are apprehending that bit of extension redly. He frequently treats secondary qualities not as objects but as perceptions identical with the mental act of perceiving. "When we have a vivid sensation of light attached or related to an intelligible circle, distant through a certain intelligible space, and made sensible by different colors, we see the sun" (*OC* 6:65, Réponse 6, also quoted in Nadler 1992, 64). The mind attaches color to the pure idea of a circle in order to perceive it as an individual body. We have here a relation between the mind and the idea-object in which the first relatum is the mind in a particular state. Thus to perceive the yellow sun is to perceive an idea of the sun yellowly. Steven Nadler thinks ascribing this view to Malebranche unnecessarily burdens him with "confusions," since Malebranche suggests that color sensations are ways of apprehending pure ideas (most often in connection with the perception of extension) (Nadler 1992, 64–65). But if ideas are abstract entities and not sense data, how could one sensibly perceive ideas? I am unconvinced by Nadler's worry here, since an alternative explanation exists. Sensation is, in a sense, the touching of ideas to the mind. Since the mind cannot perceive without being in a particular mode, then it cannot perceive without sensing. The goal of pure thought is to separate out sensation from the pure idea, although often that might not be possible. Color sensations are ways of apprehending pure ideas only in the sense that we have no perceptions without sensation. I grant that Malebranche is unclear in many of the passages, and perhaps Nadler is right to point out these rough spots, but I do not think these worries are independently serious. Malebranche uses the word "perception" multivocally to include both the apprehension of ideas *and* at some points the apprehension of material bodies (albeit indirectly). Both processes require mentation (since perception for Malebranche always involves the intellect), but the objects of perception can differ. Straightening out such worries as Nadler presents often leaves small riddles like this one.

Whereas sensations are modes, ideas are explicitly described as entities external to the mind. They can, for instance, exist independently of minds (*LO*, 229 [3.2.5]).[2] They are universal, abstract, and immutable. In his *Dialogues on Metaphysics and Religion,* Malebranche (represented by Theodore) has his opponent Aristes sum up his conception of ideas near the end of the first dialogue.

> ARISTES: I give in, Theodore. Ideas have more reality than I thought, and their reality is immutable, necessary, eternal, common to all intellects and in no way modifications of the being of the intellect which, because it is finite, cannot actually receive infinite modifications. The perception I have of intelligible extension belongs to me, it is a modi-

---

2. See McCracken 1983, 236–37.

fication of my mind. It is I who perceive this extension. But the extension I perceive is not a modification of my mind. . . . But the extension I see subsists without me. For you can think of it without my thinking of it, you and everyone else. (16, Dialogue I.9)

Ideas are "third realm" entities (neither strictly mental nor material) and the only proper vehicles to represent the external material world. As independent and immutable entities, they can underlie change, making them unambiguously rather like substances. I do need to be clear that when I say that Malebranche's ideas are *like* substances, I intend that they are "second-rate" substances and not substances per se. As Descartes notes, technically speaking only God is a substance, and Malebranche shares this conviction. This caveat explains one passage in *The Search After Truth* where Malebranche appears to deny the substantiality of ideas. "But if it be said that an idea is not a substance, I would agree—but it is still a spiritual thing, and as it is impossible to make a square out of a mind, though a square is not a substance, so a spiritual idea cannot be formed from a material substance, even though an idea is not a substance" (*LO*, 223 [3.2.3]). So Malebranche treats ideas on the continuum of things as substance-like, as being *close* to genuine substances in the sense that they are independent and simple, but does not regard them as literally first-rate substances. We should not be surprised, therefore, to see him denying that ideas are strictly substances, even though his considered view makes ideas strikingly similar to them. Additionally, in this particular passage, Malebranche is primarily concerned with denying that ideas are either material or strictly mental—the two traditional substance types. Ideas for him are decidedly third realm, and this no doubt also contributes to his desire to argue against the notion that they are *traditional* substances (mind or matter).

One might ask at this point where these "substantial" ideas reside and how the mind relates to them in perception. Given that he essentially models his conception of ideas on that of Augustine, it should be no surprise that Malebranche locates all ideas in God.[3] Malebranche also asks how ideas could come to be present to our minds. He asserts that there are (only) five possible explanations. He considers and rejects the first four, leaving only the final possibility. In short, the only substances of which we have knowledge are mind, body, and God. He argues that neither bodies nor finite

---

3. It is instructive to compare Malebranche with Augustine on this point. See *LO*, 613–14, Elucidation 10, and Augustine 1993, 2:8.43–47.

minds could produce ideas, and thus all we have left is God. He then dismisses the possibilities that God either continuously creates ideas or has bestowed us with an innate repository of the same and so finally concludes that the mind perceives ideas in a being different from itself. That being has to be in close mental union with our minds and contain an infinite store of ideas, actual and possible. Since only an infinite being can meet such requirements, we must see our ideas "in" God, in the sense that we literally see God.

> To understand this fifth way, we must remember what was just said in the preceding chapter—that God must have within Himself the ideas of all the beings He has created, and thus He sees all these beings by considering the perfections He contains to which they are related. We should know, furthermore, that through His presence God is in close union with our minds, such that He might be said to be the place of minds as space is, in a sense, the place of bodies. Given these two things, the mind surely can see what in God represents created beings, since what in God represents created beings is very spiritual, intelligible, and present to the mind. Thus, the mind can see God's works in Him. (LO, 230 [3.2.6])

Malebranche's "Vision in God" thesis has been much ridiculed, but it is nonetheless an ingenious theory. Ideas are actually ideal archetypes in God. Since it is not my purpose to here to evaluate the entirety of his philosophy, I leave this strange, exciting doctrine for others to analyze, but I would like to make one observation. Note that for Malebranche ideas "in" God are not modes of Him. Instead, they are God's substantial essence. "But, you will say, for these same reasons God would not be able to see His creatures in Himself. This would be true if ideas of creatures were modifications of His substance, but the Infinite Being is incapable of modifications. God's ideas of creatures are, as Saint Thomas says, only His essence, insofar as it is participable or imperfectly imitable" (LO, 625, Elucidation 10). This view is intriguing, since it strikes me as initially plausible that ideas in God could be modes of the divine substance. Malebranche denies this move, presumably on the grounds he uses to attack ideas as modes generally, but he provides no explicit argument against this possibility when applied to God (assuming that God not being able to directly see His creatures in Himself is a consequence with which we can live). What matters for present purposes is that ideas are robust, ontologically distinct entities; Malebranche is a convinced substantivalist about ideas, even if perception generally requires both ideas and sensation.

Granting, then, that perception involves both ideas and sensations, Malebranche still needs to argue for his claim that ideas cannot be modes. After all, it is possible that sensations are a species of ideas and hence that both are modes of the mind. Here we need to be careful. Malebranche launches an impressive array of attacks against treating ideas as modes, but not all of them are used constructively to defend his claim that ideas *must* be substance-like. I will thus break down the voluminous amount of material into two sections, one concerning what might be taken as his arguments for treating ideas as (like) substances and a second that examines his negative attacks on the Cartesian theory of ideas as modes.

3.2 Substantializing Ideas

Malebranche's strategy for arguing that ideas must be substantial is best thought of in two parts, even though he himself might not have conceived his own argument in this way. He first attempts to establish that material objects cannot be directly perceived by the soul and then that all perception is object directed (intentional). Since every thought must have an object distinct from itself, and material objects cannot fulfill this required role, ideas must fit the bill.

Malebranche writes as if his first point is obvious.

> I think everyone agrees that we do not perceive objects external to us by themselves. We see the sun, the stars, and an infinity of objects external to us; and it is not likely that the soul should leave the body to stroll about the heavens, as it were, in order to behold all these objects. Thus, it does not see them by themselves, and our mind's immediate object when it sees the sun, for example, is not the sun, but something that is intimately joined to our soul, and this is what I call an *idea*. Thus, by the word *idea* I mean nothing other than the immediate object, or the object closest to the mind, when it perceives something, i.e. that which affects and modifies the mind with the perception it has of an object. (*LO*, 217 [3.2.1])

Since the soul does not "stroll out" to the stars, and they don't seem to be coming to us, there must be intermediate ideas that we directly perceive.

Malebranche's reasoning here relies heavily on the principle mentioned in our discussion of Descartes (section 2.1) that cognition cannot occur "at a distance." What this argument does not do, however, is establish what Malebranche acts as if it does, namely, that an idea must be that *object* closest to the mind. Arnauld quarrels with the reasoning that leads Malebranche to conclude that an idea must be an object, countering that Malebranche is confusing a purely physical principle with a mental one. There cannot be action at a distance; hence, in the physical world, causality requires locality. But one cannot legitimately apply this analogously to the mental, since by definition the material and mental share nothing in common. "But why then, I will be asked," Arnauld writes,

> does everyone go along with the thought that since the soul cannot know distant objects, there must be something which makes them present to it and that therefore ideas or species are necessary?
>
> I have already given the explanation in Chapter IV. It is the comparison of bodily vision, itself poorly understood, with mental vision. The ambiguity of the word *presence* also played an important role, as I have indicated. It is quite common that the same word is applied to mind and to body, and is taken by most people in a very coarse sense suitable for bodies even when it is applied to the mind. Thus the word *presence* signifies, with regard to bodies, a *local presence*, and with regard to minds, an *objective presence*, according to which objects are said to be in our mind when they are there objectively, i.e., when they are known by it, as in definition 4. (*TF*, 37)

Arnauld's move attempts to fill a gap left by Descartes, who had no clear theory about mental causation. His point is well taken and Malebranche replies by disowning the literalness of the example. His only intent, he claims, was to demonstrate that the "presence" (in whatever sense) of something other than material objects is required for the perception of the external world.

Malebranche does not make it clear exactly what he means by "presence." Arnauld argues that if Malebranche does not mean physical locality, then he must mean some sort of cognitive (he calls it "objective") presence. Yet if it is the latter, then there does not seem to be any (stated) reason why material objects cannot be present to the mind. Locke is equally puzzled by Malebranche on this point, finally concluding in exasperation, "Explain this manner of union, and show wherein the difference consists between the union necessary and not necessary to perception, and then I shall confess this difficulty removed" (EM, 416, also quoted in Nadler 1992, 74). We might venture on Malebranche's behalf to say that presence requires sameness of ontological kind, which would be perfectly in keeping with Malebranche's deep Cartesian dualism. The reason that a physical object cannot be present to the mind stems from the fact that the object and the mind are of distinct ontological kinds. Unfortunately the drawback to this explanation of presence is that if material objects cannot be present to the mind, then neither can ideas! Ideas, recall, are abstract "third realm" entities for Malebranche. If "presence" means similarity of kind, then the mind cannot directly perceive ideas either.

Steven Nadler has proposed another possible reading of "presence" for Malebranche. Nadler argues that presence to the mind is causal in nature. "To be present to the mind is to be in a causal relationship with the mind; thus only that which can act on the mind, which can 'touch' or modify it by causing a perception in it, is visible or intelligible by itself" (1992, 76). There is some textual evidence to support Nadler's assertion. Malebranche does occasionally indicate that material bodies cannot be present to the mind because they cannot act on it (*LO*, 320 [4.11.3]). Bodies are devoid of causal powers with respect to minds not only because their essence is only passive extension but also because Malebranche adheres to a form of Descartes' causal reality principle. A cause must have at least as much reality and power in itself as is present in the effect. For minds, this means "nothing can act immediately upon the mind unless it is superior to it [the mind]" (*LO*, 232 [4.11.3]).[4] Souls, however, are more perfect and real than bodies, and hence they cannot be affected by material objects but only by "God alone." Malebranche wants ideas to be ontologically distinct from the mind yet simultaneously insists that they have robust causal powers to affect the mind. "It is certain that ideas are efficacious, since they act upon the mind and enlighten it" (*LO*, 232 [3.2.6]). Why should we not think that "third realm" ideas are like material objects and thus consider that they cannot act outside of their own ontological kind? Malebranche does not confront this issue squarely. One possible explanation has been suggested by Nicholas Jolley (1996, 542). Perhaps Malebranche is in the grips of the following argument:

---

4. Technically, of course, the Cartesian doctrine only requires *equality or superiority*, and not simply superiority as mentioned here by Malebranche.

(1) Ideas are literally in God.
(2) Everything in and about God is causally efficacious.
(3) Therefore ideas are causally efficacious.

The crux of the matter is the second premise. Malebranche does not explicitly argue that *everything* "in" God must be causally efficacious. Yet he was steeped in the medieval theological tradition that conceived of God as pure activity, which suggests that he would have accepted the notion that whatever is "in" God must also be active and hence causally active as well. Nonetheless it is difficult to see on independent *philosophical* grounds why everything in God would have to be causally potent. At some point one might muster in his defense that, confound it all, ideas just *do* affect minds. Such a response would be thoroughly Cartesian. Instead of mind/body interaction problems, Malebranche has mind/idea interaction problems.

Let us assume, for the moment, that Malebranche successfully defends his claim that material objects cannot be directly perceived by the mind. Ideas are defined by him as the immediate objects perceived by the mind, so what remains is for him to establish that *only* ideas construed as abstract entities can be present to the mind in the appropriate manner to allow for the perception/representation of the external world. Malebranche seems to recognize that the first part of his argumentation does not quite accomplish his goal; he claims in his "Response" to Arnauld that Arnauld simply did not read carefully enough (OC 6:96, also quoted in Nadler 1992, 78–79).

In short, Malebranche contends that every mental act requires an object. To be more precise, every perception is necessarily object-directed. One cannot have a thought without it being a thought of something. Note, however, that for Malebranche this discussion excludes sensation, since he believes that sense perception does not have an object distinct from the object provided by the pure understanding. Recall that the senses "particularize" the abstract objects of the intellect, so strictly speaking sensation has no object of its own. Malebranche thinks his basic point is indisputable: to perceive nothing is not to perceive at all.

> It should be carefully noted that for the mind to perceive an object, it is absolutely necessary for the idea of that object to be actually present to it—and about this there can be no doubt; but there need not be any external thing like that idea. . . . When, for example, a man imagines a golden mountain, it is absolutely necessary that the idea of this mountain really be present to his mind. When a mad-

man or someone asleep or in a high fever sees some animal before his eyes, it is certain that what he sees is not nothing, and that therefore the idea of this animal really does exist, though the golden mountain and the animal have never existed. (*LO*, 217 [3.2.1])

Arnauld, interestingly enough, agrees with Malebranche's underlying point here. "Therefore," he writes, "since it is clear *that I think*, it is also clear that I think of something, because thought is essentially thus. So, since there can be no thought or knowledge without an object known, I can no more ask what is that reason why I think of something, than why I think, since it is impossible to think without thinking of something" (*TF*, 6). They differ, however, on what it means to be the object of a thought. Whereas Malebranche takes perception and intentionality to be a two-place relation, Arnauld insists that perceiving is a nonrelational property of the mental act.

Using what he regards as the uncontested premise that all perception takes an object, Malebranche makes his case for substantializing ideas. Every mental act has an object. Some mental acts, however, have no corresponding external material object, as in the case of illusions or hallucinations. Yet even here it cannot be the case that nothing is perceived, and since by hypothesis no material object is present, it must be the case that some nonmaterial entity is present to the mind fulfilling the role of the direct object. Malebranche advances this argument in several places, sometimes with minor differences, but this rough outline is sufficient for our purposes here.[5]

The argument is generally unsatisfying, since Malebranche seems to be assuming that intentional perception is relational in order to prove that ideas must be substantial. As mentioned in the first chapter, often part of what it means to substantialize ideas is to hold that perception is inherently relational. As a consequence, Malebranche's argument appears circular. And, unsurprisingly, his inference is valid. If all mentation requires an object and the intentional nature of mentation is inherently relational, then the ideas that serve as the objects of thought must be entities distinct from the mind. Yet we have two problems to flesh out here. The first is that merely discovering that ideas must be distinct from the mind does not entitle Malebranche to conclude that they must be *ontologically* distinct. And, certainly, one might think he *cannot* conclude this at all. After all, ideas are causally efficacious on minds. Second, he has not given us a good reason to suppose that the intentional nature of mentation is relational.

5. For a full discussion, see Nadler 1992, 81–90.

Malebranche indicates how the second problem can be overcome. He provides a number of arguments against the possibility of ideas being modes and concludes that if they are not modes, perception must be relational. I examine those arguments in the next section. Arnauld, of course, fights him tooth and nail on that point. More interesting, however, is Malebranche's apparent blindness to the issue of ontological kinds. I submit that he was profoundly unclear about the exact nature of ideas as a distinct ontological kind. Evidence of his unclarity is abundant. He argues that ideas can affect minds—ideas are "present" to them. Yet minds are particular beings whereas ideas are abstract and universal. Thus when I say that one might deny that he could conclude ideas are ontologically distinct from minds, I am suggesting that he might not have thought they were distinct. That is because he was unaware of the importance of this issue. To Malebranche, ideas are essentially, if confusedly, mental entities. He does not say so, but he acts as if they are, and therein lies the problem. Given what Malebranche says about ideas alone, they must be "third realm" entities. Given what he says about their relations to minds, they cannot be. Acting as if ideas are mental entities causes him and his system problems, and it also points to a fundamental obscurity about the nature of ideas that the early moderns would have difficulty shaking. As we shall see, the nature of the metaphysical relation between minds and ideas causes Berkeley considerable distress, and I suspect what worries he does display come partially from Malebranche.

3.3 Attacking Modes

Although Malebranche does not provide us with any independent arguments as to why intentionality must be relational (aside from appeals to commonsense descriptions of mental activities), he does generate a number of often insightful criticisms of ideas as modes. His target is usually Descartes, whom he thought (despite his general genius) did not reflect carefully enough on the status of ideas and hence fell into error. Arnauld is quick to defend not only modes but also the claim that Descartes genuinely did intend to advance a theory of ideas that treats them exclusively as modes.

On an initial read of his critique of Descartes, we encounter a flurry of problems raised by Malebranche. He thinks it reasonable to ask, "How many ideas have I had in the past hour?" but there is no easy answer forthcoming from Descartes' theory. Malebranche does not restrict himself simply to posing difficult questions. He advances both metaphysical and epistemological concerns that militate against ideas being modes. He provides a number of arguments, many of them minor variations of others, and I want to consider only the most potent of them.[6] The first I call the "distinctness argument," which he lays out in Elucidation 10, Second Reply:

> To be sure, we can assert what we clearly conceive. Now, we clearly conceive that the extension we see is something distinct from ourselves. We can say, then, that this extension is not a modification of our being, and that it is indeed something distinct from ourselves. For it should be noted that the sun that we see, for example, is not the one we look at. The sun, and everything else in the material world, is not visible by itself. This I have proved elsewhere. The soul can see only the sun to which it is immediately joined, only that sun that like it occupies no place. Now, we see clearly and perceive distinctly that this sun is something distinct from us. Thus, we speak contrary to our light and consciousness when we say that the soul sees in its own modifications all the objects it perceives. (*LO*, 625)

Assuming the truth of his claim that the material world is not directly perceived, Malebranche reasons that since the modes of the soul are perceived as part of the soul (since they in fact are), it is not possible for it to represent anything as distinct and external to itself. Yet we do think of things, such as extended objects, as external to and distinct from ourselves; thus our knowledge of that externality must not stem from the modes of the soul. The argument is based on Descartes' distinction between modes and substances. A mode is that which cannot be conceived apart from its substance (*CSM* I:298, *Comments on a Certain Broadsheet*). Hence, if our idea of an extended square figure is a mode, there must be some part of representing that figure to ourselves that involves the mind or that at least does not depend solely on the body. Yet we *do* represent figures to ourselves as entirely nonmental entities. For a body to possess squareness, the body must be square. Likewise, for a person to be in pain her or his mind must be in a painful state. So, in order for an idea to be a mode, it must be possible that the soul is square and extended (or is in a square, extended state) when it represents a square figure to itself. Yet this is absurd, for it ascribes physical properties to a nonmaterial thing.

---

6. For a more complete exploration of Malebranche's arguments against modes, see Rome 1963, esp. ch. 2.

One might try Descartes' suggestion that ideas are modes contained "eminently" within the mind (*CSM* II:30–31, Third Meditation). God, after all, contains all the ideas of the world and yet is not material, so why might we not think that the soul can be square without being extended? This option suggests that ideas are in the soul in a manner somehow superior to the content represented. Malebranche considers this reply in Elucidation 10 and rejects it (*LO*, 624–25). God is an infinite being; the minds of persons are finite. He does not think it possible for finite minds to contain all the properties of every possible physical object that might be represented to it. Hence, external physical objects must be represented to the mind in another way. He further strengthens this reply by appealing to another argument he uses elsewhere against modes, namely, that if ideas were modes, we could not have ideas of the infinite.

Malebranche argues that, unlike God's mind, the human mind is finite and therefore cannot contain within itself an infinite number of essences. Yet, he protests, we do have an idea of the infinite. We can clearly conceive of an infinite number series and figures in geometry that invoke similar concepts. If ideas were modes, however, then the mind would have to be in an infinite state or perhaps represent to itself an infinite number of mental states at once. But this is impossible.

> Therefore, since the human mind can know all beings, including infinite beings, and since it does not contain them, we have a sure proof that it does not see their essence in itself. For the mind not only sees things one after another in temporal succession, but it also perceives the infinite, though it does not comprehend it, as we have said in the preceding chapter. Consequently, being neither actually infinite nor capable of infinite modifications simultaneously, it is absolutely impossible for the mind to see in itself what is not there. It does not see the essence of things, therefore, by considering its own perfections or by modifying itself in different ways. (*LO*, 229 [3.2.5])

Every state of a finite mind is not only finite but particular. Thus every time we perceive an idea representing the infinite, we have demonstrated that ideas are not modes. Now, since the mind cannot be infinitely modified, it cannot contain within itself eminently all the possible modifications that would be required to represent the external world.

Perhaps more important to Malebranche, however, are the dire epistemological consequences of treating ideas as modes. Modes lead to skepticism for a variety of reasons. First, if ideas are merely modes, then he thinks that the truths of geometry become true simply because we think them so. The interior angles of a triangle total 180 degrees. I have a series of ideas from which I deduce this truth. But since those ideas are nothing more than states of my mind, the veracity of the claim reduces to an assertion that it is so. Necessary truths, he complains, are not like this at all. Unless we have access to an external, immutable reality, we have no, and *can* have no, guarantee that what we think about the external world is true. In short, modes grant no security that things outside us correspond to our ideas (*LO*, 320 [4.11.3]).

Most of this charge rests on Malebranche's (Platonic) belief that ideas are immutable. The idea of a triangle does not change, nor could it. Since modes are merely transient states of mind, we have no guarantee that our ideas remain stable over time, especially since they now are fleeting, particular, and contingent beings. To make matters even worse, had no human mind ever thought of a triangle and its interior angles, then that necessary truth would never be! Now we might add Malebranche's claim that ideas are not only immutable but also universal. Modes are particular states of minds. As a result, there is no guarantee that when two persons think of a triangle that they are thinking of the same thing. In short, the natural consequence of treating ideas as modes is a pernicious form of skepticism. Yet we *do* know we have the same idea, he protests, and we *do* reason and act on the basis of that knowledge. We therefore have ample metaphysical and epistemological reasons for rejecting the claim that ideas are modes.

Whether or not Malebranche is right, his insistence that ideas are not modes coupled with his equally stringent insistence that ideas are joined intimately with the mind leaves us with a considerable difficulty. Ideas are not modes and they are not mental entities, but he describes them and their behavior as if they were decidedly mental. What then are we to conclude? His descriptions of them make them substantial, but they often do not behave like substances, and they cannot be modifications of substance. Within a Cartesian framework Malebranche has no other choices. As a result, I think he simply did not confront the question. And so we are left with the unpalatable task of having to carry this increasingly unclear notion of an idea into additional philosophical accounts that rely ever more heavily on it.

3.4 A New Ontology?

Left with the manifestly unclear doctrine of ideas, one might be tempted to conclude that Malebranche abandoned the substance/mode ontology altogether. Such a move would not have been surprising or even perhaps ill advised. Malebranche, however, did not make it. He, as with the rest of the early moderns, was firmly in the grip of the *core* of the old ontology. Some scholars, however, credit Malebranche with novel moves when it comes to ideas. Richard Watson, for instance, argues, "Malebranche's radical innovation is in his treatment of ideas. Concerning ideas he breaks not only with the Cartesian but also with the Scholastic ontological tradition" (1987, 109).[7] Ultimately Watson argues that Malebranchian ideas are neither modes nor substances. Here I want to be clear. I agree with Watson that there are important philosophical pressures guiding Malebranche's reasoning about the nature of ideas. I further agree that these tensions push him toward *stretching* the traditional substance/mode ontology. Ideas are "third realm" entities and like substances are neither material nor mental. Thus Malebranche did abandon traditional substance dualism. That said, abandoning Cartesian dualism does not imply the abandonment of the traditional ontology in any *important* way. All Malebranche has done is to reintroduce the possibility of a third kind of substance, a move made by others before him and arguably even by philosophers within the Scholastic tradition. Watson's analysis of Malebranche's innovation does not extend beyond the (re)introduction of this third kind of substance. "Malebranche must deny that the traditional ontological categories are complete. Ideas appear to be some kind of third representative entity that allows the mind to know material objects" (111).

Interestingly, however, instead of concluding as I have in the analysis above that ideas are *substances* of a new kind, Watson infers that ideas must be a new kind of ontological entity altogether. "[Malebranche] recognizes that his external—third entity—ideas have no place in the Cartesian ontological framework, but rather than alter that framework he tries to add to it by calling on God to be the place of representative entities that have no place in a substantial God nor in an ontological structure that is still basically that of substances and their modifications" (112). His is an odd conclusion. While simultaneously conceding that Malebranche operated entirely within the Cartesian framework, Watson denies that ideas have any place within it.

---

7. See Lennon 1993, esp. 257. Lennon stops short of endorsing Watson's position but notes the unusual moves being made by Malebranche.

Unsurprisingly, he finds more confusion and disarray in Malebranche than one might expect. "Malebranche is certainly trying to solve the problem of how we know external objects by way of ideas, by breaking out of the ontological pattern of substance and modification. But he succeeds (at least within the Cartesian framework he accepts) only in making it as difficult to understand how a mind can know external ideas as it is for the orthodox Cartesians to explain how a mind can know external material objects" (113). Watson ultimately attempts to explain the paradox of Malebranche's embracing the abandonment of the traditional ontology by invoking God. "Further, having broken with the Cartesian ontological framework, he offers no explanation of what might be a new ontological structure. Instead, he does as the orthodox Cartesians do: He appeals again to the mysterious ways of God" (114). I am sympathetic to Watson's contention that Malebranche is being pushed to test the bounds of the traditional ontology but insist that struggling with problems within an ontology is not evidence that one has abandoned it.

The evidence Watson brings to light for his reading of Malebranche is good but not compelling. Watson's reasoning runs roughly as follows (114–15). Malebranche retained several key Cartesian tenets, most notably the likeness principle and the belief that presence to the mind was necessary for understanding. Yet he denied that ideas could be modes of the mind, and this forced him to abandon the traditional categories of substance and mode. Implicitly Watson assumes that the only relations of idea-mind acquaintance available are those of mode to substance. Since direct acquaintance is required for knowledge, yet ideas cannot be modifications of mind, Malebranche must have discarded the substance/mode ontology and invented a new ontological category for ideas. This new category, with the assistance of God, allows for direct contact with the mind without the relation being one of mode to substance. As Watson rightly notes, Malebranche has no explanation of what this new ontological structure might be and so invokes God to cover over the cracks. But nothing in Watson's analysis prevents us from supposing that Malebranche took ideas to be substances of a new kind. Nothing in Malebranche precludes the possibility of substance-substance relations. Granted, mind and body cannot interact, but he has no (persuasive) story of how ideas and minds interact either. We have ample evidence that Malebranche, in effect, treats ideas as substances. They are thing-like, simple, and ontologically independent. Watson may suppose, and perhaps rightly, that Malebranche needed a completely new ontological category, but as a matter of historical interpretation, Malebranche already had a category at hand that he thought could serve his purposes. Given that Watson graciously admits that Malebranche was firmly in the grips of the Cartesian framework, including its ontology, I do not see how his supposition that Malebranche was trying out a new category is likely. Instead of concluding that Malebranche reached for this new ontology, we can simply conclude that he applied his powerful mind to mixed effect within the tradition in which he was so deeply entrenched. To say so does nothing to minimize his accomplishments. Malebranche was driven to explore the limits of the substance/mode ontology because of his theorizing about ideas. That his results pushed and pulled at that ontology are just as sure signs of his intellect as any claim that he abandoned it for a nebulous new ontology that not even he could describe.

3.5 Arnauld's Theory of Ideas

Although a few scholars today have seen fit to place Malebranche outside the traditional ontology, his contemporaries did not. Arnauld in particular was a potent critic of Malebranche who nonetheless accepted without apparent worry that they shared a common ontology. As such, some scholars have thought that the dispute between Arnauld and Malebranche concerned only representation. Arnauld is depicted as a direct realist and Malebranche as an indirect one.[8] This characterization, however, is oversimplified and misleading. As has been implicit in my arguments thus far, the two are primarily disputing the ontological status of ideas and *not* whether some form of representationalism is true. Arnauld *grants* that ideas represent material objects and in fact must do so. Malebranche characterizes their dispute as follows: "What is the issue at hand? Mr. Arnauld insists that the modalities of the soul are essentially representative of objects distinct from the soul; and I maintain that these modalities are nothing but sensations, which do not represent to the soul anything different from itself" (*OC* 6:50, also quoted in Nadler 1992, 184). I argue that we ought to take Malebranche at his word: the issue is whether representative ideas are modifications of the mind or external to it (see *OC* 9:902). This particular dispute is not of pressing concern here; even if the primary issue does revolve around direct versus indirect perception, the problem of the status of ideas nonetheless underlies that dispute. I read Arnauld as though the ontological question is primary in his

---

8. See Lovejoy 1923, 449–61, and Cook 1974, esp. 54.

thinking, mindful of the fact that others might disagree.[9] Such concerns will not affect my analysis.

Why, then, assuming that both agree that ideas need to represent, does Arnauld so strongly deny that ideas are mind-independent external entities? At the heart of his objections lies his belief that such a view in fact cuts us off from the material world altogether.

> He [Malebranche] assumed at the outset that our mind perceives material things. He was troubled only about *how*, whether through ideas or without ideas, taking the word "idea" to stand for *representative beings*, distinct from perceptions. After he has philosophized a great deal about the nature of those *representative beings*, after he has trotted them everywhere and succeeded in locating them only in God, all the fruit he gathers from them is no longer to explain to us how we *see* material things, which is the only thing he sought, but rather that our mind is incapable of perceiving them, and that we live in a continual illusion, thinking that we *see* the material things that God has created when we *look at* them, i.e., when we turn our eyes toward them, and nevertheless seeing, in their place, only the *intelligible bodies* which resemble them. Is anything more needed to destroy all credence in what the author of *The Nature of Ideas* says, whatever air of superiority he gives it? (*TF*, 51)

The point, Arnauld argues, was to explain how we perceive the material world. To conclude that we don't perceive the world reveals an (alleged) absurdity somewhere in the reasoning. Malebranche's chief error was to introduce the unnecessary complication of intermediate, external representative entities.

Contrary to some early twentieth-century readings of him, Arnauld does not treat ideas as objects in any serious sense.[10] Ideas are straightforwardly acts of perception. Part of the difficulty in interpreting Arnauld stems from the fact that Malebranche himself does not quite seem to understand Arnauld's position either. He appears to take Arnauld as arguing that ideas are objects but ones that are merely internal to the mind. According to his reading of Arnauld, the mind perceives only itself, which is suggestive of the fact that he never abandoned the opinion that ideas must be some form of

---

9. Many in fact support my view here. See Church 1970, 155, and Nadler 1992, 183–85.
10. See Lovejoy 1923, 454–55, who attributes a form of sense-datum theory to Arnauld.

object, even if mental ones (see *OC* 6:78, 170). Malebranche glosses over Arnauld's assertions that ideas are essentially *acts*. The words "idea" and "perception" simply describe two aspects of the same entity in Arnauld's view: "I have said that I take *the perception and the idea* to be the same thing. Nevertheless it must be noted that this thing, although only one, has two relations: one to the soul which it modifies, the other to the thing perceived insofar as it is objectively in the soul; and that the word 'perception' indicates more directly the first relation and the word 'idea' the second" (*TF*, 20). There is no act/object distinction for Arnauld in perception. The perception of an object refers to its modifying the mind, whereas the idea of the object refers to the fact that the activity is itself related to an external object by way of representing it. Thus, although our ordinary talk might make things confusing, we must not forget that "these are not two different entities but one and the same modification of our soul, which includes essentially the two relations" (*TF*, 20).

External physical objects are directly perceived, even though they are nonetheless represented to the mind. When I perceive a chair, it is the chair itself that stands in the basic perceptual relation to my mind. This view is occasionally difficult to interpret, as Arnauld nonetheless wants to say that the chair is represented to the mind by the idea. Yet ideas are only acts, so are material objects immediately perceived or not? If one defines "immediately" as "perceived without any representation," then the answer is no. If one defines "immediately" as without a representative entity distinct from the perceptual act itself, then the answer is yes (*TF*, 31). Essentially Arnauld *is* a direct realist, for he claims that there are no representative entities distinct from the perceptual act. His adherence to the claim that the soul can only be modified by its own operations corroborates his commitment to direct realism. The mind is an essentially active entity. It always thinks, and all of its modes are activities. He thus sees the issue to be whether or not modifications of the soul (as operations of the same) can intrinsically represent.

Now one might expect that Arnauld owes us an explanation of how perception actually works on his theory. Since he too is a Cartesian dualist, how do modes of the mind represent external material objects? His answer is uncharacteristically unsatisfying:

> If it is asked, for example, why our soul can see material things, its own body and those which surround it, even when they are very far away, it is quite a good reply to say *that it can see them because*

that is its nature and because God gave it the faculty of thinking. Once again I hold that the reply is quite good and it is for want of being content with it that we are led to imagine that our soul can see material things only by means of *representative beings,* which, being intimately united to our soul, put them into a position to be known by it. (*TF*, 113, emphasis in original)

The passage is mildly reminiscent of Descartes' claim in the Sixth Meditation that the mind-body union is more than the relationship of a sailor to his ship, but what more he cannot say (*CSM* II:56). At least this much is clear: both Arnauld and Malebranche face difficulties they are not able to overcome by marrying any theory of ideas with substance dualism. Still, though Arnauld's own theory ultimately suffers from defects, his attack on Malebranche is nevertheless potent and interesting.

3.6 Critique of Malebranche

We have already seen that Arnauld views treating ideas as substances as self-defeating in a theory that purports to explain how we perceive the material world. Positing the existence of intermediaries that we perceive as representative of the external world means that we have no direct contact with the latter. This problem is especially acute for Malebranche, who argues that we strictly perceive only the intelligible ideas (located "in" God) of external objects. In effect, when he tries to explain how we perceive the external world, Malebranche winds up telling us that we cannot do it at all. In addition to claiming that Malebranche's theory cuts us off from the material world, Arnauld also holds that treating ideas like substances is superfluous on two related grounds. The first is a straightforward application of Ockham's razor. He thinks he can better explain perception without recourse to intermediary representative entities. Second, he advances a theological argument that relies on a similar principle: that God always acts in the simplest manner.

Earlier we briefly alluded to Arnauld's accusation that Malebranche conflates local, spatial presence with a different kind of "presence" needed for mentation. Arnauld agrees that action cannot take place at a distance, but since the mental realm is nonspatial, one cannot apply this principle directly to minds and their objects. It is not the eyes but the soul that "sees," and it does perceive distant objects. Arnauld confidently asserts, "[I]t is certain that my soul has seen the sun, the stars and the other works of God countless times, as well as men, not specters but true men created by God like me: Therefore I am certain that my soul has the faculty of seeing all those things" (*TF*, 36–37). Objects are present to the soul *objectively*, in the Cartesian sense of "presenting content." Thus there is no need for external ideas to make objects "present" to the mind.[11] Malebranche is simply confusing two *different* principles and therefore must agree that "local presence is not a necessary condition of an object's being able to be seen by our soul, and consequently, local absence contributes nothing to its not being able to be seen" (*TF*, 40).

More generally, Arnauld contends that the only way it is possible to prove that representative entities are required for perception is to assume as much, which begs the question. Malebranche does appear to reason just so, blithely remarking that, "I think everyone agrees that we do not perceive objects external to us by themselves" (*LO*, 217 [3.2.1]). We have greater cause for complaint, Arnauld says, when Malebranche invokes his argument for substantializing ideas on the basis of illusions. Malebranche, recall, argues that "[F]or the mind to perceive an object, it is absolutely necessary for the idea of that object to be actually present to it—and about this there can be no doubt; but there need not be any external thing like that idea. For it often happens that we perceive things that do not exist, and that even have never existed—thus our mind often has real ideas of things that have never existed" (*LO*, 217 [3.2.1]). Arnauld responds that this too begs the question. If "idea" here means an external representative entity, there is indeed doubt. About this very passage he remarks:

> But if the proposition is conceived in these terms, not only *is it possible to doubt it,* but I absolutely deny its first part, since I see no need of that assumed *representative being* in order to know any object, either present or absent. So, to assume *that it is impossible to doubt the necessity of the representative being,* is manifestly to beg the question. As for the second part, if it is not necessary that there be something outside, similar to the *representative being,* it is no more necessary that there be something *existent* outside, similar to my perception of the sun. (*TF,* 43)

---

11. As noted earlier in the discussion of Arnauld's own theory of ideas, exactly *how* this works remains a Cartesian mystery.

Arnauld's point is subtle. If there doesn't need to be an *object* genuinely existing beyond the representative idea (since we can have ideas without external objects when we hallucinate or perceive illusions), then there need not ever be an idea beyond the perception itself in the first place. Hallucinations are examples of acts of perceiving without external objects, and they are analogous to cases of perceiving without *any* object separate from the act of perception, including, in particular, ideas. There is no reason to posit an idea beyond the mental activity of perceiving. Arguing from perceptual error can only succeed in proving representative entities by antecedently assuming they are necessary. Arnauld's argument does not, however, establish that Malebranche's conclusion is false; it only provides some reason for thinking that Malebranche's analysis about the indubitability of the existence of ideas as distinct representative entities fails.

Rightly not content with this negative point, Arnauld also advances a positive argument that he thinks conclusively demonstrates that there are no representative ideas distinct from the activity of perceiving. The proof is a theological one and runs roughly as follows:[12]

(1) God would not have put souls in bodies without allowing them to perceive bodies.
(2) Thus souls do perceive bodies.
(3) God always uses the simplest means.
(4) It is simpler to make our minds know our bodies directly than by representations.
(5) Therefore we know bodies immediately without representative entities distinct from the mind.

Forcing God to create representations of the material world not only violates Ockham's razor; it is also an affront to the power and simplicity of God's greatness. Instead of having minds and bodies, Malebranche requires God to create ideas as well, not to mention countless "bizarre and groundless laws" to accommodate them (*TF*, 47).

Malebranche, of course, denies the fourth premise, arguing that it cannot possibly be true given the nature of the soul. His reasons, however, are merely his old arguments for why ideas must be like substances. Arnauld's critique, as interesting as it is, does not fully resolve the dispute in his favor. It is one thing to argue that ideas do not *need* to be substantial to represent

---

12. Paraphrased from Arnauld, *TF*, 44–46.

and quite another to provide a theory that plausibly shows they *cannot* represent if they are substances. Arnauld fails in this latter endeavor, whatever his successes in proving the former. Thus although Arnauld has firmly established that philosophers need not be *forced* into substantializing ideas, he has not decisively demonstrated why they *ought not* to do so.

3.7 The Cartesian Debate

Despite extended wrangling concerning the nature of ideas, the Arnauld-Malebranche exchange did little to resolve the issue for other early moderns who would follow them. Indeed, those who did follow this debate found few clear answers, and many gave up entirely on resolving the deep metaphysical difficulties associated with ideas. Malebranche advanced interesting and occasionally plausible reasons for holding that ideas simply could not be modifications of the mind. His arguments for treating ideas as substances, however, fail to adequately deal with potent criticisms by the likes of Arnauld. In turn, Arnauld made a number of interesting moves in trying to cast ideas as simple mental modifications but failed to decisively meet all of Malebranche's objections. Independently, Arnauld also failed to conclusively establish that ideas could not be at least substance-like.

Despite the frustrating lack of a clear answer about the ontological nature of ideas, one element in the Malebranche-Arnauld discussion remained constant. They, like early modern philosophers in general, thought it was *important* to keep ideas in their philosophical systems. The epistemological functions played by ideas were simply too vital to the early modern understanding of the world for philosophers to abandon them. Consequently there was an often unstated imperative to solve the metaphysical problems surrounding ideas, although one might set aside those questions for a time to work on the epistemological details. Locke would take the latter route, but even in so doing he could not escape, nor did he desire to escape, the powerful influence of ontology.

4

LOCKE

Descartes' philosophy of ideas left unresolved the issue of how ideas were to be reconciled with the traditional ontology of substance and mode. A debate ensued, epitomized most famously by the Malebranche-Arnauld exchanges, but little apparent progress was made. As a result, some turned their attention away from questions of ontology altogether. By this I do not mean that ontological questions were rejected as unimportant but rather that some philosophers chose to spend their time attempting to solve other problems. Aside from the dispute about the status of ideas, there were other issues, including how ideas could represent. Perhaps, it was thought, progress could be made here, and philosophers could return to the challenges of ontology after grappling with other puzzles in idea philosophy.

Such is the motivation I attribute to Locke. While the disagreements over the status of ideas raged, Locke focused his attention on other issues. Here I will argue that he did not reject the core traditional ontology nor deny that ideas have an ontic status. He did, however, set those questions aside, fearing that they might not have answers that could be discovered by mere human beings. Thus I am arguing that Locke is committed to the importance of *an* ontology for ideas, but I am *not* arguing that Locke endorsed a particular well-defined ontological theory. The issue is not whether ideas are substances or modes. For Locke there is an answer, but it might be beyond our finite powers to know what it is. In the introduction to the *Essay Concerning Human Understanding*, he is delightfully explicit.

> I shall not at present meddle with the Physical Consideration of the Mind; or trouble myself to examine, wherein its Essence consists, or by what Motions of our Spirits, or Alterations of our Bodies, we come to have any Sensation by our Organs, or any *Ideas* in our

Understandings; and whether those *Ideas* do in their Formation, any or all of them, depend on Matter, or no. These are Speculations, which, however curious and entertaining, I shall decline, as lying out of my Way, in the Design I am now upon. . . . *We should not then perhaps be so forward, out of an Affection of an universal Knowledge, to raise Questions, and perplex our selves and others with Disputes about Things, to which our Understandings are not suited; and of which we cannot frame in our Minds any clear or distinct Perceptions, or whereof (as it has perhaps too often happen'd) we have not any Notions at all.* (ECHU I.1.2, I.1.4, emphasis mine)

Locke consciously excludes an examination of the causal processes that underlie perception.[1] He is thus essentially excluding ontology from his purview but *not* from any conviction that ideas have no ontic status (just as he does not believe that there is no underlying causal story to be told). He thinks there are causal relations in perception and that ideas have some ontological grounding but that these questions of causation and the metaphysical status of ideas might well be unanswerable.

In general, even a cursory glance should make it apparent that Locke has good reason to be wary of making any definite pronouncements about the nature of ideas. If they are substances, then their natures lie outside the realm of human knowledge. Locke tells us that we have no clear understanding of substratum, let alone substance, and hence we also would have no clear understanding of the nature of ideas should they be substances. In short, by Locke's analysis, if ideas are substances then by that very fact their formal nature must be a permanent mystery to us. If ideas are modes, then he encounters problems about how they can represent and how they can perform certain other functions he ascribes to them. The puzzles associated with marrying idea philosophy to the traditional ontology were well known to Locke. He read Malebranche and Arnauld and was well steeped in the Cartesian tradition. Thus he tries to avoid explicitly saying anything definite about the ontic nature of ideas. He simply is not sure and does not have the answers to resolve the issue either way. I contend that Locke attempts to sidestep what he perceives as a metaphysical quagmire, although perhaps

---

1. Compare *ECHU* II.33.6, where Locke starts to speculate about the cause of ideas but refuses to engage in any serious analysis. "Whether the natural cause of these *Ideas,* as well as of that regular Dancing of his Fingers be the Motion of his Animal Spirits, I will not determine, how probable soever by this Instance it appears to be so."

not with the greatest success. Yet whether Locke's sidestepping is successful or not, he does implicitly endorse the core traditional ontology for ideas.

To defend my contention that Locke had an implicit ontology for ideas, I first engage the line of interpretation that holds that Locke shunned ontology with respect to ideas in two of its most prominent forms as defended (differently) by John Yolton and Thomas Lennon. After arguing that these readings of Locke are unpersuasive, I build a case for my limited claim that Locke ought to be read as endorsing *an* ontology of ideas. The qualification is important, since it is *not* my aim to argue that Locke has *a particular* ontology in mind. Locke recognized the need for some supporting ontology but, having learned something from his predecessors, did not think he could reasonably defend any specific view. Consequently Locke bracketed those concerns even though he wrote and thought within the context of the *core* traditional ontological categories. I argue for this position by considering how Locke's contemporaries understood his work and then by engaging in a positive analysis of what Locke has to say about the nature of ideas, focusing in this positive analysis on the generally neglected "Examination of P. Malebranche's Opinion of Seeing All Things in God." There Locke is forced to confront explicitly ontological concerns about ideas.

4.1 Locke "Deontologized"

At first glance it is not obvious exactly what Yolton and his advocates want to argue with respect to Locke. Initially one is led to believe that Yolton merely wants to exonerate Locke from the charge of treating ideas as substances, as some tertium quid in perception. Ideas are perceptions and "not real beings."[2] Yet oddly enough Yolton is not arguing that Locke treats ideas as (mental) modes. Instead, we are told that Locke rejected ideas as ontological beings altogether. He "deontologized" them (1975, 158). "Had Locke seen sufficiently clearly these implications of his position, he could have written a reply to clarify the difference between his own epistemological analysis and that which used the older metaphysical categories of substance and accident. He so quietly dispensed with the traditional categories on this question that many of his critics did not appreciate the novelty which he was introducing" (1996b, 97). Locke's quiet contribution to the way of ideas, Yolton maintains, was to remove them not just from the traditional ontology but from ontology altogether.

2. See Yolton 1975, 159; Yolton 1984, 88–94; and Chappell 1994, 32.

Yet when we turn to examine what Locke actually says about the nature of ideas, it is difficult to understand what grounds Yolton's thinking. In responding to Malebranche's theory of ideas Locke writes: "So that supposing ideas real spiritual things ever so much, if they are neither substances nor modes, let them be what they will, I am no more instructed in their nature, than when I am told they are perceptions, such as I find them. And I appeal to my reader, whether that hypothesis is to be preferred for its easiness to be understood, which is explained by real beings, that are neither substances nor modes" (EM, 424). Locke neither says nor implies that ideas have no ontological status. Yet this is exactly what Yolton suggests. With respect to the text just quoted ("Examination"), Yolton writes:

> In another draft of a reply to Norris, he makes this point emphatically: "If you once mention ideas you must be presently called to an account *what kind of things you make these same ideas to be* though perhaps you have no design to consider them any further than as the *immediate objects* of perception." *The point of this last remark is that Locke did not consider ideas to have an ontological status;* he wanted to concentrate upon their role in perception and knowledge. Having Malebranche's theory as an example of a theory that gave to ideas an ontological status, Locke had a twofold reaction: he rejected Norris's attempts to fit ideas into the standard ontological categories of substance or mode, and he stressed the cognitive, awareness features of ideas. The language of "having ideas" is identified with being aware, with perceiving.[3] (1984, 94)

Exactly what it means to "deontologize" Locke is difficult to untangle. Following Chappell, one might construe Yolton in one of two ways (Chappell 1994, 32–33). First, Yolton is fond of pressing the point that ideas are perceptions themselves, indicating that ideas are merely acts of perception. Second, Yolton also indicates that ideas are the contents of perceptual acts. Lennon provides yet a third variant, which I take up in the following section.

Usually Yolton talks about ideas as acts when drawing parallels between Locke and Arnauld, trying as it were to rub them together and imbue Locke with Arnauld's philosophy by friction (see, e.g., 1984, 89–90). Arnauld tries to invoke Descartes' distinction between ideas taken objectively and formally in order to argue that "presence to the mind" means a dull form of

---

3. For comments on John Norris, see Acworth 1971.

objective presence only. On that view, an object is present to the mind ("in" it) only when the mind perceives it.

There certainly are a number of passages in the *Essay* and "Examination" that superficially support this thesis, and Yolton lists them. The best of these are from the *Essay* and run as follows:

> Whatever *Idea* is in the mind, is either an actual perception, or else having been an actual perception, is so in the mind, that by the memory it can be made an actual perception again.

> For our *Ideas,* being nothing but bare Appearances or Perceptions in our Minds, cannot properly and simply in themselves be said to be *true* or *false,* no more than a single Name of any thing, can be said to be *true* or *false.*

> To ask, *at what time a Man has first any* Ideas, is to ask, when he begins to perceive; having *Ideas,* and Perception being the same thing. (I.4.20, II.32.1, and II.1.9)

There are more, but these passages are representative.[4] The difficulty here is that these selections do not support Yolton's claim that ideas are identified with acts of perception. Locke, as with virtually all of his contemporaries, held that there could be no cognitive activity, whether thinking or perceiving, without an object.[5] Since Locke uses "thinking" and "perceiving" interchangeably in the *Essay,* this maxim applies to all instances of perception. As a result, it is easy to be misled by ambiguities in the use of perception talk. An instance of the word "perception" can refer *both* to the act *and* the object(s) of perceiving. Thus when Locke indicates, as he does in the above passages, that ideas are perceptions, he means nothing more than that ideas are the *objects* of perceptions. To confirm this, note that when Locke refers to the act of sense perception he speaks of "having ideas," as in the last of the quoted passages above. The contrast between II.32.1 and II.1.9 is telling. In the former we are told that ideas are "appearances," which is object talk.[6] The qualifier "or Perceptions" is accordingly best read as "or objects of

---

4. See also *ECHU* II.1.3, II.1.5, II.1.23, and II.10.2 as well as Yolton 1984, 90.
5. We will have cause to engage this claim further when discussing Thomas Lennon's defense of a Yolton-style reading of Locke.
6. Lennon would disagree, arguing that my claim that appearances are objects is misleading. His position will be engaged in section 4.2.

perception." His official definitions consistently indicate that ideas are objects of perception, as at II.8.8: "Whatsoever the Mind perceives in it self, or is the immediate object of Perception, Thought, or Understanding, that I call Idea" (see also, e.g., *ECHU* I.1.8). When Locke wants to describe perception itself, a fairly clear line is drawn between the acts and the ideas that are the objects of those acts. "Perception, as it is the first faculty of the Mind exercised about our *Ideas*, so it is the first and simplest idea we have from reflection" (*ECHU* II.9.1). Note that perception, when described as an act or faculty, is not an idea but *about* an idea. Given the nature of examples like these, it is unlikely that Locke identified the act of perception with an idea. At the very least Yolton requires a systematic analysis to uncover the ambiguity in the use of the word "perception" (and similar terms like "sensation"). In fact none of the cases Yolton provides to buttress his thesis survives this test; all of them either can be read, or are even best read, as taking "perception" to mean an *object* of perception.

Independently, Yolton offers another reading for what Locke intends by the term "idea." Just as frequently, Yolton argues, Locke tells us that ideas are the "contents" of perceptual acts. Yolton's favorite version of this line is that ideas are simply "conscious mental contents" (1984, 101–2). In short, Yolton takes ideas to be intentional objects that lack any ontic ground, as evinced by his puzzling language of ideas not being "entities."[7] The trick is to now parlay that into an account that makes these intentional objects "*purely*" epistemological beings without any ontic status whatsoever. I have already argued in the first chapter that such a view is implausible. I do not see how one can maintain the thesis that ideas, at least as understood by any of the early moderns, have no ontic ground at all. About *what* would we be speaking? What remains is to demonstrate that Locke did not hold this view.

The first thing we should note is that Locke's language generally does not cohere well with the view that ideas are nothing but intentional objects (which is not to deny that Lockean ideas might *involve* intentional acts and/or objects). He asserts, for instance, that ideas can either resemble or fail to resemble their external objects. Simple ideas are never false but complex ideas may well be (*ECHU* II.21.16–18). What, then, is being compared? Similarly, knowledge is garnered through the comparison of ideas. "*Knowledge* then seems to me to be nothing but *the perception of the connexion and agreement, or disagreement and repugnancy of any of our Ideas*" (*ECHU* IV.1.2). By this he means that our ideas are in genuine relations with one

---

7. Ayers and Chappell agree on this point. See Ayers 1991, 56–59, and Chappell 1994, 33.

another, and it is these relations that the mind perceives. "*First,* the one is of *such Truths laid up in the Memory, as whenever they occur to the Mind, it actually perceives the Relation is between those Ideas*" (*ECHU* IV.1.9; see also *ECHU* IV.1.8). If the mind perceives the relation without the intervention of yet a third idea, Locke calls this "intuitive knowledge." If ideas are merely conscious mental contents, then *what is it* that one compares? Ungrounded content is not enough, since it has to fill the role of relata, which falls within the category of ontology.

Perhaps more importantly, Locke claims that all ideas are *particular.* "Every Man's Reasoning and Knowledge, is only about the *Ideas* existing in his own Mind, which are truly, every one of them, particular Existences" (*ECHU* IV.17.8). What could it mean to say (using Yolton's definition of "idea") that "content" is particular? I should think that content can be detailed or abstract. Perhaps content can be particular in the sense that some ideas are particular (as in an individual instance) and others universal or general. But if so, then this makes Locke's claim that all ideas are particular implausible. And here he describes ideas as "existences," talk not consistent with the view that they are merely conscious contents. Locke writes as if ideas have an ontic ground; he simply does not know what that ground happens to be. Consider the following passage, which I think indicates Locke's leanings on this issue: "For all the Enquiries that we can make, concerning any of our *Ideas,* all that we know, or can affirm concerning any of them, is, that it is, or is not the same with some other; that it does, or does not always co-exist with some other *Idea* in the same Subject; that it has this or that Relation to some other *Idea;* or that it has a real existence without the Mind" (*ECHU* IV.1.7). Ideas "coexist" and become relata not only in relations with other ideas but also with external objects. Even here, however, a supporter of Yolton will not likely be convinced. Maybe Locke used relational talk in the absence of better language or spoke loosely to convey his point.

Perhaps so, but there is one locution Locke uses that makes my point forcibly. If Yolton is correct, then when Locke speaks of ideas being "in the mind," he cannot mean that ideas are ontically in the mind. Ideas must be only "cognitively" in the mind. Yet when we examine what Locke says, it becomes clear that he cannot be endorsing the merely cognitive sense of "in the mind." For one thing, Locke maintains the now venerable causal story of how ideas come to the mind, and for another he insists that ideas are *signs* of external objects. Consider the first point. The corpuscularian hypothesis extends all the way to the mind. "There are some Ideas, *which have admit-*

tance only through one Sense. . . . And if these Organs, or the Nerves which are the Conduits, to convey them from without to their Audience in the Brain, the mind's Presence-room (as I may so call it) are any of them so disordered, as not to perform their Functions, they have no Postern to be admitted by; no other way to bring themselves into view, and be perceived by the Understanding" (*ECHU* II.3.1). And elsewhere Locke is less metaphorical:

> First, *Our Senses,* conversant about particular sensible Objects, do *Convey into the Mind,* several distinct *Perceptions* of things, according to those various ways, wherein those Objects do affect them: And thus we come by those *Ideas,* we have of *Yellow, White, Heat, Cold, Soft, Hard, Bitter, Sweet,* and all those which we call sensible qualities, which when I say the senses convey into the mind, I mean, they from external Objects convey into the mind what produces there those *Perceptions.* (*ECHU* II.1.3)

The traditional "presence principle" is the one advanced by Malebranche. What is known is literally present or somehow united to the mind. Locke's story is entirely literal, especially when it comes to sensation. "[T]he Sensation of Heat and Cold, be nothing but the increase or diminution of the motion of the minute Parts of our Bodies, caused by the Corpuscles of other Body" (*ECHU* II.8.21). This corroborates (as do other passages) his analysis in the "Examination," where he indicates that external objects literally affect the mind, suggesting that he found it difficult to free himself from the Malebranchian interpretation of the presence principle. The reason Locke has the causal thesis is to guarantee local presence to the mind.

What seals my case here about the nature of ideas with respect to the mind is the second point. Ideas are signs. And why must this be so? "For since the Things, the Mind contemplates, are none of them, besides it self, present to the Understanding, 'tis necessary that something else, as a Sign or Representation of the thing it considers, should be present to it: And these are *Ideas*" (*ECHU* IV.21.4). As Michael Ayers notes, this passage must invoke ontic presence to the mind, otherwise the argument simply does not work (1992, 176–77). A sign must be in the mind and these signs (as ideas) are the elements of mental propositions as words are elements of verbal sentences. Yolton requires that ideas be intrinsically representative, yet Locke does not accept this claim. They become representative when used as signs present to the mind and not before. Immediate cognitive presence seems to require "local" (on a physical model) presence for Locke.

Yolton might respond by claiming that ideas qua signs are in fact intrinsically representative. This cannot be the case, however, since the representative power of ideas stems from their causal origins. How is it that this particular idea represents the redness of that (external) ball? Because the ball and I are so constituted that the ball *caused* me to be affected in a certain way. The idea represents the redness in virtue of the causal relationship between the ball and myself. Locke is explicit:

> [S]imple Ideas *are not fictions* of our Fancies, but the natural and regular productions of Things without us, really operating on us; and so carry with them all the conformity which is intended; or which our state requires: For they represent to us Things under those appearances which they are fitted to produce in us. . . . Thus the *Idea* of Whiteness, or Bitterness, as it is in the Mind, exactly answering all the real conformity it can, or ought to have, with Things without us. (*ECHU* IV.4.4)

There is no evidence that Locke thinks of ideas as intrinsically representational. We already know that the mind can "have" ideas in the memory of which it takes no notice. Are we to suppose that such ideas nonetheless represent their objects to the mind? Certainly not—not until the mind by its own actions conjures up those ideas again, and even then the mind recreates the impression of the idea (quality) on the mind. Therefore even in memory an implicit causal story is preserved. Ideas "in the mind" must be present ontically according to Locke, and hence ideas cannot be *merely* intentional objects; all ideas are ontically grounded.

It is true that Locke professes ignorance as to what ideas are beyond that they are perceptions.[8] Yet this claim does not support Yolton's thesis. Admitting ignorance of the underlying ground is not the same as proclaiming that none exists. Interestingly, Locke's commonplace assertions that he either wants to avoid or has no understanding of the metaphysics of ideas aside, he never actually *says* ideas have no ontic grounding. Given the preponderance of evidence suggesting that he must think they do, Yolton's interesting thesis about Locke must be false, providing further evidence that the early modern tale is also false.

---

8. See Yolton 1984, 94, remembering that this is an object reading of "perception."

4.2 Lennon's Locke

Yolton is not alone in endorsing views about Locke friendly to the early modern tale. One important defense comes from Thomas Lennon, who argues that, despite admitted problems in the details, Yolton essentially has Locke right. (Lennon defends "the line, if not the exact letter, of Yolton's interpretation" [2004a, 322].) Lennon ascribes to Locke what amounts to a theory of appearing. Ideas are not entities separate from their objects because ideas are simply descriptions of the objects *as perceived*. Lennon is characteristically clear with his thesis: "The central point of my paper is that an idea of x is an appearance of x, not really distinct from x" (323). The underlying point is that ideas for Locke refer to ideas qua perceived things, which is all the same as referring to objects themselves. Thus just as Yolton tells us there is no "third thing" that constitutes an idea, so Lennon argues that "'The phantasm of my pen' refers to my pen":

> But why not just "my pen"? Why mention "phantasm" in referring to my pen? The answer is that "the phantasm of my pen," like "the idea of my pen," refers not just to my pen, but to my pen insofar as it is perceived. And since Locke will never speak strictly about things except as they are perceived, i.e. except as they appear, he cannot help but use the term "idea." The necessity is philosophical, and stylistic only in the sense that it is an omnibus way of expressing a necessity attaching to the use of many other such items. (326)

Lennon fastens on Locke's frequent use of the word "appearance" in connection with Locke's theory of ideas. Ideas represent not by being a surrogate for the external object but rather by making the object "present" to the mind.[9] Lennon's reading of Locke retains the advantage both he and Yolton are seeking, namely to "save" Locke from the sense-datum fallacy (327).

There is no textual "smoking gun" in Locke that supports Lennon's thesis. The absence of *obvious* textual evidence is to my mind no bar to its truth, but we are nevertheless owed good reasons for thinking that Locke endorsed Lennon's theory of appearing for ideas. He produces four explanatory benefits that accrue from his interpretation, arguing that they render Locke more consistent and comprehensible. When coupled with the added

---

9. Lennon uses this clarifying language in an unpublished essay, "Locke on Ideas and Representation." I am grateful to Lennon for allowing me access to this and other materials of his.

bonus that his account frees Locke from the evils of a sense-datum theory, the position has initial credibility. Lennon lists the attractions of his reading:

> First, it gives us the sense of Locke's empiricism, which is grounded in the distinction between simple and complex ideas. Second, it explains Locke's ambiguous talk of ideas as objects, including the texts most frequently cited in connection with the veil of perception. Third, Locke's use of awkward metaphors is explicated in a way that both avoids the veil and is philosophically important. Finally, Locke's argument for substance is relieved of some of the obscurity often attributed to it. (2001a, 161)

Here I argue that none of these benefits requires Lennon's reading of Locke's theory of ideas and they they often reveal textual obstacles to his own view. As a result, when coupled with the textual analysis provided above in section 4.1, I conclude that although Lennon's analysis is smart, it is not *Locke's*.

The first of Lennon's advantages concerns the division between simple and complex ideas. Lennon alleges that his reading of Locke makes this distinction more comprehensible. Simple ideas are "just those with respect to which the mind must be passive, the complex all others" (161). The mind, once equipped with the ammunition of a stock of simple ideas, can actively manipulate them to produce complexes. Lennon quotes Locke: "Where the Understanding is once stored with these simple *Ideas,* it has the Power to repeat, compare, and unite them even to an almost infinite Variety, and so can make at Pleasure new complex *Ideas.* But it is not in the Power of the most exalted Wit, or enlarged Understanding, by any quickness or variety of Thought, to invent or frame one new simple *Idea* in the mind, not taken in by [sensation or reflection]" (*ECHU* II.2.2). With respect to simple ideas, the mind is passive. Once it has a stock of simple ideas, the mind may actively manipulate them into complexes. I happily grant that Lennon's explication of the difference between simple and complex ideas might well be exactly right. What is unclear, however, is how this analysis indicates that Locke endorses a theory of appearing. There are two concerns. First, this reading does not *exclude* rival theories. Second, some of what Locke says with respect to this distinction seems to *deny* Lennon's view.

In the passage from the *Essay* (II.2.2. quoted just above), Locke does not say that either simple or complex *ideas* are passive; he says that *the mind* is passive when receiving simple ideas (see *ECHU* II.21.72, also cited by Lennon). To be clear, this is the position Lennon attributes to Locke as well. I am not attributing any error to Lennon here. A finite mind cannot conjure up new simple ideas in the way that it can create new complex ideas by manipulating its stock of simple ones. The distinction is thus not one that concerns the nature of ideas but rather the nature of the mind when perceiving ideas. Understood in this way, however, the distinction (between simple and complex ideas) is compatible even with theories that make ideas robust substances. *All* ideas intromitted through the senses are passively received into the mind. Once present to the mind, the mind may manipulate its stock of ideas to form complex ideas. In this case, that would be complexes of substances. A similar story can be told if ideas are mental modifications. Hence, any advantage Lennon accrues from his reading concerning explaining passivity in the mind is also available to more ontological understandings of ideas as well.

More importantly, when Locke discusses the distinction between simple and complex, he writes as if ideas are distinct from the external objects they represent. Consider what Locke says in II.2.2 after noting that "it is not in the Power of the most exalted Wit, or enlarged Understanding, by any quickness or variety of Thought, to invent or frame one new simple *Idea* in the mind, not taken in by the ways before mentioned," namely, that no "force of the Understanding [can] *destroy* those that are there." What is it that the mind cannot destroy? According to Lennon, ideas are appearances not distinct from the object themselves. One might say that choosing not to perceive a certain presentation of an object is tantamount to its destruction, but this is to stretch the text a fair bit. *Things* are destroyed. Since Locke considers the possibility of destroying ideas (perhaps only complex ones) in cases where obviously the external object would not be, this passage at a minimum suggests that Locke is thinking of ideas as distinct from their objects. In the same paragraph Locke further reinforces this impression. "The same inability, will everyone find in himself, who shall go about to fashion in his Understanding any simple *Idea,* not received in by his Senses, from external Objects; or by reflection from the Operations of his own mind about them" (*ECHU* II.2.2). Ideas are "received" by the senses *from* external objects. The foregoing is the language of someone implicitly thinking of ideas as things (whatever they might be) distinct from what they represent. Lennon might plausibly respond that Locke is forced into a loose use of language given his available resources. That response is fair enough, but I hope I have shown that this first interpretative benefit is meager at best.

The second payoff for Lennon's thesis is that it explains Locke's "ambiguous" talk of ideas as objects. The difficulty Lennon hopes to clarify is Locke's speaking of objects of sensation as external to the mind and objects of perception internal to the mind. Thus in some passages it is unclear exactly *what* are the objects—ideas or external things. Lennon produces the clock passage as an example. "The Picture, or Clock may be so placed, that they may come in his way every day; but yet he will have but a confused *Idea* of all the Parts they are made up of, till he *applies himself with attention,* to consider them each in particular" (*ECHU* II.1.7). Locke seems to recommend that we attend to the actual parts of the clock (not the ideas) in order to understand the clock better. One traditional resolution of this problem is to attribute confusion to Locke. Perhaps Locke simply confuses qualities and ideas, as Jonathan Bennett has alleged (1996; see also Bennett 2001, 2:30–33). Lennon's analysis at least partially absolves Locke of Bennett's charge. There is no confusion when speaking about external things as the objects of understanding, since ideas are simply the appearances of the former.

Elaborating on his position in response to a challenge by Vere Chappell, Lennon appeals to a view of Paris from atop a department store, the Samaritaine. The view of Paris is an appearance, depends on minds (there are no views without viewers), and satisfies the conditions for being a thing. We refer to the view, it may be individually considered, and we can quantify over views in a meaningful sense. The issue, then, is *what* thing this appearance is and whether it is distinct from Paris as the object of perception. Lennon denies that the idea/view is distinct. "On the contrary, what one sees from the Samaritaine is just Paris, which is why the view from there is so much to be preferred to the view from Blackpool Tower, for example. Chappell and Yolton cannot disagree about this; where, then, does the disagreement lie?" (2004a, 325). Lennon clears away the putative confusion by noting that Locke's object talk is perfectly consistent when one recognizes that the appearances (the ideas) and the actual objects are not ontologically distinct.

Lennon's analysis in turn depends on what the word "object" means for Locke. Lennon anticipates this question by arguing that the word "object" perhaps never meant anything beyond "an awareness of the mind," at least according to the *Oxford English Dictionary* (325). I think Lennon is probably right on this point, but that turns out to be exactly the problem. Locke *qualifies* the word "object" in his discussions. Ideas are the *immediate* objects of perception, external things are not. In fact, the dictionary even cites as evidence under the fourth definition for "object" a letter from Locke to Stillingfleet that uses the qualifier. "Ideas are . . . the immediate objects of our mind in thinking." In Locke's works "immediate object" or its plural is used twenty-seven times. *In every case* it is associated with the term "idea" and no other.[10] In *none* of Locke's discussions of external objects (that I can find) do we find the qualifier "immediate." We thus have a decidedly more compelling reason to exonerate Locke from this particular charge. External things are objects; ideas are objects. But only ideas are *immediate* objects. Not only is there is a more compelling explanation for the problem Lennon locates but this same explanation also adduces textual evidence against attributing a theory of appearing to Locke. Locke does not treat objects and their appearances as walking hand in hand; instead, he *separates* them using a mediate/immediate distinction.

Lennon's third benefit concerns Locke's "awkward" metaphors. In fact, Lennon's analysis here is intended to defend his interpretation of Locke against those who might seek to oppose it on the grounds that Locke's metaphors commit him to a particular theory of ideas. The worry is that Locke's use of picture terms betrays at least an implicit commitment to some form of veil and hence a denial of Lennon's theory of appearing. Locke metaphorically compares ideas to images, resemblances, and pictures (in *ECHU* II.8.15, II.14.9, II.11.17, among other places). If ideas are pictures or images of things, then as such they are *distinct* from the items they resemble.

In response, Lennon musters an interesting reading of Locke. Pictures might represent by "calling attention to" something other than themselves. Hence a picture of Caesar calls our attention to *Caesar,* not merely an image of him. Similarly, when I look at a mirror I see myself and nothing else. But in all of these cases, I would note, there is something present *that is not the actual object.* In looking at a picture of Caesar we do not perceive the actual body of Caesar. Hence the formal object in perception is numerically distinct from the external thing. Lennon recognizes the constraint, but his analysis is troubling. "If this idea theory of pictures is at all plausible, then we can resolve what appears to involve a contradiction in the logic-of-ideas interpretation of Locke: an idea is a bodily state and an idea is the object as it appears to us. What this amounts to is that for him the ontology of an idea is that of a material impression, but the having of the idea, a perception, has as its object something beyond that impression" (2001a, 166). The trick now is to focus on the epistemic relation and not on the impression, which otherwise would be like "focusing on the paint and canvass and thereby

---

10. Locke uses the phrase "immediate object" four times in the *Essay*: once at the end of "The Epistle to the Reader," then again at II.8.8, IV.1.1 and IV.17.8. The other twenty-three instances appear in Locke's letters to the bishop of Worcester, in the "Examination," and in Locke's "Remarks upon Some of Mr. Norris's Books."

missing the portrait." This passage is a difficult one to understand in the context of Lennon's larger argument. Although Lennon wants us to look past the impressions, I see no good reason why we ought to do so, either on textual or philosophical grounds. Textually, I have already argued that Locke invokes a distinction between mediate and immediate perception insofar as he uses the language of "immediate objects" with respect to ideas but not to external things, and Lennon does not provide any new analysis here to tempt one to reconsider the language of the *Essay*.

Philosophically the position is troubling because earlier Lennon explicitly claims that ideas are not things (even though there is an ontology of ideas).[11] A "thing" is among the broadest categories and includes whatever exists (moods, for instance, exist and are things; they are simply not substantial things). I fail to see any good reason for thinking that appearances are not things. They might not be independent things and hence not substances, but they are certainly things. And here we find by Lennon's own lights that ideas *are* things, namely material impressions. I speculate that Lennon is concerned (as is Yolton) not to *reify* Locke's ideas (see section 1.3.1). But this *contemporary* emphasis then misses part of Locke's early modern thinking. When Lennon resists calling ideas "things," I submit that in fact he wants to resist interpretations of Locke that *substantialize* ideas, that is, that treat ideas as robust, independent things. The problem, however, is that resisting the tendency to substantialize ideas does nothing to remove the veil of perception. Modes and appearances can both be "third things" even if not substances.

A fourth and final argument remains. Lennon contends that Locke's discussion of substance can be clarified if one adopts his thesis. Lennon's view rests on an analysis of the phrase "idea of x." According to Lennon, the "of" when applied to ideas is a material genitive—the genitive of kinds. So, using his own example, to speak of a vase of gold is to stipulate a *kind* of vase, namely a golden one. Ideas of substance and mode likewise use the material genitive. The idea of substance is in fact not an idea *about* some *thing* but rather about a *kind* of idea in general. The idea of substance is the kind of idea we have when the intellect performs a particular kind of operation, namely that of collecting qualities together. As a bit of philosophy, this is first rate, and I can find no compelling reason to disagree with the function to which Lennon puts his material genitive. In fact, there is reason to think Lennon might be right, at least with respect to a few particular ideas

---

11. Lennon 2001a, 156: "Although ideas are not things, there is nonetheless an ontology of ideas (as there is of rainbows)."

Locke discusses. When Locke divides complex ideas into modes, substances, and relations, his presentation does read as if he were talking about *kinds* of ideas (see, e.g., *ECHU* II.7.3–4). But does this admission entail that Locke never thought of ideas as objects distinct from what they putatively represent? I confess I remain skeptical, especially since Lennon's insight with respect to the material genitive is relatively limited in scope; it only applies to a select few ideas and not to ideas in general.

In the aggregate, I find too much of the *Essay* simply does not read the way Lennon would have us understand it. As a result, although I confess that Lennon's sophisticated analysis provides a more *potent* reading of Locke that might well "preserve" Locke from several errors, I do not believe that his analysis captures Locke the early modern philosopher. Too much core traditional ontological talk survives in Locke. The question remains whether in interpreting Locke's theory of ideas I can do any better in defending the claim that *some* kind of ontological thinking underlies Locke's theory of ideas.

4.3 Locke's Contemporaries

Before we turn to provide a positive account of Locke's theory of ideas, it is worthwhile to briefly examine what his near contemporaries had to say, not only in their own work but more importantly in reaction to the *Essay* itself. Few disagreed about the epistemological role ideas play. Locke's definition of an idea as an object of the mind is echoed in various loosely similar forms, and he was not the only one to use "idea" in that sense.[12] The representative function of ideas was widely accepted, although *how* ideas represent naturally caused disagreement. The status of ideas remained a major issue. An anonymous writer in 1705, commenting not only on Locke but also on Malebranche and others, notes:

> By an Idea, I mean the Representation of something in the Mind. (This Definition I think, all sides are agreed in thus far, but whether

---

12. Peter Browne, for instance, calls ideas "any Representation or Likeness of the Object being transmitted from thence to the Imagination, and lodged there for the View and Observation of the pure Intellect" (1976, 58). See also Lee 1984, 2. Lee narrows the representative function of ideas to visual images, but the basic thought is the same. Lastly, of course, Descartes was the first to use the word "idea" as an object of the mind. See chapter 2 and *CSM* II:113, 127, Second Replies.

this Representation be only a Modification of the Mind, or be a Distinct Being, or Substance United to the Mind, is a Question.)

These are the only Two Hypotheses that carry any show of Probability along with them, the *latter* you will find Currently set forth by Mr. *[Malebranche]* in his *Search After Truth*. ([1705] 1996, 6)

Thus the representative function of ideas was not in serious contention, and even the disputants themselves recognized that it wasn't. Neither Arnauld nor Malebranche, for instance, denied the important epistemological role of ideas. What they quarreled about was whether such functions were carried out by ideas construed as modes or as substances. In short, the tangles highlighted during Locke's time concerned reconciling the generally accepted representative functions of ideas with their ontological status, where the choices were limited to only two. Ideas were either substances or modes. It was in this philosophical atmosphere that Locke was reared.

Not only was the thinking of the era fixed by the boundaries of the traditional ontology but all interpreters of Locke read him as bound by this metaphysic as well. This is not to say there is no room for maneuver. Perhaps one of the more interesting things about reading the commentaries of Locke's near contemporaries on the *Essay* is how divergent their interpretations of his theory of ideas can be. There is, of course, the now-famous general invective against Locke's use of the word "idea," especially the general complaint made by Edward Stillingfleet, the bishop of Worcester.[13] My focus here, however, is on ontology. I want briefly to consider a few critics and defenders of Locke and note how they interpret his theory of ideas. All of them read Locke as adopting the traditional ontology, although they understandably vary as to whether he thinks of ideas as substances or modes. A clear consensus emerges: no one thought Locke was seeking to deny the traditional ontology. Naturally, in Locke's replies to his critics he never suggests he was seeking to do so either.

Commentaries on the *Essay* give little explicit attention to the question of the ontological status of ideas, a striking feature given the volume of total responses the work provoked. Nonetheless, there are a number of clues that signal to the careful reader that Locke's commentators read him as adhering to the traditional ontology. Stillingfleet, perhaps Locke's most important adversary, never explicitly raised the issue of what ideas are. Most of their

---

13. Compare Stillingfleet 1697a, 273: "But none are so bold in attacking the *Mysteries of the Christian Faith;* as the Smatterers in *Ideas,* and new Terms of Philosophy, without any true Understanding of them. For these *Ideas* are become but another sort of Canting with such men."

disputes about ideas concerned purely epistemological questions such as whether Locke's idea philosophy could generate certainty about anything, especially about the existence of substances. Stillingfleet attacks Locke for grounding human knowledge and certainty on the observed relation among ideas. In particular, he faults Locke for supposing that our ideas of substances are nothing more than congeries of simple ideas. At this point in his critique, he reveals what he otherwise assumes all along, namely, that he takes ideas to be genuine substantial things: "A general *Abstracted Idea* of *Substance* is no *real Substance,* nor a *true Idea* of one, if *particular Substances* be nothing but a *Complication of simple Ideas*" (1697b, 27, emphasis in the original). That he understands ideas to be substances is clear by the distinction he draws between an abstract idea *as* a substance ("A general . . . idea . . . *is* no substance . . . if particular substances are nothing but a complication of simple ideas," and he completes this thought by denying that substances are complications, implicitly concluding that a general idea is a substance) and the idea *of* substance.[14] Stillingfleet goes on to explain that the word "idea" derives from the Greek "to see" ("*idein*") and is connected to the concept of an unchanging and uniform appearance. "[A]nd so the natural Sense of it is *something Visible;* from thence it came to signifie the *Impression* made in us from our Senses; and thence it was carried to the *general Notion* of a thing, and from thence by Metaphysical and abstracted speculations to the *Original Exemplars* of particular Essences, which were *Simple and Uniform* and not liable to those Changes which visible Objects are subject to" (1697b, 32). Stillingfleet's etymology stems from Plato and classical Roman authors who use "*visum*" (that which is seen) to mean "a true Idea." At no point does Stillingfleet ever suggest that there is disagreement between him and Locke about the nature of ideas. The pressing and immediate issue for him was whether ideas as used by Locke could ward off pernicious skepticism.

Stillingfleet was not the only commentator to invoke the etymology of the word "idea" when explicating Locke. Henry Lee asserts that the word in Greek means "that which is a visible representation or resemblance of the object" (1984, 2). Ideas, we are told, are thus properly only *images*. Lee's primary complaint against Locke is that the latter's use of the word "idea" is far too inclusive and thus essentially meaningless.

---

14. Obviously the lesson drawn from this passage is a weak one, given that Stillingfleet's purpose here does not relate directly to the ontology of ideas. Nonetheless, my point remains that when unreflectively discussing ideas the default view is to treat ideas as ontically grounded.

> By the word *idea* [Locke] means, he says, *whatever is the object of the understanding when a man thinks.* And this term, he says, he could not avoid frequently using, and there is no wonder at that; for if every thing that is within the reach of thought be an *idea*, then all the world, of which we have the least knowledge, must consist only of several kinds of *ideas.* And so it must come to pass that the word must be used in no certain sense. And accordingly this author makes it stand, sometimes for the thoughts, or conceptions themselves, *in* the mind, and sometimes for the *things* themselves *without* the mind, that are the objects of its thoughts. (1, emphasis in the original)

Lee reprimands Locke for not restricting the use of the word "idea" to its strict and proper signification: that of an image. In this diagnosis, Lee clearly reads Locke as one committed to the claim that ideas are all modes.[15] "By a *simple idea*, then, this author means (excepting space) the same which other philosophers do by a *single quality, property,* or *accident*, or, in one word, a *mode*, allowing some latitude for the word *mode*, so as it may comprehend *inseparable* attributes, such as unity, existence, etc., as well as *separable* qualities" (48). Lee rejects Locke's theory, of course, but what matters for our purposes here is that his engagement with Locke falls squarely within the confines of substance and mode.

As far as Lee is concerned, Locke's worries about substances are unfounded. We do have a perfectly serviceable conception of substance and, as it turns out, that conception is *exactly* the traditional one.

> This name of *substance* we give to any thing whose existence we conceive independent upon every thing else, and in which several properties or qualities are united or combined. And this, as old as it is, is taken to be a perfect definition of *substance* in general.... And now I am ready to answer all my author's queries. Have we any notion of *substance* in general? Yes, as before defined, and that as distinct as qualities in general, or *idea* either, if he mean by the word *idea* that which is the object of which he is said to have an *idea*. (110)

---

15. Lee's claim explicitly refers only to *simple* ideas, but in the larger context the assertion can reasonably be applied to *all* ideas.

Again, Lee analyzes Locke within the assumption that the formal nature of ideas must be either as a substance or a mode, for *everything* that exists must obey this (apparently) exhaustive distinction. It is difficult to clearly pin Lee down on what he takes ideas in his own conception to be, but his language suggests that images are substantival. He typically treats ideas as robust images, independent things that are somehow conveyed to the sense organs. "For when we *see* a body of any certain figure or bulk, the image or *idea* of it goes no farther than the bottom of the eye" (56). The implication is that the image is moved from the external object to the eye (much like in Aristotle's theory of perception). It is beyond my task here to defend the view that Lee held a specific kind of theory, for it suffices that we recognize that Lee's reasoning shows clear signs of accepting *as obvious* the confines of the traditional ontology of substance and mode. Lee believes that Locke takes ideas to be modes. The anonymous author quoted earlier in this section also attributes a mode view of ideas to Locke, something of which that author approves ([1705] 1996, 8). We thus find a consistent and traditional pattern of interpretation by Locke's contemporaries.

Locke ignored most of his critics, especially with regard to ontological issues. He took most seriously those attacks relating to religion and skepticism, another reminder of his epistemological priorities when he wrote the *Essay*. There is at least one important exception. John Norris, a supporter of Malebranche, wrote a brief tract criticizing Locke in May 1690, a scant five months after the *Essay* appeared. Norris's commentary is predictable. He starts by complaining that Locke should have defined "idea" before searching for its origin, but he goes on to provide some interesting analysis. He attacks Locke's doctrine that the memory is a storehouse of ideas (II.10.2), claiming that substances cannot be "stored" in the mind ([1728] 1961, 9). Although Locke did not publicly respond directly to Norris, the *Essay* was amended at this point in the second and subsequent editions. (The "Examination of P. Malebranche's Opinion of Seeing All Things in God" was most likely prompted by Norris's critique as well, judging by the invective in the [usually unpublished] first six paragraphs of the piece. There Locke attacks an anonymous follower of Malebranche. These opening paragraphs have not been included in any published version of the "Examination" of which I am aware but are available in the originals at the Bodleian Library in Oxford.) Norris spends a fair bit of time arguing that ideas cannot be modes and hence must be immaterial substances, but Locke simply ignores this part of Norris's tract. The changes Locke makes appear to commit him to making ideas modifications of the mind. Ideas are "nothing, but actual Perceptions in the Mind, which cease to be any thing, when there is no perception of them" (*ECHU* II.10.2). Locke's changes are apparently intended to shift his position away from one that could be seen as substantializing ideas.

Of those contemporaries who wrote about Locke's underlying metaphysics, I have found none who read Locke in any way other than within the bounds of the traditional ontology. Although this in itself does not constitute evidence that Locke thought of ideas within that tradition, it is at least suggestive that he was nonetheless so constrained. He certainly made no attempts to clarify his position, the absence of which is odd if he genuinely intended to reject the substance/mode ontology. I remind the reader that I am *not* arguing Locke *ought* to have adopted the traditional ontology; I am merely noting that in fact, explicitly or not, he did. The difficulties that arise stem from the incompatibility of the way of ideas and the traditional ontology, but those problems, simply because they exist, do not in and of themselves constitute evidence that Locke abandoned the ontology.

4.4 Locke's Implicit Ontology

Locke says nearly everything about ideas except what we really want to know. From his own era to the present, much has been made of the alleged many senses in which Locke uses the term "idea." Gilbert Ryle even accuses Locke of using the word in one sense such that, had it been the only sense, his philosophy would have been "a labored anatomy of utter nonentities" (1968, 17). There has been no shortage of scholars who remark in various ways how Locke must have employed multiple uses of the word "idea" when writing the *Essay* (Greenlee 1977, esp. 47, e.g.). Yet even so, none of this entails that Locke was *confused* about ideas or even about how he used the word. I grant that Locke used different conceptions of the term and for divergent purposes, but I deny that an overarching sense was missing. Locke introduces us to the word "idea" early in the *Essay*. "It being that Term, which, I think, serves best to stand for whatsoever is the Object of the Understanding when a Man thinks, I have used it to express whatever is meant by *Phantasm, Notion, Species,* or whatever it is, which the Mind can be employ'd about in thinking; and I could not avoid frequently using it" (*ECHU* I.1.8). Again, not far into the work, Locke gives us another definition. "Whatsoever the Mind perceives in it self, or is the immediate object of Perception, Thought or Understanding, that I call *Idea*" (*ECHU* II.8.8). From these minimal definitions we know several things. First, ideas are either *mental* entities that exist "in" the mind (to be specific, in the understanding) or are minimally "mental" in the sense of being specially related to minds (they are "known" even if not necessarily mental substances or mental modes).[16] Second, ideas are the objects of mental activities, including thinking, understanding, and perceiving. Finally, ideas are *immediate* objects. The first and third invoke what I have called the "presence principle." Ideas must be "present to" the mind, or "in" the mind in order to be properly perceived. Putting the three points together, ideas are that which are in immediate contact with the mind when any form of mental activity occurs. As it stands, we perhaps ought not to be surprised that some think the word "idea" has no one clear sense; the definition is amazingly broad. Locke uses it to describe images, concepts, and occasionally even qualities.[17] Yet in each of these uses, ideas are all objects in contact with the mind. As a result, one might more accurately say that Locke uses the term "idea" as a genus that covers a wealth of species. In so doing we might fault him for not being as detailed as we might like, but that hardly constitutes confusion.

The fact that Locke makes explicit reference to terms that would generally *not* be thought synonyms is important. John Sergeant uses the term "notion" to mean "the nature of the objects represented." This expression is intended to capture the meaning of the represented object, and he contrasts it explicitly with "idea," which he thinks means a similitude or image (1696, 2–3). "Phantasm" was widely used to mean "image" in relation to the imaginative faculty of the mind. And "species," of course, is a reference to the Scholastic doctrine of intentional species. On the surface, none of them is a synonym. I take the wide variety in the language used by Locke as good evidence that he did not have one narrow conception of idea in mind. Instead, he had a number, all of which loosely fit underneath the umbrella of "objects present to the mind." If this speculation is correct, then perhaps we would not be well served to suppose that all ideas must have the same ontological ground. We already have a precedent. Malebranche separates sensation from pure intellection and correspondingly argues that sensations have a different ontological nature from ideas of the intellect, so it is not unrea-

---

16. In claiming that ideas are mental entities, I am not denying that sensations for Locke are material impressions nor that ideas might have a causal origin in the body. See *ECHU* II.1.23, where Locke says that ideas are "coeval" with sensations. I take this to mean that they have similar origins and not, as Thomas Lennon argues, that ideas are, in fact, material. See also *ECHU* II.9.3.

17. Since I argue that Locke at times conflates ideas with qualities, it is worth noting that my contention that Locke's use of the word "idea" is not "all over the place" is nonetheless consistent with the presence of some difficulties in its use.

sonable to suppose Locke might have done something similar. In fact, Locke paid little explicit attention to what might ontically ground his ideas, however used, but that is no bar to our doing so in his place. His professed agnosticism about metaphysical issues leaves open the possibility that different kinds of ideas have varying ontic grounds. Thus even if one understanding of ideas dominated his thinking, we should not automatically expect that there will be only one underlying ontological ground for all ideas.

Locke's discussions in the *Essay* provide little *explicit* information about his views on the metaphysical nature of ideas. Given that he warned us that he would not be confronting such issues, we should not be surprised that he doesn't. Nonetheless, all of Locke's works are replete with references and implicit appeals to the core of the traditional substance/mode ontology. The soul, for instance, is sometimes clearly treated as a simple substance, and he provides extended discussions of our ideas of substances and modes. Naturally one might have cause to doubt Locke about the soul, since he also thinks it metaphysically possible that God could superadd thought to material bodies (*ECHU* IV.3.6). Yet even in his discussion of the possibility of thinking bodies, two things are clear. First, Locke never denies that thinking is an attribute of substance, and second, his language clearly preserves the substance/mode ontology. There can be little doubt that Locke was thoroughly steeped in the traditional ontology, and even if Locke believes that there is an in principle barrier to our knowing the nature of substance, such a view does not entail his believing that ideas *have* no ontic status, as either substance or accident (mode). Earlier commentators seem more cognizant of this point than recent ones. James Gibson, for instance, makes it a point to note the influence of the background ontology on Locke's writings: "Locke had himself inherited the current scheme of thought, for which the categories of substance and quality expressed in an exhaustive manner the ultimate nature of reality, and he never thought of questioning either its general validity or its applicability to the subject of experience" ([1917] 1960, 28). It is difficult to avoid noting the influence of the traditional ontology even in a work as self-confessedly opposed to discussing metaphysical issues as the *Essay*. Yet to indicate that Locke's thought was conditioned by the background ontology does not constitute proof that Locke thought ideas had any particular ontic status. In fact, Locke tried to be agnostic about exactly that claim, with varying degrees of success. Locke repeatedly challenges his opponents to generate a clear and distinct idea of substance. He famously does this with respect to space: "If it be demanded (as usually it is) whether this *Space* void of *Body*, be *Substance* or *Accident*, I shall readily answer, I know not: nor shall be ashamed to own my Ignorance, till they that ask, shew me a clear distinct *Idea* of *Substance*" (*ECHU* II.13.17). The inability of others (or himself) to conjure up a clear idea of substance is not an admission that ideas are not substances. Instead, it is an admission that he cannot say whether they are, and he refuses to pass judgment until someone can make it clear to him exactly what saying an idea is a substance would entail. We do not, of course, find many open pronouncements about the status of ideas. We do, however, find numerous remarks that betray leanings in different directions.

One clue we might fasten on is how he treats ideas in connection to relations. If he were to present ideas as clearly objects in two-place relations, then there would be reason to suppose he was thinking of ideas in a substance-*like* manner, since this would suggest that ideas are not dependent on other relata. Recall that claiming that an idea is "substance-like" indicates that the idea has at least one of the features associated with the core conception of a substance while lacking at least one other important feature typically associated with a substance. An idea that is volitionally but not ontologically dependent on a mind has one feature associated with the core conception but lacks another. Therefore that idea is at best only substance-like. It satisfies the independence requirement in one way (ontologically) but not in another. To think of an idea as an object in a two-place relation is to think of that idea, in at least some sense, as an independent thing. That might not be enough for ideas to qualify as robust substances, but it would mean that they share a vital feature we primarily associate with substances. Likewise, were Locke to treat ideas on the model of predicates modifying subjects (as monadic predicates), then that would constitute some evidence he viewed ideas as modes. There are a number of places where Locke sounds like he is treating ideas substantially. We have already briefly touched on one. In discussing memory Locke reports that it is a "Store-house of our *Ideas*" (in II.10.2). More compellingly, he tells us that "[t]he Mind very often sets it self on work in search of some hidden *Idea,* and turns, as it were, the Eye of the Soul upon it; though sometimes too they start up in our Minds of their own accord, and offer themselves to the Understanding; and very often are roused and tumbled out of their dark Cells, into open Day-light, by some turbulent and tempestuous Passion; our Affections bringing *Ideas* to our Memory, which had otherwise lain quiet and unregarded" (*ECHU* II.10.7). This passage reads as if Locke believes there is a two-place relation between the mind and its ideas. They are "roused" from slumber, where they otherwise reside "unregarded." Locke's language suggests that ideas in the memory are called up by certain mental actions, in turn indicating that ideas exist in some sense without the attention of the mind. Some might object that this would be odd indeed given that he commits himself to the transparency of the mind, such that it has no ideas of which it is not aware: "[I]t seeming to me near a Contradiction, to say, that there are Truths imprinted on the Soul, which it perceives or understands not" (*ECHU* I.2.5). Yet Locke's view is *not* that the mind must *be* aware of any ideas it has; rather he claims that the mind must be *or have been* aware of them. That is, Locke makes an exception for memory. "For what is not either actually in view, *or in the memory,* is in the mind no way at all" (*ECHU* I.4.20, emphasis mine). So there can be ideas (in some sense yet to be determined) in the mind without actually being "in its view."

We should be quick to recall, however, that the sense in which ideas can be in the mind without being "in view" shifts Locke firmly away from substantializing ideas. In a later edition, Locke deleted the storehouse metaphor, replacing it with the following:

> But our *Ideas* being nothing, but actual Perceptions in the Mind, which cease to be any thing, when there is no perception of them, this *laying up* of our *Ideas* in the Repository of the Memory, signifies no more but this, that the Mind has a Power, in many cases, to revive Perceptions, which it has once had, with this additional Perception annexed to them, that it has had them before. And in this Sense it is, that our *Ideas* are said to be in our Memories, when indeed, they are actually no where, but only there is an ability in the Mind, when it will, to revive them again; and as it were paint them anew on it self, though some with more, some with less difficulty; some more lively, and others more obscurely. (*ECHU* II.10.2)

But what are we to make of this passage?[18] Locke apparently believes here that ideas cannot exist without a mind. And why would he believe this? The most plausible explanation would be that ideas are modifications, states, or properties of the mind. Other scholars have come to similar conclusions.[19]

One worry about attributing this view to Locke is that it seems to deny a distinction between the act of perception and its object. As we have seen in

---

18. I read the word "perceptions" in the first sentence of the passage as meaning "objects of perception."
19. Jonathan Bennett, for one, in private conversation. Ian Tipton has defended in conversation the same reasoning with respect to Berkeley.

our discussion of Yolton, Locke often uses the word "perception" to mean "object of perception." For the moment, however, it is enough to notice that this worry is unfounded. Locke provides a nice explanation that might help clarify the situation. Ideas are the final states that result from an activity of the soul. Locke writes: "[T]he perception of *Ideas* being (as I conceive) to the Soul, what motion is to the Body, not its Essence, but one of its Operations" (*ECHU* II.1.9). When a body is moved, the final state resulting from that action is the object, as it were, of that act. Similarly, an idea is the end result (or "object") of a mental activity. The act of perception and its object are kept distinct, yet the idea-object is nonetheless a modification of the mind.

Is all of this clear evidence that ideas are modes for Locke? No, although I cannot imagine what else he could have in mind at this point. At no place does Locke explicitly deny that ideas are substantial, and he never even hints that we know nothing other than our own mental states (Alexander 1908, 30–31). Aside from those numerous passages where Locke sounds like he is treating ideas substantially, he also complicates matters by apparently endorsing a substance view when attacking adverbial theories of ideas elsewhere.

The only place Locke explicitly takes up the issue of the ontological status of ideas comes in his lengthy commentary on Malebranche's *Search After the Truth*. Here Locke directly takes up the metaphysical issues Malebranche raises about ideas. Without doubt, the "Examination" is the most significant work of Locke's we have to consider, despite the prominence of the *Essay*. In the former, Locke directly addresses the ontological problems Malebranche raises and, although not published until after his death, it was apparently written in between the first and third editions of the *Essay*.[20] Locke's directness is refreshing and illuminating.

Malebranche divides the objects of mental activity into two groups: sentiments (sensations) and ideas. Sentiments correspond to Locke's ideas of sense and the latter to Locke's ideas as they figure in intellectual thought. Locke claims to be baffled by Malebranche's claim that sentiments are modifications of the soul.

> The "sentiment," says [Malebranche], in the next words, "is a modification of our soul." This word *modification* here, that comes

---

20. Locke wrote to Molyneux on 28 March 1693, indicating that he was thinking of adding a chapter to the next (second) edition of the *Essay*. Later, on 26 April 1695, he reports to Molyneux that his critique of Malebranche is a treatise in itself, but he decided not to include it in the third

> in for explication, seems to me to signify nothing more than the word to be explained by it; v.g. I see the purple color of a violet; ... I take the word ["modification"], and desire to see what I can conceive by it concerning my soul; and here, I confess, I can conceive nothing more, but that I have the idea of purple in my mind, which I had not before, without being able to apprehend anything the mind does or suffers in this, besides barely having the idea of purple; and so the good word *modification* signifies nothing to me more than I knew before. (EM, 438)

On the surface this is classic Locke. By a "modification" Malebranche asks Locke to conceive of something about a substance (namely his mind), and this Locke refuses to do. Yet his claim that the word "modification" means nothing to him is disingenuous. Locke proceeds to argue against the modification view in a way that reveals he understands the position well enough. Ideas cannot be modes, he claims, because it would require that a unified substance (the soul) be modified in incompatible ways.

> Now I ask, take *modification* for what you please, can the same unextended indivisible substance have different, nay, inconsistent and opposite (as these of white and black) modifications at the same time? Or must we suppose distinct parts in an indivisible substance, one for black, another for white, and another for red ideas, and so of the rest of those infinite sensations which we have in sorts and degrees; all which we can distinctly perceive, and so are distinct ideas, some whereof are opposite, as heat and cold, which yet a man may feel at the same time? (439)

This passage, I think, reveals that Locke's initial trepidation with Malebranche's use of the word "modification" owes to the claims it makes on his knowledge of substances. Locke shows that he understands Malebranche's use of the term "modification" to mean an alteration, state, or property of a substance. He balks at the notion that he therefore has to know what this modification means in terms of the underlying metaphysics. Thus, without having to claim any understanding about the substance itself that is modified, he can still turn and criticize this view whatever it actually entails in

---

edition because he wished to avoid controversy and had "affection" for Malebranche. See also Locke 1976, 4:1620 and 5:1887.

terms of the underlying substance. All he knows is the represented content of the idea, be it a mode or not.

Locke's criticism is a famous one. The basic claim is that the soul cannot simultaneously be modified by the idea of white and the idea of black. So far as I can tell, the only rationale for this claim is that Locke attributes to Malebranche the view that the soul "having" the idea of white, that is, being so modified, *literally* qualifies the soul. Locke's allegation is technically wrong, since Malebranche holds that only *sensations* qualify the soul. It is, however, right insofar as what Locke means by "idea" includes what Malebranche calls sensations. Malebranche certainly does hold that sensations are literal qualifications of the mind (*LO*, 634–35, Elucidation 11). Hence, seeing white entails that the soul is white. On that thinking, the soul cannot simultaneously sense white and black because the soul itself (which is a unity) cannot simultaneously *be* white and black. It is not clear to me whether Malebranche is committed to any such view.[21] That is, I am not convinced that Malebranche would take the unity of the soul to imply anything about how it might be modified. At a minimum we should take careful note of Malebranche's distinction between ideas (which are never modes) and sensations. To perceive white might just mean that people who so perceive are in a particular state, and likewise with every other sensation. There is no obvious requirement that the modifications be mutually exclusive (indeed they cannot be). Locke's argument here will be of interest later, since his own analysis occasionally appears to merge idea and quality. If an idea impresses on the mind in such a way as literally to qualify it, then, arguably, ideas just are qualities.

Importantly, we have no explicit evidence that Locke changes his position about the ontological nature of ideas here. If that is correct, then we have reason to think that Locke's considered view is that ideas cannot be modes. In questioning the Malebranchian concept of sentiment, he outlines the possible meanings of the word as used by Malebranche: "If by *sentiment,* which is the word he uses in French, he means the act of sensation, or the operation of the soul in perceiving; and by *pure idea,* the immediate object of that perception, which is the definition of ideas he gives us here in the first chapter, there is some foundation for it, taking ideas for real beings or substances" (437). This passage is particularly telling, since his description of pure ideas, "the immediate object of that perception," *exactly* resembles his

---

21. Steven Nadler has ably argued at some length that Malebranche avoids the error of making representation literal, but this does not exonerate Malebranche from the problems concerning sensations (1992, esp. 41–43).

official definition of "idea" in *Essay* (II.8.8). Here we are told that to treat ideas as immediate objects of perception is to take them as real beings or substances. Now Locke attacks the position that *Malebranche* can say all ideas are substances on the grounds that it would mean that all sensations are perceived in God. *This complaint is not a rejection of the view that ideas are substances;* it is a rejection of Malebranche's doctrine of Vision in God. In fact, Locke concludes this paragraph by wondering why everything isn't properly an idea, given that "by this word idea he understands here nothing else but what is the immediate or nearest object of the mind when it perceives anything" (438). This remark is, of course, made in reference to Malebranche's work, but given that Locke describes ideas in the same way in the *Essay* there is reason to suppose he thinks that ideas as immediate objects are substance-like.[22] Here, in the one spot where Locke says anything explicit about ideas, they rather resemble substances.

But our puzzle deepens. There are no other *conclusive* indications that Locke thought of ideas as substances. If he did, we ought to expect at least two things. First, we should expect that he treat any act of perception as a two-place relation in which one of the relata is an idea (which is not to suggest that substances are the only things that can stand in relations). Second, we should expect that Locke give some credence to the notion of substance by minimally acting as if ideas are somehow independent beings.

Now Locke does write as if perception is relational. In one place, for instance, we are told that ideas continually parade before the mind and that the mind only considers some of them. "At other times, it barely observes the train of *Ideas*, that succeed in the Understanding, without directing, and pursuing any of them: And at other times, it lets them pass almost quite unregarded, as faint shadows, that make no Impression" (*ECHU* II.19.3). Here the perceptual relation between the mind and its ideas is decidedly two-place. Such passages abound in the *Essay*. I will go so far as to say that I think they dominate his discussions of ideas. Some might object, citing Locke's example of pleasure and pain. That example is supposedly the clearest case where Locke treats ideas as monadic predicates (aside from the memory and retention passage examined above). Yet even here Locke does not indicate that our *idea* of pain is itself a mode, even if pain itself is a modification of the mind. "By Pleasure and Pain, I must be understood to mean of Body or Mind . . . though in truth, they be only different Constitu-

---

22. This does not imply that Locke thought of ideas as abstract concepts existing in a Platonic heaven. Rather, ideas just are (behave like) thing-like independent entities.

tions of the Mind, sometimes occasioned by disorder in the Body, sometimes by Thoughts of the Mind" (II.20.2). I find it surprising that if our ideas are modes that Locke does not clearly write as if our idea of pain in particular is just a modification of the mind. Yet he does not. He distinguishes between pain and our concept (idea) of pain, at the same time maintaining only that the former is a mode of the mind. The key is that we must reflect on our experience—how the soul is modified—to fashion the idea. "For to define [pleasure and pain] by the Presence of Good or Evil, is no otherwise to make them known to us, than by making us reflect on what we feel in our selves, upon the several and various Operations of Good and Evil upon our Minds, as they are differently applied to, or considered by us" (II.20.1). Consider an example. If I were being harmed by an "evil" cause, say someone burning my arm with a brand, then my body would be in the state of being damaged ("disordered"). It is not until I reflect on that disorder (and its effects in the mind) that I am said to feel pain. We can *suffer* pain without having the idea of that pain. Now this fits Locke's analysis because he alleges that the mind cannot fail to receive impressions conveyed by the senses. The outcome is perhaps odd; namely, that we can be in pain without having the idea of pain, but I submit that Locke might have had just this result in mind.[23]

In order to make this clear, we need to examine the claim that Locke did not think ideas could exist apart from a mind (Chappell 1994, 28). Locke holds that every instance of thinking or perceiving requires an object, but the reverse is not *obviously* true for him. I want to be absolutely clear about the position I am about to take. I am not asserting that Locke reflectively believed that ideas can exist without a mind like some third substance. I *am* arguing that once we reveal some tensions in Locke's thought concerning the relationship between ideas and qualities we can see *pressures* within his thought to treat ideas as rather like substances. Consider one passage often taken as evidence that ideas cannot exist "outside" the mind:

> Want of Sensation in this case [when there is an impression on the sense organ but no notice is taken of it] is not through any defect in the Organ, or that the Man's Ears are less affected, than at other

---

23. In discussing Berkeley, Robert Muehlmann notes that sensations (like pain) can have two components, one affective (which would be the suffering aspect), one sensory. There is thus some reason to believe that this view is not entirely implausible, and I engage it further in section 7.2 with respect to Berkeley. See Muehlmann 1992, 255. As Muehlmann himself notes, he is presaged by Norton Nelkin with respect to Reid (Nelkin 1989, 65–77).

> times, when he does hear: but that which uses to produce the *Idea*, though conveyed in by the usual Organ, not being taken notice of in the Understanding, and so imprinting no *Idea* on the Mind, there follows no *Sensation*. *So that where-ever there is Sense, or Perception, there some* Idea *is actually produced, and present in the Understanding.* (*ECHU* II.9.4)

Although I grant that the passage does not explicitly allow that ideas can exist without perception, it is consistent with that possibility, although it is not commonly interpreted in this way. The part typically seized on here is not the last sentence emphasized by Locke but the one before it. No idea is formed unless the mind takes notice of it. His final conclusion does not indicate that there can be no ideas without a mind perceiving them; it only asserts the reverse. Every instance of perception involves an idea. Perhaps there is some reason for this omission. Locke tells us that the mind in the perception of simple ideas is utterly passive: "[T]he Mind is wholly Passive in the reception of all its simple *Ideas*" (*ECHU* II.12.1). Hearing a basic sound is, as we have seen, offered as an example of a simple idea by Locke. Furthermore, in addition to being passive, the mind *cannot refuse* to admit a simple idea. "For the Objects of our Senses, do, many of them, obtrude their particular *Ideas* upon our minds, whether we will or no. . . . These *simple Ideas*, when offered to the mind, *the Understanding can* no more refuse to have, nor alter, when they are imprinted, nor blot them out, and make new ones in it self, than a mirror can refuse, alter, or obliterate the Images *or Ideas*, which, the Objects set before it, do therein produce" (*ECHU* II.1.25). Note that Locke states that the objects of the senses intrude on the *mind* and not just the sensory organs. Thus Locke tells us on the one hand that the mind can refuse entrance to certain sensory ideas (by inattention or otherwise), while on the other he tells us that the mind cannot.

I submit that Locke's position here is not necessarily contradictory. The mind cannot refuse the impressions conveyed by the senses. By this Locke intends that the mind cannot refuse to be modified by qualities that affect the senses. When the senses function properly, the causal powers of external objects extend, via the senses, to the mind. The impressions conveyed to the mind are not themselves ideas but qualities. Confusion arises because in the earlier passage Locke is providing an *intellectual* interpretation of ideas in mind. I should be clear here. By "intellectual" I do not mean to imply anything about whether ideas are images. I only intend that such ideas are not qualities nor immediately sensory. In short, Locke sometimes blends qualities and ideas, especially when it comes to the underlying metaphysical issues. This point has been discussed in the literature by Jonathan Bennett and opposed by Thomas Lennon.[24] Locke himself warns us of the possibility of confusion or error on this very point in II.8.8, and I am inclined to think that Locke offered the apology for some reason, even if he is not generally guilty of conceptual confusion.[25] Allowing for the possibility that Locke at least occasionally runs ideas and qualities together, we can see that perception usually involves a two-place relation between the mind and the ideas it considers. As I briefly suggested in section 4.2, we might tell a corroborating story. Sensations (bodily impressions) are mediate objects (of perception) that are perceived only when made present to the mind by causing an idea (the immediate object) to be perceived. It would be easy to lose track of the objects to which we refer when we admit multiple kinds of them, thus explaining some of Locke's apparently loose language.

And what of the passage about memory and retention where Locke says that ideas are really nothing when not perceived by the mind? A careful rereading will satisfy us that he has a quality sense of idea in mind. I reproduce the passage for convenience.

> But our *Ideas* being nothing, but actual Perceptions in the Mind, which cease to be any thing, when there is no perception of them, this *laying up* of our *Ideas* in the Repository of the Memory, signifies no more but this, that the Mind has a Power, in many cases, to revive Perceptions, which it has once had, with this additional Perception annexed to them, that it has had them before. And in this Sense it is, that our *Ideas* are said to be in our Memories, when indeed, they are actually no where, *but only there is an ability in the Mind, when it will, to revive them again; and as it were paint them anew on it self*, though some with more, some with less difficulty; some more lively, and others more obscurely. (*ECHU* II.10.2; the last emphasis is mine).

Note the last italicized phrase. The mind "paints" ideas on itself anew. The metaphor is imagistic and strongly reminiscent of qualities. From his cri-

---

24. Bennett 1971, 25–30, and Lennon 1998, 13–21.
25. Compare *ECHU* II.21.1: "The Mind being every day informed, by the Senses, of the alteration of those simple *Ideas,* it observes in things without" and "For we cannot observe any alteration to be made in, or operation upon any thing, but by the observable change of its sensible *Ideas;* nor conceive any alteration to be made, but by conceiving a Change of some its *Ideas.*" In these passages, as elsewhere, the word "idea" is plausibly best taken as meaning "quality."

tique of Malebranche we know that Locke is inclined to take the qualification of minds literally. As a consequence, Locke is here telling us that the mind has the power to invoke states of itself that recreate the affection of a sensory quality. In this sense, ideas (understood as quality instances) do not exist when not perceived by the mind. Here "perception" again means "the object of perception." Qualities modifying the mind are actual objects of mental activity. I am emboldened by the fact that this is the *only* passage where Locke says anything remotely like this, and it is easily explained in terms of the idea/quality conflation.

Additional evidence of pressures in Locke's thinking to treat ideas as substance-like (because perception is relational) may be found elsewhere. Locke tells us that consciousness is "the perception of what passes in a Man's own mind" (*ECHU* II.1.19). Given that he admits that we can be influenced (materially affected by external objects) while asleep, it follows that the mind can be affected without consciousness or intellectual perception (*ECHU* II.1.21). This view is plausible, since something must presumably cause the mind to start functioning consciously when we awaken. Sensory qualities affect the mind even when we sleep. Another piece of evidence comes from Locke's adherence to the transparency thesis, which holds that the mind must be aware of any idea in its possession. "For to imprint any thing on the Mind without the Mind's perceiving it, seems to me hardly intelligible" (*ECHU* I.2.5). Adhering to this thesis contradicts his claim that the mind does not have to take notice of ideas conveyed to it, *unless* he intends that it is possible to perceive something of which one takes no notice. The only sense I can give to that suggestion is that Locke thinks the affection of the mind by qualities constitutes a form of perception. And so it does. The mind "perceives" whenever it has an object on which it acts. Since the impression of qualities on the mind always results in mental activity (the mind being modified), the mind always perceives in a minimal sense what is imprinted on it, hence the distinction between having ideas and "taking notice" of them. We cannot fail to perceive a sensory impression in the sense that we are modified by it, but we need not take notice of it, which involves generating an immediate object for the mind, an idea.

The end result is that because Locke does not fully separate qualities from ideas, it is not surprising that he writes as if perception is relational between minds and distinct objects. He often thinks of qualities as like ideas and as external features of the world, and so in perception there is a two-place relation between the mind and the idea "in" the object. Yet we cannot thus conclude that ideas are substances for Locke. At best we can conclude that when Locke speaks of ideas in the quality sense, he merely treats them as rather *like* substances. They have important features typically associated only (or primarily) with substances but they lack others, so we cannot conclusively hold that Locke considers ideas to be substances. What if Locke had completely separated ideas and qualities consistently in *all* of his thinking and writing? Might that have led Locke to make a clear pronouncement about the nature of ideas? I suspect Locke would have urged us to pay close attention to the distinction between mediate and immediate objects, but beyond this I have no good sense of what else he would have said. I am content to conclude that a substance interpretation at least influences his thinking about the nature of ideas. That still leaves a fundamental ambiguity in his thinking about them. When he speaks of ideas as qualities *external to us,* they at least *behave* like substances and fit well with his attack on Malebranchian modes. At other times, however, he thinks of the effect (mechanistically) of qualities on our bodies and minds, and in those few cases ideas appear to be modes (as in the memory passage). Either way, his thinking betrays a clear commitment to the traditional categories.

But what of the second element in Locke's thinking we expected to find? If Locke implicitly holds that ideas are like substances in some cases, there should be some evidence that ideas are independent of minds. Insofar as he thinks of ideas as qualities, they exist independently of minds as derivative on the mind-independent primary qualities of external objects. Consider those passages where Locke most clearly conflates qualities with ideas. "The Mind being every day informed, by the Senses, of the alteration of those simple *Ideas,* it observes in things without." And again later in the same paragraph: "For we cannot observe any alteration to be made in, or operation upon any thing, but by the observable change of its sensible *Ideas;* nor conceive any alteration to be made, but by conceiving a Change of some [of] *its Ideas*" (*ECHU* II.21.1, emphasis on "its Ideas" is Locke's). The ideas, which are "out there" in the objects, are independent of the mind. Insofar as we consider ideas of primary qualities, where he merges those qualities with ideas they would be obviously mind independent. When Locke merges idea with quality, he treats them both as relata in two-place relations and as independent of the mind.

I am intrigued by the fact that there are no clear cases where Locke denies independence. He is careful to assert that perception always requires an idea, but he never claims that all ideas must be perceived. That innovation was Berkeley's, not Locke's. It is possible that Locke simply ignored these problems, leaving them for others to grapple with as best they might. I do not believe Locke thought hard about these complications and hence also do not believe that Locke held a reflective view about the independence of ideas, all of which helps to explain why the quality-idea conflation runs so deep.

We have yet, of course, to explain how quality ideas sometimes can be modes of the mind when Locke attacked Malebranche for holding a similar view. Locke takes care to emphasize that ideas of secondary qualities, when received by the mind, do not resemble external objects. In effect, Locke here adopts the solution I provided for Malebranche above. That is, he recognizes that the mind need not be literally red when perceiving red. Thus it is possible for the mind to receive contrary impressions simultaneously. I also take this as some evidence that Locke was thinking within the confines of the traditional ontology.

It is worth reminding ourselves of Locke's agnosticism about the nature of ideas. When John Norris attacked him for not discussing the nature of ideas, Locke replied, "[A]nd as to that, I answer, no man can tell; for which I not only appeal to experience, which were enough, but shall add this reason, viz. because no man can give any account of any alteration made in any simple substance whatsoever."[26] Locke's attitude results in one passage some have cited as evidence that Locke rejected the notion that ideas are substances (Lennon 1993, 246). In his response to Norris, Locke goes on to say:

> Ideas may be real beings, though not substances; as motion is a real being, though not a substance; and it seems probable that, in us, ideas depend on, and are some way or other the effect of motion; since they are so fleeting, it being, as I have elsewhere observed, so hard, and almost impossible, to keep in our minds the same unvaried idea, long together, unless when the object that produces it is present to the senses. . . . To excuse therefore the ignorance I have owned of what our ideas are, any further than as they are perceptions we experiment in ourselves; and the dull, unphilosophical way I have taken of examining their production, only so far as experience and observation lead me, wherein my dim sight went not beyond *sensation* and *reflection*. (1894, 2:469)

The passage is admittedly difficult for me, even if a singular exception. But perhaps Locke does not deny that ideas are substances in this passage. He

---

26. Locke 1894, 2:460, "Remarks upon Some of Mr. Norris's Books." The reply to Norris was appended to his "Examination" and apparently written in 1693 (between the first and second editions of the *Essay*), although not published until after Locke's death.

may be reasonably read as denying that he *knows*. They *may* be real beings without being substances (and hence *may* be analogous to the case of motion), and at any rate he tells us that all he commits himself to is the claim that they are clearly dependent on external causes through motion (which still allows ideas to be substance-like). This last claim reflects his mechanistic corpuscularianism and reinforces the point that external qualities causally affect the mind. Thus the passage might not speak against the traditional ontology, although it raises the possibility of another interpretation. Thomas Lennon argues, partially on the basis of this text, that Locke's ideas are *material* particles (1993, esp. 247–48). The plausibility of that thesis lies outside the purview of this work (see section 4.2), but I may content myself with the knowledge that Lennon's thesis still has Locke adopting the traditional ontology.

Now, finally, we have an ontic ground for Locke's theory of ideas. Ideas, in the broad sense of his official definition, have characteristics of *both* substances and modes. That is, he sometimes acts as if they are modes and sometimes acts as if they are like substances. We can interpret this ambiguity in one of two ways. First, we might think that there are various kinds of ideas, some of which are modes, some of which are substances. Alternatively, we might conclude that Locke is simply unreflectively inconsistent. Such options come as a result of his broad and free-ranging conception of ideas, his consciously ignoring the metaphysical consequences of his theorizing, and the occasional merging of qualities and ideas. We can also explain why his contemporaries, although all placing him within the substance/mode ontology, nevertheless interpreted him in various ways. Since they were not clear about the conflation, and most commentators committed it themselves, any of a number of plausible readings may come from the texts.

Thus far I hope at a minimum to have established the reasonableness of supposing that Locke operated within the substance/mode ontology when thinking about ideas. One lesson seems clear from a careful study of Locke's theorizing. Even when one sets aside questions about ontology, the problems that arise from the poor fit between idea philosophy and ontology intrude into the epistemology. Locke occasionally makes ideas mental entities in the tradition of the later Descartes and his Cartesian followers, yet he too wishes to account for our knowledge of a nonmental world. His core problem is essentially the same one that Descartes, Arnauld, Malebranche, and others faced. How do ideas function epistemologically given the nature of the mind and body? As with Descartes, the difficulty is pressing not only because Locke maintains that resemblance sometimes figures into the process (as with primary qualities) but also because he conceives of perception as a causal process.

I conclude that although Locke did not advance early modern thinking about the ontic nature of ideas, he neither "abandons" ontology nor "deontologizes" ideas. Instead, he provides an interesting bridge between the Cartesians and Berkeley, and not just on the infamous matter of abstraction. Locke's work additionally constitutes a preservation of the core conceptual scheme associated with the Cartesian philosophy of ideas. Ideas are mental, tightly related to the mind (present to it), and represent the external world. Understanding them in their entirety is the key to unlocking the secrets of the mind. As we shall see, Locke was not alone during this period in maintaining an adherence to a core traditional ontology when thinking about the nature and function of ideas. Leibniz, often a critic of Locke, develops a distinctively different theory about ideas. Yet on closer scrutiny, Leibniz's philosophizing about ideas retains this same commitment to a traditional underlying ontology.

5

LEIBNIZ

G. W. Leibniz, like Locke, also developed his theory of ideas in the aftermath of the famous dispute between Arnauld and Malebranche. That dispute turned on the ontological status of ideas. For Malebranche ideas are abstract and substantial things that reside "in" the mind of God. They are permanent entities preserved by Him even when not in use by finite beings. Arnauld takes ideas to be temporary modes of the mind. Both figures pull Leibniz in opposite directions. He agrees with Malebranche that ideas cannot be identified with particular thoughts; ideas must be objects to which the mind is related in thinking. Yet Leibniz simultaneously takes Arnauld's side in the dispute, agreeing that ideas must be internal modifications of the mind.

What emerges, at first glance, is a difficult amalgam of incompletely stated views. Early in his career, in the "Notes on the Reply of Foucher to the Criticism of his Criticism of the 'Recherche de la Verite'" (1676 [*L*, 155]), Leibniz distinguishes between two senses of idea, and ten years later he repeats the very same distinction, making it plausible to suppose that he had a relatively stable conception of their nature. According to the *Discourse on Metaphysics* (1686), ideas can be either the form of thought or the immediate object of perception (*L*, 320; *G* 4:451). Sometimes he explicitly speaks of ideas as modes and sometimes as objects, leaving us with what Jonathan Bennett calls an "unresolved tension" in Leibniz's thinking about ideas (*NE*, xxiii; see *SSB* 6).

Conventional scholarship now indicates that these opposing forces are resolved in Leibniz's mature theory that treats ideas as dispositions. Thus Nicholas Jolley argues that Bennett's "unresolved tension" is actually a "genuine synthesis" of the views of Arnauld and Malebranche (1990, 134–35). Leibniz agrees with Malebranche that ideas are not particular thoughts but nonetheless seeks to make them mental. "Although he resists any straightforward identification of ideas with thoughts," Jolley remarks, "Leibniz does believe that talk about ideas can be reduced to talk about the mental. Leibniz brings off the reduction by explaining that ideas are dispositions to think in certain ways" (136). Benson Mates takes it as obvious that Leibnizian ideas are just mental dispositions (1986, 49, 175, 246).[1] Ideas are not particular events but are nonetheless nonabstract psychological entities. Again, idea language reduces to talk about the mental as dispositions to think in certain ways.[2]

Unfortunately what it means to say that "ideas are dispositions" is less clear than it appears at first blush. Not only is the ontic nature of Leibnizian ideas left murky but a number of unresolved philosophical difficulties are also associated with this particular theory. It is especially important that one should take care to distinguish between what ideas *are* (ontologically) and what occurs when representing is being tokened. Furthermore, one should understand that the claim that what it means to be in possession of an idea *requires* a disposition is distinct from the *identification* of an idea with a disposition. In this chapter I seek to flesh out Leibniz's ultimate ontology of ideas by investigating what it might mean to say that ideas "are" dispositions. The goal is largely prophylactic; I want to head off any possible suggestion that Leibniz's theory of ideas places him in the early modern tale or supports an understanding of the development of the way of ideas that is anti-ontological. Ultimately I contend that ideas for Leibniz are, strictly speaking, modes (i.e., mental modifications). As such his views place him cleanly within the traditional core ontology, although the focus of my discussion indicates why ideas cannot be *straightforwardly* identified with dispositions. Many modes are dispositional, but to think of ideas as dispositions engenders considerable philosophical difficulties in Leibniz and runs counter to significant textual evidence.

5.1 Resolving a "Tension"

As a student of the Malebranche-Arnauld dispute, Leibniz was clear about the competing views concerning the status of ideas early in his philosophical career. In 1676, in response to Foucher's criticisms of Malebranche, he

---

1. Note that Mates expresses the claim differently at different points. On page 49 Mates says to *have* an idea is to have a disposition; at 175 and 246 he says that an idea *is* a disposition. I go on to argue that the distinction matters. See Broad 1975, 134–35.
2. "What Is an Idea?" (1678 [*L*, 207, G 7:263–64]); see also G 2:547.

writes: "Idea can be taken in two senses; namely, for the quality or form of thought, as velocity and direction are the quality and form of movement; or for the immediate or nearest object of perception. Thus the idea would not be a mode of being of our soul. This seems to be the opinion of Plato and the author of the *Recherche*" (*L*, 155). Later Leibniz repeats this basic distinction in the *Discourse,* but he indicates a preference for the object reading he will continue to hold as late as the *New Essays.* "If the idea were the *form* of the thought, it would come into and go out of existence with the actual thoughts which correspond to it, but since it is the *object* of thought, it can exist before and after the thoughts" (109). This passage is a straightforward denial that ideas are particular thoughts (that is, particular states of thinking). Thoughts come and go, but ideas are stable objects to which the mind is related during mental activity. Thus far Leibniz seems to be in agreement with Malebranche. Yet Leibniz curiously sides more often with Arnauld, arguing that ideas must be modes of the mind. In a 4 November 1715 letter to Remond, Leibniz is unequivocal. "There is more plausibility in attacking P. Malebranche's opinion about ideas. For there is no necessity (it seems) to take them for something which is outside us. It is sufficient to consider ideas as Notions, that is to say, as modifications of our mind. This is how the Schools, M. Descartes, and M. Arnauld take them" (*G* 3:659). The standard way to resolve these apparently conflicting passages is to appeal to dispositions. Ideas are both particular objects and internal modifications, and we can make sense of this by saying that ideas are dispositions. The relevant concept here means something like "the power to act or be acted on in a certain way."[3] To say that an idea is a disposition means that the idea just is a *power* to bring about some result. Unfortunately this contemporary characterization is positively misleading when applied to Leibniz, who does not have such an understanding of the concept of power. A power, according to Leibniz, is the possibility of change (*NE,* 169). But genuine powers—active powers—also include something Leibniz calls "endeavor." The powers had by substances, for instance, include an active striving to actualize whatever faculty is possessed. "If 'power' is taken to be the source of action, it means more than the aptitude or ability in terms of which power was explained in the preceding chapter. For, as I have more than once remarked, it also includes endeavor" (*NE,* 216; see also *NE,* 169, 226). Ideas, of course, are not active substances according to Leibniz. As a result, when one alleges that

---

3. I borrow this formulation from Mackie 1972.

ideas are dispositions, we cannot charitably understand he or she to mean that ideas are (active) powers in Leibniz's sense of the term. Instead, dispositions are perhaps best understood as *abilities* or *capacities* absent any entelechy or "endeavor." Leibniz uses the word "aptitude" to describe powers that do not include endeavor.

Having an idea thus reduces to the mind having the bare possibility (aptitude) of bringing about a certain kind of change. Accordingly scholars like Mates and Jolley argue that Leibniz holds a coherent synthesis view that borrows from both Malebranche and Arnauld. Idea language reduces to mental talk, and the reduction works because ideas are mental dispositions. In "Quid sit Idea?" ("What Is an Idea?") Leibniz writes: "There are many things in our mind, however, which we know are not ideas, though they would not occur without ideas—for example, thoughts, perceptions, and affections. In my opinion, namely, *an idea consists, not in some act, but in the faculty of thinking* [Idea enim nobis non in quodam cogitandi actu, sed facultate consistit], and we are said to have an idea of a thing even if we do not think of it, if only, on a given occasion, we can think of it" (*L*, 207; *G* 7:263–64). From this and other passages it is clear that Leibniz does not attribute endeavor to the nature of ideas. They are faculties of mere capacity.

There is an additional complication, however. Leibniz also consistently indicates that ideas "express" their objects. In the *Discourse* he writes: "I believe that this disposition [*qualité*] of our soul in so far as it expresses some nature, form, or essence, is properly the idea of the thing, which is in us, and which is always in us, whether we think of it or not" (*L*, 320; *G* 4:451).[4] Leibniz's doctrine of expression is an interesting, if technical, one. In short, x expresses y if we can move from the properties of x to knowledge of the corresponding properties of y.[5] If I have an idea of a square, then my mind is in a certain dispositional state. Furthermore, from the properties of my mind so disposed, one (a supermind) could read off the properties of the square. So ideas have dispositional properties to express their objects. As such they are enduring objects themselves, as Malebranche would have it. However, they are not abstract entities, but decidedly mental beings, in accordance with the views of Arnauld. The initial case for attributing a dispositional theory of ideas, properly understood, to Leibniz is quite nice. We have, it appears, a genuine synthesis of views.

---

4. Loemker translates the word "*qualité*" here as "disposition," and Jolley follows his translation.

5. For a more thorough discussion, see Kulstad 1977, 55–76.

5.2 Ideas as Dispositions

If ideas just are dispositions, then we need to flesh out the rest of the theory. Importantly, one might argue that dispositions must be "grounded."[6] The solubility of salt (its disposition to dissolve in water) is grounded in the chemical properties of salt and water. That is, solubility depends on the relations that hold between the intrinsic properties of salt and water. Ungrounded dispositions were often held in the early modern period to be philosophically repugnant. To use a now (in)famous example, if one were to ask me why a particular substance causes people to go to sleep, merely saying that the substance has a dormitive power is unsatisfying. Similarly, if one wants to know why this idea expresses a dog as opposed to something else, merely saying that it is a disposition to conjure the content dog fails to explain anything.[7]

Whether dispositions generally must have a ground or not, Leibniz independently provides in his system a ground for the dispositional states *of the mind:* his doctrine of *petites perceptions.* There are many minute, insensible modifications of the mind at every point in time. "Besides, there are hundreds of indications leading us to conclude that at every moment there is in us an infinity of perceptions, unaccompanied by awareness or reflection; that is, of alterations in the soul itself, of which we are unaware because these impressions are either too minute and too numerous, or else too unvarying, so that they are not sufficiently distinctive on their own" (*NE,* 53; see also *NE,* 112–13, 134). These minute modifications of the mind ultimately explain why we have the dispositional properties we do, and Leibniz describes them as "alterations in the soul itself," suggesting that they are not also dispositions themselves. Assume that I have an idea of a dog (as opposed to an idea of a cat or an elephant). Since that idea just is a disposition, my having this idea means either (1) that should I somehow be able to reflect on my *petites perceptions*—the modes of my mind that ground this

---

6. This is actually a contentious *contemporary* metaphysical issue, as some hold that dispositions are intrinsic objects that do not require grounds. I do not wish to take a particular stand on this issue here, for *Leibniz* seems to recognize some need for a ground. Both Mates and Jolley, for instance, explicitly agree that at least Leibnizian dispositions are grounded. See Mates 1986, 246, and Jolley 1990, 139. For a contemporary defense of "categoricalism" (where dispositions must be grounded in nondispositional states), see Armstrong 1997, esp. ch. 5. For a nice recent overview, including some of the alternate positions, see Bird 2001, 137–49.

7. It should be noted that I am forced into using some awkward language just to express the view that ideas are identified with dispositions. The natural inclination is to attribute a disposition *to* the idea (hence saying that the idea *has* a dog disposition), which is not the view I take Jolley and Mates to be espousing.

disposition—I will learn why they express a dog and not a cat or an elephant, or (2) that merely having these modifications entails my possession of this particular idea (the reverse is not necessarily true; having an idea does not entail the possession of any particular set of modes). I want to remain neutral with respect to these options as, for my purposes here, not much hinges on which one is taken. Given this characterization, we might make a comparison between solubility and ideas.

Salt	Mind	My mind
Chemical structure	*Petites perceptions*	*Petites perceptions* x, y, and z
Solubility	Ideas	Idea of a dog
Dissolvings	Occurrent thoughts	Thinking of a dog

Salt is soluble because of its chemical structure. A mind has an idea in virtue of its *petites perceptions*. The important difference, of course, is that an idea also has an expressive ability.[8] One important advantage accrued here is the ability to explain Leibniz's contention that we have ideas even when not thinking of them and that all of our ideas are innate and internally generated (*L*, 320; *G* 4:451; see also *L*, 113; *G* 4:109–10).

Given this understanding of what it means to say that Leibniz treats ideas as dispositions, what compelling reason is there to think that he actually thought of ideas this way? There are two. The first reason for supposing Leibniz thought of ideas as dispositions is that he appears to say so in two places. Second, Leibniz's discussion of innate ideas appears to support the disposition thesis. Let us engage both reasons, turning first to analyze the former.

5.3 Reading Leibniz

Loemker's translation of the *Discourse* has Leibniz writing that ideas *are* "dispositions of the soul." This translation imports a fair bit of philosophy into the text, but virtually all of the commentators follow this translation (*L*, 320; *G* 4:451.).[9] In the French, Leibniz uses the word "*qualité*" and not the

---

8. One might immediately worry that for Leibniz *petites perceptions* are also representational. I think that is right. Compare *NE*, 54, where he says that these minute perceptions are like unconscious sensations. However, as Jolley does not emphasize the expressive role of ideas *in his account of how they are grounded* (he certainly does so elsewhere), it is not clear that this point can (or should) be held against him.

9. Interestingly, in *The Light of the Soul* Jolley notes the French word but preserves the translation of "disposition" anyway (1990, 137).

word "disposition" (which is an English cognate). As it turns out, however, Leibniz simply does not use "*qualité*" to mean disposition. He does not do so primarily because it was not seventeenth-century usage (and indeed it is not even today). In the *Thresor de la langue française* (1606) none of the sample uses of "*qualité*" plausibly means a disposition in the sense of a tendency to behave. More importantly, the *Dictionnaire de l'Académie française* (1694) also does not list any such usage for the term. At best one definition indicates that "*qualité*" might mean an inclination or habit ("Il signifie plus particulierement, inclination, habitude"), but the illustration of what this definition means indicates that it is intended in the sense of a personal character trait ("*C'est un homme qui a beaucoup de bonnes qualitez, d'excellentes qualitez, des qualitez louables, extraordinaires, & heroiques. il a de belles, de grandes qualitez. parmi quelques bonnes qualitez il en a beaucoup de mauvaises. il a une mauvaise qualité, c'est qu'il ne sçauroit garder de secret.*"). "*Qualité*" certainly has diverse meanings and Leibniz employs them all. He commonly uses it in the sense of "has value" ("Si notre illustre Auteur avoit beaucoup de compagnons en qualité et en merite" [G 3:428]), most often as a property (as with "*qualité occultes*" [e.g., G 2:534 and passim]), and even in the sense of a role ("Pour la seconde fois il ne le fir qu'en qualité de pensionnair de la France" [G 3:277]).[10] A careful search of the original French (at least in the Gerhardt edition) does not reveal even one other clear instance of "*qualité*" being used to mean disposition in the relevant sense.

Tellingly, Leibniz *does* use the French word "disposition" to mean what one would expect. In the *New Essays* in response to Locke's claim (at II.22.10) that tenderness is a disposition, Leibniz uses the word "disposition" in the sense of a tendency to behave. "[E]t quand on peut le reduire en acte à chaque occasion qui se presente, nous l'appellons disposition; ainsi la tendresse est une disposition à l'amitié ou à l'amour" (G 5:199; NE, 215). One should wonder, then, why Leibniz would not use *this* word in the *Discourse* if that were what he really meant. Since arguably "*qualité*" did not mean "disposition" and he had alternative words that he *did* use in the appropriate sense (even in the same work), I conclude that Leibniz is just not saying that ideas are dispositions at all. Ideas are *qualities* of the soul. I will subsequently argue that he intends this in the sense of a straightforward

---

10. With respect to the property characterization of the term, Andrew Pessin in private conversation reminded me that Locke in the *Essay* tends to conflate quality and property (especially in II.8), suggesting that it might have been common to identify the two in the period. If so, then this would, in turn, make Loemker's translation yet more of a stretch.

mental modification. In short, to *have* an idea involves a disposition, but an idea *is* a mode.

A second, more difficult bit of text remains to analyze. Recall that Loemker translates the passage from "Quid sit Idea?" cited above as *"an idea consists, not in some act, but in the faculty of thinking,* and we are said to have an idea of a thing even if we do not think of it, if only, on a given occasion, we can think of it" (*L*, 207; *G* 7:263–64). This passage certainly seems to say that ideas "consist" in an activated power, which could be a disposition to think. Consider the original Latin.[11] "Idea enim nobis non in quodam cogitandi actu, sed facultate consistit, et ideam rei habere dicimur, etsi de ea non cogitemus, modo data occasione de ea cogitare possimus." The verb *"consistere"* (here conjugated as *consistit*) in Latin carries the positional or architectural metaphor of "standing on" or "resting on." Thus a building may "consist" of marble either by "resting on" a foundation made of marble or by being literally composed of it. I do not wish to deny that Leibniz might well be saying here that ideas consist in a faculty, but it is not the only plausible reading of the Latin. Although the English cognate "consists" derives from the Latin *"consistere,"* it can be a misleading translation. The *Oxford Latin Dictionary* lists both "to be composed of" and "to be based or dependant upon" as definitions, but they are the tenth and eleventh entries respectively.[12] Lewis and Short indicates that *"consisto"* plus *"in"* (as occurs in the present passage) means *either* "composed of" *or* "depends upon." In common usage the word is prone to ambiguity and in philosophical parlance a special sense of the word is available that is consistent with the rest of Leibniz's claims about ideas. It is not unreasonable to think that Leibniz might have the sense of "depends on" in mind, especially since this is the only known text where Leibniz appears to say that ideas "consist" of a faculty. Additionally, there is reason to believe that Leibniz uses the word in a similarly specialized philosophical sense to mean "depends upon" elsewhere in his writings. Consider the following passage from an untitled note around 1710: "Extensionis modificatio consistit in varietate magnitudinis et figurae" (*G* 7:328). It would be odd to hold that Leibniz thinks that the modification of extension is "composed" of the variety of magnitude and figure. The more natural reading is that the modification of

---

11. I would like to thank Doug Jesseph and John Brinkley for their valuable assistance on this material.

12. The *Oxford Latin Dictionary* is a classical Latin dictionary, but there does not appear to have been any change in the use or definition of this word in the medieval period.

extension *depends* on the variety of magnitude and figure. Notice that the grammatical constructions are parallel.

In the passage in question, had Leibniz wanted directly to identify ideas with faculties, then the clearest Latin would have been "idea est facultes cogitandi," but he does not use this wording. A better translation than Loemker's might be "our ideas *depend* not on some act, but on the faculty of thinking." In that case, the phrase only indicates that Leibniz takes there to be some relation between ideas and the faculty of thinking. I am not suggesting that ideas depend on dispositions (the faculty of thinking). Rather I think Leibniz is asserting that our *having* an idea requires the faculty of thinking. I freely admit that, unlike my analysis concerning "*qualité*," the support for my position is considerably weaker in this case. In the end, all I can do is suggest that this passage might not be as convincing a support for the dispositional reading as it appears at first glance. At a minimum it is worth noting that there is only a single instance that is troubling in the face of considerable textual evidence elsewhere that Leibniz holds ideas to be modifications. Before we turn to that specific evidence, however, I want to provide a diagnosis as to why others might think that Leibniz considers ideas to be dispositions.

5.4 Ideas: Being One vs. Having One

In order to make proper sense of my reading of Leibniz in the above passages, we need to stop and be clear about an important distinction being made in the texts. Once clear about this distinction, we have a natural and plausible way to understand Leibniz even in these two initially troublesome texts. Ideas for Leibniz are modes but not *merely* modes. What separates ideas from mere modes is the clarity of their expressive capacity. We "have" ideas even when they are not actively being considered only in the sense that should they become "activated," they would express their external object.[13] Thus Jolley is absolutely right to attach something dispositional to ideas. But the relationship is not one of identity. My mind does not perpetually express a dog, but a supermind could "read" from the arrangements of my mental modes the nature of this dog. It is in this sense that Leibniz believes that one mind expresses the entire universe. The entire universe is not simultaneously *actively* represented in the mind, but the entire universe can be expressed by a single mind.

---

13. A more complete account of this "activation" follows in the next section.

I propose that Leibniz is drawing a distinction here between "having" an idea and the nature of the idea itself. To have an idea involves a certain sort of relation between the subject and some represented content. This "having" relation is a dispositional one but is something distinct from the metaphysical nature of ideas. Consider the following contrast. I have a headache. That is, there is a relation—an occurrent one—that holds between me (whatever I am) and some mode with a certain content. The headache is a case of nondispositional having and is akin to occurrent thinking. Ideas for Leibniz function similarly, except with the dispositional twist. Imagine that I have an idea of a dog. Having this idea entails that there is a relation between me and a represented dog. In this case, the relation is hypothetical. To say that I have an idea of a dog means that under certain circumstances (if such and such should occur . . .), I become aware of the particular content of a dog. A more natural example of dispositional having is temperament. One might say that I have a bit of a temper. That attribution does not imply anything about my *current* behavior (although it might suggest something about my states that ground this disposition). Rather it describes the content of my behavior or mental states given certain conditions.

The key now to understanding Leibniz's theory of ideas is separating what does the representing from the representation itself. Imagine that I have the idea of a barking dog. Having this idea does not entail that my idea "just is" the disposition to have that content (perhaps after hearing a barking dog). Rather the idea (its formal nature) is whatever it is *that enables me* to be related to that content (to "have" it). After all, one may meaningfully ask *what it is* that makes this idea an idea of a barking dog as opposed to a meowing cat or something else.

Ideas can be had both occurrently and dispositionally. Such is Leibniz's insight. To have an idea occurrently is to be in a nondispositional relation to some content. I am thinking about a barking dog now. That is, my mind is actually modified such that I have that particular content now. To have the idea dispositionally is at least this: that my mind is capable of being altered such that a particular mode of my mind actually represents a barking dog (has that particular content), regardless of whether I am aware of that content. If I have a headache in the dispositional sense of having, I might be said to have a headache even when I am, in fact, not feeling any pain. These sentences doubtless sound odd because we are forcing language into the dispositional model, but that might just indicate that headaches are not "had" dispositionally—only occurrently.

Now for Leibniz this distinction between having ideas occurrently and having them dispositionally might entail one of two things. Perhaps he intends that modes of the mind are brought into actuality from possibility. In other words, at one moment my mind is not modified (at all) in this way, and at another moment it is. This view assumes, not unreasonably, that all modes are occurrent beings. Alternatively, Leibniz's view might be that we always have all of the (our) modifications. To say that minds always have all of their modes might require that we claim that for Leibniz modes can themselves be had dispositionally, introducing further complication. It does not matter for our purposes here which is right. In either case, occurrent thought will require an activator to make the content represented by the particular mode available to consciousness. The best evidence of this interpretation comes from an analysis of his discussion of innate ideas.

5.5 Innate Ideas

The traditional reading of Leibniz makes his theory of innate ideas a dispositional one.[14] Thus Leibniz tells us that ideas are (innately) in us the same way that the veins that outline the shape of Hercules are in a block of marble (*NE*, 52). As one might expect from the foregoing, I maintain that Leibniz implicitly distinguishes between what it means to *have* innate ideas and what it is for something to *be* an idea (innate or otherwise). That is, I think the traditional reading of Leibniz is right when properly construed. He does have a dispositional theory of innate ideas: a theory of what it means to *have* innate ideas. Perhaps more importantly, on the account I provide Leibniz's dispositional theory of having ideas meshes neatly with the traditional ontology.

Leibniz's principal strategy in countering Locke's attack against innate ideas rests on his establishing that there are at least some ideas that we acquire only from within (i.e., not from the senses). "Logic also abounds in such truths, and so do metaphysics and ethics, together with their respective products, natural theology and natural jurisprudence; and so the proof of them can only come from inner principles, which are described as innate" (*NE*, 50). The question is now *how* these ideas are present within us. Here Leibniz provides us with what I call the "attention model" of having ideas innately: "It would indeed be wrong to think that we can easily read these eternal laws of reason in the soul, as the Praetor's edict can be read on his

---

14. See Jolley 1984, esp. 177. See also Yolton 1956, 58.

notice-board, without effort or inquiry; but it is enough that they can be discovered within us by dint of attention." The mind must do something to *activate* the content of the ideas held innately by us. Leibniz then argues that Lockean ideas of reflection are nothing else but "attention to what is already within us, and the senses do not give us what we carry with us already" (*NE,* 51). This assertion implies that whatever grounds the content activated by the mind is always *actually* present within us. And this is exactly Leibniz's position. Our mind is a vast repository that actually contains the ideas we have. We uncover the content represented by a particular idea when we focus our attention inwardly (as it were) on it. Consider again this passage reproduced in section 5.2: "Besides, there are hundreds of indications leading us to conclude that at every moment there is in us an infinity of perceptions, unaccompanied by awareness or reflection; that is, of alterations in the soul itself, of which we are unaware because these impressions are either too minute and too numerous, or else too unvarying, so that they are not sufficiently distinctive on their own" (*NE,* 53). Ideas (perceptions) are modes of the mind (alterations of the soul itself). We are unaware of the vast majority of the ideas we actually have. We become aware of them (and bring them to consciousness as occurrent thoughts) when we attend to them for whatever reason. Thus it would be best to say that Leibniz holds that we *have* ideas (including those that we have innately). It might well be that we have *all* of our ideas innately; this thesis has been ably argued elsewhere, and I do not pursue it here (Jolley 1984, 113; see also Russell 1900, 163). Ideas *are* modes of the mind but to *have* an idea (innately or otherwise) calls for dispositions.

Leibniz is reasonably consistent in his discussions of ideas and about what it means to have them as opposed to what they actually are. Recall that immediately after he says that ideas depend [*consistit*] on the faculty of thinking he says that "we are said to have an idea of a thing . . . if only . . . we can think of it." In the *New Essays* Leibniz has a characteristic way of reminding his readers of his view. "You will remember, too, that I have shown how ideas are in us—not always so that we are aware of them, but always in such a way that we can draw them from our own depths and bring them within reach of our awareness" (438). So when he says that "we are said to have an idea of a thing . . . if only . . . we can think of it," he is providing a description of how we *have* ideas and how we can "draw them from our depths." The pervasive nature of this kind of language in Leibniz's philosophy lends credence to the argument that he makes such a distinction. This account is also strongly reminiscent of the one Locke employs to separate perceptions from having perceptions.[15] "Having" an idea certainly does involve a disposition: the disposition to express an external object. But for Leibniz this is not what an idea *is;* a disposition is an aptitude that we *have* in virtue of having an idea.[16] Similarly, solubility is not what salt is; it is a power that salt has. Just as salt is best described by its chemical structure, so ideas are best understood as being modes of the mind. As a result, I suggest that the following is a better understanding of the relationship between ideas and dispositions than the one with which we started in section 5.2:

Salt	Mind	My mind
Chemical Structure	Ideas	The ideas I have
Solubility	Expressive ability	My power to express a dog
Dissolvings	Occurrent thoughts	My actually thinking of a dog

Importantly, the two problem texts (discussed in section 5.3) are the only passages (of which I am aware) where Leibniz clearly seems to say that ideas are to be identified directly with dispositions. I admit that other passages could be massaged to provide some limited support for the thesis that ideas are disposition, but none of them comes nearly as close to explicitly stating that ideas just are dispositions, and most often when read carefully, they indicate the opposite. So Leibniz writes (immediately on the heels of the veined marble block passage) in the preface to the *New Essays,* "This is how ideas and truths are innate in us—as inclinations, dispositions, tendencies, or natural potentialities, and not as actions" (52). Although this certainly ties ideas to dispositions, Leibniz does not indicate by any reasonable stretch that ideas *are* dispositions. Instead, he says this is what it means to say that ideas are innate in us—a rather different claim. At best, when he appears to say otherwise, he is being incautious about separating the grounds of our dispositions from the dispositions themselves.

As it turns out, as Leibniz matures he outright asserts that ideas are modes. By the turn of the century Leibniz appears to have staked out a rather firm position. For instance, in the letter to Remond in 1715 (quoted earlier) Leibniz writes "It is sufficient to consider ideas as Notions, that is to say, as modifications of our mind" (G 3:659). There is no ambiguity here.

---

15. See section 4.1.

16. Note the account I endorse here is not a *general* account of dispositions and what it means to have or activate a disposition but rather only an account of *Leibniz's* theory.

5.6 Difficulties with Dispositions

The case against the argument that Leibniz holds ideas to be dispositions can be further strengthened. The textual evidence becomes especially persuasive when we attend to the philosophical concerns that push us to reject the traditional interpretation of Leibniz. Note that my analysis here assumes an account of dispositions that requires a "ground" for the disposition. Although I recognize that in contemporary discussions the assumption may be controversial, the evidence that Leibniz provides a ground for dispositions is compelling. My aim here is only to argue that ascribing *to Leibniz* the view that ideas "are" dispositions is a mistake. In this context, I limit myself to two pressing problems. The first concerns the expressive ability of ideas. The second is a worry about Leibniz's commitment to a metaphysical hierarchy of ideas, such that complex ideas are formed from more simple ones, ultimately originating from the attributes of God.

Ideas serve to express their objects. Divorcing the expressive role of ideas from the ideas themselves eliminates the need for ideas entirely. It is difficult to explain, however, how dispositions can adequately fill the role required by ideas as expressive beings. The idea of a circle, we are told, expresses a circle ("What Is an Idea?" G 7:264). How can an *aptitude* to act or be acted on express anything? I do not see how it can. Here we need to be careful. Recall first that aptitudes for Leibniz are powers without principles of "endeavor" to internally actualize them. Clearly the thing *that has the aptitude* can express, and such capacities "do the expressings," but it seems perhaps a category mistake to hold that *dispositions* themselves express external objects.[17] What does solubility express? It certainly expresses the propensity of some things to dissolve in liquids, but this is not what we are after. We can meaningfully ask why this idea expresses a dog (as opposed to something else). If the idea of a dog is just a disposition, then the idea of a dog is the capacity to think of a dog. But an aptitude to think of x does not express x. How could a supermind read off from the aptitude to think of x the properties of x? Perhaps it could, since the aptitude is directed toward some state. Yet if it could, there would need to be a determinant directing the content of the aptitude to *a dog* instead of something else. Fair enough, we know what this is for Leibniz: the *petites perceptions* or modes that ground the disposition. But this knowledge does not do us any good, for the move

---

17. And note that the concern is independent of the particular theory of dispositions one chooses to embrace.

simply indicates that the underlying modes themselves are what actually determine what is expressed, contrary to the hypothesis. I can construct no viable case for supposing that dispositions can perform the expressive function of ideas.[18] Ideas *have* dispositional powers, and part of what it means to say that ideas can express is captured by their dispositional abilities. Nonetheless, it is a mistake to confuse the aptitude of an idea with the idea itself.

A more pressing difficulty presents itself when we consider Leibniz's adherence to the common early modern claim that ideas are compositional. Complex ideas are formed from combinations of simpler ones, and ultimately we derive our simple ideas from God.[19] There are actually two subproblems here. The first concerns whether we can make a reasonable case for supposing that dispositions are compositional, and the second involves whether we can make sense of the claim that we receive our simple ideas from God, assuming those ideas are dispositions.

Locke tells us in the *Essay* that all complex ideas are made by the mind combining several simple ideas into one compound one (II.12.1). Leibniz accepts not only the division of ideas into simple and complex but also a version of the basic Lockean story of how simple and complex ideas are related.[20] We need to be a bit circumspect here, since Leibniz does not accept the division in the same spirit as Locke does. Leibniz, for instance, holds that simple ideas are characterized by the fact that they cannot be defined and that complex ideas are those resolvable into simple ideas (*Monadology*, pars. 35 and 33; L, 646). The emphasis differs, but for our purposes nothing important hinges on the areas of divergence. The outlines of the distinction between simple and complex ideas are straightforward. I arrive at the idea of a satyr by combining the ideas of a goat and a man (or resolve the idea of a satyr into the component ideas of a goat and a man), and less obviously I arrive at the complex idea of lead by combining the ideas of a substance, a

---

18. One might object by asking for the details of how modes express. The answer, of course, is that we do not know. So one might challenge this analysis by saying that if one cannot explain how modes express, then one cannot complain that the problem with dispositions is that one cannot account for how they express. Perhaps dispositions are also primitively expressive. The point is well taken, but since Leibniz does apparently seek to ground dispositions (contemporary concerns aside), there is some reason for giving modes preferential treatment.

19. One might suppose that the compositionality of ideas here is purely objective and not formal. If so, I grant that the force of this last argument will be greatly diminished. It is plausible to suppose, however, that there must be some link between the objective content of ideas and their formal nature, hence reinvigorating the issue. None of the early moderns had any developed theory about what the nature of the connection between the objective and formal was, and so I believe these considerations are relevant and pertinent.

20. See *Monadology*, par. 33; L, 646; G 6:612; and *NE*, 120–21, 212; L, 285.

color, a certain degree of weight, ductility, hardness, and so forth (*ECHU* II.12.6). The only explicit hesitancy Leibniz shows concerns what constitutes the stock of simple ideas; he thinks that Locke is overly generous.

Any interpretation of Leibniz's theory of ideas needs to provide a reasonable explanation of his understanding of the division of ideas and their compositional nature. Unfortunately, it is difficult to see how we can combine and decompose dispositions given Leibniz's claims about ideas. We would be adding two distinct *aptitudes* to generate a third. Let's be careful about what this means. Recall that the relevant sense of an aptitude for Leibniz is a power (a "possibility of change") without an internal principle of endeavor. Faculties are possibilities of change that would result from an act. The most charitable case I can conjure is something like the following. Perhaps aptitudes are compositional like my ability to drive a vehicle is composed of the ability to turn the steering wheel, manipulate the pedals, and so on. Yet even here there must be some guiding principle of organization. Simply conjoining random steering with pedal pushing does not (always) produce driving. So we need not only the mere capabilities but also some (special) *way* to put them together. Unfortunately this drives us back to our former problem, the need for a determinant. I confess that I must struggle to give any meaning to the claim that aptitudes are composed of other aptitudes in the sense that our idea of lead is composed of the ideas of substance, color, ductility and the like without appealing to something outside of powers to make it work.[21]

Another approach to this problem might be to compare dispositional powers with ordinary properties. After all, Locke arrives at complex ideas by simply conjoining properties (think of his lead example again). Leibniz discusses complex ideas by forming their definitions out of simpler ideas, so there is no reason to suppose that we are not just conjoining dispositional properties. On a given occasion, when I think of a dull white, fusible, ductile substance I am thinking of lead. But this will not quite work. The problem arises when we recall that Leibniz holds that we have our ideas *prior* to being aware of them. "For I believe I have shown that in so far as they [ideas] contain something distinct they are in us before we are aware of them" (*NE*, 111). This view coheres with his theory of *petites perceptions*. As a result, we

---

21. Again, one might challenge this analysis by inquiring whether Leibniz has any better story when it comes to how modes are added or combined with one another. As I've suggested, I take the early moderns to think of the compositionality of ideas as involving the manipulation of content (images), which then had to be (in some unspecified way) reflected in the formal nature of ideas as well. At a minimum the issue is neutral between dispositions and ideas.

cannot construct an account that relies only on merging occurrent thoughts but must include the passive dispositional aptitudes. Thus imagism cannot be what Leibniz has in mind since we do not have an image to manipulate if ideas are dispositions—at least not until there is actual thought. The disposition to think of lead is already present in the mind and must be made by combining the aptitudes to think of substance, color, and so on. Furthermore, the complex idea of lead must be able to be decomposed into more "simple" dispositions.

Here again, I am at a loss as to how to make sense of this process without making the grounding mental modes do all the work. How can an aptitude (contemporary "power") be reduced to other aptitudes? We do not think that solubility reduces to another set of powers but to nondispositional chemical properties. Salt is soluble because of the structure of sodium chloride and water and how they interact (relate). We might perhaps say that a passive power of sodium chloride when conjoined with a power of water gives us solubility, but what are these underlying powers? Dispositions are relational; given a certain situation, a particular result occurs. There is no further analysis of *powers* required. To make matters worse, there is no clear way to make sense of the notion that some dispositions are complex when others are not except by appealing to their grounds, which only serves to deny the hypothesis that ideas are dispositions.

We might say that since I have the ability to think of a goat and the ability to think of a man, ipso facto I have the ability to think of a satyr. But the ability to think of a satyr is more than merely thinking of a man and a goat; I have to join the ideas in a certain way (goat on bottom, since there are mythological creatures with the lower body of a human and the head of a goat that are not satyrs). What can explain *how* the abilities are joined? Dispositions by themselves do not do the trick. Dispositions merely indicate that given an occasion, a certain result follows. If we want to know *why* a particular result follows under those situations, we need to examine the grounds of the disposition. (We might, as Hume would later, just study the regularities in nature as brute facts, but Leibniz does allow for that possibility.) As in the case expression, it turns out that the mental modes are doing all the actual work. Differences in the modes and how they are related can explain differences in the ideas we have. The mode or modes associated with a whitish color alone gives us the disposition to think of this whitish color. But those modes properly adjoined to others expressing substance, ductility, and the rest give us the disposition to think of lead. In short, all of the compositionality occurs at the level of the modes. Similarly, when decomposing a complex idea, we must look to the grounding modes to distinguish its parts. Whatever intuitive explanatory force the dispositional view gets in terms of explaining the compositionality of ideas it gets derivatively from the modes that ground those dispositions. Hence there is good independent reason to suppose that Leibniz ought not be thinking of ideas as dispositions.

One complication arises, however. Leibniz says that some allegedly simple ideas are really in fact relations. This difficulty leads us directly to our final—and most damaging—problem: Leibniz's claim that our simple ideas come from God. Some of the ideas that Locke lists as simple Leibniz characterizes as "merely relations" (*NE*, 145). We get an interesting result when we compare these claims to others made by Leibniz in which he indicates that simple ideas are relations that derive from the attributes of God. The overall picture is fairly easy to construct. God alone affects us from without (*Discourse on Metaphysics, L*, 321; G 4:453). As Leibniz puts it in his Paris notes from April 1676, "Ideas are in God insofar as the most perfect being consists in the conjunction of all absolute [i.e., positive] forms or possible perfections in the same object" (*L*, 163). We thus ultimately derive our ideas from God's ideas, but they are not transferred to us. Rather our ideas are "reflections" of God's, and thus our simple ideas are related to those of God's. In a seldom-referenced work from after 1707 in which Leibniz comments on Locke's criticism of Malebranche, Leibniz remarks, "I believe that one may say that these [ideas] are only relations that result from the attributes of God" (*G* 6:576).[22] For the moment we know two things about Leibniz's position. First, God has (simple) ideas, and second, our ideas stem from God's.

From these insights a difficulty emerges. Dispositions, even according to Leibniz's own discussions of the concept of an aptitude, involve potentialities and not actualities. In particular, Leibniz contrasts aptitude with act. God, of course, is pure act (*NE*, 114). So if ideas *are* dispositions, how can a God of pure act have ideas as passive potentialities? He cannot. I find this a fairly decisive objection against treating ideas as straightforward dispositions.

Defenders of the dispositional theory might not surrender so easily. I can conceive of two possible responses to this problem concerning the activity of God. The first is that perhaps Leibniz uses the word "idea" equivocally when applied to God and created minds. Perhaps idea is like Leibnizian

---

22. See Rutherford 1995, 104, who makes a similar point without using this particular passage.

power. Just as there are active and passive powers, so too there might be active and passive dispositional ideas. The most immediate trouble with this response, however, is that it appears to fly in the face of Leibniz's commitment to the claim that created minds differ from God only by degree and not in kind. Jolley in particular is in a poor position to make this distinction between active and passive dispositional ideas since his analysis of Leibniz rests heavily on the continuity between created mind and God.

> Leibniz gives a radically new twist to this thesis [that man is made in the image of God]. By virtue of his metaphysics he is in a position to claim that human knowledge resembles divine knowledge in its extensive aspect; since every mind expresses the whole universe according to its point of view, there is a real sense in which it is omniscient. Such omniscience is of course unlike divine omniscience in that it is, for the most part, extremely confused; but Leibniz need not deny that, in the case of a priori truths, human knowledge can be close to godlike in its quality. (1990, 9)

On this point I think Jolley is almost certainly correct. Leibniz is firmly committed to a robust doctrine of the image of God. As he writes in the *The Principles of Nature and of Grace, Based on Reason* (1714), "As for the reasonable soul or *spirit*, there is something more in it than in monads or even in simple souls. It is not only a mirror of the universe of creatures but also an image of divinity. The spirit not only has a perception of the works of God but is even capable of producing something which resembles them, though in miniature" (*L*, 640). It is difficult to see how Leibniz could make a principled exception for ideas given his strenuous commitment to the claim that created souls share even in the same capabilities as the divinity. It is simply not plausible to suppose that Leibniz uses the term "idea" equivocally.

Alternatively, one might try to finesse the claim that there is nothing potential in a purely active God. In one sense God is pure act, but in another, the divinity can be said to contain potentiality. The distinction might be thought of as parallel to Leibniz's distinction between moral and metaphysical necessity. Leibniz tells us that God is free with respect to the creation of this world because He could have opted not to create at all. Since He did create, His moral perfection required that this be the best of all possible worlds. But in terms of God's raw omnipotence, there was no *metaphysical* bar to His creating any of a number of other possible worlds. God, qua morally perfect being, could only create the best world. God, qua perfectly powerful divinity, could create any world he desired to bring into being. We might try to tell a similar story with respect to divine potential. Although God is pure act, there is a sense in which God could have done otherwise. And this metaphysical possibility is within the power of God and hence represents a *sense* in which God contains potentiality: the sense in which God has unrealized dispositional features. Now God will, in fact, never create a world less than perfect, but because metaphysically speaking He has the ability to do so, there is a sense in which God is not purely active.

Consequently one might then contend that God has passive, unrealized aptitudes in a fashion similar to that of created beings. There is an extreme difference in degree, of course, namely that, *in fact*, God never actually *is* passive. But it is metaphysically possible for God to be passive, if He were to will Himself to be so. But God is not this way as it would deny His perfection. The underlying point, however, remains: there is a sense in which Leibniz can hold that we were created in the image of God even though we have passive dispositions.

Engaging this particular line of response is difficult not because it is potent but rather because it is hard to provide textual evidence to refute a position that seems so deeply anti-Leibnizian in spirit. First, Leibniz would most likely deny that there is a sense in which God has passive potentials simply because God could have done otherwise. That God could have done otherwise is an indication of *our* limited understanding of the nature of God. God's nature, like his propensity to act, is absolute. As Leibniz reveals, "It is essential to substances to act, to created substances be acted upon" (*NE*, 305). Thus Leibniz introduces two senses of power discussed earlier (section 5.1). Genuine, active powers include within them an active internal principle of endeavor toward some particular aim. Passive powers do not. God, a purely active being, has powers only in the active sense. As a consequence, conceived absolutely, Leibniz's God has no potentialities. Every idea God has, He has occurrently and not dispositionally. To seek to deny this is to undercut several of Leibniz's more important distinctions. It is possible, I confess, that a more plausible story might be told in defense of the reading of Leibniz in which God contains potentialities. I am prepared to change my mind if confronted by such a more persuasive account, but as it stands now, I do not believe this line of response is promising.

One might yet wonder, however, whether my proposed solution—that ideas are mental modes for Leibniz—is any better off. Modes are arguably more passive than dispositions. But the problem is only apparent. In the Paris notes (April 1676, *L*, 163), Leibniz tells us that from the conjunction of an infinite number of absolute (i.e., positive) simple forms, modes result (i.e., ideas). Thus the simple forms in God (the essence of God) generate modes. God's attributes are expressed *in us* as mental modes, which in turn ground our dispositions to think on those ideas and compound them into complex ideas. The passivity of ideas is accordingly a generated feature and not intrinsic to God. In short, ideas qua modes only *result* from the simple attributes.

5.7 Ideas as Modes

Given that the textual support for supposing ideas to be dispositions is questionable and that there are positive reasons of a philosophical nature for thinking that Leibnizian ideas cannot be dispositions, why should we hold that at least for the later Leibniz ideas are simply modes? There are several reasons. First, virtually all of the putative benefits of identifying ideas with dispositions can be retained. Ideas are modes, but these modes ground dispositional properties. What it means to *have* an idea involves a disposition to think, and I do not want to deny any of the analysis presented by the likes of Jolley and Mates on that score; however, we must keep carefully separate what ideas *are* from what it is to *have* them. What is innovative and challenging in Leibniz's thought remains untouched.

Second, taking ideas to be modes provides Leibniz with reasonable ways to consistently answer the philosophical worries we have considered here. Modes can easily accommodate the expressive function of ideas, and there are no unusual conceptual difficulties that arise from plugging modes into the simple/complex distinction. The compositionality problem can also be solved in a way that at least the early moderns would have thought straightforward. Since we actually have all of our modes and the mind only focuses its attention on some of them, the complexity of an idea will be dependent on the range and arrangement of modes on which the mind focuses. All the basic building blocks are present; how the attentive faculty of the mind stacks those blocks determines the complexity of an idea. There is more to be said here, of course, but a detailed analysis of Leibniz's theory of complex ideas lies beyond the scope of this work. Lastly, and perhaps most importantly, this reading provides us with a way to understand Leibniz's thinking concerning a divinity of pure act and its relation to the ideas we have.

As a result of our analysis in this chapter, it is reasonable to conclude that Leibniz, for all of his innovations, was a traditional thinker when it came to the ontology of ideas. His interesting and important introduction of dispositions into his theory of what it means to have an idea does not produce a theory that denies that the formal nature of ideas falls squarely within the core categories of substance and modification. No Leibniz scholar to my knowledge has explicitly argued that Leibniz was an anti-ontologist with respect to ideas. I hope to have shown that the thought that Leibniz endorsed a dispositional account of ideas does not push him in that direction either.

6

BERKELEY

With Locke and Leibniz we see the continuation of serious dissonance between the way of ideas and the traditional substance/mode ontology. Locke recognized the difficulties and sought to avoid them. Leibniz perhaps introduced important novelties into the way of ideas, but he did not explicitly engage concerns about their ontological nature. The Irish philosopher George Berkeley, however, confronted the metaphysical problems more explicitly. In that process he encountered no less difficulty than his predecessors. In fact, some of his most interesting and ingenious philosophy stems from the conflict between the epistemological roles of ideas and their ontic grounding. Nevertheless, like those before him, Berkeley did not seek to abandon the ontology of substance and modification. Instead, he *stretched* it, if you will, to make room for a new category *within* the traditional ontology. Ideas for Berkeley had features of substances *and* of modes, but instead of outright rejecting ontology and the substance/mode ontology in particular, he altered it. As a result, despite some appearances to the contrary, Berkeley did not abandon ontology with respect to ideas. He modified and improved it, but his thinking never became "extra-ontological," let alone anti-ontological.

Berkeley's metaphysics is rich. Understanding his theory of ideas is complicated, however, by the fact that at times Berkeley himself is still grappling with the fit between the epistemological roles of ideas and their ontological foundation. My goal here is to support an interpretation of Berkeleian ideas that treats them as objects and to simultaneously deny that they must be strongly distinct from (i.e., independent of) minds. After making this argument, I engage the scholarship that alleges that Berkeley makes his ideas rather like modifications of the mind. The literature on the topic is large, and I do not pretend to engage all of it, only enough to make my reading of

Berkeley plausible. The key element in this discussion will be the relationship of dependence that ideas have on minds. I then explain why these two interpretations are compatible, generating a complete theory of ideas for Berkeley. Along the way we shall see how this reading leaves Berkeley within the substance/mode tradition yet outside the early modern tale.

Establishing the plausibility of my reading of Berkeley is, I recognize, not enough. There might be additional concerns about my thesis, and I thus also defend the claim that reading the early moderns through the lens of the traditional substance/mode distinction yields interpretive and philosophical insights hidden by the early modern tale. So in subsequent chapters I engage several important issues in Berkeley scholarship within the framework of my reading of Berkeley's theory of ideas that I offer here in this chapter. In the course of these discussions I also address the most serious objections to my reading. In particular, I consider Berkeley's much maligned theory of divine ideas, his attack on abstraction, and his claim that ideas are heterogeneous. In each of these areas, avoiding the early modern tale results in what I claim is a more charitable reading of Berkeley that gives him a more philosophically potent system.

6.1 Minds and Ideas

Ideas, Berkeley tells us, are *"inert, fleeting, dependent beings,* which subsist not by themselves, but are supported by, or exist in minds or spiritual substances" (*PHK* 89, emphasis in the original). Given this characterization, in which Berkeley appears to deny ontological independence for ideas, we might expect him to think that ideas are adverbial (or perhaps adjectival, if one thinks of minds and ideas as more like balls that are red than mental acts of a particular sort).[1] They are "in the mind" and "dependent beings," so what else *could* they be? Furthermore, he tells us in no uncertain terms that *only* spirits are proper substances.[2]

---

1. See section 7.5 for a more complete treatment of the fleeting nature of ideas.
2. That spirits are traditional substances for Berkeley has been challenged by several scholars, most notably Steve Daniel and Robert Muehlmann (on separate and unrelated grounds). See Daniel 2000, 621–36; Daniel 2001a, 239–58; Daniel 2001b, 55–68; and Muehlmann 1992, esp. ch 6, 170ff.; and Muehlmann 1995, 89–106. It does not fall within the purview of this book to engage all of the complications surrounding Berkeley's theory of mind, which I take to be somewhat more traditional than either Daniel or Muehlmann do. For extended engagement of the views of Daniel and Muehlmann, see Hight and Ott 2004.

> From what has been said, it follows, there is not any other substance than *spirit,* or that which perceives. But for the fuller proof of this point, let it be considered, the sensible qualities are colour, figure, motion, smell, taste, and such like, that is, the ideas perceived by sense. Now for an idea to exist in an unperceiving thing, is a manifest contradiction; for to have an idea is all one as to perceive: that therefore wherein colour, figure, and the like qualities exist, must perceive them; hence it is clear there can be no unthinking substance or *substratum* of those ideas. (*PHK* 7)

Ideas, then, apparently cannot be proper substances. Since Berkeley appears to operate within the traditional ontology, only one alternative remains: ideas must be modes. Richard Watson illustrates this kind of thinking. "Berkeley is bound to the all-inclusive ontological type-distinction between substance and modification. He adheres to this pattern particularly in saying that ideas depend on minds in that their being is being perceived by a mind. *Ideas,* for Berkeley, *must be mental modifications*" (1987, 124, emphasis in the original). Unfortunately, Berkeley appears to work just as hard at *denying* that ideas are modes. Near the beginning of the *Principles*, in section 2, we are told that the mind is "a thing entirely distinct" from ideas. One main theme in his works is that the activity of the mind contrasts with the passivity of ideas. In light of this contrast, it is difficult to allow that he thinks modes are sufficiently distinct from minds to qualify as ideas. Section 49 of the *Principles* seems to clearly deny that ideas are modes. "I answer, those qualities are in the mind only as they are perceived by it, that is, not by way of *mode* or *attribute,* but only by way of *idea*" (see *3D,* 237). Again in section 89 he reaffirms the distinction between minds and ideas. "*Thing* or *being* is the most general name of all, it comprehends under it two kinds entirely distinct and heterogeneous, and which have nothing common but the name, to wit, *spirits* and *ideas.*"[3]

Perhaps the most notorious element of Berkeley's theory is that ideas are "in the mind." The superficial suggestion is that ideas are either somehow parts of the mind or states of the same. Yet Berkeley repudiates this suggestion, saying that ideas being "in" the mind means nothing more than that they are perceived by it. But if the mind and its ideas are strongly distinct, then one naturally is led to believe that they can exist separately, a position

---

3. Luce makes much of this progression, ultimately arguing that ideas cannot be construed as mental entities at all (1963, esp. 24–32).

Berkeley famously rejects with his *esse* is *percipi* doctrine. We thus have a tangle of apparently inconsistent views. Minds and ideas are entirely distinct, but ideas are dependent on minds for their existence, all the while so existing only "in" the mind. It should be clear, then, that part of unraveling the status of ideas for Berkeley must involve characterizing the relationship that holds between ideas and spirits.

Despite his insistence that only spirits are proper substances, Berkeley often speaks of ideas as if they were robust and independent things. Ideas are "objects" of the mind. The impression that he thinks of them as being like substances is difficult to shake, and many commentators understand Berkeleian ideas in this way. Ultimately the position Berkeley ends up adopting, however odd it might be, is that ideas fall somewhat short of being genuine substances. I argue here that ideas for Berkeley are *quasi* substances (and hence not *proper* substances). That is, they behave like substances except for the fact that they are ontologically dependent on minds. In particular, they are "external" to the mind, by which I mean that ideas are not modifications (nor proper parts) of the mind and that there exists a two-place relation between the mind and its perceptual objects. This reading allows Berkeley to claim volitional independence for ideas (the "external" ideas of sense are not under my control) while denying them ontological independence. In summary, Berkeley implicitly denies that the substance/mode ontology is exclusive or exhaustive without actually denying the basic ontology itself. Instead, he bends it to allow for a new kind of entity, and in so doing, he does not think that he is in any way denying the legitimacy of the traditional distinction. The final test of my interpretation comes when, in light of my analysis here, I endeavor to explain his puzzling endorsement of certain radical metaphysical claims.

6.2 Ideas as Objects

The most prevalent characterization of Berkeleian ideas in contemporary scholarship is simply as "objects."[4] Kenneth Winkler, in his excellent book, makes his position clear right at the start. "I hope to show that Berkeley's tendency to treat ideas as objects is a powerful one; in later chapters I will show how the tendency is expressed in his case for immaterialism. I think Berkeley's tendency to treat ideas as objects is not only powerful but domi-

---

4. See Harry Bracken (to take just one example), who characterizes Berkeleian ideas as "objects to mind" (1963, 9).

nant; it is, I think, virtually the only one governing his understanding of the word 'idea'" (1989, 4). Winkler's claim strikes me as basically correct, but his understanding of what it means for an idea to be an object is not sufficiently clear. In claiming that ideas for Berkeley are objects, Winkler is presumably implicitly denying the assertion that Berkeley sees ideas as (perceptual) acts. The rival view, most notably defended by George Pitcher, holds that ideas for Berkeley *should* be construed as "adverbial" (Pitcher 1977, esp. 189–203, 1969, 198–207, and 1981, 221–27). I stress the word "should" since even Pitcher backs off from saying that Berkeley himself really did endorse such a view of ideas. If ideas are adverbial on minds, then they are modes of the mind. Pitcher's worries notwithstanding, I think Berkeley did at times seriously consider ideas to have traits that can only be understood if ideas are thought of as, or rather like, modes. The debate among most scholars, then, has centered on whether Berkeley's ideas are objects or acts.

Initially there is some reason to doubt that ideas can be modes. Consider the grammar of modes. One might think that whether something is a mode is purely dependent on how it is expressed in language, such that all monadic predicates represent modes. So "is red," "being a father" and "being near Niagara Falls" would each express a mode because their grammatical structure is one place. Yet Berkeley would deny that any of these are genuine modes, since being a father and being near a place involves more than what is required to simply be red. Being a father, for instance, implies a relation to another specific person or persons, despite the grammar. Being a mode goes deeper, and in one way this makes Berkeley understandably nervous. He believed (as many did before him) that something cannot be a mode without being predicated of its subject. Thus red cannot be a mode because it would have to be predicated of me (my mind). In other words, I would *be* red if I perceived or owned that quality. "[I]t may be objected, that if extension and figure exist only in the mind, it follows that the mind is extended and figured; since extension is a mode or attribute" (*PHK* 49; see also *3D,* 237). In response to just this criticism Berkeley tries to separate his understanding of ideas from that of mere modes. On the first pass, therefore, we have reason to expect that he will favor object talk over mode talk.

Ian Tipton once kindly pointed out to me how infrequently Berkeley uses the term "mode" in his writings. He should have made the point far stronger. In Berkeley's complete works the word "mode" appears in a scant ten paragraphs and its plural in only twenty-six. Of these combined instances more than half are negative uses either articulating or attacking the view that extended substance underlies or supports material modes.[5] The rest all are innocuous uses.[6] The phenomenon is striking. Berkeley does not *even once* use the word "mode" to positively describe his own theory of ideas. He appears to be consciously avoiding the term and reserving its use primarily for the discussion of the views of his contemporaries.

Without doubt the one word Berkeley uses frequently to describe an idea is "object." Virtually all of his official pronouncements about ideas reflect an understanding of ideas as objects. "Note that when I speak of tangible ideas, I take the word idea for any immediate object of sense or understanding, in which large signification it is commonly used by the moderns" (*NTV* 45). As we have already seen, this characterization is not uncommon among early modern philosophers. Locke, Malebranche, and others accept some version of this definition and treat ideas as objects of perception. In Berkeley's private notebooks, we can clearly see how this conception of ideas is present in his thinking.

> 427 We see the Horse it self, the Church it self it being an Idea & nothing more
>
> 427a The Horse it self the Church it self is an Idea i.e. object immediate object of thought.

There are numerous other examples, all of which essentially conform to those offered here (e.g., *PHK* 1, *PC* 643, *PC* 808, *3D*, 230 and 249). Immediately, however, we encounter conceptual difficulty. The act/object distinction is not straightforwardly an *ontic* distinction. Simply because something is identified as an act does not necessarily imply that it is not an object. As a result, employing the distinction will not tell us anything of significant value about the *ontological* status of Berkeley's ideas. Consider the following sentence:

> A mind M perceives an idea of a red ball.

According to the traditional act/object analysis as I understand it, this sentence means:[7]

---

5. See *PC* 711; *PC* 785; *PHK* 16; *3D*, 190, 198, and 237; *S* 162, 249.
6. For instance, "modes of light," in *TVV* 40, 41, 44; "modes of speech," in *PHK* 52 and *PC* 176; and "modes of living," in Berkeley 1948–57, 9:154.
7. I am not, of course, implying that any of the early moderns would have understood things this way. The formalization is only meant to help *us* be clear about what the position entails.

$(\exists x)(\exists y)[(x \text{ is a mind}) \cdot (y \text{ is an idea of a red ball}) \cdot (x \text{ perceives } y)]$

This formalization seems right, except we do not know the status of y, other than that we are quantifying over it. If we can quantify over modes, and the moderns certainly did,[8] nothing in the logical analysis of the sentence bars one from holding that ideas are modes. In general, nothing prevents modes from being the objects of awareness, either in cognition or perception. Barring unusual cases where the modification of the mind is its own object, nothing logically precludes one from supposing that in cognition we are contemplating objects that are simply modes of our own mind. Thus even if ideas were modes, they could still be objects, and indeed objects entirely consistent with what Berkeley says about the nature of ideas. If so, then merely characterizing ideas as objects does not determine whether they are ontologically independent of minds. Prima facie, one ought not to expect that invoking the act/object distinction by itself will enable us to make progress in solving the ontological problems surrounding ideas.

Why then do many assume that if an idea is an object, it cannot be a mode of the mind? Winkler certainly seems to accept this entailment. His central claim is that "ideas are objects distinct from (that is, not identical with) the acts or operations of the mind; they are not viewings or perceivings but objects viewed or perceived" (1989, 6). Following George Pitcher, we might distinguish two kinds of distinctness, strong and weak (1969, 198–207). Two things are weakly distinct when they can be described as separate objects but there is some ontological dependence between the two. Correspondingly, modes are weakly distinct from their substances. They can be described as separate objects, but modes depend on minds for their existence. Two things are strongly distinct when they can be separately described and are ontologically independent of one another. Thus I am strongly distinct from my computer, since I do not require my computer to exist and vice versa. Now we can ask whether Berkeleian ideas, as understood by Winkler, are strongly or weakly distinct from minds. Initially, the most plausible view would be that ideas are only weakly distinct from minds. After all, Berkeley tells us that ideas cannot exist without a mind and that ideas are decidedly dependent beings. Yet if this is the case, then the "distinctness" Winkler emphasizes between the idea and the mind is not sufficient to prevent ideas from being objects that are also modes. A "viewing" can be the

---

8. See sections 1.3 and 1.3.1.

object of the mind, just as any other mode can be as well. Oddly, however, Winkler denies this move, arguing that "If ideas are weakly distinct from the mind it does not follow that they are modifications of the mind" (1989, 297). Just so, there is no *entailment,* but is there another possibility? Winkler cites *PHK* 49 as evidence for his claim that just because ideas are weakly distinct from the mind does not mean they are, on Berkeley's view, modifications of it, but he provides no alternative. Instead, he simply confronts Berkeley with the charge of "metaphysical embarrassment." Ideas are weakly distinct from both the mind and its acts, but their ontic status is scandalously mysterious.

What about the alternative? Might ideas be strongly distinct from minds? Interestingly enough, Winkler does not argue for strong distinctness despite the fact there might be some reason to suppose that Berkeley does take minds and ideas to be strongly distinct. Berkeley dwells on certain differences between minds and ideas and consistently urges that these differences are important. One example comes late in the *Principles,* in section 142: "*Spirits* and *ideas* are things so wholly different, that when we say, *they exist, they are known,* or the like, these words must not be thought to signify anything common to both natures."[9] We know that ideas are completely passive and spirits likewise active (*3D,* 231). Yet the passivity issue is not what ultimately drives Berkeley's thinking here. Instead, Berkeley is trying to preserve the commonsense distinction between the external world and our mental lives. "When I speak of objects as existing in the mind or imprinted on the senses; I would not be understood in the gross literal sense, as when bodies are said to exist in a place, or a seal to make an impression upon wax. My meaning is only that the mind comprehends or perceives them; and that it is affected from without, or by some being distinct from itself" (*3D,* 250).[10] If Berkeley wants to hold on to *this* kind of division between minds and ideas, it appears he must be thinking they are strongly distinct from one another. If ideas are simple modes of the mind, then they (minds and ideas) must share *some* commonality. After all, for something to modify something else, at least sameness of ontological kind seems required.[11] Here we find that something (through ideas as passive vehicles)

9. See also *3D,* 231, and *PHK* 89 and 2. In these passages Berkeley uses the phrase "entirely different from" to separate minds and ideas.
10. Note Berkeley's use of the Cartesian example of the wax imprint, in turn borrowed from Aristotle. The continuity of thinking is striking.
11. I go on to argue in section 8.10 that Berkeley occasionally allows this ontological commonality to bleed into his thinking about the content of ideas as well.

affects minds "from without." If we take Berkeley seriously here, it follows that ideas are not really mental entities at all. They are neither mental substances nor modes of the same. The sense in which they could be "fleeting, dependent beings" starts to lapse into incoherence. Since I would rather have mystery than incoherence, I conclude that Berkeleian ideas are only weakly distinct from minds but in a sense that remains to be explored; we have a mystery to be solved.

Returning to the original problem, why might one be so quick to apply the act/object distinction to ontic issues? A reasonable conjecture is that the act/object dichotomy has traditionally been associated with an implicit internal/external pairing. The assumption that if ideas are identical with perceptual acts then they must be internal to and dependent on the mind leads us to naturally conclude that if ideas are objects then they must be external to and independent of the mind. Although perhaps a psychologically natural inference, it does not follow. Completing this move is especially difficult with Berkeley, who independently denies the existence of matter. Without an external material reality to ground our intuitions about perception, we seek an alternative that resembles it, that is, a reality that is external and independent. I think a sort of underlying material realism undergirds our intuitive understanding of the act/object distinction. Importantly, Berkeley shares this sense of realism about ideas. That is, Berkeley also thinks of the act/object distinction at least partially in terms of the internal/external pairing. Ideas, as objects, are external to the mind. "External" in this context means in a two-place relation with the mind in which ideas are not a mode of the mind. As he says, ideas affect the mind "from without."

One might object that my claim here ignores Berkeley's allusions to ideas of reflection (in, e.g., *PHK* 13, 25, 35, 68, and 74). Apparently not all ideas come from without. The point is well taken but misses the force of my claim. All ideas *ultimately* come from a source independent of our minds. Ideas of reflection (a memory might be an example) themselves originate from previous sensory experience. As a result, if they are ideas, they have a sensory content of a particular kind. Since ideas can only be like other ideas (*PHK* 90), and sensory ideas are the exemplar for ideas in general, it follows that calling an idea an idea of reflection is a reference to how we access sensory content. We can have direct experience (seeing a visual image) or reflective experience (calling to mind a visual image). Thus although Berkeley frequently runs together "ideas of sense or reflexion" (in *PHK* 13, 25, 35, 68, and 7, for instance), he does explicitly restrict the use of the word "idea" when it comes to nonsensory content. In section 89, he notes that

> [w]e comprehend our own existence by inward feeling or reflexion, and that of other spirits by reason. We may be said to have some knowledge or notion of our own minds, of spirits and active beings, whereof in a strict sense we have not ideas. In like manner we know and have a notion of relations between things or ideas, which relations are distinct from the ideas of things related, inasmuch as the latter may be perceived by us without our perceiving the former. To me it seems that ideas, spirits and relations are all in their respective kinds, the object of human knowledge and subject of discourse: and that the term *idea* would be improperly extended to signify everything we know or have any notion of.

We do *not* have ideas of a mind or of anything else other than that which can be described as having sensory content. None of this denies that Berkeley holds that we have ideas of reflection. I am only noting that such ideas will be restricted in content if they are to be ideas at all on Berkeley's view. If that is right, then my claim that ideas generally invoke an internal/external pairing with the mind remains reasonable, given that ideas *ultimately* originate from a source other than the mind. Even so, learning that perception (broadly construed as all mental activity) involves two-place relations with objects usually, but not always, "outside" the mind does not tell us much about the ontic nature of ideas.

We are still left asking exactly what it means to treat an idea as an object. And if ideas are objects, what *are* these objects Berkeley calls "ideas?" At the start of his analysis, Winkler only indicates that they are objects as distinct from perceptual acts. Winkler resists characterizing Berkeleian ideas as mental, suggesting that for Berkeley they cannot therefore be modes. Instead, we are told that Berkeley regards ideas as genuine entities. "An idea is an entity, a real thing, and the relation between an idea and the mind is a genuine relation between two distinct items. An idea is an object of thought in a sense demanding that the object exists whenever it is true to say that a thought is directed towards it" (1989, 7). Presumably then Berkeley thinks that perceptual acts are not themselves "real entities" that exist and so ideas cannot be adverbial on minds. But if ideas are "real things," are they therefore substances? Winkler does not say in the course of his analysis, until the very end of his book, where he confesses that on his reading "ideas have no clear place in the framework of traditional ontology" (309–10). I take this to imply that he does not consider ideas to be proper substances, although he stops short of giving Berkeley a role in the early modern tale. But then what *are* ideas for Berkeley? Winkler does not discuss the ontic status of ideas, and so all we know according to him is that they are real things that are neither substances nor modes. They are simply "objects."[12] At this point, we know that ideas are objects that function as arguments in two-place relations and that they are weakly distinct from minds, which entails that they are not ontologically independent of them. Dependence, however, is traditionally expressed only in terms of the substance-modification dichotomy. As I have endeavored to demonstrate, establishing that ideas are objects does not exclude them from being modes, and some commentators still urge that Berkeleian ideas are indeed modifications of minds.[13] So might they be right? Might ideas be mere modes?

6.3 Ideas as Modes

Although I argue that Berkeley does not take ideas to be modes, there are several places where Berkeley seems to characterize ideas as modifications of the mind. That is, he apparently denies that a genuine distinction exists between the perceptual act and its object. Consider the following passages.

> *PHK 7* [F]or to have an idea is all one as to perceive.

> *PC 609* The distinguishing betwixt an idea and perception of the idea has been one great cause of imagining material substances.

> *PC 656* Twas the opinion that Ideas could exist unperceiv'd or before perception that made Men think perception was somewhat different from the Idea perceived, yet it was an Idea of Reflexion whereas the thing perceiv'd was an idea of Sensation. I say twas this made 'em think the understanding took it in receiv'd from without which could never be did not they think it existed without.

> *PC 585* Qu. if there be any real Difference betwixt certain Ideas of Reflexion & others of Sensation, e.g. 'twixt perception & white,

---

12. Moreover, Winkler endorses a particular kind of phenomenalistic interpretation of Berkeleian ideas. I think Winkler's account is smart but mistaken. I address his reading in section 6.6.

13. Aside from George Pitcher, Philip Cummins (1975, 55–72) and Richard Watson (1987, esp. 124) have defended this view. Alan and David Hausman defend a loosely similar view of Berkeleian ideas (1995, 47–66).

> black, sweet, etc. wherein I pray you does the perception of white differ from white. Mea . . .

These passages to varying degrees appear to deny the legitimacy of the distinction between act and object. The denial of this distinction is important to scholars who wish to attribute an adverbial view of ideas to Berkeley.

The most well-known advocate of an adverbial analysis of ideas is probably George Pitcher, who argues that ascribing an adverbial account to Berkeley does the least amount of philosophical violence to the plausibility of his system. He first argues that Berkeley is independently committed to three mutually inconsistent claims (J), (K), and (L).

> (J) The mind perceives ideas.
> (K) The mind is wholly distinct from its ideas.
> (L) The alleged distinction between (i) the perceiving of an idea and (ii) the idea perceived, is a bogus one; there is no such distinction.[14] (1977, 189)

(J) and (K) are claims made explicitly in Berkeley's published works and (L) is the important (alleged) denial of an act-object distinction in perception.

Pitcher eventually decides to jettison (K) and allow that ideas are not strongly distinct from minds because they are, in fact, modes of the same. His reasoning depends on the claim that accepting (K) requires Berkeley to admit that ideas can exist unperceived (201–2). Any view of ideas (of sense) that makes them "wholly distinct" from the mind without collapsing into an adverbial theory requires that it is at least possible for some idea to exist without a mind. This result is not an immediate disaster, for one might retreat to the position that although it is possible for ideas to exist without a mind, in fact they do not. But, as Pitcher rightly notes, the retreat is *ultimately* a disaster. Berkeley would then owe us some account of why (and how) ideas happen to exist only when perceived (given that there is no logical necessity that they be perceived on the current assumption). Berkeley, of course, provides no such analysis, and it is difficult to even imagine what he might say in response to such a challenge. Thus Pitcher rejects any act-object analysis that would support (K), instead opting to reject (K) and assert that Berkeley at a minimum *should* have embraced an adverbial theory of ideas.

---

14. This analysis appeared earlier in article form. See Pitcher 1969.

> I conclude that Luce's "act-object" interpretation of Berkeley saddles our philosopher with a hopeless position. My suggestion, then, is that we allow Berkeley to abandon proposition (K), with its act-object analysis of the perceiving of ideas, and have him adopt instead the adverbial analysis implicit in proposition (L). This move has the great advantage of allowing him to retain the necessary non-existence of unperceived ideas as part of his system. Furthermore, everything else of importance that Berkeley wishes to maintain can be accommodated within the adverbial analysis. (202–3)

Pitcher's analysis rests on the contention that Berkeley needs (L) (the denial of the act-object distinction) and is not, or should not be, deeply wedded to the claim that ideas are distinct from the minds that perceive them. Acts of perception are identical to their objects.

The most commonly cited evidence for the identity claim is *Principles* 5, where Berkeley is characteristically bold.[15] "Light and colours, heat and cold, extension and figures, in a word the things we see and feel, what are they but so many sensations, notions, ideas or impressions on the sense; and is it possible to separate, even in thought, any of these from perception? For my part I might as easily divide a thing from itself." Pitcher takes the passage (combined with its matching passage in the *Three Dialogues* [195]) to be decisive based on two arguments Berkeley goes on to offer. The first argument depends on the passivity of perception. When I perceive a sensory idea, my mind is passive with respect to that idea. As a result, Pitcher reasons that there is no *act* of perceiving the idea at all. Thus there can be no distinction between act and object in a case where there is no identifiable act. Pitcher recognizes that this line of reasoning is unacceptable, since it depends on a rather stringent conception of what it means to act. On this reading, acts would have to be directly caused by a volition. Even Berkeley would not likely adopt the position that one must be positively willing in order to be acting, since the implications of such a position border on the absurd. To use Pitcher's own example, Berkeley would be forced to admit that there are no distinctions between active and passive actions, such that there is no distinction between falling on an ant and the ant being fallen on in cases where my falling was not preceded by a volition (193).[16] As a result, Pitcher rests his case on Berkeley's second line of reasoning.

---

15. Pitcher 1977, 191, relies on the passage heavily. More recently, Lennon follows a similar pattern of analysis, defending a theory of appearances for Berkeley (2001b, esp. 657–60).

16. The *events* might be distinct, but Pitcher does not engage the distinction between acts and events in his analysis on this point.

The matching passage in the *Three Dialogues* comes early in the work, where Philonous speaks on behalf of Berkeley. "To return then to your distinction between sensation and object; if I take you right, you distinguish in every perception two things, the one an action of the mind, the other not" (195). Two pages later he gets around to attacking this distinction by using the example of pain. "Besides, since you distinguish the active and passive in every perception, you must do it in that of pain. But how is it possible that pain, be it as little active as you please, should exist in an unperceiving substance?" (197). If we are to distinguish ideas from perceivings, then we must do so in every case. But at least for some cases, like perceiving pain, suggesting that the idea might exist outside the mind is allegedly absurd.

Berkeley's argument relies on his claim that sensations are ideas, and advocates of the adverbial reading of Berkeley will likely be quick to point out that we need not posit a separately existing entity in these cases. There is no "chill" separate from my feeling it. We tend to naturally use the language of "sense" and "feel" to describe external objects. I can feel the needle being inserted into my arm and one might easily be misled into thinking that I am actually feeling the needle. Yet we would be better off saying we feel the sensation *caused* by the needle, which is not necessarily the needle itself. In that case, there is no bar to our saying that we perceive the caused modification in our mind and *that* is the object to which our mind is directed when feeling pain. The pain passage becomes more compelling when we note that Berkeley draws much of his inspiration from Malebranche. Recall that Malebranche divides sensory objects into two kinds: sensations and ideas.[17] Sensations, however, are explicitly modes. A reasonable conjecture is that Berkeley collapses the sensation/idea distinction and preserves the critical feature of sensations as modes. As we have seen, a long line of Cartesians thought of ideas as modes, including Descartes himself.[18] Such a simple appeal to authority, however, is neither convincing nor consistent with Berkeley's temperament as a philosopher.

I think something more limited is going on in this passage in the *Three Dialogues*. We need to be rather careful before attributing to him the claim that perceptual acts are *identical* with their objects (I am not even sure I know what this ultimately means), when a weaker, more plausible position is available. When Philonous clarifies Hylas's distinction between act and object, he does so cautiously. "So that if there was a perception without any

---

17. See section 3.1.
18. Watson makes this observation and uses it as evidence that Berkeley thought of ideas as modes (1987, 124).

act of the mind, it were possible such a perception should exist in an unthinking substance" (196). Berkeley, of course, denies the consequent, concluding that the antecedent is therefore also false. But what is the negation of this statement? It does not follow that if there is no perception without an act of the mind, that act and object must be identical. Instead, all that follows is that every case of perception must be accompanied by a mental act. This consequence expresses dependence, not necessarily identity, and therefore one cannot conclude that ideas must be modes. Pain, we are told, cannot exist "*in* (i.e. be dependent upon) an unperceiving substance," but that does not logically preclude instances of pain from being (or being like) substances. The point is that Berkeley's apparent denial of the act-object distinction is not an assertion of the *identity* of act and object but instead an assertion of the necessary *dependence* of act on object and object on act in perception.[19]

It is telling that in the *Principles* 5 passage Berkeley discusses the impossibility of *separating* idea from perception ("and is it possible to separate, even in thought, any of these from perception? For my part I might as easily divide a thing from itself."). Even in thought we find the two so conjoined by necessity that we cannot imagine one without the other. The assertion of unimaginable separability does not make them identical. His final comment is rhetorical flourish, for saying that he *might* as well divide a thing from itself implies that in this case one would *not* be doing so, although it would be similarly difficult. In general, all of the selections from Berkeley that some scholars read as endorsing strict identity between act and object can be more plausibly read as expressing the essential *dependence* of object on mind. Thus we are told that to have an idea is all one as to perceive, that is, one cannot have an idea without perceiving (*PHK* 7). I might similarly say, in explaining the concept of parenthood to an alien, that being a parent is all one as having children (although one ought not to confuse this concept of mere parenthood with that of being a *good* parent). That is, if you want to understand what it means to be a parent, you may substitute the concept of having children for parent, since the two are logically dependent on each other. Berkeley's big target in all of these passages is the notion that ideas can exist

---

19. Compare Tom Stoneham's analysis of what he calls the "simplest model of perception" (SMP). SMP is technically neutral between adverbial and nonadverbial accounts while preserving the two-place nature of perceptual relations (2002, esp. 53–56). Asserting that Berkeley's apparent denial of the act-object distinction is in fact a denial of their logical separability (and nothing stronger) coheres with Stoneham's account, although he does not pursue the particular line I do here.

unperceived. If we stay focused on that as the main issue, my weaker reading of these passages is more appropriate than the identity reading.

Interestingly, in the original 1710 edition of the *Principles,* the last line of section 5 reads as follows: "In truth the object and the sensation are the same thing, and cannot therefore be abstracted from each other." In revising the work, Berkeley *removed* this important line from the text. The last line of the 1734 edition reads: "Hence as it is impossible for me to see or feel anything without an actual sensation of that thing, so is it impossible for me to conceive in my thoughts any sensible thing or object distinct from the sensation or perception of it." The difference is striking. The 1710 edition suggests an identification whereas the 1734 version does not, instead emphasizing how sensation cannot be thought of as distinct from (i.e., independent of) the object. I take this change to be at least consistent with my thesis and, more strongly, as constituting corroborating evidence.

There are additional positive reasons for thinking that ideas cannot be mere mental modes. First is what I call the "content argument." One of the key roles ideas play is that of explaining the content of our various mental activities. If ideas are meant to genuinely provide us with additional information about our mental states, then they cannot be straightforwardly identical with them.[20] Even here this might not exclude ideas being modes, so long as the object mode is sufficiently distinct from the act of mentation. I can reflect on my own state of mind without any difficulty. But Berkeley qualifies this claim. One *cannot* have an *idea* of one's own mental states, since the mental is active and ideas are passive. What I have when I contemplate my own mental states is a "notion." Alternatively, Berkeley could admit that we have ideas that represent the *effects* of a mental action, but representing an effect does not capture the entire content of the act (*PHK* 27). Unfortunately Berkeley does not provide us with much theory about notions; all he does is strongly separate them from ideas.[21] About the act of perceiving itself, Berkeley is adamant that the relation is two place. "It is therefore evident there can be no *substratum* of those qualities but spirit, in which they exist, not by way of mode or property, but as a thing perceived in that which perceived it" (*3D,* 237; see also *3D,* 230). An idea is a (separate) thing perceived by the mind. As a result, Berkeleian ideas cannot be modes. Note, however, that nothing here indicates that ideas are not decidedly dependent just *like* modes.

20. Winkler advances a similar argument (1989, 6).
21. Daniel Flage (1987) has made a book-length study of the doctrine of notions, but the issue otherwise lies outside the scope of our discussion here.

Consider the companion passage denying that ideas are modes from section 49 in the *Principles*. "I answer, those qualities are in the mind only as they are perceived by it, that is, not by way of *mode* or *attribute,* but only by way of *idea.*" This passage has been resisted by many commentators on the grounds that there is no other possibility than that they are modes given Berkeley's claims elsewhere that act and idea are not distinct. Now, however, we have another option, and one that coheres well with all of his other claims. Ideas are not modes but are merely ontically dependent, which explains why some might be misled into thinking that Berkeley is endorsing a mental modification view.

I must confess, however, that there is another reason why one might nonetheless wish to hang on to an adverbial understanding of ideas for Berkeley. If ideas are modes, then Berkeley has an immediate and intuitive answer to the question of why he thinks ideas must be dependent on minds. The *esse* of ideas is *percipi* because ideas are literally modifications of the mind. If ideas are not modes of the mind, then it is reasonable to ask why Berkeley was so thoroughly convinced that ideas had to be such dependent beings. To partly answer this question, however, requires that we stop and consider the assertion lying behind it. Might Berkeley think that ideas are dependent *because* they are modes of the mind? It seems unlikely, even if it were true that Berkeley had an adverbial theory of ideas. The dependent nature of ideas *seems* to be an assumption he holds deeply; his commitment to it seems to trump his metaphysical engagements with the nature of the mind, although I grant that I doubt any quality argument could be adduced for this claim. An adverbial theory would explain why ideas are dependent on minds but would not in itself explain why Berkeley seems so obviously convinced of the claim. The explanatory gap left by adverbial theories strikes me as especially clear given the preceding discussion that strongly indicates that Berkeley wished to separate himself from those analyses. As a result, I fail to see how such a theory really has any serious explanatory superiority.

So why did Berkeley think that ideas must be dependent on minds? The simplest answer is that he, like his philosophical predecessors, built this feature into the concept of an idea. Oddly enough, even Pitcher recognizes the point. "Ideas of sense—like all other ideas, are, for Berkeley, necessarily mind dependent. It is a conceptual truth that there can be no such thing as a free-floating idea" (1977, 93). Descartes, Locke, and even Berkeley all tell us that ideas are the *immediate* objects of perception. How could such objects exist without being perceived? Berkeley only touched on this issue long enough to say that the dependence of ideas "is what everybody will allow.... I think an intuitive knowledge may be obtained of this, by anyone that shall attend to what is meant by the term *exist* when applied to sensible things" (*PHK* 3). Berkeley was, of course, right when he said that everyone agreed with this claim. It was not an assertion for which he thought he needed to argue. Instead, the dependence of ideas was a foundational premise he thought obviously true because, in part, *everyone* thought it was obviously true.

We have yet to put the finishing touches on what he means by "way of idea," but the pieces are beginning to fall into place. I submit that traditional scholarship has been misreading the force of Berkeley's assertion that we err when distinguishing between idea and perception (*PC* 609). Pitcher's interesting and powerful analysis is largely responsible for the tradition of reading Berkeley this way, but I hope to have shown that, at a minimum, we are not forced into making Berkeley an adverbialist about ideas. We have a better way of reconciling the various texts, one that doesn't weaken any of his explicitly held positions. When Berkeley writes as if ideas are perceptual acts, he is in fact only seeking to express his insight that ideas are essentially dependent on minds. Reading him this way preserves his philosophical analysis, although we have yet fully to reconcile these claims with others that suggest ideas are substances. At a minimum, by embracing my weaker reading we can save Berkeley from obvious inconsistency.

6.4 Qualities

Why does Berkeley think that ideas are ontologically dependent yet not mental modes? The answer, I think, lies partially in his contention that qualities are ideas. According to contemporary scholarship, Berkeley is rather notorious for his conflation of qualities and ideas. "Qualities, as hath been shewn, are nothing else but *sensations* or *ideas,* which exist only in a *mind* perceiving them; and this is true not only of the ideas we are acquainted with at present, but likewise of all possible ideas whatsoever" (*PHK* 78). It is important to note, however, that Berkeley is perfectly conscious of the distinction he denies. That is, he thinks he has reasons for supposing that qualities are nothing more than ideas. Thus we ought not to accuse Berkeley of confusion, even if it were to turn out he was ultimately in error.

The basic story about qualities and their relationship to ideas Berkeley likely derived from his reading of Locke. Most of that story Berkeley finds plausible. Locke holds that ideas are a kind of intermediary that give us all the information present about the qualities of things and theorizes that qualities might as well be expressed in terms of the ideas they generate within perceivers (the primary and secondary quality thesis). For Locke, what it means to be a (secondary) quality essentially involves the ideas caused within us. Berkeley, however, who thinks he has good reasons to deny the existence of an independent material world, does not have to account for correspondence between ideas and external things. As a result, if qualities can be explained essentially in terms of ideas, it is a short step to simply reducing qualities *to* ideas. Without a material world, what role could qualities play if distinct from ideas? None. Thus we ought not find Berkeley's conflation initially unreasonable.

What matters for our purposes, however, is that the identification of idea and quality was more of a meeting than a reduction. Berkeleian ideas have features reminiscent of material qualities; he does not merely turn qualities into ideas. And so Berkeley has Philonous tell Hylas: "I am not for changing things into ideas, but rather ideas into things" (3D, 244). In a materialist ontology, qualities are the "vehicles" (Locke's "powers" grounded in the microstructure of material things) that report about an independent, external reality. Skepticism arises because there is a purported gap between the vehicles and the reality they represent. There does not appear to be any mechanism by which we can guarantee that the ideas we perceive accurately represent reality because reality and what represents reality are distinct items. On Berkeley's view, however, ideas/qualities *still* report a nominally independent, external reality, just not a material one, and this allows him to circumvent skepticism. Locke's representative vehicles *become* reality in Berkeley's system. Ideas and qualities represent, as it were, themselves. Since we immediately perceive them, skepticism is averted. We are passive with respect to many of the ideas we perceive, having no control over them. Berkeley thinks that the world according to his immaterialist principles is just materialism without the matter. "Hence it is evident the supposition of external bodies is not necessary for the producing our ideas: since it is granted they are produced sometimes, and might possibly be produced always in the same order we see them in at present, without their concurrence" (*PHK* 18). His world is *just like* the material world; the order and arrangement of what we experience remains unchanged on his view. Since Berkeley does not deny that the world appears to be external to us, in an important sense *it really is external*. Now here I mean "external" in the weak volitional sense of "not created by the (i.e., our) mind" and not in the sense Berkeley concerns himself to deny, namely that of "ontologically independent of all minds." Berkeley himself makes this clear: "And so may you suppose an external archetype on my principles; *external,* I mean, to your own mind; though indeed it must be supposed to exist in that mind which comprehends all things" (*3D*, 248). Ideas are things, and just as materialists assert for physical objects, these idea-things are ordered and stand in relations to one another. They behave remarkably like physical objects ("ideas into things").

In light of this explanatory model, it is worthwhile to briefly take note of Berkeley's unusual theory of perception. For each of the senses there is a smallest perceptible unit, called a *minimum sensibilium.* No matter the purported physical object or event, our perception of it consists of a large number of these minimum sensibilia. A direct result of this is that there are no invisible/insensible parts to things in our universe. This consequence is important to Berkeley, since it helps guarantee that skepticism will be sealed out of his system. Nothing physics posits will be in principle undetectable. As for the advances of microscopes and telescopes all the rage in his time, his reply is sharp. "[F]or when we look through a microscope we neither see more visible points, nor are the collateral points more distinct then when we look with the naked eye at objects placed in a due distance. A microscope brings us, as it were, into a new world: it presents us with a new scene of visible objects quite different from what we behold with the naked eye" (*NTV* 85). Berkeley's universe is genuinely external, just not independent from us in the way a materialist would suggest. We might not find his theory of minimum sensibilia attractive, but the picture is coherent. Since his *New Theory of Vision* was the first of his major philosophical works to be published, the fact that he puts so much emphasis on the sensibility and externality of the perceived world in his subsequent works is significant.

This kind of reading of Berkeley is not original to me, although I think I have discovered reasons for accepting it that are stronger than those heretofore proposed. A. A. Luce casts Berkeley as a realist, at one point noting that Berkeley "is talking about ideas that *are* stones, trees and books" (1963, 30). The world "outside" the mind is real—it is just not material. Berkeley's critique of matter is a critique of the possibility of a *material substratum.* That is, he is primarily concerned to deny that ideas could be ontically dependent on anything other than spirit. But this goal, as stated, indicates nothing about the nature of the dependence. Berkeley is actually quite clear about what he means.

> That there is no substance wherein ideas can exist besides spirit, is to me evident. And that the objects immediately perceived are

ideas, is on all hands agreed. And that sensible qualities are objects immediately perceived, no one can deny. It is therefore evident there can be no *substratum* of those qualities but spirit, in which they exist, not by way of mode or property, but as a thing perceived in that which perceives it. . . . If there be anything which makes the generality of mankind averse from the notions I espouse, it is a misapprehension that I deny the reality of sensible things: but as it is you who are guilty of that and not I, it follows that in truth their aversion is against your notions, and not mine. I do therefore assert that I am as certain of my own being, that there are bodies or corporeal substances (meaning the things I perceive by my senses), and that granting this, the bulk of mankind will take no thought about, nor think themselves at all concerned in the fate of those unknown natures, and philosophical quiddities, which some men are so fond of. (3D, 237–38)

The only thing here that is at all confusing is his persistent claim that ideas are "in" substances. Even so, the argument is straightforward.

(1) For an idea to exist is for it to be perceived.
     Or: ideas can only exist "in" the mind.
(2) Only ideas are immediately perceived.
(3) Qualities are immediately perceived.
(4) Therefore qualities are ideas.
(5) Therefore for a quality to exist, it must be perceived (be "in" the mind).

Now Berkeley takes qualities to be *things*. He urgently repeats his claim that what we perceive—sensible qualities—are real things. He additionally stresses that the recognition of this truth will not significantly alter our understanding of how the ordinary world appears to us. This result is only possible if qualities retain *some* form of independence from the mind, by which I mean that they are not "controlled" by our wills (what I call volitional independence). When we open our eyes in the morning the sky is still blue, no matter how hard we wish to perceive it as yellow. In that sense, ideas are independent of our minds, but this form of independence is not an ontological notion.

Thus Berkeley takes ideas to be quasi substances: (ontologically) dependent things whose primary relation to the mind is two place without being modes of it (i.e., "external" to the mind). The view is plausible given Berkeley's desire to simultaneously eliminate skepticism by reducing qualities to ideas. Once we accept his assertion that qualities must be ideas, Berkeley's only escape from solipsism is to forcibly bend the substance/mode ontology to allow for a category of volitionally independent and "external" entities that retain a measure of ontological dependence.

6.5 Unperceived Existence

A crucial test of the viability of my interpretation is how well it handles certain notorious problems. In the remainder of this chapter I start my defense by briefly introducing the first of those issues: the problem of unperceived existence. I then move on to engage a rival reading of Berkeley (Winkler's phenomenalistic interpretation) before delving deeply into more complicated problems in chapters 7 and 8.

At first blush it rubs common sense the wrong way to claim that when we leave a room it and its contents wink out of existence. The nature of the world and how we perceive it strongly suggests the opposite. If I leave a clock alone and unobserved for several hours, I return to find that it has kept the proper time despite its apparent nonexistence in the interim. Given our analysis of Berkeley's theory of ideas, he now has some resources to account for this phenomenon more plausibly.

Importantly, Berkeley makes sure that the existence conditions for any idea require only *a* mind, and not all minds. Hence, my clock continues to exist so long as *some* mind perceives it. "Wherever bodies are said to have no existence without the mind, I would not be understood to mean this or that particular mind, but all minds whatsoever. It does not therefore follow from the foregoing principles, that bodies are annihilated and created every moment, or exist not at all during intervals between our perception of them" (*PHK* 48). As Ronald Knox has popularized in his limerick, what ultimately guarantees the continuity of objects unperceived by finite minds is God.[22] Berkeley does not seriously discuss the role of God in preserving continuity until late in the *Three Dialogues*, where he marries the role of God with the externality of ideas.

---

22. Knox's limerick: "There was a young man who said 'God / Must think it exceedingly odd / If he finds that this tree / Continues to be / When there's no one about in the Quad.' A second limerick follows: "Dear Sir: Your astonishment's odd; / I am always about in the Quad. / And that's why the tree / Will continue to be, / Since observed by / *Yours faithfully*, GOD."

> When I deny sensible things an existence out of the mind, I do not mean my mind in particular, but all minds. Now it is plain they have an existence exterior to my mind, since I find them by experience to be independent of it. There is therefore some other mind wherein they exist, during the intervals between the times of my perceiving them: as likewise they did before my birth, and would do after my supposed annihilation. And as the same is true, with regard to all other finite created spirits; it necessarily follows, there is an *omnipresent eternal Mind*, which knows and comprehends all things. (230–31)

Berkeley sees two challenges here. First, how to explain the continuity of unperceived objects across time, and second, how to explain why they behave independently of us, both when perceived and not. He solves the second problem with his realization that ideas are both mind dependent (ontologically) yet volitionally independent ("external") and the first by positing an omnipresent deity that perceives all things. Presumably then, God perceives every idea throughout its functional existence, making the world of ideas one filled with permanent ideas.[23] Exploring the exact nature of this divine order of ideas will occupy us at length in the next chapter, so I limit the following discussion of God to certain circumspect claims.

Although invoking God to provide continuity in the world would be a pleasant solution, there are difficulties, since Berkeley elsewhere indicates that God does not sense as finite minds do. "There is no sense or sensory, nor anything like a sense or sensory, in God. Sense implies an impression from some other being, and denotes a dependence in the soul which hath it. Sense is a passion; and passions imply imperfection. God knoweth all things as pure mind or intellect; but nothing by sense, nor in nor through a sensory" (S 289).[24] If God does not sense ideas, then how can He preserve their existence? Berkeley already provides the answer. Like virtually all of his contemporaries, Berkeley uses the term "perception" and its cognates in a broad sense to capture all mental activity.[25] His usage includes sensing, thinking, pondering, and so forth. Sensing, as Berkeley notes, implies both the exercise of a passion *and* the reception of the object from an external source. Since God is the source of all ideas, clearly God does not sense. Yet

---

23. I am not alone in this interpretation. See Luce 1942, 4, and Berman 1986, 41–45.
24. See Thomas 1976, 163–68. That God does not sense even though God perceives has not been as widely noted as it ought to be.
25. Compare the similar discussion of "idea" with reference to Locke in section 4.3.

God can nonetheless be aware of our ideas of sense without actually sensing them. "God May comprehend all Ideas even the Ideas which are painfull & unpleasant without being in any degree pained thereby. Thus we our selves can imagine the pain of a burn etc. without any misery or uneasiness at all" (*PC* 675). Berkeley clearly allows perception without sensation. More importantly, the view allows God and finite minds to be aware of the numerically same ideas.[26] God creates every idea that we perceive (the order of which obeys what we call the laws of nature), although such creation does not entail that God experiences or senses them; it merely implies that God is simultaneously aware of them.

Thus Berkeley accounts for the nominal independence of the perceived world by asserting that God preserves the existence of ideas. Ideas are nevertheless (ontologically) dependent beings. Now this picture makes the relationship between ideas and finite minds admittedly unusual. In his quest to preserve some of our ordinary intuitions, Berkeley had to make certain emendations to the traditional ontological categories. Before we can further explore the fruits of Berkeley's labors on this score, however, we first need to engage one last potent rival interpretation.

6.6 Phenomenalism

To this point the picture I have been sketching of Berkeley's metaphysic is thoroughly idealist. There are no things that we perceive that are not actual ideas. Kenneth Winkler, however, has urged that Berkeley is in fact a kind of an early phenomenalist (1989, esp. ch. 6). Broadly speaking, "phenomenalism" applies to any theory according to which objects (like bodies) are constituted of phenomenal items, or sensa. I readily admit that in general terms Berkeley is not far from phenomenalism. Winkler's phenomenalism, however, holds that any statement about a sensible thing is equivalent to a set of counterfactual conditionals about ideas. As a result, what is essential to sensible things is that they are *perceivable* and not just perceived.[27] Additionally, the meanings of statements depend on the truth conditions expressed in the counterfactual language about minds and ideas (193). The

---

26. I amend and expand on this claim at length in the following chapter.
27. This leaves room for positivistic phenomenalisms. To say now that dinosaurs once roamed the earth would be cashed out in terms of counterfactuals about sensory evidence perceivable now (e.g., fossils). What would be essential to asserting that dinosaurs did exist is that evidence be perceivable to us *now*.

primary appeal of Winkler's phenomenalism stems from its ability to independently explain the persistence of unperceived objects without invoking the divine. So my statement "The clock is on the table in my study" is equivalent to a presumably complex set of counterfactuals including ones that describe what I would perceive were I now in my study. Hence Winkler ultimately concludes that Berkeley *consciously* endorses this form of phenomenalism: "These imperfections are to be expected, I think, in the writings of a philosopher who was one of the first to see the promise of phenomenalism" (200). From this point forward, I will use the word "phenomenalism" to refer to Winkler's specific theory and not to the broad sense of the term, primarily because Winkler himself does not further qualify the word. I recognize, however, that the term "phenomenalism" in contemporary usage covers more positions than just Winkler's.

If indeed Berkeley were a phenomenalist, that revelation would not critically undermine my contention that ideas are quasi substances. Even Winkler's phenomenalism is technically compatible with my analysis about the nature of Berkeleian ideas. It is not, however, the best of marriages. On my view, one of the reasons Berkeley is attracted to the claim that ideas are substance-like is that he needs to explain how the perceived world is independent of our will. The clock exists even when I fail to perceive it because God perceives it *and* because its nature or perceptual content is independent of me. A main motive for embracing phenomenalism is that it allows (but admittedly does not require) one to make sense of the world without God. As it turns out, however, I think that Berkeley cannot be a phenomenalist. Attributing such a view to him presents a number of philosophical problems and is unconvincing in light of a careful analysis of the texts.

At first glance, two philosophical reasons arise for rejecting phenomenalism as an interpretation of Berkeley. The first difficulty stems from the nature of counterfactuals. One might think that counterfactuals must be *grounded* (as I have discussed previously, especially in section 5.2). If a counterfactual is true, then that is because there is some nonconditional truth that "underlies" it.[28] Thus if one were to say truly that "If this sugar were put into the water then it would dissolve," that can be true only in virtue of other nonconditional truths about sugar and water. In this case, the counterfactual is true because of the chemical properties of sugar. When

---

28. My sense is that few contemporary philosophers seriously argue that counterfactuals do not require a ground in the sense that some have argued for ungrounded dispositions. See Armstrong 1997, esp. ch. 5, and Bird 2001, 137–49. Nonetheless, as I shall argue shortly, that need not be a restriction on Berkeley.

we turn to analyze sensory statements, however, we run into a problem. Consider Berkeley's example about the table. Winkler claims that the statement "There is a table in my study," is equivalent to "If one were to go into the study, one would see a table." But then what nonconditional truth grounds this counterfactual? We certainly cannot say that there truly is a table in the study, and not just because it seems to beg the question. More probingly, the claim that "There is a table in my study" is itself a sensory claim according to Berkeley. As such it also has a counterfactual reading and accordingly is not itself a nonconditional ground. In fact, no sensory claim at all can ground any other, since they are all supposedly equivalent to counterfactual conditionals about what we would experience under certain circumstances. Berkeley, of course, does have an out: God could ground these counterfactuals. What explains why I have certain experiences instead of others depends on nonconditional truths about how God is now. Yet if we must rely on God to make phenomenalism plausible for Berkeley, much of the impetus to endorse the theory in the first place is vitiated.

Yet it strikes me that Berkeley, who does not have any reflective theory of counterfactuals, might just as well deny the starting assumption. Just as some argue that there might be ungrounded dispositions, so one might suggest there are ungrounded counterfactuals as well.[29] To say "There is a table in my study" only asserts as a brute fact that two sets of sensory experiences are regularly conjoined. Berkeley was arguably interested in removing the metaphysical pretensions of the scientists of his day. One of those pretensions was the claim that every event in the experienced world had to be reduced to some underlying mechanistic or metaphysical cause (Brook 1973, esp. 3). Science is not about efficient causes but simply about discoverable uniformities. Yet if we reduce counterfactual talk to mere discoverable uniformities, one might well wonder how this supports phenomenalism at all. If the point of analyzing "There is a table in my study" is only that we learn to regularly associate certain ideas with one another, then the counterfactual nature of the claim drops out entirely. The sentence now means only when I do x, I will have a y-type experience. "There is a table in my study" means nothing about what would happen *were* I to go there. After all, there is no "there" to which to go when I am absent from "it." Instead, it is shorthand I use to describe a regularity in the order of ideas I perceive. Thus at the end of our analysis, we might confront the phenomenalist reader of Berkeley with a dilemma. Either counterfactuals require a ground, in which case the

---

29. See section 5.2ff. for a more complete discussion of grounding dispositional properties.

view looks implausible, or they do not. And if not, then the best reason for denying they do pushes one to a position where it appears Berkeley does not need counterfactuals at all, removing yet more of the impetus for endorsing phenomenalism.

A second problem emerges, however, when we remember that phenomenalism attempts to characterize the meanings of sentences in terms of the sensory evidence one could have for them.[30] What it means to say that there is a table in the study depends on the truth of various counterfactuals about what I would experience under certain conditions. That relationship seems clear enough. We could presumably list all the counterfactuals and then conjoin them, providing the meaning for the original declarative statement. Yet therein lies the problem. How are we to know what sensory statements count as evidence for the truth of any given claim? Does the meaning of "There is a table in my study" depend on who sees or touches it? Does it depend on being able to see the desk in the ultraviolet spectrum? There seems to be no nonarbitrary method for determining *which* counterfactuals are genuinely relevant. It is even possible that we will discover new kinds of sensory evidence in the future, yet it sounds odd to say that the meaning of a sentence would change were we to make a new empirical discovery. At the very least such an account is un-Berkeleian. Berkeley does not seem to rest his account of meaning on complexes of counterfactuals, although this point will require further textual proof.

I am not arguing that either concern absolutely defeats the phenomenalist interpretation. They do, however, make it more difficult to imagine why one would think that Berkeley endorses such a view. As it turns out, I think Berkeley did briefly entertain a phenomenalist account. Ultimately, however, he rejected it, and the textual evidence of this strikes me as unusually clear. Most of the statements cited as evidence that Berkeley embraced phenomenalism come from early entries in his notebooks. Here is a sample of some of his musings that are suggestive:

> + 293a Bodies taken for Power do exist when not perceiv'd but this existence is not actual. When I say a power exists no more is meant than that if in the light I open my eyes & look that way I shall see it i.e. the body etc.

---

30. I learned of this argument from Jonathan Bennett. See Bennett 1979, 45–64.

M.P. 185a Colours in the dark do exist really i.e. were there light or as soon as light comes we shall see them provided we open our eyes. & that whether we will or no.

+ 52 Bodies etc do exist even when not perceiv'd they being powers in the active Being.

These entries, and others like them, all indicate that Berkeley did flirt with a broadly phenomenalist understanding of the existence of sensory objects. Note, however, that I have provided Berkeley's own system of marginalia prior to the entry numbers.[31] The proper interpretation of the " + " sign has engendered considerable controversy and requires a brief aside to consider properly.

6.6.1 An Aside About Signs

Discovering the proper interpretation of the " + " sign is all the more important now since a surprisingly large amount of the evidence used by Winkler comes from entries with this symbol.[32] Luce originally wrote of the sign that "I am inclined to think that Berkeley used it as a sort of *obelus,* setting it against those entries which he found he could not use, whether because (a) irrelevant to his final argument, or personal, or trivial, or (b) representing discarded views" (1970, 8). He subsequently added that although he believed this to account for 95 percent of the occurrences of the sign, he was "not entirely satisfied" on this point. Much later he qualified his claim even further, reducing the number of "clear" cases of rejection to about one third of the total entries marked with the " + " symbol. Nonetheless, arguably the standard reading of the sign still treats it as *some* form of hesitancy or rejection, whether an indication that Berkeley thought the statement false in some way or merely that he wanted to set that particular line of reasoning aside. In his introduction to Berkeley's philosophical works, Michael Ayers writes that "The symbol ' + ' indicates a 'black list' consisting of entries for which Berkeley had no further use, often, but not always, expressing rejected possibilities" (Berkeley 1975, xxi–xxii).

---

31. The "M" and "P" stand for "matter" and "primary and secondary qualities" respectively, according to his notes.
32. My thanks to Walter Ott (and the *Canadian Journal of Philosophy*), who graciously agreed to the republication of this material, with revisions, originally coauthored with him and applied in another context. See Hight and Ott 2004, 8–11.

There are some reasons for supposing that something like a rejection mark might be an appropriate understanding of the symbol. Among the entries with the "+" are *PC* 422 and 356 ("No word to be used without an idea"), *PC* 450 ("Motion on 2nd thought seems to be a simple idea"), and *PC* 623 ("An extended [sic] may have passive modes of thinking, not active"), all claims that Berkeley goes on to reject in his published works. *PC* 378 is an ancestor of one of his arguments that eventually appears in the *Principles*. A portion of that entry is as follows:

+   1. All significant words stand for Ideas
       2. All knowledge about our Ideas
+   3. All ideas come from without or from within.
       4. If from without it must be by the senses & they are call'd sensations.
+   5. If from within they are the operations of the mind & are called thoughts.
       . . . .
+   8. All our ideas are either sensations or thoughts, by 3.4.5.
       . . . .
+   13. that thing wch is like unto another thing must agree wth it in one or more simple ideas.
       14. whatever is like a simple idea must either be another
+   simple idea of the same sort or contain a simple idea of that same sort. [By] 13.

Here Berkeley attaches the "+" symbol to certain premises and not to others. Tellingly, he attaches the sign to subsequent lines that depend on earlier premises marked with the plus sign. At a minimum, Berkeley is being hesitant about endorsing the claims he marks with the "+" symbol. I am *not* interested in demonstrating that the sign is univocally a rejection (I am not confident that such a proof is even possible); I only wish to establish that *frequently* the sign is so used. The evidence is sufficiently compelling that one may not legitimately simply appeal to entries marked with a "+" as if they unproblematically reflect Berkeley's considered views. In short, we ought not refer to his unpublished works as evidence for any *considered* position at all and certainly not without corroborating evidence from his published works.

Bertil Belfrage has since cast doubt on the standard interpretation, arguing that Luce's reading of the sign as an obelus is mistaken (1987, 217–30).

Stephen Daniel has taken Belfrage's analysis seriously and as evidence to justify his liberal use of the notebooks entries.[33] The "black list" interpretation of the symbol is attacked as textually unsupportable. According to Belfrage, of the 188 entries with the "+" sign only around 50 indicate allegedly *obvious* rejections. The rest are either unclear or controversial for various reasons.

Many of the passages containing references suggestive of phenomenalism are marked with the "+" sign. That in itself, as Belfrage has argued, is not necessarily a good reason to suppose that Berkeley later rejected them. But it is also no reason to suppose that Berkeley endorsed them either. Even Belfrage's own view stops short of that. He argues that the *Notebooks* should be read not as a single evolving philosophical position but rather as a collection of "different philosophical standpoints which were set forth at different times in Berkeley's life" (226). Belfrage has an important point. Even if one fully accepts all of Belfrage's claims concerning the interpretation of the offending sign it does not follow that they represent Berkeley's mature, considered views. Without additional evidence confirming that these entries are among those Berkeley accepts, the countervailing evidence in the particular case of phenomenalism makes it more plausible to assume that they number among those he really did set aside or reject. At a minimum, we should be hesitant to give *special* weight to any "+" marked entry in the *Notebooks*.

6.6.2 Against Phenomenalism

Despite the foregoing analysis of the *Commentaries*, occasionally we do find passages in the main works that remind one of phenomenalism. In section 3 of the *Principles* Berkeley writes: "The table I write on, I say, exists, that is, I see and feel it; and if I were out of my study I should say it existed, meaning thereby that if I was in my study I might perceive it, or that some other spirit actually does perceive it." Berkeley does not go on to develop this into a theoretical position; rather he instead notes that the essence of sensible things is to be *perceived*, and not, as phenomenalism requires, merely *perceivable*. As it turns out, Berkeley endorses another unrelated view that gen-

---

33. In private correspondence Daniel has asserted that Belfrage's article has "refuted" Luce's interpretation of the "+" sign. Whether that is the case is open to debate, but it must be noted that Daniel has the admirable desire to preserve as much of *Commentaries* as good scholarship will allow and thus believes that any possibility that allows us to employ the entries seriously compels us to do so. Although I am sympathetic, I believe that changes required elsewhere to accommodate this methodology come at too high a price.

erates examples that look a lot like phenomenalism. He tells us that the "laws of nature" are a set of rules we can use to *predict* sensory experiences.

> Now the set of rules or established methods, wherein the mind we depend on excites in us the ideas of sense, are called the *Laws of Nature:* and these we learn by experience, which teaches us that such and such ideas are attended with such and such other ideas, in the ordinary course of experience.
>
> This gives us a sort of foresight, which enables us to regulate our actions for the benefit of life. (*PHK* 30–31)

In the context of this analysis he provides us with an interesting example that some might take as evidence of phenomenalism.[34] "[F]or the question, whether the earth moves or no, amounts in reality to no more than this, to wit, whether we have reason to conclude from what hath been observed by astronomers that if we were placed in such and such circumstances, and such or such a position and distance, both from the earth and the sun, we should perceive the former to move among the choir of the planets, and appearing in all respects like one of them" (*PHK* 58). However, the conditional expressed here is decidedly not phenomenalist. Instead, Berkeley is seeking to explain why sensible phenomena appear to have causal connections in a universe that nonetheless is purely immaterial. This analysis is not about the meaning of statements but about their truth and relationship to other sensory claims. As a result, when Berkeley says that the table exists in the study and explains the claim by noting that if we should walk into the room we would perceive it, all he is really doing is explaining the truth of the claim in terms of the connections between perceived ideas. Why, before I walk into the study, do I believe I will perceive the table? Answer: because God has so regulated the flow of ideas such that we can reliably *predict* that we would have such a sensory experience. None of this unequivocally supports phenomenalism, and I believe I have provided a viable alternative to explain passages like these.[35]

---

34. Winkler takes this passage as some evidence for his view, although he does call it "defective as a statement of phenomenalism" (1989, 199).

35. At *3D*, 238, Berkeley brings up another example (the bent oar case) that some might think is suggestive of phenomenalism (although Winkler himself does not directly appeal to it). As this case is even weaker than the astronomical one discussed above, I have omitted a detailed analysis of it. As a gloss, the oar passage is not about the *meaning* of "The oar is bent" but rather concerns the nature of his error in *supposing* that the oar is bent. Here again, what is at issue is the connection of sensory ideas and the judgments we make on their basis and not the construction of meaning from counterfactuals.

One passage appears to more directly support Winkler's thesis. When writing about creation in the *Dialogues*, Berkeley presents the following analysis:

> HYLAS: What shall we make then of the Creation?
> PHILONOUS: May we not understand it to have been entirely in respect of finite spirits; so that things, with regard to us, may properly be said to begin their existence, or be created, when God decreed they should become perceptible to intelligent creatures, in that order and manner which he then established, and we now call the Laws of Nature? You may call this a *relative*, or *hypothetical existence* if you please. (253)

Here we have perhaps the closest thing to an instance of Berkeley endorsing phenomenalism. I do not deny that this passage has a phenomenalist air about it, but it is an oddity. Instead of being representative of a deeper commitment to phenomenalism, I think it is a case where he did not carefully think things through. That is, in general his Mosaic account of the Creation is basically an ad hoc exercise.[36] Consider the core claim (C) Berkeley advances: "Things properly begin their existence when God decrees they should become perceptible to intelligent creatures." We might interpret (C) in one of two ways. The sensible object becomes perceptible when God makes the decree, or, alternatively, God decrees the time at which intelligent creatures could perceive the object, were they doing the right things. There is an ambiguity between the time of the decree (first reading) and the time mentioned *in* the decree (second reading). Phenomenalist interpreters will favor the latter option, since it relies on a counterfactual analysis. Either way, however, Berkeley's theory of the Creation runs into some theological problems.

Consider the first interpretation. At the time of the decree, things become perceivable to intelligent creatures should they do the right things, be in the proper spot, etc. This reading entails that God did not make the decree about what humans could perceive until they were created. So during the first few days, while God is making the earth, the trees, and lower animals, God apparently has no idea what he is going to do a few days later. After all, *on this reading*, he cannot make the decree at the outset of creation. Berkeley certainly would have rejected the notion that God had no idea what he was going to do in the last days of the Creation. Yet the alternative only makes

---

36. Here I am echoing parts of Jonathan Bennett's (unpublished) analysis on this issue.

matters worse. If God immediately decreed the time at which things would become perceivable to humans, we find that God is acting arbitrarily. Assume that on day 1 God willed the following statement to be true on day 3: *If any created spirit were now to do certain things, then it would have certain kinds of ideas.* Presumably God knows that there will not be any created spirits on day 3, so why make the statement true *then*? The existence of sensible things just is their being perceived, so what possible reason could God have for making the statement true then, and not some other time, either later or earlier? As philosophical theology I think Berkeley would have been disturbed by the consequences. Phenomenalism does not make Berkeley's account of the Creation theologically more tempting.

Part of what compels me to believe that his analysis here is ad hoc is how he presents the entire account. The always-confident Philonous usually explains new objections away by invoking points already established earlier. He does not do this here. Nor does he indicate that the issue is apiece with some other objections raised elsewhere. Lastly, his conclusion is not that he is *correct* but rather that no one can do better. Here is the finish to the passage quoted immediately above, discussing his account of Creation:

> But so long as it supplies us with the most natural, obvious, and literal sense of the Mosaic history of the Creation; so long as it answers all the religious ends of that great article; in a word, *so long as you can assign no other sense or meaning in its stead;* why should we reject this? Is it to comply with a ridiculous sceptical humor of making everything nonsense and unintelligible? I am sure you cannot say, it is for the glory of God. For allowing it to be a thing possible and conceivable, that the corporeal world should have an absolute subsistence extrinsical to the mind of God, as well as to the minds of all created spirits: yet how could this set forth either the immensity or omniscience of the Deity, or the necessary and immediate dependence of all things on him? Nay, would it not rather seem to derogate from those attributes? (253, emphasis mine)

As a bit of Berkeley, the passage is unusual. It is not a confident assertion of the truth of his immaterialist doctrines; rather it is a defense on the grounds that no one has a better answer. As long as his account preserves religious ends and we can assign no other (better) meaning, then we ought to just sit back and be happy with what we have. I take his unusual tone—and the theological difficulties present—as evidence that this passage is not a carefully thought out representation of his systematic beliefs.

The crowning bit of evidence that Berkeley rejected phenomenalism, however, comes in the *Dialogues*. Berkeley has Hylas present Philonous with the perfect opportunity to make his intentions clear.

> HYLAS: Yes, Philonous, I grant the existence of a sensible thing consists in being perceivable, but not in being actually perceived.
> PHILONOUS: And what is perceivable but an idea? And can an idea exist without being actually perceived? These are points long since agreed between us. (234)

Hylas invites Philonous to make his phenomenalism pellucid. Instead, Berkeley explicitly declares that such a move is useless. Bennett rightly calls this an "anti-phenomenalist skirmish" (1971, 150), and Winkler's reply is unsatisfying.[37] Winkler asserts that the passage is compatible with phenomenalism, but he does not provide any analysis to support his claim, instead relying on a "long list of reasons which are not, I admit, decisive even in the aggregate" (201; see also 227). The logic of the exchange seems fairly clear. Hylas starts by asserting:

> (1) A sensible thing exists = an idea is perceivable.

Winkler's phenomenalism would have Berkeley interpret this as:

> (1P) A sensible thing exists = if a situation were to occur, then an idea would be perceived.

But Philonous *does not adopt this interpretation*. Instead, he takes a stronger position:

> (1S) A sensible thing exists = there is an idea such that, if a certain situation were to occur, then it would be perceived.

Recall that Berkeley adopts the *esse* is *percipi* thesis. If there *is* an idea, then it is being perceived. Conjoined with that thesis, (1S) does *not* allow the existence of unperceived objects, whereas (1P) does. (1S) stipulates that there

---

37. See Winkler 1989, 227, and Bennett 2001, 2:189–96.

is an extant idea—and hence that it is perceived—whereas (1P) does not. To say that a sensible thing exists only commits one to the truth of the counterfactual(s) according to phenomenalism. Thus the sensible thing could exist even if not now actually perceived, so long as the counterfactual remains true. (1S) sticks to the idealist claim that without actual perception, an idea cannot exist. Berkeley is even good enough to *explicitly state* in the exchange that the existence of sensible things requires actual perception.

In summary, I grant that Winkler's phenomenalism might have some positive features that make it philosophically desirable in general, but in the context of the rest of Berkeley's metaphysics, it leaves much to be desired. Traditional idealistic approaches are more plausible, especially in terms of what Berkeley actually says, and ultimately the textual evidence strikes me as fairly conclusive. Most of the passages that seem to flirt with phenomenalism can be readily explained by other features of his thought. Most importantly, although he did briefly entertain phenomenalism, when he finally seriously confronted its possibility, he outright rejected it. I therefore conclude that Berkeley was not a phenomenalist.

6.7 Berkeley and the Early Modern Tale

There are a number of philosophers who see Berkeley as playing a vital role in the early modern tale (although I hope I have provided an interpretation of the nature of ideas in Berkeley's ontology that is plausible and fruitful enough to throw doubt on that ascription). Interestingly, some give Berkeley a role in part precisely because they understand him as groping toward exactly the sort of the theory I attribute to him. Richard Watson writes:

> Berkeley's treatment (deriving from Malebranche) of the relationships between mind and idea, and between mind and notion, is illuminated by a consideration of the extent to which he takes these relationships for granted in the Cartesian way (as substance to modification), and of the extent to which he sees difficulties in the relationship between substance and modification. Berkeley's solution to Cartesian problems by the introduction of an entity external to substance and modification is, like that of Malebranche before him, not successful; Malebranche belittles, and Berkeley denies, the dualism of substances, but neither philosopher can break entirely

with the ontological pattern of substance and modification. (1987, 24)

Watson notes more or less the same tensions driving Berkeley's ontology of ideas as I do, except that I think Berkeley's solution has more merit than Watson admits. More importantly, however, Watson argues on the basis of this alleged failure that Berkeley is a part of a tradition that pushes away from ontology with respect to ideas. Claiming that ideas for Berkeley must be mental modifications (124), Watson proceeds to argue that this ontology of ideas was incapable of supporting the epistemological roles ideas play. He thus sees Berkeley as a failed idea ontologist, one well on the way to "deontologizing" ideas (127–28). For Watson, Hume completes the early modern tale, "breaking" with the traditional ontology, but Berkeley plays a vital role in the story. I defer the discussion of Hume until the final chapter; it is enough for the moment to note Berkeley's pivotal role.

John Yolton in fact pushes Berkeley further down this epistemological road than Watson. He reads Berkeley as *already* having made the leap away from ontology with respect to ideas. Yolton reduces Berkeley's language of "exist in the mind" to "is known" or "is perceived," where the reduction is an epistemological one. "The being of objects in the mind is not a notional existence. It is, as it was for Descartes, an epistemic existence. *Esse est* [sic] *percipi*, 'to be is to be perceived,' is clearly a translation of 'to be is to exist in the mind'" (2000, 96).[38] I have, in effect, spent the majority of this chapter arguing against such readings of Berkeley. Unlike Yolton, I take the word "in" to express ontological dependence, a view I take to have better textual support and more philosophical respectability.

In a similar vein, recent scholarship has increasingly tended to read Berkeley as an epistemologist first and an ontologist second. Daniel Flage is an excellent representative of this line of thinking. I hasten to note, however, although sympathetic at times with the claims of Watson and Yolton, Flage's views are differently motivated.[39] I readily confess that his approach is not without merit, but it does strike me as somehow missing part of what is important and even plausible in Berkeley's thinking. I cannot fully make this case until given the opportunity in the next chapters to explore some of the consequences of my ontological reading of Berkeley, but is it worth

---

38. As a point of accuracy, note that Berkeley consistently writes "*esse* is *percipi*" and does not use the Latin "*est*."

39. Flage cites Yolton's thesis about Berkeley while building his own distinct account (2004, 34).

briefly exploring Flage's approach. "The alternative approach I propose is epistemological. On such an approach, Berkeley asks what is known and introduces ontological commitments only on the basis of what is known. Ideas are nothing more than 'objects of human knowledge'" (2004, 26). On one level Flage and I do not disagree. We both hold that Berkeley *has* an underlying ontology of ideas; we differ on the importance and role of that ontology in his thinking. For Flage, the ontology is added afterward to support the epistemological roles idea play. I read Berkeley as seeking to use ontology as the means to solve a variety of problems, metaphysical *and* epistemological. Berkeley is an immaterialist first; some of the epistemological problems that arise from his metaphysics need to be engaged, but they appear only *after* the system is in place. Berkeley is an ontologist happy to reap epistemological rewards.

Flage would likely object that I am missing the point. The *Principles of Human Knowledge,* after all, has a title with an explicit epistemological reference. Yet it should be no surprise to anyone familiar with early modern philosophy that within the work epistemological and metaphysical issues are often blurred and hard to separate. I read the *Principles* as an attempt to ground a reasonable (perhaps even "commonsensical") epistemology inside his immaterialist ontology. As such, epistemological concerns are often going to have pride of place in the book but only because Berkeley needs to demonstrate that his metaphysical system can accommodate our experiences of the world. A metaphysical system that cannot explain the world as we experience it is a poor theory.

Flage contends that Berkeley builds his ontology on epistemological foundations (2004, 59).[40] One of Flage's core arguments is that ordinary objects are nothing more than appearances, mere sensible things. "If my account is correct, Berkeley holds that ordinary objects *are nothing but* collections of ideas of sense" (2004, 54, emphasis mine). But this formulation of Berkeley's view, which I do not dispute, misses a rather important feature of his thinking. Ordinary objects in the world are not merely ideas of sense—they *are also real things.* That is, Berkeley tells us that sensory ideas *constitute* reality (*PHK* 35–36). And he is quite clear about this.

PHILONOUS: You mistake me. I am not for changing things into ideas, but rather ideas into things; since those immediate objects of percep-

---

40. See Flage 2007. I am grateful to Flage for having allowed me to read this material in advance of its publication.

tion, which according to you, are only appearances of things, I take to be the real things themselves. (244)

One might wish to press me further. The fact that Berkeley is turning ideas into things is evidence that he is grounding his ontology (things) in his epistemology (ideas). Thus Flage notes that the appearance of ideas as real things does not occur until *Principles* 33, where it is invoked to separate imaginary things from real ones. It is, in essence, serving an epistemological end as well as an ontological one. But there is more to knowing the world than perceiving ideas. We also learn to anticipate ideas based on previous experience and discover regular patterns in the ideas we perceive. These epistemological discoveries depend on the nature of reality—the order of ideas whose nature it is to be perceived. To be fair to Flage, I am not certain our views are that far apart, for he also claims that the *esse* is *percipi* principle is a "principle of ontological commitment" (2004, 59). Flage does not deny that Berkeley's thinking operates within the traditional ontology; he simply believes that Berkeley's ontology is limited by epistemological constraints. What is real is limited by what is known. Although I agree that there is an important connection here, I am more inclined to believe that, for Berkeley, what is known is limited by what is real. It just so happens, however, that the two sets closely overlap in Berkeley's philosophical system.

My primary concern here is only to note the role that some scholars have given to Berkeley in the early modern tale. I doubt Flage would consciously place Berkeley in the tale, but his thinking is representative of a larger movement to read the early moderns as epistemologists first and ontologists second (if at all). It is this tendency I am resisting.

Up to this point I have provided a positive account of Berkeley's theory of ideas that preserves and reconciles two apparently conflicting tendencies in his works. Berkeley writes as if ideas are *like* modes because he emphasizes the ontological dependence of ideas on minds, and he writes as if ideas are *like* substances because he thinks of them as robust objects that in perception appear volitionally independent of minds. As a result, Berkeley emerges with a view that makes ideas what I call "quasi substances." In effect, Berkeley is stretching the traditional ontology of substance and mode by creating a category that shares features of both without fully being either. The most prominent nontraditional alternative, Winkler's form of phenomenalism, is not a viable candidate. As a result, we have not only an independent case for positively thinking that Berkeley endorsed this view but also significant evidence that its rivals are unacceptable.

Making sense of the positive account I have provided is not enough. The real test of the theory is how well it accommodates and explains important features of Berkeley's metaphysics, for I have maintained from the outset of this study that reading the early moderns in light of the substance/mode ontology will provide us with interpretive and philosophical benefits. I have chosen to spend most of my effort on Berkeley on this score because he has been considered a key figure in the early modern tale and because the philosophical payoff is considerable. I argue that Berkeley's fantastical metaphysical system is in fact more plausible (without saying that it is *true*) given our ontological approach. The following two chapters consequently engage several important topics in light of my reading of Berkeley's theory of ideas, demonstrating its interpretative power and philosophical promise.

7

DIVINE IDEAS

It has long been thought that Berkeley cannot consistently help himself to a theory of divine archetypal ideas in order to explain our perception of the sensible world. Positing the existence of such ideas in God allegedly creates skeptical problems, difficulties about the continuity of sensible objects, puzzles about the privacy of ideas, and worse. Introducing divine ideas allegedly inserts an intermediary between minds and ultimate reality, creating another veil of perception in a new form. Ardently committed to removing skepticism, Berkeley cannot endorse any theory that even hints at representationalism. J. D. Mabbott concludes, "It does not seem likely that Berkeley himself believed in Divine Ideas, at least as a necessary part of his system" (1968, 373). These ideas allegedly raise more problems for Berkeley than they solve. Worse yet, they are not even adequate to the challenges they are supposed to overcome. Thus Leopold Stubenberg has insisted that an archetypal theory of divine ideas for Berkeley is "a complete failure," unable to provide a stable, continuous, unfragmented world (1990, 226). In general, most commentators have argued that Berkeley ought not to have defended a theory of divine ideas at all.[1]

Much of the skepticism regarding Berkeley's theory of divine ideas derives from a reluctance to assiduously follow Berkeley through his reasoning about the nature of ideas and their relation to genuine substances. The topic of divine ideas and the alleged embarrassment they constitute to Berkeley accordingly provides us with an ideal opportunity to show how the early modern tale is frequently uncharitable to the early moderns. My task here is

---

1. See Acton 1967, 1:301. Acton alleges that archetypes lead Berkeley back into skepticism. See also Stack 1970, esp. 71; Tipton 1988, 344ff.; and Warnock 1982, 124. Winkler is an unusual exception, but even there the view he attributes to Berkeley is a weak version of an archetype theory (1989, 228–32).

to construct a theory of divine ideas in light of Berkeley's ontology, thereby demonstrating the philosophical and textual advantages of our traditional ontological approach. In short, I argue here that technically Berkeley did not endorse a divine *archetypal* theory at all; he does not believe that God has an original order of ideas of which our own ideas are copies. Instead, the sensory ideas perceived by finite minds are numerically identical to God's divine ideas.[2] Thus although one might (misleadingly) call Berkeley's theory of divine ideas an archetypal theory, this label does not imply that there are always distinct archetypes and ectypes in his ontology.[3] This realization in turn makes not only Berkeley's theory of divine ideas more plausible but also renders the rest of his metaphysics more consistent and reasonable.

Along the way we shall have opportunity to engage a number of concerns that might be pressed against the quasi-substance account of Berkeley's ideas. The most important of these worries is what I call the "privacy problem," an issue that will arise naturally in the course of the discussion about divine ideas. This chapter is therefore meant also to be an extension of the argument of chapter 6.

7.1 Divine Ideas and Archetypes

At a minimum it is clear that Berkeley does hold some form of a theory of divine ideas, archetypal or otherwise. Historically, divine archetypes are the ideas of God that represent (or for Berkeley, constitute) genuine reality; they are the "originals" of what we perceive. Their counterparts, ectypes, are copies of these original archetypal ideas. Berkeley knew of archetypes from both Locke and Malebranche. For Locke, our ideas generally are derived from genuine things or properties we encounter in the world. As Locke writes in the *Essay*: "*First, By real Ideas*, I mean such as have a Foundation in Nature; such as have a Conformity with the real Being, and Existence of Things, or with their Archetypes. *Fantastical or Chimerical*, I call such as have no Foundation in Nature, nor have any Conformity with that reality

---

2. To my pleasant surprise, I am not the first to argue for this explicit thesis. See Raynor 1987, 611–20, esp. 613. Jonathan Dancy (I think unintentionally) suggests a similar view when he asserts that God perceives every idea. Hence, our ideas are simply a subset of those of God's (1987, 71).

3. Daniel Flage has recently attributed a theory of archetypes to Berkeley, but his theory is not one strictly of divine ideas as archetypes. Instead, archetypes on Flage's account are ordered sets of ideas (which are not themselves ideas) accessed only notionally. There is much to recommend Flage's account and although I think we agree substantively, my emphasis here is on individual divine ideas (not common sense objects or collections). As a result, a detailed treatment of Flage's position lies beyond the scope of this chapter. See Flage 2001, 7–31.

of Being, to which they are tacitly referr'd, as to their Archetypes" (II.30.1). Locke, of course, thinks of *most* archetypes as objective, external, *material* things, which ideas represent either by causation or by resemblance.[4] Malebranche, unlike Locke, invokes ideas as archetypes for the material world. That is, physical objects are "reflections" or even ectypes (images) of God's ideas. Consider two representative passages from the *Dialogues on Metaphysics and on Religion,* in which Malebranche's mouthpiece Theodore speaks:

> Ideas have an eternal and necessary existence, and the corporeal world exists only because it pleased God to create it. Thus, to see the intelligible world, it suffices to consult Reason which contains intelligible, eternal, and necessary ideas, the archetype of the visible world. (9, Dialogue I.5)

> Consider attentively the clear idea of extension. It is the archetype of bodies; it represents their nature and properties. Is it not evident that all the possible properties of extension must be simply relations of distance? (38, Dialogue III.10; see *LO,* 320 [4.11.3])

Malebranche concludes that when we perceive, we "see" the very archetypes in God, hence the name for this doctrine: "Vision in God." When Berkeley talks about divine ideas, one immediately wonders whether he might not be flirting with the Malebranchian position that our ideas just are the archetypes in God. "[D]o I not acknowledge a twofold state of things, the one ectypal or natural, the other archetypal and eternal? The former was created in time; the latter existed from everlasting in the mind of God" (3D, 254). Positive remarks about archetypes, however, are relatively rare in Berkeley's works, and the majority of those references are negative.[5] When not negative, they are typically grudging remarks about terms and language use. Thus after Johnson presses Berkeley about an archetypal understanding of ideas, Berkeley replies, in a 24 March 1730 letter, that "I have no objection against calling the ideas in the mind of God archetypes of ours. But I object against those archetypes by philosophers supposed to be real things, and to have an absolute rational existence distinct from their being perceived by any mind

---

4. Locke also speaks of some archetypes as complex ideas, as in the case of abstract notions like incest and adultery (*ECHU* III.5.3).

5. Archetypes are mentioned three times in the *Principles* (sections 45, 87, and 99), twice as many times in the *Dialogues* (pp. 206, 212, 214, 240, 248, and 254–55), and a few times in the correspondence with Johnson. See also *PC* 823.

whatsoever; it being the opinion of all materialists that an ideal existence in the Divine Mind is one thing, and the real existence of material things another" (Berkeley 1948–57, 2:292).[6] The reluctance of Berkeley to use the language of archetypes is not surprising given that he generally wants to distance himself from the accounts of Locke and Malebranche. Despite superficial appearances here that Berkeley accepts a robust archetypal understanding of God's ideas (such that they are the originals of our own sensory ideas), there are powerful reasons for thinking that Berkeley wants to make the distance great enough to allow him to deny this traditional understanding of God's ideas as archetypes.

A divine archetypal theory of ideas presumably solves several pressing problems for Berkeley. First, it provides a solution to what is commonly known as the problem of privacy. Two persons perceive the very same thing in an immaterialist world when their ideas are properly related to the one archetypal idea in God. Second, it removes worries about unperceived parts of the world, since God is always present to perceive everything. As an extension of the last point, it preserves the continuity of sensible objects as well. The objects intermittently perceived by finite minds remain constant without blinking in and out of existence. Unfortunately, as we have already seen, most Berkeley scholars believe that none of these problems can be effectively overcome by Berkeley's theory of divine archetypes and furthermore that new difficulties arise from it. Since this archetypal theory introduces our own finite ideas as intermediaries between our understanding and the archetypal ideal reality, Berkeley allegedly would be smuggling in a representative theory that he himself argues engenders skepticism. Even if our ideas are perfect copies of the archetypes in God, we nonetheless are *not* directly perceiving reality.

All of these alleged inadequacies, however, stem from an incomplete understanding of Berkeley's theory of divine ideas. I demonstrate that Berkeley does not believe that the archetypal order is inside the mind of God in any sense that implies inherence or that these archetypal ideas are modes. Instead, Berkeley holds that ideas fall into the hybrid ontological category of quasi substance. Ideas are dependent on minds but nonetheless distinct from and "external" to them. The resulting theory of archetypes survives the above objections, is broadly consistent with the rest of Berkeley's philosophical system, and provides his immaterialism with greater resources.

---

6. Given the amount of careful time and space Johnson gives to the issue of archetypes, Berkeley's response is curiously brief.

7.2 "In" the Mind of God

Recall that ideas for Berkeley are decidedly dependent beings. Their *esse* is *percipi*. As a result, some divine order of ideas must be maintained by God to preserve the perceived connected and continuous nature of the sensible world.[7] Yet now an issue arises as to *where* this order "resides." Here I want to revisit my earlier analysis of the nature of ideas but this time from the perspective of Berkeley's language about being "in the mind." The conclusions I ultimately reach are exactly the same, but the difference in approach might be helpful for some and in any event makes the analysis concerning divine ideas more lucid.

Some interpreters of Berkeley's theory of divine ideas have emphasized that he posits an archetypal ideal order "inside" the mind of God. This characterization might mean that ideas are "in" the mind in a metaphorically spatial sense as a color is "in" an object or a chair is "in" a room. Thus one might say that ideas are "in" the mind of God in the sense of being a part of God. Berkeley writes, "the real tree existing without his mind is truly known and comprehended by (that is *exists in*) the infinite mind of God" (3D, 235). The parenthetical remark with emphasis *is Berkeley's*. Given that Berkeley is apparently telling us that reality is in the mind of God, it should not be surprising that some commentators have taken him seriously.[8] For instance, Berkeley explains the continuity of sensible things by appealing to their real existence "in" God: "When I deny sensible things an existence out of the mind, I do not mean my mind in particular, but all minds. Now it is plain they have an existence exterior to my mind, since I find them by experience to be independent of it. There is therefore some other mind wherein they exist, during the intervals between the times of my perceiving them.... it necessarily follows, there is an *omnipresent eternal Mind*" (3D, 230–31). Ideas exist in minds. Yet to suppose that "in" here should be read as inherence or to treat ideas as monadic properties of minds is an error. Berkeley explains that by "in the mind" he means nothing more than *ontological dependence*. God's ideas are "external" to the mind of God in the sense of being distinct relata in a two-place relation with the mind, implying only

---

7. This claim does not necessarily imply that archetypes are themselves continuously existing beings. The divine order of ideas can be continuous in terms of the content they represent (their appearances) without the ideas themselves being necessarily permanent. When Berkeley says that part of the state of things is "archetypal and eternal" (3D, 254), that is a reference to the *order* of ideas and not to the nature of the ideas themselves. See section 7.5.

8. For instance, Peter Wenz argues, "Nowhere does Berkeley deny the existence of archetypal *ideas,* archetypes existing *within* the mind of God" (1976, 541, emphasis in the original).

that they are neither modes nor proper parts of the divine mind. They are perceived directly but depend on the constant perception of God for their existence.

We have here two different conceptual distinctions that run closely together. I preserve the slightly misleading language because it is Berkeley's. Using the same language will help us unravel some otherwise confusing passages. First, there is the distinction between an idea being "in" and "without" the mind. An idea is "in" the mind if it is dependent on the mind for its existence. An idea is "without" the mind if it does not rely on that mind to sustain it.[9] Here we need to be careful, since Berkeley sometimes blurs ontological and volitional independence. In one sense, all the sensory ideas a finite mind has are "without" because they are independent of the will, even though the idea itself is still dependent on some mind or other for its existence. Berkeley sometimes expresses this by saying that sensory ideas affect the mind "from without." A finite mind may perceive a sensory idea not under its volitional control *and* have that idea be "in" the mind. As a consequence, the idea is both "in" and "without" the mind. Such assertions are not contradictory but rather reflect an infelicitous use of language, since the "without" here implies only that the idea is independent of the will and not that the idea can exist independently of a mind.

Yet a second potential distinction lurks. Ideas may be either internal ("in") or external to the mind. Note that this distinction implies nothing about ontological dependence. An idea is "external" to the mind if it is both distinct from the mind and in a two-place relation with it. Sensory perception is an external relation. The ideas we have are distinct from us. Berkeley's insight is to note the unusual nature of this relation. The existence of one of the *relata* (the idea) depends on the relation actually holding. Apart from some perceptual relation the idea does not exist. Therefore when we perceive, we are related to a distinct but (ontologically) dependent entity. It is natural to think that this dependence is on the mind that is participating in the particular relation in question, but this does not necessarily follow. One might well perceive an idea that is actually being sustained by another mind or whose sustenance is overdetermined. As a result, "external" ideas can be neither modes nor proper parts of a mind. On the other hand, an idea is "internal" to the mind if its relation to the mind can be reduced to a monadic property. Berkeley does not think ideas are internal to the mind in this sense.

---

9. Thus the distinction is only a conceptual one, since Berkeley denies that ideas can exist "without" the mind in this sense.

In *Principles* 49 Berkeley distinguishes between the dependence of ideas (being "in" the mind) and their being modes (being "internal" to the mind).

> [I]t may be objected, that if extension and figure exist only in the mind, it follows that the mind is extended and figured; since extension is a mode or attribute, which (to speak with the Schools) is predicated of the subject in which it exists. I answer, those qualities are in the mind only as they are perceived by it, that is, not by way of *mode* or *attribute*, but only by way of *idea;* and it no more follows, that the soul or mind is extended because extension exists in it alone, than it does that it is red or blue, because those colours are on all hands acknowledged to exist in it, and nowhere else.[10]

Ideas are not modes of the mind and thus are not present "in" the mind in that sense. Then what does it mean to say that qualities are "in" the mind "as they are perceived by it?" "In" expresses nothing more than ontological dependence. Berkeley uses this odd phraseology to distance himself from materialist confusions, but his position is unmistakable. "When I speak of objects as existing in the mind or imprinted on the senses; I would not be understood in the gross literal sense, as when bodies are said to exist in a place, or a seal to make an impression upon wax. My meaning is only that the mind comprehends or perceives them; and that it is affected from without, or by some being distinct from itself" (*3D*, 250). When perceiving a sensory idea, the mind is *affected* by another source, making ideas dependent but decidedly external (in the Berkeleian sense). God's archetypal order is a set of ideas external to His mind, but "in" it in the sense that the ideas depend on His perceiving them for their existence.[11] This example is not an isolated use of the language I am attributing to Berkeley. "Again, the things I perceive must have an existence, they or their archetypes, out of [i.e., external to] my mind: but being ideas, neither they nor their archetypes can exist otherwise in [i.e., are dependent on] an understanding: there is therefore an understanding" (*3D*, 240).

One might object, however, that I have left out an alternative possibility.

---

10. The claim is essentially repeated at *3D*, 237.
11. This claim is not to imply that ideas, even archetypes, *causally* affect God. Here Berkeley means nothing more than God and His ideas are in a two-place relation, one in which God preserves ideas by perceiving them.

Perhaps Berkeley takes ideas to be a special kind of monadic property.[12] In *Principles* 49, when he says that ideas are not in the mind by way of mode or attribute, he might mean that the following proposition (P) is false:

(P) ($\forall$x)(x is in substance S entails S is x).

If an idea were a mode or an attribute, this proposition might be true, but ideas are predicated of the mind in such a way that this proposition remains false. Hence ideas could be a kind of thing predicated of the mind such that the mind does not become what is predicated of it. Having an idea of blue means that the mind has a monadic predicate without itself being blue. I agree that Berkeley needs to keep P false, but I deny that he can allow ideas to be predicated monadically of minds. There are two reasons for this denial. First, I have no sense of what it might mean ontologically for an idea to be predicated of the mind yet not be a mode or part of the mind. There is no textual evidence of which I am aware that suggests he is thinking in this way. Second, attributing this view to Berkeley immediately introduces skeptical problems. If the ideas that finite minds have are properties of those minds they are thus numerically distinct from those of God. That would make the ideas we directly perceive distinct from the divine ideas that constitute sensible reality. Berkeley cannot consistently allow any such result without serious risk of skepticism, since the ideas we perceive would then constitute an intermediary between the real world and our knowledge of it.

Berkeley's antiskepticism runs deeper than simply his denying the existence of a material substratum. In the preface to the *Three Dialogues Between Hylas and Philonous*, Berkeley makes the stakes quite high. "*Upon the common principles of philosophers, we are not assured of the existence of things from their being perceived. And we are taught to distinguish their real nature from that which falls under our senses. Hence arise* scepticism *and paradoxes. It is not enough that we see and feel, that we taste and smell a thing. Its true nature, its absolute external entity, is still concealed*" (167, emphasis in the original). Anything that separates us from the real nature of things produces skepticism. The claim is perhaps more obviously true for material substances, but it would nonetheless cause embarrassment if it turned out that the ideas we perceive are not in fact real things but only copies of them. Even if one were to suppose that our ideas were copies of God's ideas, doubt could reemerge concerning the perfection of the copies. And Berkeley does

---

12. My thanks to Scott Ragland for raising this concern.

not believe his system will allow for *any* doubt. "*If the principles, which I here endeavour to propagate, are admitted for true; the consequences which, I think, evidently flow from thence, are, that* atheism *and* skepticism *will be utterly destroyed*" (168, emphasis in the original). He is consistent on this point. While engaging Hylas on this very issue, Berkeley has Philonous remark: "It is your opinion, the ideas we perceive by our senses are not real things, but images, or copies of them. Our knowledge therefore is no farther real, than as our ideas are the true representations of those originals. But as these supposed originals are in themselves unknown, it is impossible to know how far our ideas resemble them; or whether they resemble them at all" (3D, 246). The explicit target here, of course, is material archetypes, but the point also applies perfectly well against immaterial archetypes. Any view that creates a numerical difference between the ideas that constitute genuine reality and the (sensory) ideas had by finite minds will engender skepticism. It will always be misleading to say of Berkeley's theory of divine ideas that it is an archetypal theory, even if Berkeley himself on occasion uses that language as well.

Berkeley sometimes argues against archetypes precisely because they are said to be without the mind, and these cases have caused some confusion. "But if they are looked on as notes or images, referred to *things* or *archetypes* existing without the mind, then we are involved all in *scepticism.* We see only the appearances, and not the real qualities of things" (PHK 87). Yet note the parallel use of language. "Without the mind" here means "independent of the mind." Berkeley attacks archetypal views (like Locke's) because they posit archetypal orders that are independent and hence on the other side of the veil of perception.[13] As we have seen, he clarifies his position in the letter quoted above to Samuel Johnson: "I have no objection against calling the ideas in the mind of God archetypes of ours. But I object against those archetypes by philosophers supposed to be real things, and to have an absolute rational existence distinct from their being perceived by any mind whatsoever; it being the opinion of all materialists that an ideal existence in the Divine Mind is one thing, and the real existence of material things another" (Berkeley 1948–57, 2:292–94). To make sense of this remark it is necessary to introduce Johnson's earlier line of questioning as a back-

---

13. Geneviève Brykman has ably argued that archetypes play no role in Berkeley's immaterialism because he uses them only polemically to distance himself from the *material* archetypal views of those like Locke and Malebranche (1987, 103–12). I agree that Berkeley does attempt to distance himself from this kind of archetypal theory but insist that this does not otherwise deny him the use of a theory of divine ideas.

ground. In his letter of 5 February 1730, Johnson pressed Berkeley to clarify his position on the nature of divine ideas. He mistakes Berkeley's insistence that ideas are an "exterior existence" for a theory of archetypes.

> From those and the like expressions, I gathered what I said about the archetypes of our ideas, and thence inferred that there is exterior to us, in the divine mind, a system of universal nature, whereof the ideas we have are in such degree resemblances as the Almighty is pleased to communicate to us.... The divine idea, therefore, of a tree I suppose (or a tree in the divine mind), must be the original or archetype of ours, and ours a copy or image of His (our ideas images of His, in the same sense as our souls are images of Him) of which there may be several, in several created minds, like so many several pictures of the same original to which they are all to be referred. (Berkeley 1948–57, 2:285–86)

What is unusual about this exchange is that Johnson is expanding and enlarging on questions he had already asked in a previous letter (10 September 1729). Berkeley, however, simply refused to address those questions. Only after Johnson continues to voice his concerns does Berkeley finally relent and respond with two short sentences, neither of which actually endorses the reading Johnson advances and attributes to him. Berkeley's real concern about archetypes stems from his fear that insofar as they are not dependent on minds they could introduce skepticism. If archetypes (as Berkeley would say, "if you wish to call them that") are independent, then they *are* without the mind of God and constitute reality. As a result, sometimes Berkeley denies the possibility of archetypes, as when he attacks Lockean versions that marry ontological independence to them. At other times Berkeley is willing to allow the use of the term but only because it aptly describes divine ideas as originals that constitute reality. I cannot explain why Berkeley refuses to straightforwardly admit to Johnson that God's ideas are numerically identical to the ideas of sense had by finite minds (and hence refuses to deny that God's ideas are strictly speaking archetypes in the sense of being originals of which we have copies), but the exchange is suitably odd as to convince me that something is amiss in the correspondence.[14]

With the complications about the language of archetypes behind us, the

---

14. One possible explanation is provided by Berkeley himself, who complains of being ill in his first response to Johnson. Nonetheless, his illness had passed by the time he authored the second letter, which is still mysteriously cryptic concerning the issue of archetypes.

main point is straightforward. Only God's divine world of ideas is genuinely continuous.[15] As God is an atemporal being, the continuity to which I refer is for *us* as finite minds and not a reference to how God perceives the world. Presumably God perceives all ideas immediately and nontemporally; the reference to the continuity of God's ideas is thus shorthand for how God preserves the world as it appears temporally to finite minds. As a result, if our (individual) worlds are to be continuous and independent of us as well, they must be identical with God's world. If we recall a few of Berkeley's central claims, the conclusion seems hard to deny. Berkeley asserts:

(1) We know the appearances of things.
(2) The appearances of things constitute their reality.
(3) Therefore we know the reality of things.

When we add,

(4) Genuine reality is contained only "in" God,

we are driven (with or without Berkeley's consent) to the conclusion that what we know is contained "in" God. Now, however, we see that this implies only that what we see is *preserved* by God (ontologically) in an "external" set of divine ideas (making them volitionally independent of finite minds). Importantly, this does not imply that ideas are enduring beings, but only that the continuity we perceive is maintained (in whatever form) by God. What follows is that we, like God, directly perceive these ideas. We directly perceive an external but mind-dependent reality.

The claim that our sensory ideas are numerically identical to God's archetypes might spark some controversy. David Yandell, for instance, has already argued that it must be false that God perceives the same ideas finite perceivers do (1995, 414–15). Yet this opinion traditionally relies, as it does with Yandell, on the commonly held view that ideas are "in" minds in some literal sense. Berkeley famously says that God knows or has ideas, but they are not carried to Him "by sense" as it is with finite minds (3D, 241, and S 289). We can feel or sense pain, but although God knows pain, He does not sense or feel it as we do. Hence, we cannot perceive the very same ideas God does. Yet this conclusion simply does not follow. It follows only that we do not come to have ideas in the same *way* God does. We "sense" pain; God

---

15. Here I intend "continuous" not in the mathematical sense of "not discrete" but rather in the ordinary sense of "not gappy."

"knows" pain, but there is no suggestion that the pains in question are numerically distinct. It is possible that the difference can be explained by the nature of the relation and not the nature of the relata. The worry, of course, is that if ideas are like modes of the mind, God could not help but feel (sense) pain as we do if He has the idea of pain. But if God's ideas (like all sensory ideas) are external to the substance of God then nothing prevents the relation between God and His archetypes from being different from that of finite ideas and those same archetypes. *And this is exactly the kind of distinction Berkeley invokes.* Consider PC 675: "God May comprehend all Ideas even the Ideas which are painfull & unpleasant without being in any degree pained thereby. Thus we our selves can imagine the pain of a burn etc. without any misery or uneasiness at all." Here the suggestion is that God knows the ideas we sense in a similar manner to how we remember or imagine past pains. Berkeley makes the point generally as well. "God knows or hath ideas; but His ideas are not convey'd to him by sense, as ours are" (3D, 241). The *object* of perception is the same; the *nature of the relation* varies. Robert Muehlmann has already argued at greater length for a similar kind of interpretation, claiming that for Berkeley sensation has two distinct components (1992, 254–55). The first is "hedonic" or sensory and the second is affective. In the case of a pain sensation, the affective element would be the suffering. The upshot is that God can have concepts (ideas) of pain (be related to a perceptual object) without actually enduring pain. Our concepts of pain are concepts because having one involves a different kind of perceptual relation from experiencing a sensation.

All of the traditional interpretations of Berkeley on divine ideas run into this problem (the dicey relationship between God and sensory contents like pain). Although the textual evidence strikes me as compelling, at a minimum readings like Muehlmann's and my own have the virtue of being more charitable to Berkeley. The point remains that asserting numerical identity between our sensory ideas and God's ideas is epistemologically necessary from Berkeley's point of view to defeat skepticism and is at least theologically defensible on the grounds that the nature of the perceptual relation varies for God and finite minds.

Although we now have the position clearly laid out before us, one might object that my reading leaves Berkeley with an incomprehensible view. What exactly does it mean to say that ideas are "external" to but dependent on God? Since ideas are dependent they cannot be substances (and Berkeley tells us that spirit is the only proper substance anyway). And Berkeley indicates in *Principles* 49 that ideas are not modes. So what are they? I think it is clear that Berkeley has carved out a new ontological category, which again I call "quasi substance." A quasi substance is ontologically dependent on other proper substances yet simultaneously distinct from them. This understanding of ideas is coherent and fits well with the rest of Berkeley's system. Motivating this reading of Berkeley in relation to archetypes will occupy us for the remainder of this chapter.

7.3 Permutations

At this point we can formulate four kinds of possible divine idea theories based on the two distinctions mentioned earlier. They are:

(1) *God's ideas are in God and internal to Him.* Divine ideas are both dependent on God and either a mode or proper part of God.

(2) *God's ideas are without God and internal to Him.* Divine ideas can exist without God (they are independent of Him) but are nonetheless somehow a mode or proper part of God. One might make sense of this view by arguing that some parts of God are not essential to Him, although such a claim would engender considerable controversy.

(3) *God's ideas are in God and external to Him.* God's divine ideas depend on Him for their existence, but they are neither a mode nor a proper part of God. Such ideas would be related to God in a relation that was at the very least two place, making them distinct from the nature of God despite their being ontologically dependent on Him.

(4) *God's ideas are without God and external to Him.* This is the familiar Lockean view where divine objects do not depend on God perceiving them. If there were material archetypes, they would fall under this category.

Berkeley, by his own reasoning, can only plausibly endorse the third of these alternatives, but let's examine the other possibilities first to see why they are unsuitable.

Malebranche endorses (1). Our ideas are intellectual concepts in the substance of God. Hence his "Vision in God" thesis. We literally perceive God's ideas within His substance. Berkeley works hard to distance himself from

Malebranche and not only for political reasons. In a 27 November 1710 letter to Percival, he writes "As to what is said of ranking me with Father Malebranche and Mr. Norris, whose writings are thought too fine spun to be of any great use to mankind, I have this to answer: that I think the notions I embrace are not in the least coincident with, or agreeing with, theirs, but indeed plainly inconsistent with them in the main points, insomuch that I know few writers whom I take myself at bottom to differ more from than them" (Berkeley 1948–57, 8:41). To be certain, Berkeley's views do differ from that of Norris and Malebranche and in several important respects. However, his commitment to a divine order of ideas created by God is decidedly Malebranchian, and I speculate that he gained this insight from the famous Frenchman. That is, Berkeley takes Malebranche as his starting point when theorizing about ideas and then diverges from him as he adds his own insights. Importantly, none of Berkeley's reasons for denying an affinity with Malebranche has anything to do with the nature of divine ideas. Yet given that the views are reasonably close in origin, why is Berkeley so adamant about their differences? Although there is a political subtext, Berkeley also has genuine and reasonable objections to other features of Malebranche's philosophy.

> Few men think, yet all will have opinions. Hence, men's opinions are superficial and confused. It is nothing strange that tenets, which in themselves are ever so different, should nevertheless be confounded with each other by those who do not consider them attentively. I shall not therefore be surprised, if some men imagine that I run into the enthusiasm of Malebranche, though in truth I am very remote from it. He builds on the most abstract general ideas, which I entirely disclaim. He asserts an absolute external world, which I deny. He maintains we are deceived by our senses, and know not the real natures or the true forms and figures of extended things; of all which I hold the direct contrary. So that upon the whole there are no principles more fundamentally opposite than his and mine. (3D, 214, added in the 1734 edition)

Berkeley lists his complaints. (1) Malebranche relies on abstract ideas. (2) He asserts the existence of an external material world, which serves no explanatory purpose and is odious to God's simplicity of design. And (3) he preserves the structures that allow for the same pernicious skepticism that Locke engendered with his views.[16]

Nicholas Jolley has highlighted the first point, rightly arguing that Malebranchian ideas in God share the same problematic indeterminacy as Lockean abstract ideas do (1996, esp. 544–48). I engage Berkeley's views on abstraction in more detail in the next chapter, but it is also clear why he objects to (2) and (3). He denies the duality of worlds between the mental and physical and similarly rejects the skeptical dangers he sees arising from such a division. Berkeley will not advocate any theory that maintains an intermediary between minds and ultimate reality.

Yet are these differences enough for us to conclude, as Berkeley does, that "there are no principles more fundamentally opposite than [Malebranche's] and [his]?" I have my doubts. Berkeley was perhaps too eager to argue that his principles conformed to the beliefs of the common person and insofar as Malebranche's views were already popularly thought of as unusual and decidedly not mainstream, it only makes sense that Berkeley would labor diligently and vociferously to distance himself from the shadow of Malebranche. It was not until after he received critical reviews of his main works that he added pointed sections to later editions trying to separate himself from the likes of Norris and Malebranche. Furthermore, Berkeley's system, especially the underlying theory of ideas, nonetheless has some affinities with Malebranche's doctrine of Vision in God.

So then why not conclude that, despite his protestations, Berkeley did accept that God's ideas are in God and internal to Him and therefore hold that divine ideas are modes or proper parts of God? I take the reasons to be fairly straightforward. The most pressing one concerns the passivity of God. God is an entirely active being, *purus actus,* and ideas are essentially passive and inert. To allege that God's ideas are a mode or part of God is to allege that a part of God is passive, a conclusion Berkeley would be loath to allow. Furthermore, in *Principles* 49 Berkeley seems to rule out the possibility that ideas are either modes or (as would apply to God) attributes, in part because he thinks that such modifications literally qualify the subject. God certainly

---

16. Interestingly, Berkeley does *not* explicitly distance himself here from Malebranche's occasionalism as one might otherwise expect. Consider *PC* 548: "We move our Legs our selves. 'tis we that will their movement. Herein I differ from Malbranch." His resistance to occasionalism in the published works is more circumspect, as in 3*D*, 237, where his separation is cautious. "I have nowhere said that God is the only agent who produces all the motions in bodies." The complications of Berkeley's views about occasionalism need not delay us here.

does not take on the properties of the ideas He perceives (at least not all of them); hence this account cannot be right. Thus Berkeley has reason to distance himself from the position that God's ideas are in God and internal to Him not just because of its affinity with Malebranche but also because there are philosophical concerns that militate against supposing that divine ideas are modifications of God.

Berkeley cannot endorse either the suggestion that God's ideas are without God and internal to Him or the suggestion that God's ideas are without God and external to Him (options 2 and 4 listed above for possible divine idea theories) since both of these deny the dependent nature of ideas. The *esse* of ideas is *percipi*. *All* ideas are fundamentally (ontologically) dependent beings, even those (perhaps especially those) perceived by God. If God's ideas constitute sensible reality, then even if our ideas were perfect copies of those divine ideas we would still not directly perceive reality. The problem of skepticism dominates Berkeley's thinking—so much so that the introduction to the *Principles* presents the work as one that promises to eliminate it. His skeptical worries preclude him from endorsing any theory that would reintroduce a veil in a representative theory of perception.

That leaves the theory that God's ideas are ontologically dependent on and external to the divine mind. I hasten to emphasize here that the dependence of God's ideas does not imply that God's ideas are dependent in any way on finite minds. They are, nonetheless, essentially dependent beings. God created an ideal order external to Himself and during sensation we directly perceive those very divine ideas.[17] And what should we say about Berkeley's occasional invocation of archetype/ectype language? On my analysis, ectypes only exist for ideas of the imagination. The sensory ideas we perceive simply *are* reality. The distinction nonetheless makes sense because we do dream and hallucinate and otherwise have ectypal ideas of the imagination. Berkeley is not as lucid as one might like in his published works, but in his notebooks he makes a fortuitously explicit claim: "Ideas of Sense are the Real things or Archetypes. Ideas of Imagination, Dreams, etc. are copies, images of these" (*PC* 823).[18] A more compelling bit of supporting evidence

---

17. A point of clarification. One might object that this interpretation reintroduces an intermediary in perception since God must have had ideas of the divine archetypes before He created them (hence we do not directly perceive God's ideas at all). As I hope is already clear, this is a misunderstanding. God's ideas—our sensory ideas—just *are* the originals. In this sense Berkeley's divine ideas are not properly archetypes at all (because there is no original/copy distinction). God perceives all of them continually (for however long they exist). The ontic nature of ideas (external but dependent beings) places them (figuratively) "outside" of God's mind, but they are no less God's ideas.

18. Note that the " + " mark does *not* appear next to this entry.

would be hard to find. If our sensory ideas were ectypes in any way then Berkeley would have effectively reintroduced the veil of perception he has labored so hard to remove. We therefore have good reason not only to reject the alternatives but also to endorse (3) as Berkeley's considered view. The real test of my interpretation, naturally, will come when we examine how well it handles the problems that theories of divine ideas allegedly cannot overcome. I turn now to those challenges.

7.4 Defending Berkeley's Theory of Divine Ideas

There are a number of difficulties, as mentioned earlier, in attributing any theory of divine ideas to Berkeley, yet overall my reading is a decidedly stronger contender than any of the traditional theories attributed to Berkeley inside the early modern tale. I do not wish my defense of this account of Berkeley to be confused with a defense of its overall philosophical merit, but I do argue that my interpretation makes him more philosophically respectable than the alternatives. Berkeley's position on these matters is more sophisticated than generally recognized.

My interpretation lets us solve one problem immediately. In an immaterialist world where we directly perceive divine sensory ideas we are in perfect contact with the world as it is. Thus Berkeley could reasonably think that his metaphysical system in fact eliminates skepticism. That my reading of Berkeley explains his conviction is, to my mind, nearly worth the price of admission alone. Yet some might still have certain concerns about my interpretation.

7.4.1 Privacy

A straightforward consequence of asserting that ideas had by finite minds are numerically identical to those of God is that we might not always be able to tell whether any of "my" ideas are exclusive or "private" to me. It might be the case that the very (sensory) idea I perceive now is also being perceived by another finite mind (in a case where two persons perceive the same divine idea). As a consequence, "my" ideas are not logically dependent on my perceiving them, which straightforwardly denies the privacy of ideas. This line of reasoning runs directly counter to a traditional understanding of Berkeley as a thinker who encodes the privacy of ideas into the foundations of his philosophy.[19] In his excellent study of Berkeley, Robert Muehlmann explicitly defends the privacy thesis at some length. Early in *Berkeley's Ontology* Muehlmann writes: "I take *idealism* to be *two* theses: *first,* sensed *qualities* cannot exist apart from, **and are unique to,** the mind of one who perceives them; *second,* sensible *objects*—apples, stones, trees, books, and 'houses, mountains, rivers'—cannot exist apart from the mind of *some* percipient or other" (1992, 13, bold emphasis mine). Muehlmann believes that Berkeley's idealism requires that sensed qualities "are unique to" the mind that perceives them. I do not contest the fact that this is a natural thought, but that does not mean that Berkeley either endorsed this thought as his final position or that his theory entails it. The *esse* is *percipi* thesis holds that ideas require minds to exist; it does *not* require that an existing idea be related to only one mind at a time. In one sense the privacy thesis is *trivially* false, since God perceives all the (sensory or archetypal) ideas I do as a part of his omniscience.[20] Hence my sensory ideas do not really logically depend on my having them anyway, since God ultimately preserves them. The logic strikes me as compelling.

Naturally, Muehlmann's position is more sophisticated than this first gloss, and he provides an argument for the claim that sensory ideas are private. The argument, in short, depends on Berkeley's purposeful conflation of first sensations (i.e., qualities) and ideas and then of acts of sensation and the objects of sensation. As to the first move, Muehlmann is most certainly right. Berkeley straightforwardly identifies sensations with ideas.

> Light and colours, heat and cold, extension and figures, in a word the things we see and feel, what are they but so many sensations, notions, ideas or impressions on the sense; and is it possible to separate, even in thought, any of these from perception? (*PHK* 5)

> Qualities, as hath been shewn, are nothing else but *sensations* or *ideas,* which exist only in a *mind* perceiving them; and this is true not only of the ideas we are acquainted with at present, but likewise of all possible ideas whatsoever. (*PHK* 78)

---

19. As we shall see shortly, Stoneham is just one example of those who think that Berkeley's ideas are essentially private insofar as they are "relativized" to particular minds (2002, 171).

20. Berkeley allows that God can *perceive* sensory ideas without actually *sensing* them (*PC* 675). Dancy defends what is in effect a stronger view, namely that God perceives all possible ideas (1987, 70–72).

Berkeley consistently treats ideas and sensations as the same kind of object. They are both mind-dependent entities whose *esse* is *percipi*. On this point we agree.

Muehlmann, however, errs when he further argues that Berkeley conflates the act of sensation with the object of sensation.[21] Now I should say at the outset that this is no gross error; there are plausible reasons for being tempted into this position, not the least of which is that Berkeley appears to have carelessly flirted with endorsing it.

The most important bit of text comes in the *Three Dialogues* with what Muehlmann calls the "tulip-smelling argument":

> PHILONOUS: Make me to understand the difference between what is immediately perceived, and a sensation.
> HYLAS: The sensation I take to be an act of the mind perceiving; beside which, there is something perceived; and this I call the *object*. For example, there is red and yellow on that tulip. But then the act of perceiving those colours is in me only, and not in the tulip. (195)

On Muehlmann's reading this is the start of an argument designed to show that there is no distinction between act and object when it comes to sensations (smellings, suffering pains, etc.). Hylas raises the distinction in an attempt to defend a mind-independent external reality. It is thus natural to suppose that Berkeley would attack this move by denying the posited distinction. Initially one might be led to think that this is his strategy:

> PHILONOUS: I see you have no mind to be pressed that way. To return then to your distinction between *sensation* and *object*; if I take you right, you distinguish in every perception two things, the one an action of the mind, the other not.
> HYLAS: True. (195)

This exchange appears to be the start of a discussion of the relevant distinction between act and object. In fact, however, it is not. Instead, Philonous turns to engage the concept of an active mind during perception. I will now

---

21. Muehlmann's language here is occasionally confusing, as he typically writes of the conflation as one between "sensation" and "object of sensation." That he means *acts* of sensation in the first case is clear from the context of his analysis. I speculate that this infelicity of language might well have contributed to his erroneously endorsing the act-object distinction in Berkeley's analysis of perception, even though I grant that the view is superficially plausible.

reproduce an extended bit of the relevant core of the remaining argument with omissions.

> PHILONOUS: In plucking this flower, I am active, because I do it by the motion of my hand, which was consequent upon my volition; so likewise in applying it to my nose. But is either of these smelling?
>
> HYLAS: No. . . .
>
> PHILONOUS: But I do not find my will concerned any farther. Whatever more there is, as that I perceive such a particular smell or any smell at all, this is independent of my will, and therein I am altogether passive. Do you find it otherwise with you, Hylas?
>
> HYLAS: No, the very same. . . .
>
> PHILONOUS: Tell me now, whether *seeing* consists in perceiving light and colours, or in opening and turning the eyes?
>
> HYLAS: Without doubt, in the former.
>
> PHILONOUS: Since therefore you are in the very perception of light and colours altogether passive, what is become of that action you were speaking of, as an ingredient in every sensation? And doth it not follow from your own concessions, that the perception of light and colours, including no action in it, may exist in an unperceiving substance? And is not this a plain contradiction?
>
> HYLAS: I know not what to think of it.
>
> PHILONOUS: Besides, since you distinguished the *active* and *passive* in every perception, you must do it in that of pain. But how is it possible that pain, be it as little active as you please, should exist in an unperceiving substance? In short, do but consider the point, and then confess ingenuously, whether light and colours, tastes, sounds, &c. are not all equally passions or sensations in the soul. You may indeed call them *external objects,* and give them in words what subsistence you please. But examine your own thoughts, and then tell me whether it be not as I say? (196–97)

At the end of his analysis of this same extended passage, Muehlmann concludes that the "traditional" way of reading the passage, namely, as an argument that denies any distinction between acts of sensation and the objects of sensation, is the best. Muehlmann therefore claims that Berkeley takes as established that "in the immediate perception of the proper objects of sense, no distinction can be drawn between a *sensation* and an *object* of that sensation" (1992, 197, emphasis in the original). Muehlmann grants that there is a distinction between perception and commonsense objects but maintains that when it comes to the *proper* objects of *sensation* (objects that are the specific and immediate objects of a particular sense modality, like light and color to sight), there is no distinction between *smelling* and the *proper* object of smelling.

Applying this analysis to the larger privacy problem, we might construct an argument for the claim that ideas must be unique to a mind. Muehlmann does not himself offer up this explicit argument nor is his analysis concerning the tulip-smelling argument specifically targeted at the uniqueness of perception. I believe, however, that it is a reasonable argument that anyone following Muehlmann's interesting analysis might be tempted to employ. Hence it deserves consideration.

(1) Berkeley identifies ideas and sensations (qualities).
(2) Berkeley identifies acts of sensations and the proper objects of sensations (qualities).
(3) Sensory acts are unique to their percipients.
(4) Hence ideas are unique to their percipients.[22]

If Muehlmann is right, this argument constitutes a serious objection to my thesis that finite minds directly perceive God's divine ideas as sensible reality. In private correspondence Muehlmann has confessed that the uniqueness claim "seems straightforwardly to follow from Berkeley's identification of 'idea' with 'sensation,' an identification that is more obvious in the *Three Dialogues* than in the *Principles*."[23] As I have already indicated, I think that Muehlmann is *right* when he claims that Berkeley identifies ideas and sensations (qualities). The issue, however, is whether this identification entails that ideas (and sensations) are unique to their percipients.

The key premise is (2). Unlike Muehlmann, I do not think Berkeley identifies sensory acts and the objects (proper or otherwise) of sensations. With respect to this conclusion I essentially agree with Winkler's analysis of the same passage (1989, 7–8). Berkeley's intent in the "tulip-smelling argument" is to show that *minds are passive in sensory perception*. The motivation for Berkeley to do this is clear and compelling. He wants to defend a view that he thinks is like commonsense realism, which requires that his theory preserve the volitional independence of our sensory experiences (i.e., that the

---

22. My thanks to Tapio Korte for helping me to clarify the formulation of this argument.
23. I want to thank Robert Muehlmann for generously allowing me to reproduce some of our correspondence.

sensory world appears in our experience as independent of our wills). As a result, when Hylas presents the distinction between act and object as a distinction between two items, "the one an action of the mind, the other not," Berkeley needs to demonstrate that the former item (that the mind is always active and never passive during perception) is not strictly true, at least in one important sense. There are two senses in which minds are active. The first is with respect to the actual perception of an idea. The mind is always active when perceiving (it is doing something). But there is a second sense in which the mind may be passive, namely in terms of the *generation* (or origination) of the ideas it perceives. Some of the ideas a finite mind perceives are perceived involuntarily. Thus, the mind is passive with respect to the cause of the idea (as opposed to ideas of the imagination, which the mind generates itself). In sensory perception minds must be passive. If he fails to prove that minds are passive in this sense, then solipsism and skepticism are not far away. Berkeley holds that sensory ideas constitute the real things of the world. But if my ideas and yours are both private and unique to us, there is no meaningful sense in which we can both perceive the same real world. In effect, the uniqueness claim undermines Berkeley's deeply held antiskepticism.

This understanding of Berkeley's aim seems well confirmed by how the passage unfolds. Philonous moves from the introduction of the distinction to a discussion not of the putative identity of act and object but of the *activity of the mind* in perception. As it turns out, we learn that in sensing (seeing and smelling and the like), the *sensing* is not the drawing of air into the nose or such actions but the perceiving of the proper objects of that sense. It is at this point that Muehlmann may allege that the identification is being made. What it is to smell just is to perceive the proper object of smell. Yet this is, to my mind, manifestly not the emphasis of the argument. When Berkeley says through Philonous that "*seeing* consists in perceiving light and colours" (197), his intention is not to make an identification but to note the essentially dependent and passive nature of the sensory process. That is, seeing is a species of perceiving—a species that takes proper objects. This speculation is confirmed by Philonous's next speech, where he notes that the perception of light and color includes "no action in it." And in the following speech (extending the analysis to pain) the lesson is that sensations like pain are all equally "passions or sensations in the soul" that cannot exist in an unperceiving substance. That is, sensations are *ontologically* dependent on minds, just not *volitionally* dependent. I thus submit that Berkeley's goal in these passages is to preserve the volitional independence of the sensory world in his system.

We have not, however, reached the end of the matter. Muehlmann might draw some comfort from the 1710 edition of the *Principles,* where in the last sentence of the fifth paragraph Berkeley writes: "In truth the object and the sensation are the same thing, and cannot therefore be abstracted from each other." There can be little doubt that *here* Berkeley is flirting with exactly the position Muehlmann wishes to ascribe to him. But as we have seen (in section 6.3), Berkeley *removed* this passage from subsequent editions. What he replaced it with—"Hence as it is impossible for me to see or feel anything without an actual sensation of that thing, so is it impossible for me to conceive in my thoughts any sensible thing or object distinct from the sensation or perception of it"—indicates that he cannot *separate* the object from the sensation. This rendition is consistent with the *esse* is *percipi* principle. Why would Berkeley remove an *explicit* identity claim that is perfectly clear and replace it with a weaker claim that does not even suggest the same identity? One plausible answer is that Berkeley recognized that the identity claim was a mistake. If he kept the identity claim, then he could not reasonably defend the volitional independence of the experienced world inside his system, a claim he trumpets in both the *Three Dialogues* and the *Principles.*[24]

Perhaps the problem is a matter of emphasis. Muehlmann underscores Berkeley's adherence to the identification of sensation and the objects of sensation and then proceeds to note the difficulties that this move makes for his metaphysics later. I, alternatively, wish to downplay the early identification in order to preserve more of Berkeley's subsequent moves. I am not entirely resistant to this characterization, but I think my view has important benefits. Textually I can explain why he flirted with the view and then rejected it, *and* I can provide Berkeley with a more philosophically potent system in the final analysis. The conjunction strikes me as convincing. At the end of the day, when faced with two plausible readings of the text, we ought to prefer the one that remains historically sensitive while improving the quality of the philosophical insights.

Another important position that Berkeley defends would be threatened were we to accept Muehlmann's identification. As we saw in section 6.2 (as well as in section 5.5), Berkeley argues that God can perceive our pains without actually sensing them. This argument implies that the *object* is distinct

---

24. Muehlmann provides his own explanation for why Berkeley removed the last line of *PHK* 5 from the 1734 edition, arguing that "it proves too much" when his point was only to preclude the possibility of sensory qualities existing independently in matter (1992, 141ff).

from the sensation: "God May comprehend all Ideas even the Ideas which are painfull & unpleasant without being in any degree pained thereby" (*PC* 675). Berkeley *needs* the distinction to explain how God can be omniscient and yet not suffer. On my reading, his mature theory solves this problem quite well. The objects of perception and sensation are the same; it is the nature of the relation that varies.

To my knowledge, at no time does Berkeley ever assert that sensory ideas are wedded to particular individuals.[25] He carefully maintains in his final published works the view that ideas depend for their existence *only on some mind or other*. Ideas of imagination may still remain unique to the mind that conjures them, and thus Berkeley can continue to do some justice to our intuitions about the privacy of ideas but only insofar as they extend to the imagination. Certain passages *can* be reasonably read as endorsing privacy for ideas but none of them explicitly so. More importantly, to preserve the coherence of his larger system and to be charitable to Berkeley, none of them *ought* to be read that way.

No doubt it is a natural inclination to treat all ideas as private (as being like our "own" images) and so Berkeley (or contemporary readers) might occasionally lapse. Yet Berkeley can even explain why we have this tendency in the first place. The alleged uniqueness of ideas is a holdover from materialism. On Locke's view, for instance, ideas are private intermediaries between our minds and the external material world. The objective nature of the world is preserved by the material objects, not our ideas, and hence the difficulty is not as apparent. But the cost of uniqueness is representationalism and skepticism. Because we have some propensity to think of the world materialistically, it is understandable why one might easily slide into thinking that our ideas are unique to us. It might sound odd to say that our sensory perceptions are not genuinely private, but Berkeley can simply exhort us to set aside the vulgar confusions that stem from this mistaken adherence to materialism. If God is the author of the sensible world, in what sense *could* our ideas be genuinely private? At least God would always share them.[26] The only ideas that are truly our own are those we conjure ourselves.

25. One might object that although Berkeley does not explicitly assert this, he does so implicitly. At *PHK* 4 he writes that we perceive nothing other than "our own ideas or sensations." On my reading of Berkeley, however, the ownership of an idea is nothing more than being in a particular two-place relation with it. Here, as elsewhere (e.g., *3D*, 248), Berkeley is asserting only that this relation holds for a certain person. When I say that I am having an idea, I mean that I am in a particular relation with that idea. When I speak of "my" ideas, I refer to the set of ideas that are relata in perceptual relations with me. Possessive pronouns fix one end of the relation, nothing more. I find nothing odd or unusual about this given Berkeley's system.

26. Again, this does not entail that God senses as we do. See *PC* 675.

Even so, one might think that Muehlmann has additional resources to resist my analysis. Since Muehlmann does not use the "tulip-smelling" argument to explicitly push for the uniqueness of ideas to particular minds, perhaps there is a better way of characterizing his position, one that is tied to its explanatory power. According to Muehlmann, Berkeley's adherence to the uniqueness of ideas does philosophical work inside his system. It explains why Berkeley would think that ideas generally must be mind dependent in the first place. Ideas are like sensations, and since sensations like pain are (apparently) private, it follows that ideas must be private as well. There is an order of exposition in Berkeley's thinking about this issue. In order to show that commonsense things like mountains and cherries are mind dependent, he first endeavors to demonstrate that sensory qualities are mind dependent. So Muehlmann might well respond this way: what is *your* explanation for why Berkeley is so confident that ideas and sensations are mind dependent?

The question is a fair one, and my answer is straightforward. Like most of the other moderns, Berkeley simply could not imagine an idea without an owner (just as there can not be the *experience* of color without something doing the experiencing). We do not *need* an additional reason to make the view reasonable. On Muehlmann's account, because sensations are private, it follows that they are dependent. Thus since ideas are like sensations, ideas must be private and dependent as well. On my interpretation, Berkeley perhaps *at first* believed the privacy account (in the *Notebooks* and the early edition of the *Principles*) but then *later* came to realize the disaster that accompanied such a claim. Fortunately, Berkeley had an out. Ideas could still be dependent without being unique to a particular mind. This feature is true for sensory ideas generally, so it could be true for sensations as well. My account explains why Berkeley backed down from the claim made in the 1710 edition of *PHK* 5 and why explicit references to uniqueness are nowhere else to be found in his later works.[27] It is worth noting that in all of these challenges, none of the concerns is a straightforwardly *philosophical* worry. They are *textual* concerns. Given that I believe I have made a plausible case on textual grounds for my reading, we should prefer my account precisely because of the philosophical advantages we can accrue without sacrificing allegiance to what Berkeley actually wrote.

27. Berkeley explicitly takes up the issue of whether two finite minds can perceive the same house in the *Three Dialogues* (3D, 247), but that discussion is not strictly about the uniqueness of my ideas. Instead, the passage concerns whether multiple minds are able to perceive the same common sense objects (like houses). For a fuller treatment of that passage, see Hight 2007a, esp. 448–50.

As a small afterthought, assuming that my account is correct, one might have some qualms about the nature and number of divine ideas. One could ask whether God has an idea for each bit of content that *could be* perceived (including those that in fact never are) or only ideas for those things *actually* perceived by finite minds (at some time or other). I do not have an answer here, nor am I certain that Berkeley has one (see Dancy 1987, 70–72). Presumably Berkeley would opt, ceteris paribus, for the response most consistent with the simple nature of God, saying that God does not need to preserve ideas where there is no demand to do so. Perhaps God's omniscience indicates that God perceives all possibilities. I see no obstacle to or serious defect in either option. There might well be many more divine ideas if God preserves all those that simply *might* be perceived, but that in and of itself presents no difficulty. Even if God must maintain an idea for every qualitatively distinct potential experience, that admission does not undermine the textual or philosophical advantages of my reading.

7.4.2 *Privacy Revisited: Stoneham's Relativized Ideas*

One might question my analysis of the privacy of ideas in another way, this time with explicit reference to the claim that finite minds perceive the numerically same ideas as God. This challenge to my account comes from Tom Stoneham, who urges that God cannot possibly perceive the numerically same ideas as finite minds because ideas are intrinsically relativized to the individual perceiving minds. God cannot perceive the same idea as a finite mind because simply changing the perceiving mind ipso facto changes the idea as well. When it comes to what it means to be perceived, Stoneham rejects a cluster of views he calls "theocentric" (2002, 170). These are views that ascribe to God some role in sustaining and hence perceiving ideas. He notes two problems with assigning God such a role. The first is familiar: God does not sense. Hence God cannot perceive ideas of sense. I have already addressed this worry, arguing that the *object* is the same but the nature of the perceptual relation varies, thus allowing for finite minds to perceive the numerically same ideas as God. The second issue, Stoneham's contention that ideas are "relativized qualities," however, raises a new challenge to my position. The view that God and finite minds sometimes perceive the numerically same ideas, Stoneham argues, "faces the further problem that it needs us to make sense of a particular idea being in or being perceived by more than one mind. If, as I have argued, an idea is a relativized quality, such as the-green-of-this-grass-to-me-now, then God cannot stand in the same relation to it as the finite subject of that idea" (171). The argument depends on Stoneham's contention that ideas are relativized qualities. As should be obvious, I deny that this characterization of an idea is Berkeley's. So, to begin with, why does Stoneham think otherwise?

Stoneham arrives at this view first by analyzing why Berkeley was committed to the perceptual dependence of ideas. For Locke, "free-floating" qualities were unacceptable, since allowing such detached qualities would preclude us from being able to describe the world. Meaningful propositions typically state relations between sensible things, and unless qualities are "tied" to something (e.g., a substratum) we cannot make clusters of quality attributions at all. To use Stoneham's example, unless yellow and a sweet smell are grounded in something, we have no way of knowing whether our visual sensation of yellow is connected to our sweet olfactory experience and indeed whether either of them are related to a rose or something else. Locke simply could not imagine qualities that were not qualities of anything (167). Such is Locke's picture. Berkeley, however, finds the inherence relation equally as mysterious and thus adopts a different theory of the objects of quality predication. What ties down qualities for Berkeley are *minds*. To group several disparate qualities we do not require some mind-independent material substance; we only require a mind to organize the qualities together. Such a view need not commit Berkeley to literal predication (such that perceiving yellow makes the mind yellow) since he provides a separate theory of quality predication that identifies qualities and ideas.

Stoneham's account is plausible and intuitive, but I think it is not Berkeley's. Stoneham's analysis depends on the traditional understanding of an idea being "in" the mind. He assumes that an idea can only be in one finite mind. The assertion is reasonable if one construes "in" more literally (as if ideas qualify or are a part of the mind), but as we have seen Berkeley uses "in" to mean merely ontological dependence. To say that an idea is "in" a mind only indicates that that mind at least partially is involved in sustaining that idea. Nothing logically precludes more than one mind from sustaining an idea. Indeed, common sense demands otherwise, since how else might we be certain that we are engaging one another in the same world? If I cannot perceive *any* of the ideas you perceive, solipsism and skepticism, repugnant to Berkeley, are yet again not far away.

What "ties down" qualities in Berkeley's system is *God*. God arranges and orders the ideas we perceive (and who perceives them). If we try to conceptualize the system without God, then what we are left with is something like a brute-fact Humean trope theory. We simply realize that the universe is ordered such that certain qualities come bundled together in regular patterns. But *I* do not organize those bundles (and you do not either). Instead, we all discover more or less the same regularities in the ideas/qualities we perceive. There is, to my mind, no compelling need in Berkeley's system to assume that perception *must* be private. Indeed, there are good reasons to think he needs to deny exactly that it is. The first I have already mentioned: it is necessary to avoid skepticism. Second, Berkeley wants to preserve (to the extent he can) our commonsense understandings of the world. Relativizing ideas denies what Berkeley explicitly asserts, namely that we can meaningfully say that we (i.e., multiple distinct minds) perceive the same thing. To be certain, the exact sense in which this claim is true is unusual, since we are referring in this case only to specific ideas in the same sense modality (Berkeley's heterogeneity thesis denies that we see the same objects we feel). Furthermore, since Berkeley takes commonsense objects to be congeries of ideas, there are complications about when and whether two minds perceive the "same" commonsense object. Yet neither of these complications denies that two minds perceive the numerically same ideas of sense. The commonsense assertion Berkeley retains is that your senses function like mine, and you see (immediately) exactly what I see (and so on for the other sense modalities). There might be difficulties with whether you "see" the same *house* I do, since a house is a large collection of ideas and strictly speaking we do not (immediately) "see" *houses* at all, but there is no difficulty over whether you see the same immediate square patch of red that I do.[28] To deny that we can perceive the same immediate objects is to deny our most fundamental assumptions about how the world works.

Lastly, it is worth noting that Stoneham's depiction of Berkeleian ideas is motivated by an alleged story of how Berkeley explains what ties qualities together. The relativized nature of ideas for Berkeley is not the conclusion of an *argument* that forces one to accept that they are relativized given either what Berkeley says or other positions he holds. Instead, the supposition that ideas are relativized qualities is a smart (but I think false) *hypothesis* meant to explain how Berkeley "ties down" qualities into commonsense objects. Stoneham offers a similar analysis (64–71) of the pain argument we engaged in the previous section, but beyond that he provides no textual evidence that Berkeley believes that ideas (as the immediate objects of perception) are either private or relativized. I have argued at length in this chapter that

---

28. Pappas denies my claim here, arguing that for Berkeley we immediately perceive common sense objects (2000, esp. 172–78). That extended engagement lies beyond the scope of this work. For a detailed treatment, see Hight (2007b).

precisely the reverse is the case. To maintain a maximal number of his other philosophical claims, one must reject the notion that he regards ideas as private, and the texts reasonably support the hypothesis that he did not so regard them.

7.4.3 Continuity and Inertness

Despite my defense of Berkeley against the charge that ideas are private, one might press related concerns. One worry is the problem of continuity for sensible objects. Since my ideas only exist when perceived, if those ideas are dependent only on me then their existence is fragmented at best. But if there is no privacy for my ideas because they are numerically identical with those "in" (i.e., ontologically dependent on) God or other minds, then the continuity of sensible objects is guaranteed, or at least explained. The tree I see outside my window is the "same" tree as I saw five minutes ago, because its continuity is preserved in a divine world of ideas to which I have access. One might object, as Stubenberg does, that this view only guarantees that *something* exists when I close my eyes but not necessarily the same tree as I saw earlier (1990, 225). Note that the challenge here concerns not sensory ideas as the immediate objects of perception but commonsense objects that are complex congeries of ideas. There is no inconsistency between my analysis of Stoneham's concern and my response here. For Berkeley, Stubenberg's complaint is not a worry. It may simply happen that God continuously creates numerically distinct but qualitatively similar divine ideas over time. From our perspective, whether there is one set of numerically identical ideas or a larger set filled with distinct but qualitatively identical ideas, nothing changes. On the other hand, if we do discover qualitative differences, then the sameness of the tree becomes a verbal dispute, based on how one wants to capture "sameness" without respect to qualitative identity.[29] Since we have no access to other methods that could guarantee an answer, Stubenberg is asking for an answer no finite mind can provide. Whether it is one idea or many that preserves the apparent continuity of the sensible world, all we really know is that the world appears continuous. Generally speaking, so long as I perceive divine ideas—and the tree I perceive now and the one I perceive later are qualitatively identical—there are no other issues to resolve.[30] The trees are the same trees in the only sense of "same" that mat-

---

29. See 3D, 247, where Berkeley claims that such disputes about sameness are idle.
30. I develop and extend this same point about judgments of diachronic identity with respect to Berkeley's theory of bodily resurrection in Hight 2007a, esp. 448–53.

ters. When I perceive differences in my ideas over time, I can track certain patterns and continuities in what I sense, and no other pretensions or abstractions will tell me more about the world as I perceive it. The world as perceived is neither fragmentary nor discontinuous. Only philosophers invoking disreputable abstractions might think otherwise. As a result, the initial worry most have about Berkeley's system—that it makes our world(s) fragmentary and discontinuous—depends on concerns that simply do not apply. We *do* notice a regularity and constancy in our perceptions, and that is enough for Berkeley.[31]

The most frequently cited worry, however, stems from Berkeley's firm claim that ideas are utterly inert (Mabbott 1968, 372). God allegedly causes me to have the sensory ideas I do. Yet those ideas cannot be caused by the divine ideas in God, since ideas are passive. What role, then, do divine ideas play in the ontology? Should we not use Ockham's razor to remove this odious appendage to his system? Stubenberg also raises this as a difficulty. "This consideration suggests that God's ideas, construed as archetypes, play no role in the explanation of the sensory ideas of created beings. Thus, paradoxically, divine ideas appear as dispensable ontological baggage" (1990, 224).

We might, however, see a reason for reintroducing divine ideas if we consider the difference between divine and finite knowledge of reality. If God is going to cause me to have an idea, and that idea is a real thing, then God must be creating something independent of my volition. God does not need archetypes to cause me to have ideas, but *we* need divine ideas to perceive a real, continuous, unfragmented world.[32] If Berkeley's immaterial world is to be continuous and ultimately real, then he needs to establish it in a way that allows our access to it while preventing skeptical problems. The order of ideas set down by God is Berkeley's hypothesis about how this works. As a result, divine ideas are created by God *for us,* not simply for Himself. This also helps to explain why people can err in perception. When we err, we do not create ideas that inadequately resemble reality. Instead, we make poor inferences on the basis of the "real" ideas themselves. Error

---

31. Berkeley even argues for the existence of God on the basis of this regularity. Since he argues *from* continuity *to* the existence of God, that is a good signal that he does not think he can completely characterize the divine realm. After all, he cannot use as premises in his arguments claims about a reality created by a being he is trying to prove exists. The divine ideas of God are an explanatory *result*, a hypothesis used to explain the sensible experiences we have.

32. That the divine order is required *for us* and not God also helps remove worries about why God would have a set of ideas that are temporally ordered. God, as an atemporal being, does not require temporal ordering. What ordering exists is for our benefit.

is the result of mental operation and does not create or distort the order of reality by introducing new "false" ideas. Ideas of imagination are dependent on our wills,[33] as Berkeley says, and are less real only because of that dependence on our mental activity.[34] As a result, Stubenberg's criticism applies only if one *preserves* the numerical distinction between the ideas "in" God and those in finite minds. Since I deny that distinction, the worry does not arise.

Mabbott, in presenting a similar objection to Berkeley, considers the possibility that our ideas are numerically identical with the divine ideas of God. He dismisses this option because it "is still open to the objection that things passive and inert can be no part of God" (1968, 372). Yandell pursues the same course, explicitly identifying the claim with Malebranche's "Vision in God" doctrine. "Our ideas, since they are ideas of sensation, cannot therefore be perceived by God. Moreover, Philonous has said in the Second Dialogue that we do not perceive God's ideas (3D, 215). There is plainly no doctrine of vision in God, nor any doctrine that we perceive God's ideas, in Berkeley's theory" (1995, 414). Others have engaged the possibility of identifying our sensory ideas with the ideas of God and rejected it as well.[35] Yandell's claim that in the *Three Dialogues* Philonous denies that we perceive God's ideas is puzzling, since that passage does not seem to support his claim.

> From all which I conclude, *there is a mind which affects me every moment with all the sensible impressions I perceive*. And from the

---

33. 3D, 235, represents Berkeley's basic, unreflective view. Ideas of the imagination are dependent on our wills, ideas of sense are not. A serious problem arises here, however, since at one point (PC 548) Berkeley appears to argue that we can cause nonimaginary ideas when we will the voluntary motion of our limbs. Berkeley also introduces a robust conception of free will to deflect the problem of evil (3D, 237), further complicating the issue by requiring that he have a system that preserves the volitional independence of reality while maintaining free moral responsibility for agents in their actions. Berkeley clearly needs a criterion for distinguishing among perceptions of one's own actions, one's own imaginings, and the ideas one's voluntary actions cause in others. I have no acceptable solution to this problem, although Stoneham does an excellent job of discussing the variants (2002, 192–99).

34. There is yet another related difficulty. For Berkeley there is no such thing as misperception, only mistaken judgments based on perception. If I perceive a mirage, Berkeley is committed to the claim that I am accurately seeing an idea, and a divine idea. Yet such ideas are not "real" on Berkeley's view because they are not connected to other ideas in an orderly (natural) fashion (see PHK 33). So why would God create such ideas that cohere poorly with the rest of the divine order? What explains why we *appear* to "misperceive"? Even without a theory of divine ideas this puzzle confronts Berkeley, and so I do not take it to weigh against my interpretation.

35. See Grey 1952, 338–49. The topic of Grey's paper runs only tangentially to the one here, but it is instructive to see how his analysis concerning putatively public objects brings him close my view.

> variety, order, and manner of these, I conclude the Author of them to be *wise, powerful, and good, beyond comprehension*. Mark it well; I do not say, I see things by perceiving that which represents them in the intelligible substance of God. This I do not understand; but I say, the things by me perceived are known by the understanding, and produced by the will, of an infinite spirit. (215)

Here Berkeley denies (1) anything representational and (2) that we see ideas *as a part of the intelligible substance of God*. He does not deny that we perceive divine ideas. The interpretation I am presenting requires that one read Berkeley's divine ideas as external to God's being, but because of their inertness this is precisely what we should expect! After all, how *could* passive ideas be any part of a necessarily active being? They cannot. I take this to be more evidence that my reading is right. Malebranche, of course, puts the divine order within God, and Berkeley is clear about his objection to this alternative.

> I do not understand how our ideas, which are things altogether passive and inert, can be the essence, or any part (or like any part) of the essence or substance of God, who is an impassive, indivisible, purely active being. Many more difficulties and objections there are, which occur at first view against this hypothesis; but I shall only add that it is liable to all the absurdities of the common hypotheses, in making a created world exist otherwise than in the mind of a spirit.[36] (3D, 213–14)

Divine ideas are needed to bring order and ground reality for finite spirits. Both of these tasks can be accomplished without undermining the divine nature of God by simply moving the ideas "outside of" (i.e., they are not a part of the substance of) Him.

One might, however, seek to extend the original criticism. Positing divine ideas does not explain how two persons can perceive the "same" idea. Berkeley says that the existence of an archetype "serves all the ends of identity, as well as if it existed out of a mind" (3D, 248).[37] Yet although this

---

36. Note again that the word "in" in the last sentence only means *ontological dependence* and does not indicate that the created world is literally (located) inside the mind of God. Indeed, arguing that the world, as a mental order of ideas, must have a physical location would be a category mistake.

37. Here Berkeley is attacking the Lockean notion of "out of a mind," where independence is assumed. That is, Berkeley claims his view is just as good as one that posits mind-independent archetypes.

might work for Locke, whose material archetypes are causally empowered and independent of all minds, how can causally inert ideas explain how two persons perceive the same idea? This problem becomes pressing since Berkeley clearly thinks that divine *ideas* bear the explanatory weight here. Fortunately, we already have the resources to answer this objection. When two minds perceive the (qualitatively) same idea(s), they are both directed *by God* to the same (at least qualitatively identical) idea(s). God causes us to perceive the ideas we do, but that need not entail that there are archetypes that serve as causal intermediaries. The divine idea itself causes nothing; it is what is passively perceived. Now we say, for the sake of convenience, that "our" ideas are the same as that of others because they "match" the divine idea, but strictly speaking that language is misleading, since from our standpoint we cannot distinguish between ideas that are numerically identical and those that are distinct but qualitatively identical. Thus, without invoking numerical diversity or a causal role, divine ideas do explain how diverse persons can perceive the "same" thing. The "thing" perceived is the divine idea and its qualitative content. Whether that means you and I perceive numerically one idea or two does not matter to Berkeley, who thinks the question bears no philosophical weight.[38] The distinction between the two cases deserves emphasis. All that I am attributing to Berkeley is the claim that our sensory ideas are numerically identical to those of God. It need not follow (and indeed, does not) that the ideas had by two *finite* minds are therefore numerically identical as well. That is logically possible, but it is not required by Berkeley's system.

7.5 Fleeting Ideas

One last, general concern awaits attention. Berkeleian ideas, and hence divine ideas as well, are "inert, fleeting, dependent beings" (*PHK* 89).[39] The assertion that ideas are transient is not unique to Berkeley. Spinoza quotes Bacon in Letter 2 to Oldenburg as holding that the intellect frequently takes things to be constant that are in fact fleeting (*CWS* 1:167). Leibniz is fond of referring to fleeting modes and modifications (*PE*, 266, 267). Locke describes mixed modes as "fleeting and transient" (*ECHU* II.22.8). Berkeley and Hume both refer to ideas specifically as fleeting beings. Perceptions for Hume are "fleeting copies" (1999, 201). Yet one does not find any analysis

---

38. For an extended defense of this claim I attribute to Berkeley, see Hight 2007a, esp. 448–53.
39. See *3D*, 205, where ideas are "perpetually fleeting and variable."

as to *why* ideas were thought of as fleeting. The supposition that *all* ideas must be fleeting and changeable is so ingrained in the secondary literature that it seems no one has stopped to investigate seriously what this might mean.

So what is the exact nature of the worry? Berkeley posits the existence of an archetypal order of divine ideas that is "eternal" (3D, 254). If ideas are all by their nature fleeting in the sense of "passing swiftly," it is difficult to make sense of how divine ideas—that are nonetheless ideas despite their divine relation—could also be eternal. Hence the suggestion is that God's ideas must be distinct in kind from those perceived by finite minds. As I have argued here, there are textual and philosophical reasons for believing that Berkeley's finite minds perceive the numerically same sensory ideas as God. This thesis is problematic if ideas are all fleeting. The worry, however, extends beyond this particular context. For Hume, the fleeting and unconnected nature of perceptions helps to generate his famous problem reconciling the distinct existence of perceptions with the lack of connections among them. For if what we take to be commonsense objects are successions of fleeting but actually unconnected perceptions, then how are we to make sense of the claim that there are really commonsense objects at all? The "fleeting" nature of ideas appears troublesome.

The difficulty is avoidable. I propose a reading of Berkeley's claim that ideas are all "fleeting, indeed, and changeable" (3D, 258) that is both consistent with the use of the term generally in the early modern period as well as consistent with Berkeley's philosophical pronouncements. I suggest here that Berkeley's claim that ideas are fleeting and changeable originated only as a reference to the appearance of the sensible world as one that continually changes. That is, ideas are fleeting in relation to us, but that does not imply anything about the metaphysical nature of the ideas themselves, aside from the short duration of their relation to our mind. As a result, the alleged fleeting nature of ideas does not conflict with his theory of divine ideas. Lastly, I conclude by providing what I think is a reasonable explanation for why none of the early moderns thought it necessary to defend explicitly the claim that ideas are fleeting beings.

7.5.1 Idea Orderings

What did the early moderns *mean* when they claimed that ideas were fleeting? At first glance, "fleeting" seems to mean "passing swiftly" or "exists in a transitory state for only an instant." In fact, many of the uses of the word in the period mean exactly that. In the *Natural Dialogues,* however, Hume describes mortal existence as "fleeting," but he certainly did not intend that mortals exist only for an instant. One can discern at least two distinct uses of the word "fleeting" in the early modern period. The more familiar one is that of "short duration" implying a brief or only instantaneous existence. But the word "fleeting" also implies instability and relative changeableness, which is not quite the same thing as being of instantaneously short duration. The difference matters.

When Berkeley refers to ideas as fleeting, he is referring not merely to individual ideas but to ideas as a part of a coherent order or sequence. In so doing he is able to reconcile his claim that God's ideas are in a sense eternal with the claim, reiterated by him, that ideas are fleeting and changeable (fleeting in the sense, as we have just seen, of changing with respect to the rest of the order of ideas; thus, to repeat, to say that ideas are fleeting is not to say much about *ideas* but only about our relation as finite minds to an order of ideas).[40]

There are four arguments I want to advance to defend the claim that ideas need not be intrinsically fleeting and as inconstant as one might at first glance believe. The first concerns contemporary usage. Berkeley's contemporaries all use the language of fleeting ideas in ways that reveal that the claim is not about the metaphysical nature of ideas at all. Second, I advance a parity of reasoning argument. A critique that Berkeley uses against materialism would apply with equal force against his own views, unless his attributions of fleetingness do not imply that ideas are literally instantaneous existences. Third, there are passages where Berkeley appears to say that ideas are not *equally* fleeting, suggesting a more nuanced view. Finally, an analysis of parts of the *Siris* strongly suggests that Berkeley's claims about fleetingness apply to the sequence of ideas and not the ideas themselves.

7.5.2 *The Argument from Contemporaries*

When discussing the metaphysical nature of ideas, the natural starting position most of the early moderns adopted was that of Plato; his ideas exist as eternal realities. Hence to deny Plato's claim one might reasonably say that ideas are fleeting and transitory. After all, a common appeal to our ordinary sensory experience reveals a torrent of new and changing sensory ideas.

---

40. We should expect this result, since Berkeley independently holds that our concept of time is constructed out of the succession of changing, distinct ideas. Thus to say that an idea is fleeting in a temporal sense conflicts with his theory of time.

Leibniz argues against Malebranche in exactly this way, asserting the existence of "fleeting modifications of our souls" rather than "external ideas" that are "external realities" (*PE,* 266, 267). There is no implication that these modifications must be instantaneous existences; the use is intended to provide a contrast to Platonic (and hence Malebranchian) immutable ideas.

Locke, however, most clearly demonstrates that the attribution of "fleeting" to ideas does not necessarily entail that ideas are nothing but quickly fading entities. More importantly, Berkeley's own account resembles the larger part of Locke's, especially when it comes to the concepts of duration and time. Time, Locke opines, is only understood through the idea of duration, which is derived from our noticing that "there is a train of *Ideas,* which constantly succeed one another in [the] Understanding" (*ECHU* II.14.3). Berkeley similarly argues that our concept of time is derived only from the succession of ideas we perceive (*PHK* 98). Yet from this claim Locke does not infer that ideas must have uniformly brief existences. Instead, Locke first considers a thought experiment where a person perceives steadfastly only one idea, concluding that if such were possible, the person would have no sense of time. He then considers a case he believes is confirmed in actual experience—one in which a person fixes on an idea while other ideas pass in succession without notice (*ECHU* II.14.3). Ideas must change to give the impression of time, indicating that some ideas might be relatively more fixed than others. Ideas need not all be fleeting in the ontological sense.

To make matters more clear, Locke even defines "instant" as "*that which takes up the time of only one Idea* in our Minds" (*ECHU* II.14.10). An instant is thus effectively associated not with the idea itself but with the *change* in an idea. Until the idea gives way to another, there is no sense of time. Consequently, just as Berkeley suggests, an instant for one person might well appear as several instants to another, again suggesting that the fleetingness of ideas is a feature of the order and succession of them and not something intrinsic. When Locke writes in his "Remarks upon Some Books of Mr. Norris" that "ideas are so fleeting," he almost immediately clarifies the claim in the same paragraph when he admits that an individual idea might persist in cases where sensory objects are present to the sensory organs (1812, 10:17.256). Locke and Berkeley are remarkably consistent with respect to this feature of ideas.

Other examinations reveal a similar story. Ideas are continually referred to as "fleeting," "transitory," and so on but equally consistently only in reference to their succession and ordering. Since Berkeley takes many of his cues from Locke and other early modern figures, it is plausible to suppose in the absence of countervailing evidence that his use of such language also conforms to those of his peers. The remaining three considerations I take to remove any serious doubt that Berkeley had a nonstandard conception of these terms in mind. Where he departs from early modern usage Berkeley is typically quite clear about it.

7.5.3 The Parity of Reasoning Argument

In the *Three Dialogues* Berkeley has Philonous argue that the supposition of a material substratum does not make sense because it is not possible to have an idea, which is fleeting and changeable, of a permanent and unchanging substance.

> PHILONOUS: How then is it possible, that things perpetually fleeting and variable as our ideas, should be copies or images of any thing fixed and constant? Or in other words, since all sensible qualities, as size, figure, colour, &c. that is, our ideas are continually changing upon every alteration in the distance, medium, or instruments of sensation; how can any determinate material objects be properly represented or painted forth by several distinct things, each of which is so different from and unlike the rest? Or if you say it resembles some one only of our ideas, how shall we be able to distinguish the true copy from all the false ones? (205–6)

On one level Berkeley is perfectly consistent in employing the likeness principle here, since he readily admits that we do not have ideas of mental substances either. The problem, however, is that this same argument can be used against his claim that there is an eternal archetypal order. If an idea can only copy or represent something to which it is like in kind, and ideas cannot represent material things *because* material objects are constant when ideas are not, then ideas cannot represent or copy eternal, divine ideas either. We might simply attribute confusion to Berkeley here, or perhaps suppose that he missed this particular tension. But I prefer to contend that Berkeley's reference to the eternality of archetypes is a reference to the eternality of the archetypal *order*.[41] The order and arrangement of the divine

---

41. Recall that my position is that Berkeley has a theory of divine *ideas* that are not themselves archetypes with corresponding ectypes. A theory of archetypes will be a theory of the order of ideas or of sets of ideas. Daniel Flage has ably argued for an archetypal theory like this already (2001).

ideas is constant and eternal even if the individual ideas are not. Note that the *Three Dialogues* passage where Berkeley speaks of eternity is most naturally read as a claim about the order or sequence of ideas and not about the ideas individually. "[D]o I not acknowledge a twofold state of things, the one ectypal or natural, the other archetypal and eternal? The former was created in time; the latter existed from everlasting in the mind of God" (254; see *PHK* 30–33). The "archetypal and eternal" reference is to the *state of things* and not to the individual ideas.

In order to free Berkeley from what is otherwise an easily recognizable error, I submit that his attribution of fleetingness is best read as he technically wrote it. We cannot have ideas of substances because substances do not form changing sequences like ideas do (not to mention the fact that ideas are passive and substances are not). Similarly, we cannot, strictly speaking, have ideas of archetypes either.[42] In essence, Berkeley's objection is that no *sequence* of ideas can represent a substance since by hypothesis we can only know that there is a sequence if there are changes within that ordering. Since no changes occur during the existence of a substance, no collection of ideas can possibly represent it. No individual idea can represent a substance without the idea *being* a substance, unless we want to violate the likeness principle.

7.5.4 Because Berkeley Says So

The third reason for thinking that ideas are not all equally fleeting by nature is that Berkeley says that they are not. The ideas of sense we as finite minds have are, of course, fleeting and changeable, but they are not nearly as fleeting as other ideas we have.

> PHILONOUS: But on the other hand, it is very conceivable that they [ideas] should exist in, and be produced by, a spirit; since this is no more than I daily experience in myself, inasmuch as I perceive numberless ideas; and by an act of my Will can form a great variety of them, and raise them up in my imagination: though it must be confessed, these creatures of the fancy are not altogether so distinct, so strong, vivid, and **permanent,** as those perceived by my senses, which latter are called *real things*. From all which I conclude, *there is a mind which affects me every moment with all the sensible impressions I perceive.* And

---

42. Flage concludes precisely this same point (2001, 7).

from the variety, order, and manner of these, I conclude the Author of them to be *wise, powerful, and good, beyond comprehension.* Mark it well; I do not say, I see things by perceiving that which represents them in the intelligible substance of God. This I do not understand; but I say, the things by me perceived are known by the understanding, and produced by the will, of an infinite spirit. And is not all this most plain and evident? Is there any more in it, than what a little observation of our own minds, and that which passes in them not only enableth us to conceive, but also obligeth us to acknowledge? (3D, 215, bold emphasis mine)

Berkeley clearly has a distinction in mind between the relative permanence of sensory ideas and those of the imagination. Ideas are fleeting for Berkeley because they are constantly changing before our mind. We might extrapolate from this passage to speculate that references to fleeting ideas are references to the sequence or order of ideas. The above passage can then be reasonably read as indicating that ideas of imagination tend to be unstable, fragmented, and hence fleeting and changeable (although I freely grant this requires reading a bit into the text). The ideas of sense we have change as we experience the world as a rapid sequence of sensory contents, but this is nonetheless more "permanent" because the order of the ideas we perceive is neither fragmented nor unstable but instead regular and predictable. Furthermore, as Locke also notes, a sensory idea can be maintained in the awareness longer when the putative external object is thought to be before us. My thesis also has the advantage of allowing (but not requiring) Berkeley to defend the reasonably commonsense claim that when we stare fixedly at a sensory object, we are seeing the "same thing" (numerically and qualitatively) the whole time. I can find no other consistent and plausible way to defend the coherence of his claims given his assertions about the fleeting nature of ideas.

7.5.5 *The* Siris *Argument*

A final consideration helps to confirm my hypothesis. In the *Siris,* Berkeley attempts to ground his own immaterialism in the history of ancient philosophy. He describes what he means by the changeable and fleeting nature of ideas by aligning himself with those ancients (presumably Heraclitus) who characterized reality as "flowing." He then sets up a distinction between individual acts of sensation and the intelligible whole.

In effect, if we mean by things the sensible objects, these, it is evident, are always flowing; but if we mean things purely intelligible, then we may say on the other hand, with equal truth, that they are immovable and unchangeable. So that those who thought the Whole, or {τὸ πᾶυ}, to be {ἑστώς}, a fixed or permanent One, seem to have understood the Whole of real beings, which in their sense was only the intellectual world, not allowing reality of being to things not permanent. (S 349)

The distinction being drawn is between *individual parts of reality* and *the entire order of nature*. Individual sensible things, ideas, are fleeting and changing because the order of nature expresses a dynamic principle. But that principle, the order of nature, is itself an unchanging and permanent whole. This reading captures quite well what Berkeley appears to invoke in his discussions of divine ideas. The individual divine ideas, like all ideas, are changing. But the order of divine ideas is itself an eternal and immutable structure. Thus Berkeley can consistently hold that God's ideas—as an ordering—are eternal even if the individual ideas are relatively fleeting with respect to finite minds.

Assuming that these four considerations are individually or collectively compelling, one might still ask why ideas were thought to be "fleeting, indeed, and changeable." When Berkeley says that ideas are fleeting and transient, he means nothing more than that ideas are always found by experience to be in constantly changing sequences or orderings. The early moderns, including Berkeley, provide no argument for that claim (that ideas are fleeting) because they all equally thought the claim sufficiently obvious to not warrant defense. *Of course* the ideas and impressions we have vary constantly. No sense modality gives us any indication otherwise. Furthermore, ideas must be a part of a fleeting order or sequence to provide us finite mortals with an understanding of duration and time. Without these alterations we would have no sense of change or growth. Our knowledge of the world hinges on this metaphysical truth. In other words, it was just obvious.

As a result, when Berkeley discusses the nature of divine ideas and calls them "eternal," there is no problem or inconsistency with his assertion about the fleetingness of ideas. God's ideas constitute an eternal and atemporal order. Inside of that order the individual ideas may appear *to us* to be fleeting and transient, but that is because God constructed the sequence to appear that way. My solution to this apparent worry, hopefully like my general analysis concerning Berkeley's theory of ideas, might not be exciting or deeply illuminating, but I think it gets Berkeley right in the way we want to get Berkeley right: it preserves the quality of his philosophy at the same time as it preserves the historical integrity of the texts.

8

ABSTRACTION AND HETEROGENEITY

Given that we have a rough fix on how Berkeley treated ideas and of the significant philosophical benefit this reading provides to our understanding of Berkeley's theory of divine ideas, we are now in a position to take note of other important developments in the ontology of ideas as they culminate in Berkeley. If I am right that Berkeley treats ideas as individual quasi substances, then we ought to expect some additional "fallout" from that view. That is, my interpretation should make a difference more broadly in his philosophical system given the centrality of ideas within it. Indeed it does. Here I highlight two additional areas where his ontology of ideas impacts his thinking. The first concerns abstraction, which I will consider initially, and the second his odd belief in the heterogeneity of ideas (best captured by his claim that we do not see the numerically same objects which we touch). I want to emphasize again that it is not my intent to *defend* Berkeley's views on abstraction and heterogeneity but rather to provide a more compelling explanation than has hithertofore been offered for *why* he endorsed such unusual, radical claims. If it also turns out that Berkeley's positions are also more philosophically respectable, so much the better.

8.1 Abstract Ideas

Berkeley thinks ordinary folk make a serious mistake when they unreflectively suppose that commonsense material objects exist independently of their being perceived and understood. He even diagnoses the error: "If we thoroughly examine this tenet, it will, perhaps, be found at bottom to depend on the doctrine of *abstract ideas.* For can there be a nicer strain of abstraction than to distinguish the existence of sensible objects from their being perceived, so as to conceive them existing unperceived?" (*PHK* 5). Berkeley takes this issue to be of such importance that he devotes nearly the entire introduction of the *Principles* and considerable space elsewhere to attacking abstract ideas.

The topic of abstraction is relevant to my argument for two primary reasons. First, as I endeavor to demonstrate, at least part of what drives Berkeley to reject the conceivability of abstract ideas is his conception of ideas generally as quasi-substantial things. I will out of necessity need to rehash some well-worn ground about the debate between Berkeley and Locke, but my purpose in so doing is to highlight how Berkeley's thinking about ideas influences his philosophical position on abstraction. Second, what Berkeley has to say about abstract ideas is relevant to the more important discussion of heterogeneity. As a result, we need to be clear about why Berkeley rejects abstract ideas before we can fully understand why he also thinks that ideas are radically heterogeneous. As a final aside, one might argue that any serious treatment of ideas in Berkeley cannot omit reference to abstraction.[1] I am not certain that the supposition is correct, but those who hold that opinion will not be disappointed here.

8.2 Kinds of Abstraction

Various commentators have identified as many as four different kinds of abstract ideas in Berkeley. Most scholars, following an influential article by E. J. Craig (1968, 425–29), identify three: (1) single quality abstract ideas, where the idea is an individual property separated from its particularities, (2) common quality abstract ideas, where one property seen in many instances is isolated and attended to selectively (determinables, such as color in general), and (3) full representation abstract ideas, where the idea somehow manages to contain the content of every possible instance of a selected property.[2] To these three initial types, George Pappas adds a fourth, namely (4) highly generalized ideas of fundamental concepts, like being or existence (2000, 44). My aim here is not to provide a comprehensive analysis of the

---

1. George Pappas, for instance, argues at book length that Berkeley's attack on abstraction is crucial to understanding the *esse* is *percipi* principle and the rest of Berkeley's metaphysics (2000, esp. ch. 2). The arguments of this chapter do not directly engage or contest Pappas's core claims, as the centrality of abstraction is of less importance to this study than the impact of Berkeley's ontology of ideas on his abstraction doctrine.

2. Pappas is more specific, arguing that type 3 abstract ideas are general ideas of *bodies* rather than qualities (2000, 43).

abstraction doctrine in Berkeley. In fact, although I believe that my analysis has wider application, I will restrict myself primarily to one relatively small piece of the puzzle: Berkeley's attack against what most commentators call the "separation" model of abstraction found in Locke. The goal is to demonstrate that Berkeley's ontological approach to his theory of ideas—and the unique particulars of his theory as established in chapters 6 and 7—provides some insight into his attack against abstraction. I contend that Berkeley's conviction that abstract ideas are impossible in large part flows directly from his understanding of the ontological nature of ideas.

Achieving clarity with respect to the abstraction doctrine requires that we answer not one but two questions. First, what are abstract ideas supposed to do? Then, exactly what are they, that is, what is their nature? Given that Berkeley most explicitly attacks Locke's version(s) of abstraction, we may safely take Locke's views on the matter as a starting point. Abstract ideas, first and foremost, are entities that play a key role in Locke's semantic theory. Abstract ideas are supposed to reveal how a single word can refer to and denote a large and diverse number of individuals. Semantic theories need to be able to explain the function of general words and how they get their meanings. Abstract ideas provide that explanation.

> The Mind makes the particular *Ideas,* received from particular Objects, to become general; which is done by considering them as they are in the Mind such Appearances, separate from all other Existences, and the circumstances of real Existence, as Time, Place, or any other concomitant *Ideas.* This is called *abstraction,* whereby *Ideas* taken from particular Beings, become general Representatives of all of the same kind; and their Names general Names, applicable to whatever exists conformable to such abstract *Ideas.* (*ECHU* II.11.9)

We have, then, a *particular* idea that serves as the representative of a large number of things of that same kind. The idea is of an unusual sort, however, since one must separate from the idea all the "circumstances" in which one finds it. As it turns out, the process involves more than just this stripping of circumstances; it also involves the deliberate omission of detail.

> There is nothing more evident, than that the *Ideas* of the Persons Children converse with (to instance them alone), are like the Persons themselves, only particular. . . . The Names they first give to

> [their nurse and mother] are confined to those Individuals; and the Names of *Nurse* and *Mamma,* the Child uses, determine themselves to those Persons. Afterwards . . . they frame an *Idea,* which they find those many Particulars do partake in; and to that they give, with others, the name *Man,* for Example. And *thus they come to have a general Name,* and a general *Idea.* Wherein they make nothing new, but only leave out of the complex *Idea* they had of *Peter* and *James, Mary* and *Jane,* that which is peculiar to each, and retain only what is common to them all. (*ECHU* III.3.7)

So now we have a procedure for forming abstract ideas. We omit those details that are not shared by all of that kind. That is, we leave out "the shape, and some other Properties signified by the name *Man,* . . . retaining only a Body, with Life, Sense, and spontaneous Motion, comprehended under the Name *Animal*" (*ECHU* III.3.8). One point seems clear: Locke thinks of general words as being like proper names that refer to particular abstract ideas. One would use the word "George" to name a particular person. Similarly, one uses the word "animal" to name a particular idea, an abstract entity (Warnock 1982, 72–73).[3] Locke posits the existence of abstract ideas as the referents of general words. As a result, abstract ideas function as the bearers of indeterminate (nonparticular) content.

There is another perspective from which to view Locke's theory and from which to judge the dispute between Locke and Berkeley. Locke's abstract ideas function in analogous ways to Aristotle's secondary substances. Recalling our early discussion of Aristotle on substance (section 1.1), primary substances are particulars that are predicable of nothing, and all else is said of, or is "in," them. Secondary substances, however, are particular substances that are also predicable of other things. The clearest case of a secondary substance is a genus predicable of a species. So we say of a dog that it is an animal (predicating animal of dog). This theory makes the species dog a (second-rate) substance, because things are said of it, one key marker for a substance. Nonetheless, we may also predicate dog of particular canines. To make room for these kinds of things, Aristotle classified species as "secondary" substances. They function like things but are not substances per se. Now consider Lockean abstract ideas. Ideas that are predicable of other ideas are abstract. Take the case of a triangle. The idea of a particular triangle is a substance. It refers to something else but is "said of" nothing else. Triangu-

---

3. See Bennett 1971, 22–25.

larity (the abstract idea of a triangle) *is,* however, said of many other ideas; namely, those particular ideas that are also of triangles. We do say of the idea of a scalene triangle that it nonetheless is an idea of a triangle. As a result, we might think of Locke as treating abstract ideas as rather *like* secondary substances. Additionally, it lends weight to my earlier assertion that Locke is under some pressure to think of ideas as substantial beings.[4]

Berkeley, no matter how one interprets him, seems reasonably clear about Locke's doctrine; he simply disagrees with it. His own gloss of Locke's separation account is reasonable and accurate.

> It is agreed on all hands, that the qualities or modes of things do never really exist each of them apart by itself, and separated from all others, but are mixed, as it were, and blended together, several in the same object. But we are told, the mind being able to consider each quality singly, or abstracted from those other qualities with which it is united, does by that means frame to itself abstract ideas. For example, there is perceived by sight an object extended, coloured, and moved: this mixed or compound idea the mind resolving into its simple, constituent parts, and viewing each by itself, exclusive of the rest, does frame the abstract ideas of extension, colour, and motion. Not that it is possible for colour or motion to exist without extension: but only that the mind can frame to itself by *abstraction* the idea of colour exclusive of extension, and of motion exclusive of both colour and extension. (*IPHK* 7)

At another point in the introduction to the *Principles* Berkeley even uses Locke's own example of abstracting "man" and "animal" to flesh out the position (*IPHK* 9). Just like we can say of a man that it is an animal exclusive of its other properties, so we can say of an isosceles triangle that it is a triangle, without reference to the length of sides, its color, and so forth. We can, as a result, see that Berkeley and Locke are genuinely locking horns, as it were, on the same issue.

And what of the nature of abstract ideas? With respect to at least those abstract ideas formed by separation (admitting but bracketing other types), we already know that these abstract ideas, like ideas generally, are particular entities formed through a careful process of detail omission.[5] More than

---

4. See chapter 4.
5. There is some disagreement among scholars as to exactly what Locke meant by abstract ideas, perhaps owing to some obscurity in the details of Locke's expression. Although I am aware of rival accounts of Locke (including, e.g., those that invoke selective attention models), in this

this, as it turns out, we do not need to know. The core of Berkeley's attack rests on the claim that abstract ideas must be particular entities, as Locke grants. So, although Berkeley freely admits that he understands the role abstract ideas are meant to play in Locke's semantic theory, he denies there can exist any such thing to fill that role. Understanding his rejection of abstract ideas depends on recognizing what *Berkeley* thought abstract ideas to be.

8.3 Berkeley's Attack

Berkeley opposes abstraction because he thinks the doctrine postulates the existence of impossible entities. A first rough pass at Berkeley's reasoning is as follows. All ideas (abstract or otherwise) are particular, determinate entities. Representation requires resemblance. Therefore abstract ideas must represent through resemblance as well. And what is being represented, according to (Berkeley's) Locke, by (for example) the abstract idea of a triangle? Something that is indeterminate with respect to its particular shape. Yet there cannot be indeterminate *things,* triangles that have no particular shape. As a result, abstract ideas represent impossible things. Since one cannot represent an impossible thing, abstract ideas cannot exist. Strictly speaking, of course, Berkeley does not think ideas represent a material world. Instead, he takes ideas to be the things we immediately perceive. The story remains the same. Because Berkeley thinks of ideas as individual quasi substances "external" to the mind, they must be fully determinate with respect to all of their properties (as all material things would be, if they existed). Locke cannot simultaneously assert that abstract ideas are both particular and indeterminate if they are robust things. Given this rough overview as a guide, let us turn and carefully examine the textual evidence to reassure ourselves that this picture is the right one. My interpretation is rather mainstream in most respects, although it importantly diverges from some readings in its emphasis on the *reasons* why Berkeley rejected abstraction.

For our purposes, Berkeley identifies two broad kinds of abstraction in the *Principles.*[6] The first he finds unproblematic. "I do not deny absolutely

---

discussion I am primarily concerned with what *Berkeley* took the abstraction doctrine to be (and thence why he opposed it) and not with the technical merits of Locke's alleged actual position.

6. I am not seeking to deny that there are other distinctions (including Pappas's four types). I am only highlighting a new distinction among ideas relevant to my contention that the ontic nature of ideas generally is germane to his criticism of abstraction. See Pappas 2000, 40–44.

there are general ideas, but only that there are any *abstract general ideas*" (*IPHK* 12). A general idea is one that, although fully particular and determinate, is made to be a *sign* of all ideas similar to it in some respect. The idea is not a sign of some abstract entity but rather a sign directly for all the ideas of that kind that can actually exist (*IPHK* 12). The second kind of abstraction is the one he finds objectionable. Abstract ideas in this sense are ideas that represent indeterminate particulars. Even in his description of his positive view of how general words get meaning we can detect the difficulty Berkeley finds with abstraction: he does not think abstract ideas could possibly exist.

As a result Berkeley advances a broad argument against abstract ideas.

(1) Whatever is impossible is inconceivable.
(2) Abstract ideas are impossible.
(3) Hence abstract ideas are inconceivable.[7]

The first premise appears explicitly in Berkeley's writings several times. In the first draft of the introduction to the *Principles* he notes: "It is, I think, a receiv'd Axiom that an Impossibility cannot be conceiv'd" (*MI*, 75). Similarly, in the published version of the introduction he writes: "But I deny that I can abstract one from another, or conceive separately, those qualities which it is impossible should exist so separated" (*IPHK* 10). Lastly, consider *Principles* 5, where Berkeley makes the same claim in a slightly different way. "So far I will not deny I can abstract, if that may properly be called *abstraction,* which extends only to the conceiving separately such objects, as it is possible may really exist or be actually perceived asunder. But my conceiving or imagining power does not extend beyond the possibility of real existence or perception." Here we are told that what *may* be conceived depends on what is actually (logically) possible, and then the negative point is reiterated. Recall that for ideas, their *esse* is *percipi,* so features about perception directly reflect features about fundamental reality. Thus when Berkeley says that our power to conceive does not extend beyond what may be perceived, he means if two ideas are inconsistent, then one cannot conceive them together.

Although I find that Berkeley clearly endorsed this premise as true, I produce this evidence because not everyone agrees that the conditional here works this way. Willis Doney in particular claims that Berkeley argues *from* inconceivability *to* impossibility, reversing the order of explanation, citing

---

7. See Winkler 1989, 33–34. Winkler generally reads Berkeley as I do here, although his explanation of *why* Berkeley takes abstract ideas to be impossible differs somewhat (especially in emphasis) from my own.

section 10 of the introduction as evidence (1983, 295–307).[8] Doney carefully notes two interesting features of Berkeley's attack. First, in his own words, Berkeley's stated target seems to be the claim that the mind has the power to frame abstract ideas and not that abstract ideas are straightforwardly impossible. "And that is the opinion that the mind hath a power of framing *abstract ideas* or notions of things" (*IPHK* 6). Second, section 10 does not really establish that abstract ideas are impossible, and so read my way it is allegedly difficult to make proper sense of what Berkeley thinks he is doing. If Berkeley doesn't assert the second premise (that abstract ideas are impossible), what would be the *point* of his arguing that whatever is impossible is inconceivable? Furthermore, the first (and starkest) example supporting my position was eliminated from the published version of the introduction, and one might reasonably take this as evidence that Berkeley rejected that line of reasoning.

The preponderance of the evidence does not support Doney. Instead, I find that I can admit most of the points he thinks support his view without altering my own. First, Doney's claim that Berkeley's target is powers of the mind and not the metaphysics of ideas strikes me as misleading. Berkeley intends to explain *why* the doctrine of abstract ideas is absurd. Why is it that those who think they can frame abstract ideas are in fact confused? The answer is because (as we discover) they are attempting to frame ideas of impossible entities. If we look back on his descriptions of how abstraction allegedly works for Locke, we find that abstract ideas are formed on the basis of the observed qualities of things. We move from perceiving traits to forming ideas (*IPHK* 8). To say that Berkeley wants to discover whether humans have this mysterious faculty of abstracting *does not deny my reading of what he is doing*. That we do not possess this faculty is the *conclusion* of his argument. As a result, we should not be surprised that he states this as his goal.

Furthermore, Doney relies on a controversial interpretation of which he himself is aware. His contention that section 10 is meant to state a considered conclusion is difficult to accept. When Berkeley writes, "But I deny that I can abstract one from another, or conceive separately, those qualities which it is impossible should exist so separated," Doney reads this as indicating that "it follows that we cannot know that [two qualities] cannot exist apart without knowing that [each quality] cannot be conceived apart" (1983, 299). Doney's case relies on the dubious assumption that inconceivability

---

8. Doney explicitly attacks Pitcher and E. J. Craig, both of whom defend interpretations that are consonant with mine. See Pitcher 1977, esp. 62–70, and Craig 1968, 425–37.

entails impossibility. Even if we accept this claim as true, however, it does not help his cause. Berkeley could easily hold that, as a matter of what we *know*, conceivability is the only guide to possibility without relinquishing the claim that what *explains* why we cannot conceive of certain sorts of things depends on whether those things are metaphysically possible.

As for Doney's second claim that my interpretation does not make sense of the passage, observe that Berkeley does try to indicate why abstract things are impossible. He does not do so explicitly in section 10 because he has not finished his discussion of the topic; he continues examining the question for another eight sections and picks it up again later in the *Principles*. Why Berkeley takes abstract things (ideas) to be impossible will occupy us next. For the moment, I think it sufficient to rely on the texts as a whole to support my contention that Berkeley argues from impossibility to inconceivability, at least insofar as he wishes to explain why people cannot have genuine Lockean abstract ideas.

So now let us turn to the second premise: abstract ideas are impossible. This claim is certainly the more controversial premise, but Berkeley thinks his task an easy one. In a note to himself in the *Philosophical Commentaries*, Berkeley writes about bringing the "killing blow" against Locke's theory of abstraction (*PC* 687). Section 125 of the *New Theory of Vision* repeats his forceful complaint against Locke. He attacks abstraction in most of his major philosophical works, starting with his earliest works on vision, and in every case where he does so one is struck by the almost casual certainty that bursts forth from his analyses. Berkeley thinks he has fastened on a clear inconsistency.

The most offensive passage in Locke to Berkeley's mind is the now famous "triangle passage." Locke writes: "For example, Does it not require some pains and skill to form the *general Idea* of a *Triangle*, (which is yet none of the most abstract, comprehensive, and difficult,) for it must be neither Oblique, nor Rectangle, neither Equilateral, Equicrural, nor Scalenon; but all and none of these at once. In effect, it is something imperfect, that cannot exist; an *Idea* wherein some parts of several different and inconsistent *Ideas* are put together" (*ECHU* IV.7.9).[9] What is wrong with this passage? Berkeley emphasizes in his quotations of Locke (especially section 13 of the introduction to the *Principles*) the phrase "all and none," suggesting that Lockean abstract ideas are impossible because they describe entities that violate the law of excluded middle (Bennett 1971, 38). A triangle can be

---

9. Berkeley quotes this passage in *NTV* 125 and again in *IPHK* 13.

either scalenon, equicrural, or right but not all of them at once. That much certainly seems right. Particular things cannot have more than one quality from a set of mutually exclusive ones. We might call this principle the *law of saturation*. An entity can only possess one of a set of incompatible properties. Yet why would Berkeley think that Locke's abstraction doctrine violates *this* claim? A reasonable and charitable reading of Locke would hold that the abstract idea of a triangle is simply silent on the issue of the specific properties of its interior angles and the lengths of its sides (emphasizing the so-called selective attention model of Locke's theory of abstraction). In that case, an abstract idea would be one that *could* represent any of these kinds of specific triangles but that in fact is itself none of them.

Pitcher urges that Berkeley's imagism is to blame for the attack on abstract ideas. He ascribes the following principle to Berkeley:

> (a) If an idea of x lacks the representation of some feature F, it must therefore be the idea of x that lacks F. (1977, 70)

The reason Berkeley believes (a) is presumably that all ideas are images. The image of something must reflect what it is an image of, and therefore one might reasonably hold that if an image of a dog failed to represent its color, then the dog itself must also fail to have any color. Yet as even Pitcher notes, (a) is simply not true for images. I might conjure an image of Lassie to myself that omits the characteristic color scheme of the collie without supposing that Lassie herself has no particular coloration. We conjure images in exactly this way all the time. When I think on the image of the face of the president I do so without representing his eye color, but this does not mean that the president has no eye color.[10] It is, perhaps, doubtful that most images even *can* be completely determinate; we simply lack the power as finite minds to form images that are perfectly detailed.

There is some evidence that Berkeley did take all sensible ideas to be images. In the draft introduction he writes: "Any Name may be used indifferently for the Sign of any Idea, or any number of Ideas, it not being determin'd by any likeness to represent one more than another. But it is not so with Ideas in respect of Things, of which they are suppos'd to be the Copies & Images. They are not thought to Represent them otherwise, than as they resemble them" (*MI*, 83). Although this appears in the draft, and he is nominally describing the views of others, Berkeley does so approvingly.

---

10. Warnock makes a similar point (1982, 67–68).

Throughout his published works one can detect imagistic influences, although I nonetheless maintain he adheres to a theory of divine ideas that is somewhat at odds with a strictly imagistic theory (compare *PHK* 33 and *3D*, 194). Pitcher's analysis thus appears initially plausible. Yet it nonetheless seems odd that this alone would push Berkeley to read Locke so uncharitably. After all, Berkeley did in all likelihood read the whole of the *Essay*, and it is manifestly uncharitable to fasten on one poorly phrased passage. As we will see, in other places Berkeley makes it explicit that he is aware of this other reading of Locke. If we can unearth another reason for rejecting the triangle passage that does not depend on the particular phrasing present therein, then we ought to seriously consider it as a superior reading of Berkeley's thinking. Such a reading is suggested by my contention that Berkeley thought of ideas as quasi substances.

I do not believe Berkeley endorsed merely (a); instead, I think he believed something *stronger*.

(b) Every determinable must have a determinant.

That is, Berkeley takes all ideas to be both particular and fully determinate. For example, the determinable "color" must be either red, or green, or blue, and so forth. An idea must be *some* specific color (to include a determinate hue and brilliance, etc.). For Berkeley, there is no such thing as an idea that is "silent" on some property. If I am right, then Berkeley has a better reason to parade the triangle passage, since the phrase "all and none" is doubly objectionable. On the one hand, no particular thing can violate the law of saturation, but on the other, no particular thing can be indeterminate either—possessing "none" of the available properties.

We have already seen that Berkeley considers ideas to be robust things. It should therefore be no surprise that ideas cannot be silent with respect to certain qualities, since it is metaphysically impossible for a particular thing to exist that is indeterminate. I think Berkeley took this point to be so blindingly obvious that he believed little more needed to be said on it. There is, additionally, significant evidence that Berkeley was focusing his attack on the *indeterminate* nature of abstract ideas. Berkeley attributes the source of the error to abuse of language, noting that even Locke thinks of abstraction as arising partially from a desire to name things.[11] Berkeley's diagnosis is noteworthy. "Let us therefore examine the manner wherein words have con-

---

11. Berkeley cites *ECHU* III.6.39 and "elsewhere" in the *Essay*.

tributed to the origin of that mistake. First then, 'tis thought that every name hath, or ought to have, only one precise and settled signification, which inclines men to think there are certain *abstract, determinate ideas,* which constitute the true and only immediate signification of each general name" (*IPHK* 18). The emphasis is original! The error is to think that abstract ideas can be *determinate.* Why? Answer: in the descriptions of abstract ideas, they are anything but determinate. Thus we have an inconsistency, and not merely the inconsistency of a triangle that is both scalenon and not, but the more general (and problematic) inconsistency of positing an idea that is both determinate and indeterminate. We now have a stronger reason for supposing that Locke is in trouble in the triangle passage.

More generally, Berkeley thinks—not unreasonably—that particularity entails determinateness. If a *thing* (like a rock or a chair) is particular, then it is fully determinate. If ideas are things in the same sense (and Berkeley is not for turning things into ideas but *ideas into things*), then they too must be fully determinate as all genuine particular substances are. In the introduction to the *Principles* we can see a progression in his argument. First, he describes the illegitimate process of abstraction as involving the creation of ideas that determine no particular existence.

> For example, the mind having observed that Peter, James, and John, resemble each other, in certain common agreements of shape and other qualities, leaves out of the complex or compounded idea it has of Peter, James and any other particular man, that which is peculiar to each, retaining only what is common to all; and so makes an abstract idea wherein all the particulars equally partake, abstracting entirely from and cutting off all those circumstances and differences, which might determine it to any particular existence. (*IPHK* 9)

It is worth pausing to note that this process Berkeley describes just is the more charitable reading of Locke where abstract ideas are "silent" about certain qualities. Apparently Berkeley was aware of this move and rejected abstraction anyway. The triangle passage is illustrative of another, more general, problem than the one suggested by Locke's perhaps unfortunate choice of words. In the original draft version of the introduction, Berkeley goes on to provide an example of what this process seems to require. He makes the alleged absurdity readily transparent. "Suppose now I should ask whether you comprehended in this your Abstract Idea of Man, the Ideas of Eyes, or

Ears, or Nose, or Legs, or Arms, you will own it to be an odd & mutilated Idea of Man wch is without all these. Yet it must be so to make it consistent with the Doctrine of Abstract Ideas, there being particular Men that want, some Arms, some Legs, others Noses etc" (*MI*, 69). Here we find that Berkeley explicitly holds that the abstract idea of Man is itself a man without limbs and other features. Ideas are always self-predicating. They are so because ideas just are the "things" in the world. He provides a more striking example, also only in the first draft, immediately afterward. "In like manner Man by leaving out of his Idea of a Line the particular Colour & Length comes by the Idea of a Line, which is neither black, nor white, nor red &c nor long nor short, which he calls the Abstract idea of a Line, & which, for ought I can see, is just Nothing. For I ask whether a Line has any more than one particular Colour & one particular Length, wch being left out, I beseech any one to consider what it is that remains" (*MI*, 71). The problem, as Berkeley sees it, is that abstract ideas posit the existence of things that are "nothing." There are no lines without a particular color or length and since he later "shows" us that lines and bodies are nothing but sensible ideas, it follows that there are no ideas of lines like this either. One might be worried about why Berkeley removed these passages, but they are consistent with the material that does make it into the published versions. Both are incorporated into the final draft in varying ways (for example, a near facsimile of the abstract idea of a man example finds its way into section 10 of the introduction). He apparently chose to emphasize different examples (highlighting, for instance, one about motion instead of the line). Interestingly, he also chose to emphasize the inseparability of qualities when presenting his examples. Motion, for instance, cannot be abstracted or separated from a particular speed (fast or slow) or thing in motion. So what could this "motion" be if abstracted from all those things that make it particular? Berkeley's answer is clear: nothing. He essentially uses a different route to the same final conclusion, but both examples rely fundamentally on the claim that ideas, as particular things, must be determinate. Berkeley concludes near the end of section 10 in the introduction that "I deny that I can abstract one from another, or conceive separately, those qualities which it is impossible should exist so separated" (*IPHK* 10). We cannot have an idea of motion alone, just like we cannot have an idea of a man that has no color or particular limbs, because *such things do not exist.* We therefore have a more reasonable and charitable interpretation of Berkeley's claim that abstract ideas are impossible than the one typically ascribed to him.

Given that whatever is impossible is not conceivable, Berkeley can now conclude that abstract ideas are inconceivable. People, especially those learned men fond of words, are simply confused when they claim to make use of Lockean abstract ideas. Ideas, even abstract ideas, are particular things and as such must be determinate. Abstract ideas as described by Locke and others are decidedly not determinate. Hence such things are impossible and in turn inconceivable.

We can now go back and recast the attack on abstraction in terms of Berkeley's rejection of Locke's treatment of abstract ideas as secondary substances. Any idea, if it can possibly exist, must be a genuine or primary (quasi) substance. Abstract ideas are predicable of many other ideas without being any of those ideas. Thus the abstract idea of a triangle is itself not scalene nor right nor equilateral. But Berkeley believes that all ideas are fully particular and determinate, which precludes them from being secondary substances. Furthermore, Locke is asking the impossible when he asks us to separate species out from their instances, since a species cannot so exist. What is motion without a thing moved? Nothing. And what is dog without any particular dogs? Again, nothing. To ask us to talk about them is to ask the impossible and hence they must be inconceivable. The ready applicability of Aristotle's primary/secondary substance distinction to the Locke/Berkeley debate provides an additional indication to my mind that both figures are well within the conceptual bounds of the traditional ontology.

8.4 Berkeley's Solution: General Ideas

If my interpretation is correct, then I must briefly establish that the positive view Berkeley endorses is consistent with my claim that his ideas are all determinate particular quasi substances. Fortunately this is relatively easy to do. A general idea for Berkeley is a particular one made to be the sign for a set of similar or related ideas. As a consequence, my idea of a particular right triangle may be used by me to represent all triangles, but in that use the idea remains fully determined. With respect to the line example, Berkeley provides his own analysis.

> He draws, for instance, a black line of an inch in length, this which in itself is a particular line is nevertheless with regard to its signification general, since as it is there used, it represents all particular lines whatsoever; for that what is demonstrated of it, is demonstrated of all lines or, in other words, of a line in general. And as

> that particular line becomes general, by being made a sign, so the name *line* which taken absolutely is particular, by being a sign is made general. And as the former owes its generality, not to its being the sign of an abstract or general line, but of all particular right lines that may possibly exist, so the latter must be thought to derive its generality from the same cause, namely, the various particular lines which it indifferently denotes. (*IPHK* 12)

Berkeley allows us to use ideas in ways that might not mention or employ certain qualities but does not allow us to employ ideas that are themselves indeterminate. Thus he freely admits that when doing geometry we might not mention all the qualities present. "And here it must be acknowledged that a man may consider a figure merely as triangular, without attending to the particular qualities of the angles, or relations of the sides. So far he may abstract: but this will never prove, that he can frame an abstract general inconsistent idea of a triangle" (*IPHK* 16). We may, as Berkeley indicates, consider a figure without *attending* to some its qualities, but the idea itself must nonetheless *have* all those qualities. The mention of Locke's "abstract general inconsistent idea of a triangle" is misleading and has encouraged scholars to see him as being uncharitable to Locke. It is true that Berkeley is not one to pass by an easy shot that he thinks might be rhetorically persuasive. Nonetheless, he has a deeper point. How we use ideas might tempt us into thinking that they are incomplete or indeterminate, but we know that ideas must be fully determinate.

We now have a more complete picture of the nature of abstraction. Berkeley's conviction stems from his prior commitment to the substantial nature of ideas. This commitment explains why he thinks abstract ideas are impossible. Abstract ideas are indeterminate, when all ideas must be particular and hence determinate. So Locke's claim that all ideas are particular is inconsistent with his contention that abstract ideas are conceivable. My interpretation also helps make better sense of Berkeley's superficially unkind reading of Locke in the triangle passage. He does seize on an infelicitous phrasing and exploit it for rhetorical gain, but he nevertheless offers a deeper and perhaps accurate criticism of Locke's general program. We ought not read Berkeley's attack on abstraction through the distorting lens of this one passage when he elsewhere demonstrates sensitivity to more charitable understandings of Locke.

None of this makes Berkeley *right*, of course. At a minimum I hope to have provided an additional reason for thinking that my interpretation of

Berkeley's theory of ideas is correct. If my reading is accurate, then his attack on abstraction is more comprehensible, based on his understanding that ideas are individual quasi substances. They are particular *things* that must be determinate. Still, what Berkeley has to say about abstraction underdetermines what theory of ideas we should attribute to him, and so I turn to examine in some considerable detail a final vexing issue in Berkeley scholarship: his claim that ideas are heterogeneous. If I am successful in establishing that my interpretation makes better sense of *both* his attack on abstraction *and* his unusual metaphysical claims about heterogeneity, then in conjunction with the previous analysis about archetypes I will have minimally established that my thesis about Berkeley's theory of ideas has independent philosophical merit. In turn, this conclusion strongly suggests that Berkeley in particular ought not be read as an anti-ontologist contributing to the early modern tale, since all of this analysis requires that Berkeley is committed, albeit loosely, to the constraints of the traditional ontology.

8.5 Perceptual Heterogeneity

Berkeley believes that "we do not see the same object that we feel" (3D, 245).[12] No object of one sense is identical with any object of another.[13] He makes the point boldly. "*The extensions, figures, and motions perceived by sight are specifically distinct from the ideas of touch called by the same names, nor is there any such thing as one idea or kind of idea common to both senses*" (NTV 127, emphasis in the original). The thesis, popularly called the heterogeneity thesis, is clear enough, but his reasons for supposing it to be true are decidedly less transparent. In what follows, I explore why Berkeley felt so confident about the truth of perceptual heterogeneity and attempt to reconstruct some of his analysis that is not explicitly presented in order to complete his account. Much of the following analysis may appear at times to be a large digression, and I ask for the reader's patience until I am able to tie the narrative to the ontology of ideas. At the end, we will see that Berkeley's views on the nature of ideas directly contribute to his embracing the heterogeneity thesis.

12. The following analysis is a modified and updated version of an argument I made in a previously published article. See Hight 2002.

13. Berkeley generally restricts himself to the claim that visible and tangible objects are distinct, and I shall limit myself to this as well, although it is sometimes important to remember that the thesis extends to all the senses.

Many philosophers think Berkeley's views about distance perception drove him to endorse heterogeneity. D. M. Armstrong reports that "he is *forced* into holding such a view, because he thinks that the objects revealed by sight are merely two-dimensional while touch alone gives us access to ordinary three-dimensional objects" (1960, 35, emphasis in the original). The argument relies on Berkeley's prior premise that distance is never immediately seen.[14] Even if one can learn to represent three dimensions by sight (as we presumably do with pictures), the content of what we immediately perceive by sight has two dimensions while the content of what we strictly feel has three.[15] Hence, we do not see and touch the "same" things.[16] Our spatial ideas of sight and those of touch have no relations to one another.

Unfortunately, Berkeley's premise that distance is never immediately seen does not logically entail heterogeneity. Two-dimensional properties are a subset of three-dimensional ones, just as two-dimensional geometry is a subset of three-dimensional geometry.[17] It cannot be merely because the dimensionalities differ that heterogeneity is true. Perhaps Armstrong meant to be reporting Berkeley's state of mind when he mentioned the position as "forced," for he comes to a similar conclusion as I do (1960, 36–38). The actual content of our ideas of sight and touch is irrelevant. Suppose Berkeley underestimates the richness of what we visually perceive, such that we do perceive distance immediately.[18] The question remains whether the space perceived by sight is numerically identical with that perceived by touch. The contingency of the relations between the seen and the felt is the real issue. Berkeley holds we could feel roundly when we see squarely, even if sight and touch have similar content (see Warnock 1982, ch. 2). Thus his position that sight is two dimensional while touch is not fails to explain his adherence to the heterogeneity of ideas.

14. Pitcher makes a similar argument (1977, 25–28).

15. One might deny my passing assertion that the content of what we immediately perceive by sight is two dimensional. David Berman argues in a discussion concerning disembodied sight that "the sighted mind could have no notion of visual shape or size" (1999, 33). Berman's analysis is controversial, but in any event the point is not vital to my claim here. So long as the immediate visual content (whatever it might be) is distinct from the content presented through touch, my point stands.

16. "Same" here is purposely vague. Its meaning depends on the theory of perception one uses.

17. By this I mean only that two-dimensional objects and properties can be represented in three-dimensional space. Alternatively, however limited the content of what is immediately presented in vision might be, it can be represented in richer depictions of space and space-time.

18. James J. Gibson actually argues that we do perceive visual distance immediately (1976, 87).

Alternatively, one might think Berkeley's strategy in the *New Theory* forced him into accepting heterogeneity. After introducing the issue, but before arguing for the thesis, he briefly skirmishes with abstract ideas at *NTV* 122–26. Only after disposing of abstraction does he turn and argue seriously that the heterogeneity thesis is true. One might suppose Berkeley is thinking along the following lines. If there were common sensibles, what could they have in common? What intrinsic characteristic would the ideas of sight and touch share? Abstract ideas are the only readily viable candidates. If extension is a common sensible—to use Berkeley's example—then an idea of it must be abstractable from both our visual and tactual experiences. But Berkeley is antecedently committed to denying abstract ideas.[19] The only other remotely plausible candidate is a material substratum, and he would not allow that as a live option either. Thinking he has exhausted the alternatives, Berkeley concludes there can be nothing shared in common between ideas of sight and touch. If we cannot abstract, then ideas cannot share content, and hence the ideas of different modalities must be radically distinct.

Although an interesting and reasonable conjecture about part of Berkeley's thinking, this argument suffers from the same flaw as the distance account. His objections to abstraction do not entail the truth of heterogeneity. As it turns out abstraction does not depend on the truth of heterogeneity either. If one takes the heterogeneity of ideas seriously, then one must apply the divisions among kinds of ideas as deeply as they can go. Allowing Lockean abstract ideas into Berkeley's system does not affect the thesis. What common element do we see and feel in the case of extension? The abstract idea itself is not available. An abstract idea is still an *idea* perceived by some sense. When I feel the length of the book and attempt to abstract from that experience, I am abstracting from a *tactual* experience. I am not yet entitled to assume that I am abstracting from a tactual-visual experience or an experience that extends beyond what I sense with that particular modality. Hence the phrase "abstract idea of extension" fails to disambiguate an abstract tangible idea of extension from an abstract visible idea of extension.

To conclude that the truth of the heterogeneity thesis is independent of abstraction, however, we need to establish further that rejecting abstraction is compatible with accepting the homogeneity of ideas. Showing that accepting the latter does not entail accepting the former is a relatively weak claim

---

19. I do not assume here that his reason for denying abstract ideas is related to his conception of ideas.

and correspondingly easy to do. Assume that homogeneity is true. As a result, when we see and touch the extension of an object, we are accessing the numerically same quality. We need not think abstraction is true to account for this phenomenon. It just so happens that the idea of extension associated with this object can be translated into two different sensory languages: a tactual and a visual one. The idea remains particular, and it cannot be understood absent *some* sensory "language," but it just so happens that in our sensory lives we are multilingual. Of course this straightforwardly denies Berkeley's thesis, but it is entirely possible. As a result, we have no independent reason to suppose that the rejection of abstraction in itself drove Berkeley to endorse heterogeneity. His views concerning the perception of distance and abstract ideas provide no reasons for endorsing a radical divide between kinds of ideas. Nonetheless, he thought it was true. Let us turn to what Berkeley says and evaluate his reasons for so thinking. The *New Theory* presents us with three separate arguments.[20]

8.6 The Molyneux Thought Experiment

In the first argument Berkeley uses in defense of heterogeneity, he appeals to a thought experiment first raised by William Molyneux. "But it has been, if I mistake not, clearly made out that a man born blind would not at first reception of his sight think the things he saw were of the same nature with the objects of touch, or had anything in common with them; but that they were a new set of ideas, perceived in a new manner, and entirely different from all he had ever perceived before" (*NTV* 128). Part of the reason this constitutes an initially compelling case for Berkeley is that he subscribes to the view that the contents of the mind are self-transparent. That is, one cannot entertain two ideas and not know whether they are identical. Thus Berkeley thought that the subject described by Molyneux would have to come to some definite conclusion. Either he would recognize the similarity in the ideas or he would not. Although the case has an undeniable intuitive appeal, as an argument it falls short. Even were such a person ("Molyneux Man" for short) unable properly to judge the nature of things by sight alone, that in and of itself would not constitute proof of heterogeneity. If correct about the divergence between the ideas of sight and touch, Berkeley needs a

---

20. Atherton tells us that there is a fourth, less explicit, argument concerning the perception of motion (1990, 193). As it concerns the Molyneux Man and does not add a new line of reasoning, I consider it with my analysis of the Molyneux Man.

conceptual test that will confirm his hypothesis. He needs more than the mere fact that a Molyneux Man would not be able to recognize objects by sight, since there might be other factors that could explain such a failure.[21] Rather he needs the stronger claim that such a person would never be able determine the matchups between the felt and the seen *by sight and reason alone*. Determining the matchups by this process would require an alternate experiment. Imagine another subject blind from birth who later acquires her sight ("Molyneux Woman" for short). However, at the moment sight is restored, the person loses all tactual and kinesthetic abilities, preventing her from using mere correlation to make tangible-visual matchups. If ideas are heterogeneous, such a Molyneux Woman should not be able to figure out the visible-tangible correspondences *ever*. I think Berkeley believes this, but he does not in fact argue for this stronger claim.

Independently, it is hard to see how Berkeley's original thought experiment accomplishes much. If perceptual heterogeneity is true, then the connections between the seen and the felt will be contingent. Thus Berkeley needs to motivate the *possibility* of connections between experiences like felt squares and visible circles, but the Molyneux case does not speak to this issue. Pitcher remarks, "Thus, a world in which tangible squares answered to what we, in our world, would call visible circles would be a world that is very radically different from our actual world, and its laws would have to be so fantastically complicated, that it is uncertain whether any coherent description of it could possibly be formulated. It is, therefore, uncertain that it *is* a possible world" (1977, 57). Imagining a coherent physics that conjoins felt squares to seen circles is daunting, yet it is what Berkeley requires. The inability of the Molyneux Man to match up his visual and tactual sensations provides no direct evidence of the sort of radical contingency Berkeley needs.

8.7 The Argument from Difference in Content

The second argument Berkeley advances in the *New Theory* comes in the next paragraph at 129: "*Secondly,* light and colours are allowed by all to

---

21. There are several possible alternate explanations. The most compelling involves recent advances in our understanding of how visual abilities develop. We now know that the pathways in the brain associated with proper vision form in the early months of infancy. Individuals who do not have sight during the first year of life do not properly develop those pathways in the brain. As a result, congenitally blind persons who have had their sight restored might not pass the Molyneux test on account of a deficiency in the structure of the brain and not because ideas are radically heterogeneous.

constitute a sort or species entirely different from the ideas of touch: nor will any man, I presume, say they can make themselves perceived by that sense: but there is no other immediate object of sight besides light and colours. It is therefore a direct consequence that there is no idea common to both senses." Essentially, Berkeley argues that ordinary people will grant that what they strictly perceive by sight and touch are in fact distinct. He admits that there is a "prevailing opinion" that by sight we perceive considerably more than just light and color, but he thinks he has already proven earlier in the *New Theory* that those cases are instances of mediate perception (130). Yet, again, this argument does not support Berkeley's conclusion. Having distinct phenomenal contents does not entail heterogeneity. Perhaps the content of a single idea is presented differently to (has different effects on) various senses. Berkeley is here *describing* heterogeneity, not explaining why it is true. If by sight I perceive only light and color and by touch only solidity and shape, then what prevents the idea of a triangle from affecting my eye in one way and my tactual senses in another? The content will differ but that *alone* does not guarantee the sort of radical heterogeneity Berkeley seeks to establish.

In short, I do not think much philosophical substance lies here.[22] At best we might reconstruct the argument Armstrong uses to claim that Berkeley is forced into accepting the heterogeneity thesis, but as we have seen that line of reasoning fails. Most of the mileage Berkeley gets from the argument stems from its intuitive and not its philosophical appeal.

8.8 Adding Visible and Tangible Lines

Of more interest is Berkeley's last explicit argument. He claims that if extension in particular is common to both sight and touch, then one ought to be able to add visible and tangible lines together. But this cannot be done; hence ideas of visible and tangible extensions share nothing in common. They are not the same sort of idea, despite the similarity in name. Berkeley confidently asserts this point in section 131: "A blue and a red line I can conceive added together into one sum and making one continued line: but to make in my thoughts one continued line of a visible and tangible line added together is, I find, a task far more difficult, and even insurmountable: and I leave it to the reflexion and experience of every particular person to

---

22. Pitcher seems to disagree. Compare Pitcher 1977, 53–54. I concur with Atherton that Pitcher reads too much into this argument (Atherton 1990, 188).

determine for himself." This is less an argument than a challenge—he thinks no opponent can perform the task.

Armstrong provides the obvious reply when he asks "Can I not pace out part of a distance, and then measure the remainder by the eye?" (1960, 56). Margaret Atherton challenges Armstrong's example by questioning whether it is a genuine case of adding a tangible to a visual line (1990, 190). She rightly points out that what he is doing is measuring a tangible distance and *estimating* a visible distance. Hence Armstrong has not met the challenge, although we have still to determine whether Berkeley is correct. Perhaps Armstrong might reply that in fact Berkeley is estimating distance in *both* cases, tactually and visually. Yet even so, it is difficult to see how this sort of estimation could rise to the challenge set by Berkeley. What reason do we have to think that visual estimations are of a kind with tactual ones? At best the issue remains clouded.

To add two lines in this fashion, Atherton contends one would need an inconceivable measuring device whose units are neither visible nor tangible. This move is meant to mirror Berkeley's own reasoning earlier in the *New Theory*. He holds that we measure distance in terms of sense modality–specific points, his "minimum sensibles." The distance between two tangible locations is a certain number of tangible points; the distance between two visible places is a visible line consisting of visible points. Now the problem arises. "[B]ut if they are one tangible and the other visible, the distance between them doth neither consist of points perceivable by sight nor by touch, i.e. it is utterly inconceivable" (112).

Why is a distance measuring device that is neither visible nor tangible inconceivable? Atherton answers, "There is no unit of measurement that will allow you to get from a point that is visible to one that is tangible" (1990, 163). We might challenge her by considering some unusual olfactory abilities. The world might be constructed such that each tangible and visible point is associated with a particular kind of smell, thus permitting one to measure distance by comparing the differences in smells. It seems reasonable to suppose, then, that by smelling a point felt but not seen and then a point seen but not felt, I could still accurately judge the distance between them. Now this case would not bother Atherton or Berkeley, for they would doubtless describe my measuring as being completely within the olfactory realm. I fixed one of the points visually and the other tactually, but the distance being measured is between, as it were, two olfactory points. Olfactory points presumably only provide *cues* to visible and tangible distances. Atherton's point is thus not that there cannot be a measuring device that is neither visible nor tangible but rather that there cannot be a measuring device that is *both* visible *and* tangible, that would take us directly from a tangible point to a visible one.

Yet this is precisely what is at issue! One might attribute our inability to add visible and tangible lines to something other than their being radically distinct. Contingent psychological limitations in humans comes to mind (we might be able to think "in" only a single sense modality at a time). Berkeley cannot expect his readers to be convinced of a conceptual truth on the basis of an empirical result. At best our alleged inability to add visible and tangible lines can only confirm an antecedently assumed hypothesis. Admittedly, this result is not what one would expect, and being led to recognize its truth is a powerful psychological ploy. Berkeley uses this argument not as a careful reason for accepting the heterogeneity of ideas but as persuasive tool to convince his lay readers. We have yet to penetrate to the heart of what motivates Berkeley on this issue.

8.9 Heterogeneity and the Nature of Ideas

To this point we have seen that Berkeley's explicit arguments in defense of perceptual heterogeneity seem to amount more to intuitive appeals than rigorous reasoning. Nonetheless I think that Berkeley understood where the work had to be done. For perceptual heterogeneity to be true, he needs to establish that the contents presented by ideas of different senses themselves are not merely distinct but incommensurable. Incommensurability is implied by the *complete* distinctness of the ideas. He clearly thinks that they are incommensurable, but why? Pointing to differences in the intrinsic features of presented sensory content will not validate his thesis. It generates plausible and intuitive examples, but there *should* be more. There is.

In this discussion we have left unexamined an important element of perception: the things that *bear* content, namely the ideas themselves. If "internal" features of content cannot explain heterogeneity, perhaps extrinsic ones can. When discussing representation and content, Berkeley treats ideas like robust things: quasi substances. He makes them "external" to the mind (see chapters 6 and 7) and accounts for perceptual heterogeneity. If sensory ideas are themselves quasi substances of distinct kinds, then asking someone to add a visible line with a tangible one is analogous to asking someone to add pain (something mental) to a cubical block (something material). The reason such acts cannot be performed is attributable to the *ontological* nature of the bearers of the content and not to either limitations of the mind or the objective contents of ideas themselves.

In order to make my analysis plausible, I need to establish two claims. The first I have already done in the preceding two chapters, namely demonstrate that Berkeley thought of ideas as quasi substances or as entities in their own right external to (even if ontologically dependent on) the mind. Second, I need to indicate why *this* view would lead him to heterogeneity when, say, an adverbial theory of ideas would not. It is to the latter of these tasks we now turn.

8.10 Ontology to Heterogeneity

Why does Berkeley's conception of ideas as "external" (that is, as standing in two-place relations with minds such that they are not modifications of minds), dependent things encourage him to endorse perceptual heterogeneity? If my thesis is to have any explanatory power, it must be the case that had Berkeley thought of ideas as, say, adverbial on minds, then that would have undercut his reasons for thinking that perception is heterogeneous.

In order to make this clear, I want to use Berkeley's third argument as a guide. He claims that a visible and a tangible line are incommensurable and cannot be added together. Why might he think this? If ideas are modifications of the mind, they (the visible and tangible ideas) share at least one thing in common: they both qualify (or are ontically "in") the same mind. If touch and sight are radically incommensurable, then the content of those ideas can only be correlated, not shared. Recall that Berkeley's claim is rather strong: the two lines *cannot* be added together. Now the mind for Berkeley is an active unity.[23] Given this feature, what is the cognitive limit that explains why the mind, while simultaneously being modified by the ideas of tactual and visual lines, cannot add them together? Berkeley has no explicit answer. If he had one, however, it would have to be something internal to the mind, which might deny its unity. That is, if he thought of ideas as adverbial while thinking about perceptual heterogeneity, then he would be compelled to deny the fundamental unity of the mind in order to explain why the mind cannot add the lines together. I cannot see any other way out for him. As a result, perceptual heterogeneity is not compatible with an adverbial view of ideas.

23. See *PHK* 89, quoted earlier, where he describes spirits as active indivisible substances. His writings are replete with such references.

The picture changes, however, if we attribute a quasi-substantial conception of ideas to Berkeley. If ideas are quasi substances, then the problem of adding the lines is shifted, as it were, "outside" the mind. An idea would then be an external thing in the sense that the mind perceives it in a two-place relation that is not a modification or proper part of the mind. We know the mind can perceive ideas from diverse senses at the same time since it can correlate sensations. What bars the mind from "sharing" the content of distinct sensory ideas is the very nature of the ideas themselves. I submit that Berkeley thought of ideas as sufficiently like substances that when one divides them into kinds, those kinds are basic. Thus just as one cannot merge the mental with the material because they share no more fundamental features, so one cannot merge the content of ideas of various sense modalities. Since reality consists of ideas ordered and created by God, and perceived differences in real (sensory) ideas are veridical, there is no deeper metaphysical level to which one can push. If God created ideas in different kinds, then those differences are fundamental.

That Berkeley thinks of sensory ideas as divided into fundamental substantial kinds is discernible in the texts. When he describes the differences among the senses, he often explains what he means in terms of kinds. "But it will not hence follow that any visible figure is like unto, or of the same species with, its corresponding tangible figure" (*NTV* 143).[24] Why would Berkeley say that visible figure is not "of the same species" as tangible figure? After all, they are both figures. We have already ruled out the possibility that abstraction ultimately explains this move. So what else might explain why two bits of content must belong to separate species? I submit that the answer is that their vehicles belong to distinct ontological kinds. In short, the missing piece of the puzzle is that Berkeley took the differences between the contents of the various senses to be grounded on ontological differences in kind among the ideas. The reason these ontic discrepancies affect content is that Berkeley thinks representation requires likeness. In effect, Berkeley encodes content into his ontology of ideas. This blue idea cannot be added to this idea of extension because visual ideas are a kind of being distinct from tactual ones. Therefore there can be no point of overlap in their content except by mere correlation.

Robert Muehlmann has recently challenged my interpretation of Berkeley here on the grounds that my view essentially forces Berkeley to beg the

---

24. Berkeley often distinguishes among sensory ideas in terms of their being more or less "of a species." See *NTV* 129, 140, and 142.

question.[25] If we ask why Berkeley would think that the encoding of content into the ontology of ideas establishes the heterogeneity of ideas—why the identification of content and ontic status shows that tangible and visible ideas are specifically distinct—the answer appears to be nothing more than that they are distinct. This presentation of the interpretation I am advancing is uncharitable, even were it to turn out to be technically true. Not every petitio principii is a gross error; sometimes it takes great thinkers to make great mistakes. Granting that ideas are quasi-substantial and that Berkeley reduces qualities to ideas, it follows that the content of ideas (whether or not this is distinct from the ideas themselves qua qualities) will also be volitionally independent yet ontically dependent on minds. Their volitional independence indicates that their phenomenal appearance has nothing to do with me (beyond my contribution to sustaining the existence of the ideas) and in particular with my mind. Abstraction will not solve the problem either. But on the hypothesis that the merging of quality and idea extends to the ontological level, we have a reasonable *explanation* for the heterogeneity thesis. Ideas (and their contents) are real things. The contents of ideas differ based on the sense modality to which they are attached. Hence, the ideas qua real things differ as well. If we then ask, *why* do the ideas of different sense modalities differ, I think Berkeley would have no other answer than to say that in his experience they *do* differ. Touches are not like smells or colors. Hence tactual ideas are not like olfactory or visual ones. All of these ideas might be classified as *mental,* but as we have learned this is misleading, since they are mental only in the limited sense that they are all objects that may be perceptually related to minds. There is no sense that ideas are *ontologically* like minds. In fact, they cannot be since ideas are passive and minds are not. That this argument might be question begging is unfortunate, but it does not undermine the explanatory power that this account has, nor does it undermine my claim that we can better understand Berkeley by thinking of him as a philosopher operating within the limiting categories of substance and modification even as he introduces quasi substances. In fact, Muehlmann agrees that Berkeley is best read this way (as a metaphysician who thinks that "specific" differences entail distinctness of ontological categories); he simply defends an alternative understanding of Berkeley's strategy concerning the heterogeneity thesis. Muehlmann's position, unfortunately, is quite complicated and a meaningful analysis of it

---

25. Robert Muehlmann, "Seeing Berkeley in Depth" (unpublished manuscript).

would take us too far afield from our concerns here.[26] Let me be clear about the upshot of my analysis. That Berkeley's motivation for endorsing the heterogeneity thesis might be circular is not the point. I have aimed here to provide a plausible account for why Berkeley endorsed the heterogeneity thesis at all, given that the reasons he actually advances in the *New Theory* fall manifestly short of accounting for it. Pointing to the influence of the ontological nature of ideas in Berkeley's theory provides a reason for him to endorse heterogeneity, even if that reason might otherwise hide certain defects in his thinking. I am not confusing my analysis here with a philosophical defense of Berkeley's heterogeneity thesis, and the reader ought not do so either, although I think some philosophical progress has been made.

So now we can go back and complete the arguments Berkeley provided. Why can the Molyneux Man not ever make the required matchups without some conjunction of the senses? Answer: the *formal* nature of visual ideas is incompatible with that of tactual ones. Berkeley too closely connected the ontic status of ideas with their representative function. This move led him to believe that differences in content had to be reflected in the ontological nature of the ideas that bear that content. Given this belief as a starting point, heterogeneity is neither unexpected nor all that implausible, especially in light of why he rejects abstraction. Berkeley's implicit conception of ideas as quasi substances undergirds his rejection of abstract ideas as impossible entities and enables him to coherently maintain heterogeneity. None of this analysis is possible, however, if we accept Berkeley's role in the early modern tale. A Berkeley that is seeking to "abandon" ontology seems another world away from the Berkeley we see here reasoning deftly about abstraction, divine ideas, and heterogeneity.

With Berkeley comes an important change. He wants to operate within the traditional substance/mode ontology, but he finds he cannot properly fit ideas into either category. He inherited a tradition, most notably through Malebranche, that guided his reasoning about ideas and metaphysics generally. But guides are not straightjackets. Berkeley's radical metaphysics may be seen as an attempt to save the philosophy of ideas *within* the ontology of substance and mode. Although he ultimately might not have been clear

---

26. In short, Muehlmann's hypothesis, as I understand it, is that Berkeley uses the heterogeneity thesis disingenuously (because Muehlmann's Berkeley does *not* think strong heterogeneity is true) to lead his readers to accept the core claims of his immaterialist metaphysic, which he *does* believe. I readily confess that Muehlmann's analysis is both interesting and smart; I am less convinced that he is right. A fair and proper treatment of his book-length argument for his thesis is simply beyond the scope of this discussion.

about all aspects of the nature of ideas, to admit this is not to say that he ever abandoned the ontology. Berkeley never explicitly does so; on the contrary, he labors to preserve the old conceptual framework. His system, however, cannot properly hold that ideas are dependent yet genuine substances. As a result, he was driven to adopt increasingly unusual positions until he ultimately defended a radical form of heterogeneity among kinds of ideas. Here I have sought—and found—explanatory power in his dedication to the outlines of the traditional ontology. But Berkeley paid a price for his ingenious metaphysics. Its counterintuitive conclusions generally encouraged later philosophers to misread his commitment to the traditional ontology and misread its importance more generally to the philosophy of ideas.

9

HUME AND IDEA ONTOLOGY

For many adherents of the early modern tale, Hume represents the final break from the traditional ontology. Richard Watson, for instance, writes of the transition from Malebranche and Berkeley to Hume in just this way.

> Attempts to escape the weight of ontological status for ideas are characterized as attempts to break out of the ontological pattern of substance and modification. Everything is either a substance or a modification. As long as this principle is adhered to, the way of ideas is doomed. One could say that ideas are nothing or at least that they are not entities, or one could try to introduce a new ontological entity. But as Malebranche and Berkeley illustrate, it is difficult to characterize such an entity. There is another alternative. Everything might be of the same ontological status. . . . I introduce Hume now, near the close of this study, not as a monist who reduces all ontological categories to one, but as a philosopher who breaks entirely with the ontological structure of substance and modification.[1] (1987, 127–28)

A fairly standard reading of Hume is that he is the first systematic critic of the doctrine of substance. The *Treatise of Human Nature,* especially book 1, part 4, initially seems to lend itself to being read that way. I do not deny that Hume was a critic of the concept of substance. But being a critic of the concept and its use by his contemporaries does not entail that Hume dismissed ontology. My relatively modest goal in this chapter is to demonstrate

---

1. See also Yolton 2000, 139–40, who argues for a similar progression. Daniel Flage likewise argues that Hume does not subscribe to a substance ontology for ideas, arguing that Hume's perceptions are only "theoretical primitives" without positive characterization (1990, 19–20).

that Hume did *not* "break" from the traditional ontology. There is good reason to believe that Hume operated within the ontology of substance and modification, at least with respect to ideas and impressions (perceptions), despite concerns about how his intellectual predecessors used those concepts.

Hume was influenced by Berkeley with respect to the nature of ideas. There might be some dispute about how profound the influence is, but it is present. He accepted Berkeley's reduction of qualities to ideas (what Phillip Cummins has since called "no-quality nominalism"—the view that qualities are not ontologically distinct from individuals [1996, 49–88]), he accepted Berkeley's critique of abstract ideas, and he also embraced the important claim that we have no epistemic access to anything beyond perceptions. Yet Hume also saw the tension of which I believe Berkeley was aware: that perceptions as independent existences cannot simultaneously be modifications of mental substances. But whereas Berkeley sought to reconcile these features of perceptions by positing a new special status for them, Hume could not see his way to accepting them both. Persuaded by the likes of Bayle that a unified simple substance cannot account for the changes we experience in perception, Hume separated mental substances from perceptions completely. As he himself would confess, this separation of mental substances from perceptions presented him with insuperable difficulties.[2] Yet despite the problems Hume faced, I contend that none of his reasoning involved *abandoning* the traditional ontology for ideas.

Hume believed that the mind consists solely of perceptions; there is no substance in which these perceptions inhere. Thus it is quite clear that Hume rejects a substance account *of the mind*. Hume's claim eventually commits him to the view that perceptions are substances themselves.[3] But he also says that perceptions are dependent entities that do not exist when not perceived, which plausibly inclines one to think that perceptions are *not* substances. After all, such things would not be *independent* entities in the sense required for substancehood in the traditional ontology. To complicate matters, Hume is also a skeptic about substance. Since there is no antecedent impression from which we may derive our idea of substance, it must be that the concept is conceptually thin. These sorts of concerns that Hume expresses have led some to include him in the early modern tale. Perhaps, one might speculate, Hume joined Berkeley at the pinnacle of early modern

---

2. I refer, of course, to Hume's famous concerns expressed in the appendix to the *Treatise*, esp. *T*, 633–36; *N*, 398–401. For a discussion of Bayle's influence, see Smith 1964, 325.

3. I am not the first to advance this kind of thesis with respect to Hume; see, for example, Anderson 1966, esp. 3–15.

thought in this respect. The difficulties with the status of ideas in fact indicate that perceptions ought not be thought of as having any ontological status at all. Yolton draws the parallel between Hume and Berkeley in exactly this way. "'Existence in the mind' for Berkeley turns out to mean 'known' or 'understood.' Hume offers a similar suggestion for 'present to mind.' The mind adds to my object-perceptions the belief in their continued existence" (1984, 163). On Yolton's analysis, presence to the mind is an *epistemological* relation only. Thus Hume is characterized along with Berkeley as a philosopher who moved away from ontology with respect to ideas.

This characterization is as erroneous with respect to Hume as it is with respect to Berkeley. Strongly influenced by his Irish predecessor, we have reason to believe that Hume was driven by many of the same pressures that led Berkeley to the conclusion that ideas are quasi substances. Perceptions are existences that are distinct from minds without being modifications of them (Hume uses the word "independent" to describe perceptions in this sense), but they are nonetheless ontologically dependent on those minds for their existence. Although I believe that Hume resisted the pull to think of perceptions as quasi substances, he nonetheless provides a sort of capstone to the development of the early modern ontology of ideas, just not one in the service of the early modern tale. Hume *recognizes* the problematic fit between the ontology of ideas and their epistemic roles but nevertheless preserves the core ontology of substance and mode *when applied to ideas*. I recognize that the claim is controversial, but I base my contention on what Hume actually says at various places in the texts. Although at one point Hume indicates that substances and perceptions are distinct, he nevertheless consistently treats perceptions elsewhere as independent entities. He might intend to be a critic of the concept of substance, but at the end of the day Humean perceptions are still things with some sort of ontological standing.

9.1 Perceptions as Substances

Let us start with an analysis of the nature of perceptions. Hume is fortuitously clear on this point, arguing that perceptions are distinct, individual existences that underlie higher levels of change. As such they appear to qualify as substances. This realization turns out not to be as important for Hume as it is for some of the other early moderns, because Hume takes the content of the concept of substance to be exceedingly thin. We have no idea or impression of substance. Hence learning that something is a substance turns out to be of minimal value. This analysis explains Hume's consistent criticisms of the concepts of substance used by his contemporaries. He doesn't like to invoke essentially fictionalized concepts. Philosophers who "read into" substance more than they are entitled are basically telling stories on Hume's view. We thus help ourselves to fictions like identity over time by inserting elements into the notion of substance to which we are not entitled. In order to understand Hume's thinking about the nature of perceptions, however, we first need to do some background work.

9.1.1 Two Principles

Hume divides the sensible world into ideas and impressions; together both of them exhaust the category of perceptions. "All perceptions of the mind are of two kinds, viz. impressions and ideas, which differ from each other only in their different degrees of force and vivacity" (*T*, 96 / *N*, 67 [1.3.7]). Furthermore, we only have perfect ideas of things that may be perceived, which again are only perceptions. Hence, we can only have perfect perceptions of perceptions. "We have no perfect idea of any thing but of a perception" (*T*, 234 / *N*, 153 [1.4.5]). All of this signals Hume's underlying commitment to the way of ideas. Ideas and impressions constitute the entirety of what must be mastered to acquire knowledge about the world. The particularities about the relationship between ideas and impressions (the famous "copy thesis," namely, that all ideas derive from a corresponding impression) need not delay us here.

There are, however, two important principles that Hume invokes when discussing the nature of perceptions. The first is the conceivability principle. Whatever can be conceived is logically possible. "'Tis an established maxim in metaphysics, *That whatever the mind clearly conceives includes the idea of possible existence,* or in other words, *that nothing we imagine is absolutely impossible.* We can form the idea of a golden mountain, and from thence conclude that such a mountain may actually exist. We can form no idea of a mountain without a valley, and therefore regard it as impossible" (*T*, 32 / *N*, 26 [1.2.2]).[4] The contrapositive also holds. Whatever is absolutely impossible is inconceivable. Therefore whatever implies a contradiction cannot be conceived. "'Tis in vain to search for a contradiction in any thing that is distinctly conceiv'd by the mind. Did it imply any contradiction, 'tis impossible it cou'd ever be conceiv'd" (*T*, 43 / *N*, 33 [1.2.4]).

---

4. See *T*, 236 / *N*, 155 (1.4.5), and *T*, 250 / *N*, 164 (1.4.5).

The second principle I call the "difference-existence principle." Wherever the mind can discern difference, the mind can conceive of separate existences. "First, We have observ'd, that whatever objects are different are distinguishable, and that whatever objects are distinguishable are separable by the thought and imagination" (*T*, 18/*N*, 17 [1.1.7]).[5] Unsurprisingly, this principle also holds in the inverse: whatever is separable is distinguishable. "And we may here add, that these propositions are equally true in the *inverse*, and that whatever objects are separable are also distinguishable, and that whatever objects are distinguishable are also different" (*T*, 18/*N*, 17 [1.1.7]). One might think that two putatively distinct objects that are, in fact, numerically identical might nevertheless be (mistakenly) distinguished from one another. Certainly we distinguished the morning star and evening star before learning that the two bodies are the same planet. Why should any rational person accept this principle?

Hume's difference-existence principle, however, is meant to apply only to perceptions and not generally (say to material objects or other nonideas). Where we *detect* no difference in sensory content we posit no plurality in objects. Why would we? The morning star/evening star case is disingenuous because there is a detected difference, namely *when* we see planet. As a result, the principle is generally defensible within his philosophical system. We only distinguish things when we detect difference. That we sometimes *mistakenly* detect differences when there are none does not undercut the principle.

9.1.2 Determinate and Individual

Like Berkeley, Hume holds that all existing things are fully determinate. When applied to perceptions, it follows that each and every idea and impression must be fixed in terms of their qualities. Hume starts with the case of impressions in the *Treatise*. "Secondly, 'tis confest, that no object can appear to the senses; or in other words, that no impression can become present to the mind, without being determin'd in its degrees both of quality and quantity. The confusion, in which impressions are sometimes involv'd, proceeds only from their faintness and unsteadiness, not from any capacity in the mind to receive any impression, which in its real existence has no particular degree nor proportion" (*T*, 19/*N*, 18 [1.1.7]). The explanation is then ex-

---

5. See *T*, 24/*N*, 21 (1.1.7) ("*all ideas, which are different, are separable*" [emphasis in the original]) and *T*, 634/*N*, 399, appendix.

tended to include ideas as well at the start of the next paragraph. "Now since all ideas are deriv'd from impressions, and are nothing but copies and representations of them, whatever is true of the one must be acknowledg'd concerning the other.... An idea is a weaker impression; and as a strong impression must necessarily have a determinate quantity and quality, the case must be the same with its copy or representative." We now know that perceptions are individual and fully determinate entities. When we apply the two preceding principles to these entities, it follows that they possess the key features of traditional substances.

One might think that Hume is actually slightly cagey on this point about the ontological status of perceptions. In the section entitled "Of the Immateriality of the Soul" (1.4.5), Hume addresses the question of the nature of perceptions indirectly as a part of his argument that the soul is not a substantial unity. Considering the challenge that one might think that there are substances, defined only as independent existences, Hume responds by noting that on this definition every perception becomes a substance.

> For thus I reason. Whatever is clearly conceiv'd may exist; and whatever is clearly conceiv'd, after any manner, may exist after the same manner. This is one principle, which has been already acknowledg'd. Again, every thing, which is different, is distinguishable, and every thing which is distinguishable, is separable by the imagination. This is another principle. My conclusion from both is, that since all our perceptions are different from each other, and from every thing else in the universe, they are also distinct and separable, and may be consider'd as separately existent, and may exist separately, and have no need of any thing else to support their existence. They are, therefore, substances, as far as this definition explains a substance. (*T*, 233 / *N*, 153 [1.4.5])

Applying the conceivability principle to the difference-existence principle, we learn that it is conceivable that everything that is separable in thought may in fact be distinct. Perceptions—whether ideas or impressions—are all separable in thought. Hence perceptions (which, we should carefully note, are *objects* of some sort) are all possibly distinct from one another. At a minimum this is enough for Hume to conclude that perceptions could all individually exist apart from everything else. But this analysis depends on the supposition that a substance is to be defined as "*something which may exist by itself*" (*T*, 233 / *N*, 153 [1.4.5], emphasis in the original). I believe

Hume endorses this point but thinks it does not entail much. If *that* is all a substance is, then all perceptions are substances.

Some might object that Hume is in fact being hesitant about substance and that the passage above is intended as a reductio on the assertion that perceptions are substances. Watson, for instance, alleges: "As a *reductio*, Hume argued that if independent existence is the criterion of a substance, then his perceptions are substances. Although perceptions are all ontologically of the same kind and type, and although ideas represent by being like impressions, perceptions are neither substances nor modifications" (1987, 152). On Watson's view, Hume is unsure not merely about what perceptions are but also about whether they even exist. Watson concludes, "Hume instead denies the possibility of the knowledge and even of the existence of substances" (130). However, the only serious support for this view, I think, comes from reading Hume in this section ironically, since Hume explicitly concludes that perceptions count as substances. And some believe that there is a reason to think that this might be so. Close on the heels of the passage where Hume reasons that perceptions are substances he seems to explicitly deny the same thesis.

> Thus neither by considering the first origin of our ideas, nor by means of a definition are we able to arrive at any satisfactory notion of substance; which seems to me a sufficient reason for abandoning utterly that dispute concerning the materiality and immateriality of the soul, and makes me absolutely condemn even the question itself. We have no perfect idea of anything but of a perception. A substance is entirely different from a perception. We have, therefore, no idea of a substance. (*T*, 234 / *N*, 153 [1.4.5])

I do not think that this passage repudiates the claim that perceptions are substances. Some might respond to my claim with incredulity. After all, what else could "A substance is entirely different from a perception" mean? Well, one should note at the outset that if Hume wanted to assert that perceptions could not be substances, he could have said so more clearly. Worse yet, Hume elsewhere explicitly makes claims that *entail* that perceptions are independent objects, just like substances. Thus there is good reason to at least *look* for another understanding of the passage. After all, if we take the passage to deny that perceptions are substances, then we have much work to do to explain why Hume says what he does elsewhere (and much *more* work than trying to understand a single apparently contrary bit of text, as in this case). So what is going on in the passage?

Instead of denying that perceptions are substances, the key sentence emphasizes the point that substances are not perceptions, that is, we do not *perceive* substances. And that claim is not only true but also coheres well with the line of argument actually found in the section. In the context of the extended passage, Hume reasons (1) we have no (perfect) idea of anything other than perceptions, (2) substances are not perceptions, and hence (3) we have no (perfect) idea of substances. This, I find, is a natural way to read the passage, and it has the virtue of rendering Hume internally consistent, since he elsewhere *reaffirms* the claim that substances exist and perceptions are substances. This verity is perhaps nowhere more obvious than in the appendix where Hume gives voice to his concerns about where his thinking has led him. "In short there are two principles, which I cannot render consistent; nor is it in my power to renounce either of them, viz. *that all our distinct perceptions are distinct existences, and that the mind never perceives any real connexion among distinct existences*" (*T*, 636 / N, 400). Hume makes clear from the preceding analysis in the appendix that his "distinct existences" assertion qualifies perceptions as substances provided one takes a substance to be a simple, individual existence. And here he is quite explicit: he cannot free himself from this particular claim. Hume finds that he has no positive idea of a substance separate from a collection of qualities but nonetheless concludes that, given the traditional definition, perceptions in fact do qualify as substances. There is no reductio ad absurdum here. Hume is carefully following the consequences of believing that substances are independent existences. It simply follows that his perceptions so construed are all substances. This result is not initially worrying because Hume finds that there is not much *to* the claim that something is a substance.

We should note that a weaker claim is present in Hume's analysis of perceptions as well: perceptions are distinct from minds. That is, perceptions form two-place relations with the minds that perceive them. Perceptions are neither modes of minds nor do they inhere in any suspect thing like a mind or a substance. For Hume, minds perceive ideas more in a part-whole relation (since minds are bundles of perceptions). Even as Hume distances himself from a substantial account of the mind, he preserves the language of perceptions as distinct things. Definitions of substance seem inadequate because they do not create a suitable contrast class. If substances are independent existences, then as established above, no thing of which we can conceive (i.e., no perception) fails to be a substance. Hume's insightful analysis is not a *denial* that perceptions are substances; rather it is an assertion that such a claim does not amount to much.

As Robert Anderson notes in his analysis of the same argument (1966, 9), Hume indicates that this reasoning applies only to actually existing objects. Perceptions *may* be considered substances *if* they so exist as conceptually separable entities. But Hume is clearly committed to the existence of perceptions if he is committed to the existence of anything. As noted above, Hume takes perceptions to be entities that are always particular and determinate. In discussing personal identity, Hume advances the following argument, also cited by Anderson: "'Tis still true, that every distinct perception, which enters into the composition of the mind, is a distinct existence, and is different, and distinguishable, and separable from every other perception, either contemporary or successive" (*T*, 259/*N*, 169 [1.4.6]). The argument clearly reveals that Hume thinks perceptions are genuine existences. The issue is *what sort* of existences. Hume is seeking to separate perceptions from minds because he finds that he can make no sense of the claim that perceptions inhere in substance, the mind in particular (were the mind to be a substance). That leaves perceptions as independent existences in their own right, satisfying the demand of the traditional definition of substance that requires them to be ontologically independent. As he argues in the appendix:

> In general, the following reasoning seems satisfactory. All ideas are borrow'd from preceding perceptions. Our ideas of objects, therefore, are deriv'd from that source. Consequently no proposition can be intelligible or consistent with regard to objects, which is not so with regard to perceptions. But 'tis intelligible and consistent to say, that objects exist distinct and independent, without any common *simple* substance or subject of inhesion. This proposition, therefore, can never be absurd with regard to perceptions. (*T*, 634/ *N*, 399])

As perceptions are distinct and independent entities, they must be substances, and this is exactly the conclusion at which Hume arrives.

9.1.3 Concepts of Substance

The preceding discussion importantly depends on the claim that Hume thinks that the concept of substance is in fact meaningful.[6] Here we need to

---

6. My assertion is controversial. Daniel Flage, for one, disagrees. "Hume argues that the Cartesian definition of substance is too broad, and therefore, the substance/accidents distinction is *unintelligible*" (1990, 71, emphasis mine).

be careful. There is a difference between a concept that is *meaningless* and one that has meaning but a meaning so thin as to be of relatively little value. Hume thinks of the concept of substance in the second manner. The mere fact that Hume positively ascribes perceptions the status of being substances should be ample evidence of this truth, but the point is worth further exploration to satisfy ourselves that this is Hume's view.

Hume's initial engagement of the concept of substance comes in the form of a challenge. "I wou'd fain ask those philosophers . . . whether the idea of *substance* be deriv'd from the impressions of sensation or reflexion?" (*T*, 15–16 / *N*, 16 [1.1.6]). I can recall learning as an undergraduate that the answer is neither and that hence we have no idea of substance at all. Thus in his introduction to his edition of the *Enquiry*, Tom Beauchamp similarly writes that "Hume maintains that terms such as 'substance' have been employed in philosophy without clear meaning and that resultant controversies are burdened by meaningless terms" (19). Although in general Beauchamp is right, this is not what Hume actually concludes about *substance*. Hume reveals that we have no idea of substance "distinct from that of a collection of particular qualities, nor have we any other meaning when we either talk or reason concerning it" (*T*, 16 / *N*, 16 [1.1.6]). That we have no idea distinct from a collection entails that we *do* have a meaningful conception of substance, namely exactly that of a collection of qualities. Perhaps this is "no *clear* meaning" (emphasis mine), but it most certainly *is* meaningful. Importantly, in the *Enquiry* Hume does not specifically name substance as one of his targets. Substance is hardly mentioned much at all in this later work, no doubt primarily because of Hume's inability to resolve the puzzles surrounding substance and identity.[7] It is therefore hasty to conclude that Hume takes the concept of substance to be entirely meaningless or unintelligible.

The point of Hume's skepticism about substance concerns the concept of an underlying unity. On reflection, Hume finds that he has no idea of this unity. Alternatively, without this union the concept of substance becomes a sort of fiction constructed from the conjunction of particular qualities.

> The idea of a substance as well as that of a mode, is nothing but a collection of simple ideas, that are united by the imagination, and have a particular name assigned them, by which we are able to recall, either to ourselves or others, that collection. But the differ-

---

7. The word "substance" in its ontological sense occurs rarely in the *Enquiry*. The word is used in this way most notably in section 7, pars. 11 and 19, and then again in section 12, par. 11. The other appearances of the word are unrelated to the sense of the word relevant to this discussion.

ence betwixt these ideas consists in this, that the particular qualities, which form a substance, are commonly refer'd to an unknown *something,* in which they are supposed to inhere; or granting this fiction should not take place, are at least supposed to be closely and inseparably connected by the relations of contiguity and causation. The effect of this is, that whatever new simple quality we discover to have the same connexion with the rest, we immediately comprehend it among them, even tho' it did not enter into the first conception of the substance. (*T,* 16 / *N,* 16 [1.1.6])

Hume's depiction of substance here is consistent with his earlier claim that substances simply pick out independent distinct existences. A particular set of qualities may be given a name and considered a distinct entity in its own right. In fact, this is precisely what we do in ordinary language. If, on the other hand, we deny that a collection is a robust entity in its own right, then we content ourselves with the idea that there are nonetheless underlying "connexions" that bind those qualities together. The key to this analysis is the notion of *union.* The disparate qualities are somehow joined together. It is this collection that constitutes our idea of a substance for Hume, and we most certainly possess *that* concept (the concept of a union of perceptions). Yet because the nature of this union is so mysterious, the actual content of the concept of substance is surprisingly thin. Thus Hume's attack on theism (that all theists are ultimately atheists, invoking Spinozism) centers on his contention that inherence in a unified substratum is incoherent. He complains that substances must be altered based on the qualities that modify them (such as extensions that would, *per impossible,* cause substance to expand or contract) and that they cannot simultaneously support incompatible qualities (*T,* 243–44 / *N,* 159–60 [1.4.5]). A single substance conceived of as a unity is incompatible with our understanding of qualities.

The problem is all the worse when it comes to the idea of a person, since we find no unvarying unity when we reflect on the nature of the self. Here Hume argues that the "fiction" of an underlying substance in fact conceals the conflation of identity with succession (*T,* 254–55 / *N,* 165–66 [1.4.6]). The point, however, remains the same. We *have* a conception of substance, but the one we have is inadequate for its intended uses. Hence, Hume's concern about our idea of substance does not conflict with his assertion that perceptions nevertheless are substances.

One might interject that the story I am telling about Hume mischaracterizes what is going on. Instead of arguing that Hume has a "thin" conception of substance that remains within the core view of the substance/modification ontology, why should we not conclude that Hume is introducing a new set of criteria for something to be a substance? I understand why one might be tempted to advance such a proposal, but I resist it for two reasons. First, the revised view is equivalent to a position already articulated by his contemporaries, so there does not seem to be any compelling need for Hume to bring forward a new theory of substance. If his goal is to *critique* the concept as used by his contemporaries, then such a move would be exceedingly odd. One does not typically criticize the concepts of others by redefining those concepts from the outset. Second, the language Hume uses is remarkably consistent with that of his early modern contemporaries and predecessors; further, when he introduces new terms and conceptual distinctions, he typically is quite clear about them (as with the idea/impression division of perceptions). I thus hold fast to my claim that Hume believes he is engaging his contemporaries on their own conceptual ground, especially with respect to ontology.

At this point we need to address one further concern about Hume's concept of substance. According to what I have described as the "core" traditional ontology, substances are both independent and *enduring*. Although Hume clearly fastens on the former, what of the latter? At one point Hume explicitly endorses the common view that ideas are fleeting beings. "To begin with the coherence; we may observe, that tho' these internal impressions, which we regard as fleeting and perishing, have also a certain coherence or regularity in their appearances" (*T*, 195 / *N*, 130 [1.4.2]). Noting that impressions might be fleeting, however, need not entail that there is no sense in which they endure. Independently, I want to extend the analysis of Berkeley's conception of ideas as "fleeting" beings offered in section 7.5. There I argue that the transitory nature of ideas is a reflection of a changing *order* of perceptions. Even in the passage just cited, Hume recognizes a distinction between individual impressions and the higher-level order in the same. Yet Hume is clearer than Berkeley when it comes to perceptions underlying change. Recall that the endurance criterion captures the "thing thought" for substance. Hume certainly treats perceptions like robust *things*. We need only watch Hume at work to see this element in his thinking. For instance, ideas and impressions underlie change because Hume holds the familiar theory of simple and complex perceptions.

> There is another division of our perceptions, which it will be convenient to observe, and which extends itself both to our impressions

> and ideas. This division is into simple and complex. Simple perceptions, or impressions and ideas, are such as admit of no distinction nor separation. The complex are the contrary to these, and may be distinguished into parts. Though a particular colour, taste, and smell, are qualities all united together in this apple, it is easy to perceive they are not the same, but are at least distinguishable from each other. (*T*, 2 / *N*, 7–8 [1.1.1])

Impressions need not be permanent (or even stable over time) to underlie change; they only need to be continuants under some change—the constituents, if you will, of the world. That they play this role should not be controversial (the more pressing and difficult issue being whether they are independent). Our complex idea or impression of an apple depends on the underlying ideas or impressions of taste and smell and so on. Thus a certain color impression underlies the more complex impression of the apple. Now the point is not that the simple impression needs itself to change; rather it only needs to endure long enough to allow the presence of change. Simple substances, in fact, *will not* change in themselves, except insofar as they are created or annihilated. Our endurance criterion requires nothing more, and Hume's ideas and impressions seem to meet this criterion.

9.2 Dependent Perceptions

Although it appears that Hume's perceptions are at least substance-like (in the core sense of the concept), some philosophers nonetheless continue to assert that for Hume perceptions cannot be genuine substances. Hume consistently denies that perceptions are *in fact* ontologically independent. They depend on minds (specifically mental faculties) for their existence. The dependence of perceptions is an intriguing position for Hume to hold, since he simultaneously maintains that minds are constituted by perceptions. Furthermore, as we have already seen, Hume argues that perceptions are independent existences distinct from the mind. How does Hume tie these claims together? First, we need to remind ourselves that Hume takes the mind to be composed of perceptions. Then we may more profitably turn to examine the evidence for thinking that he believes perceptions to be dependent entities. I argue that Hume is driven by separate lines of reasoning to incompatible positions. He has no recourse to Berkeley's position of treating ideas as quasi substances, for that view appears to require a substance account of the mind. Thus Hume believes that perceptions are substances *and* that they are dependent beings, without any way of ultimately reconciling the two. This difficult ending place, however, is the result of Hume *adhering* to the traditional ontology for ideas, not abandoning it.

9.2.1 The Bundle Theory of the Mind

Saying that Hume has a bundle theory of the mind is now commonplace.[8] The details of the view, however, are important to our questions here. The exact nature of the relationship between minds and perceptions will determine what one may reasonably say about the status of both. The most famous passage comes from the section "Of Scepticism with Regard to the Senses." "As to the first question; we may observe, that what we call a *mind*, is nothing but a heap or collection of different perceptions, united together by certain relations, and suppos'd, tho' falsely, to be endow'd with a perfect simplicity and identity" (*T*, 207 / *N*, 137 [1.4.2]). Minds are collections of perceptions. But what is the relation between the mind and its perceptions? Hume continues in the same passage: "Now as every perception is distinguishable from another, and may be consider'd as separately existent; it evidently follows, that there is no absurdity in separating any particular perception from the mind; that is, in breaking off all its relations, with that connected mass of perceptions, which constitute a thinking being." Perceptions are independent of the mind, but in a strict sense. We can, *in thought*, separate the mind from any particular perception. As a result, the mind is not necessarily dependent on any particular perception. That is, no perception is individually essential to the mind. This realization does not, however, entail that perceptions can exist without a mind that somehow perceives it. We shall turn to that issue shortly.

Hume describes the mind as a "succession" of ideas. The illusion of an underlying unity is fostered by the uniform and consistent appearance present in this succession. "The mind is a kind of theatre, where several perceptions successively make their appearance; pass, re-pass, glide away, and mingle in an infinite variety of postures and situations.... The comparison of the theatre must not mislead us. They are the successive perceptions only, that constitute the mind" (*T*, 253 / *N*, 165 [1.4.6]). Hume again asserts the thesis that minds are composed of perceptions, but this time he claims that minds are successive perceptions *only*. The passage from the chapter on

---

8. John Biro, to name just one example, calls the bundle theory "famous" (1993, 49).

skepticism with regard to the senses explicitly indicates that the mind is its perceptions *and* certain "uniting" relations. Perhaps the second formulation is a bit of a slip, since Hume consistently ascribes powers and faculties to the mind.[9] It hardly makes sense to ascribe powers and faculties to *individual* perceptions (and in fact he does not [see Biro 1993, 56]), so these faculties must arise from the relations that allegedly unite the perceptions in question. They could, of course, arise from a unified substantial self, but Hume excludes that possibility. That the mind has faculties is important because one of those faculties is that of perception. Minds also *perceive* impressions and ideas. Minds are thus both constituted by perceptions and form a perceptual relation with them.

We are accordingly driven by Hume to the conclusion that the mind is constituted by its perceptions *and* certain faculties or powers. Hume is persuaded by Berkeley's analysis that all ideas and impressions are fundamentally dependent beings. We are sometimes led, of course, to think otherwise, but this does not deter Hume from endorsing the dependent nature of perceptions. "Whoever wou'd explain the origin of the *common* opinion concerning the continu'd and distinct existence of body, must take the mind in its *common* situation, and must proceed upon the supposition, that our perceptions are our only objects, and continue to exist even when they are not perceiv'd. Tho' this opinion be false, 'tis the most natural of any, and has alone any primary recommendation to the fancy" (*T*, 213 / *N*, 141 [1.4.2]). Hume admits that we perceive only perceptions, and hence the "false opinion" can only refer to the claim that perceptions exist when not perceived. He indicates that our perceptions are generally dependent on our sense organs, as evidenced by the simple trick of pressing one's eye to conjure a double image. Such experiments, says Hume, are enough to convince us "that our perceptions are not possest of any independent existence" (*T*, 210–11/*N*, 140 [1.4.2]; see also *T*, 5/*N*, 9 [1.1.1]). Although Hume insists that we can *conceive* of perceptions as existing independently from minds, *in fact* they do not exist independently. The two views are not necessarily inconsistent. The former insists only that perceptions are distinct from minds (and not modifications of them), while the latter makes a claim about the actual ontological nature of ideas and impressions. What is missing is a discussion

---

9. For instance, here are a few references, virtually at random: the mind has the power to produce ideas (*T*, 23/*N*, 20 [1.1.7]), has feelings and operations (*T*, 576/*N*, 368 [3.3.1]), and has operations that are "natural and necessary" (*T*, 266/*N*, 173 [1.4.7]). The *Treatise* is replete with references to the faculties of the mind.

of what constitutes a *perceiver*. Minds are bundles of ordered perceptions, and perceptions are entities perceived, but what is doing the perceiving?

9.2.2 On the Unintelligibility of Substantial Minds

Hume's insight, I argue, is that the obvious candidate—a substantial mind understood as an immaterial unity—is not the right answer to the question of what is doing the perceiving. But the problem is not that minds cannot be substances or that substances are impossible entities; rather the problem concerns the positive intelligibility of the question of what the nature of a substance (like the soul) is. Because substances are not perceptions, we cannot ascribe any positive content to the concept of a substance. Hume's strategy is to show that any conception of the soul as an immaterial substance requires us to admit by parity of reasoning the possibility that the soul is a material substance—a heretical view endorsed only by the likes of Spinoza. Hume provides three arguments to support his position.

First, Hume reasons that arguments that can be used against Spinoza's conception of substance also can be used against the doctrine of an immaterial soul. A unified substance that *underlies* change does not itself change, but this is exactly what is required on an inherence theory of quality predication. On this view, just as Spinoza's properties literally qualify the one substance, for a mind to have the idea of a particular extension also literally extends the mind.

> First, It has been said against *Spinoza* . . . that a mode, not being any distinct or separate existence, must be the very same with its substance, and consequently the extension of the universe, must be in a manner identify'd with that simple, uncompounded essence, in which the universe is suppos'd to inhere. But this, it may be pretended, is utterly impossible and inconceivable unless the indivisible substance expand itself, so as to correspond to the extension, or the extension contract itself, so as to answer to the indivisible substance. This argument seems just . . . and 'tis plain nothing is requir'd, but a change in the terms, to apply the same argument to our extended perceptions, and the simple essence of the soul. (*T*, 243–44 / *N*, 159–60 [1.4.5])

The concern here is not that the word "substance" is meaningless but rather that its meaning is so thin as to preclude any serious distinctions from being raised about its application. Thus what applies to Spinoza applies equally to the posits of theologians.

Hume's second argument is an extension of his earlier claim that all perceptions count as substances if by substance we mean nothing more than a distinct thing that can exist by itself. Given the nature of matter, every bit of matter will qualify as a substance. From this it follows that matter is never a mode. This argument is not a reductio ad absurdum on the possibility of substances but an argument designed to show that material monism and mind/body dualism labor under the same constraints. Hume concludes this argument by noting that "consequently the one hypothesis labours under the same difficulties in this respect with the other" (T, 244/N, 160 [1.4.5]). Thus the point is that because matter and mental substances are parallel in this respect, if one accepts the latter theory then there is no reason to reject the former. If you want immaterial, indivisible substantial souls, you must accept the possibility that material monism might undermine or replace the theory entirely. As Hume concludes, "we cannot advance one step towards the establishing the simplicity and immateriality of the soul, without preparing the way for a dangerous and irrecoverable atheism" (T, 244/N, 160 [1.4.5]).

The final argument is the venerable one that a single unified substance cannot be simultaneously modified by inconsistent qualities, as seems otherwise necessary. "The round and square figures are incompatible in the same substance at the same time. How then is it possible, that the same substance can at once be modify'd into that square table, and into this round one?" (T, 244/N, 160 [1.4.5]). The question, Hume believes, has no satisfactory answer, but neither does the parallel question when applied to souls and their perceptions. Hume continues in the same passage: "I ask the same question concerning the impressions of these tables; and find that the answer is no more satisfactory in one case than in the other."

Hume moves on to explore other options about the nature of mentality, including the possibility that thought is simply an action of the soul. Dismissing this alternative as well, Hume finally concludes that it is not possible to ascertain the nature of the soul. "To pronounce, then, the final decision upon the whole; the question concerning the substance of the soul is absolutely unintelligible: All our perceptions are not susceptible of a local union, either with what is extended or unextended.... And as the constant conjunction of objects constitutes the very essence of cause and effect, matter and motion may often be regarded as the causes of thought, as far as we have any notion of that relation" (T, 250/N, 163 [1.4.5]). Materialism might explain the affects of the soul as well as it explains anything else, which is to say not well at all. What matters for our purposes, however, is that this skeptical conclusion is *not a rejection of the traditional ontology.* Hume does not conclude that the soul cannot be a substance; he concludes that the concept of substance is so thin that the question resolves into unintelligibility. By this he means that the concept is not robust enough to justify making any confident pronouncements that might matter to us, whether they concern the soul or material objects.

Hume's insight, unfortunately for us, is only a negative one. We do not have access to the nature of the mind, its essence "being equally unknown to us with that of external bodies," and "it must be equally impossible to form any notion of its powers and qualities otherwise than from careful and exact experiments" (*T*, xvii / *N*, 5). In light of this analysis, Hume's aim is quite clear. Although he does not think it possible to discern the true (ontological) nature of the mind, we can understand regularities in its operations. He seeks to show that the human mind—whatever that might be—has regular and constant machinery (Hume 1875, 166). Yet even if the mind cannot be a simple unified substance, it does not follow that there are no substances or that the traditional ontology has been abandoned when it comes to perceptions.

One might wish to press me on this issue.[10] Perhaps there is an alternative to the traditional ontology here. The Hume of the *Treatise* holds that the mind is nothing but an ordered collection of perceptions without necessary connections or mysterious substances; it is just a collection of perceptions ordered by the principles of the association of ideas. What role *could* such a thin conception of substance play? Although I recognize the force of this worry that might arise from my reading of Hume, and the traditional way of reading Hume lends credence to this concern, we cannot escape the underlying problem. If the mind is "nothing but" a collection of perceptions, *then what are perceptions?* They exist. They must have *some* ontological status for the theory to be meaningful. And so the question is: what is that status? I take Hume's answer to be that perceptions are substances. The answer might seem unsatisfactory because he also believes perceptions to be dependent, but at least Hume is aware of this tension. For those who might think that I am trying to hammer my ontological reading onto Hume, I can only stop and ask how they can account for the persistent tendency of Hume to talk about perceptions as distinct, independent entities. I do not deny

---

10. My thanks to Daniel Flage for raising this objection.

that Hume is a critic of the concept of substance and especially its use by his contemporaries. But having an epistemological focus does not eliminate the need for an underlying ontology.

9.2.3 Perceivers and Perceptions

We have yet, however, to find an answer to the question about the nature of perceivers in Hume's ontology. From the preceding we should already know that Hume is not going to tell us much that we will find satisfying. Fortunately for this study, we do not require a complete answer or even necessarily a consistent one. Hume tells us that perceptions are mind dependent. Perception is a faculty of the mind, and minds are collections of perceptions related in certain ways. But as Hume famously concluded, none of his thinking revealed the necessary connections or relations among perceptions that characterize a perceiver or a self. Throughout this analysis, however, Hume holds on to the claims that all perceptions are things and distinct existences (and hence at least like traditional substances in those important respects) as well as dependent ones. The fact that he recognizes a problem with this nest of claims is actually evidence of his commitment to the core conception of the traditional ontology. The conflict between these claims only arises from the traditional view that substances are both enduring (distinct existences underlying change) *and* independent (not dependent on other kinds of things for their existence). Had Hume abandoned the traditional ontology with respect to the nature of perceptions it would be more difficult to see what the problem actually is.

Examine Hume's conflicting principles carefully:

> In short there are two principles, which I cannot render consistent; nor is it in my power to renounce either of them, viz. *that all our distinct perceptions are distinct existences,* and *that the mind never perceives any real connexion among distinct existences.* Did our perceptions either inhere in something simple and individual, or did the mind perceive some real connexion among them, there wou'd be no difficulty in the case. For my part, I must plead the privilege of a sceptic, and confess, that this difficulty is too hard for my understanding. (*T,* 636/*N,* 400)

The first principle articulates the claim that perceptions are substances (for as Hume argues, whatever is distinct may exist independently). The second principle expresses Hume's inability to locate the dependence of perceptions in their relations to other perceptions. If perceptions were not independent, what might that mean in terms of the traditional ontology? Hume gives us the possibilities. Perceptions might inhere in simple substances. Such an alternative would in effect deny that perceptions are substances but preserve his claims that they are dependent. Alternatively, we might explain the dependence of perceptions by appealing to necessary "connexions" or relations. This option would enable us to accept Berkeley's view that ideas are quasi substances. They would be distinct and independent from minds but nonetheless dependent on minds construed as necessary collections of perceptions. But Hume finds himself unable to adopt Berkeley's answer because he finds on introspection no necessary relations of any sort.

Thus when Hume provides an initial account of the self, he seeks a unifying faculty for the disparate perceptions that constitute the mind. One candidate for this role is memory. If, following Locke's theory of personal identity, we as persons were constituted by necessary connections among perceptions (that we call "memory"), that is, if certain perceptions by their content and nature were necessarily a part of a particular collection, then Hume's dilemma fades away. But here again, the problem is that our perceptions do *not* demonstrate this kind of dependence. Hume sees the need for perceptions to be dependent—and indeed baldly asserts that they are dependent on a number of occasions—but cannot figure out how to make them dependent given his prior claim that perceptions are distinct and individual existences.

It is in part because I think my hypothesis explains the seriousness of Hume's dilemma as expressed in the appendix that I believe that Hume did not depart in his thinking from the traditional ontology. Indeed, it is precisely *because* Hume weds himself to the ontology of ideas and impressions—his thinking lies *within* the confines of an ontology of substance and mode—that he finds himself in such a quandary.

9.3 Concluding Remarks: The Demise of the Early Modern Tale

The aim of this endeavor has been to debunk the early modern tale and provide an account of the development of the way of ideas that acknowledges the important role ontological concerns played in that development. I hope to have succeeded in this project in at least two ways. First, I hope I have made a good case for accepting that, as a matter of good history of philosophy, the developments in the "way of ideas" from Descartes to Hume simply do not entail that we read any of the moderns as abandoning or "deontologizing" ideas. Second, I hope I have shown that by embracing the early modern tale we risk impoverishing our understanding of the early moderns. If Berkeley, Locke, and Hume (among others) have gained philosophical power and respectability as a result of my analysis, that is largely because I have been unwilling to surrender them to a fairy tale designed for mainly contemporary interests. Although I have not the space to make the argument here, I think this lesson extends to other philosophers as well, modern and contemporary. It does not pay to ignore ontology.

The early modern tale is one designed both to avoid the deep difficulties of metaphysics and "save" the early moderns for contemporary philosophy. Our fairy tale fails on both accounts. The problems of ontology are inescapable—and I believe that is just as true now as it was for the early moderns. Idea epistemology without ontology leaves the systems of the best early modern minds potentially more confused and less relevant. Trying to preserve Locke from a sense-datum fallacy is an admirable aim, provided that first, we are *confident* that invoking sense data is a fallacy and provided that we do not allow our contemporary interests to mask other historical insights yet to be gleaned. Great minds can provide illumination in their failures as well as their successes; we do not shame or belittle Locke by detailing the struggles he had with ideas. Sometimes our own analyses are improved by respecting the historical conditions that guided the thinking of the early moderns. Thus I have tried to argue that Berkeley's metaphysical system is not quite as fantastical as some might believe. He might not be right, but he has resources to employ in defense of his system that can be easily overlooked if we are intent on forcing on him a contemporary "epistemology as first philosophy" perspective. If I am right, and Berkeley was also strongly motivated by deeply metaphysical concerns (which is not to exclude epistemological ones), then new understandings of his controversial claims may emerge. I submit that Berkeley's theory of divine ideas, his attack on abstraction, and his heterogeneity thesis are all more potent when viewed in this light. As a result, Berkeley has more philosophy to teach us than we might have otherwise thought.

Even how we read Hume depends on the mindset with which we come to the texts. When I was a younger philosopher (in several senses), Hume held little attraction for me. I had no use for figures who wished to set our theories of knowledge and belief adrift, unconnected to ontology. I still believe in the relevance of ontology, but now I have come to see Hume as a philosopher interested in fixing our epistemological place by exploring its natural and metaphysical boundaries. Those boundaries might involve thin concepts, distant borders, and difficult problems, but the enterprise makes sense to me. Hume is not merely a critical skeptic; he has a positive agenda that respects the need for an ontological ground, even if that ground does not take center stage.

In tracing early modern discussions about the nature of ideas from Descartes forward to Hume, it is clear that much of the friction generated in those debates derives from the conflict between the epistemological roles ideas play and the metaphysical nature of those same ideas. Conflicts typically can be resolved in several ways. Here I have argued mainly that the early moderns did not seek to "deontologize" ideas as an answer to their problems. To suppose that they did is not only to mischaracterize some of the early moderns but also to miss some brilliant philosophy. Denying the spectacular metaphysical speculations of the early moderns is to rob us today of what they did best.

REFERENCES

Acton, H. B. 1967. "George Berkeley." In vol. 1 of *The Encyclopedia of Philosophy*, ed. Paul Edwards. New York: Macmillan.
Acworth, Richard, ed. 1971. "Locke's First Reply to John Norris." *The Locke Newsletter* 2:7–11.
Adams, Robert Merrihew. 1975. "Where Do Our Ideas Come From?" In *Innate Ideas*, ed. Stephen Stich, 71–87. Berkeley and Los Angeles: University of California Press.
Alexander, Samuel. 1908. *Locke*. London: Constable.
Alston, William. 1976. "The Representative Function of Ideas in Locke." Unpublished manuscript.
Anderson, Robert. 1966. *Hume's First Principles*. Lincoln: University of Nebraska Press.
Anonymous. [1705] 1996. *A Philosophick Essay Concerning Ideas, According to Dr. Sherlock's Principles*. New York: AMS Press.
Aristotle. 1984. *Complete Works of Aristotle*. Ed. Jonathan Barnes. 2 vols. Princeton: Princeton University Press.
Armstrong, D. M. 1960. *Berkeley's Theory of Vision*. New York: Cambridge University Press.
———. 1997. *A World of States of Affairs*. New York: Cambridge University Press.
Arnauld, Antoine. 1990. *On True and False Ideas*. Trans. Elmar J. Kremer. Lewiston, N.Y.: Edwin Mellen.
Arnauld, Antoine, and Pierre Nicole. 1996. *Logic; or, The Art of Thinking*. Trans. and ed. Jill Vance Buroker. New York: Cambridge University Press.
Atherton, Margaret. 1990. *Berkeley's Revolution in Vision*. Ithaca, N.Y.: Cornell University Press.
Augustine. 1993. *On Free Choice of the Will*. Trans. Thomas Williams. Indianapolis, Ind.: Hackett.
Ayers, Michael. 1991. *Locke: Epistemology and Ontology*. New York: Routledge.
———. 1992. "Are Locke's 'Ideas' Images, Intentional Objects, or Natural Signs?" In *John Locke: Theory of Knowledge*, ed. Vere Chappell, 153–86. New York: Garland.
Belfrage, Bertil. 1987. "A New Approach to Berkeley's *Philosophical Notebooks*." In *Essays on the Philosophy of George Berkeley*, ed. Ernest Sosa, 217–30. Boston: D. Reidel.
Bennett, Jonathan. 1971. *Locke, Berkeley, Hume: Central Themes*. New York: Oxford University Press.
———. 1979. "Analytic Transcendental Arguments." In *Transcendental Arguments and Science*, ed. Peter Bieri, Rolf P. Horstmann, and Lorenz Krüger, 45–64. Dordrecht: D. Reidel.
———. 1996. "Ideas and Qualities in Locke's *Essay*." *History of Philosophy Quarterly* 13:73–88.
———. 2001. *Learning from Six Philosophers*. 2 vols. New York: Oxford University Press.
Berkeley, George. 1948–57. *The Works of George Berkeley, Bishop of Cloyne*. Ed. A. A. Luce and T. E. Jessop. 9 vols. London: Nelson.

———. 1975. *Berkeley: Philosophical Works, Including the Works on Vision.* Ed. Michael Ayers. Totowa, N.J.: Rowman and Littlefield.
———. 1987. *George Berkeley's Manuscript Introduction.* Ed. Bertil Belfrage. Headington, U.K.: Doxa.
Berman, David. 1986. "Berkeley's Quad: The Question of Numerical Identity." *Idealistic Studies* 16:41–45.
———. 1999. *Berkeley.* New York: Routledge.
Bird, Alexander. 2001. "Review of *Dispositions: A Debate* and *Dispositions.*" *The British Journal for the Philosophy of Science* 52:137–49.
Biro, John. 1993. "Hume's New Science of the Mind." In *The Cambridge Companion to Hume,* ed. David Norton, 33–63. New York: Cambridge University Press.
Bracken, Harry. 1963. "Berkeley and Malebranche on Ideas." *The Modern Schoolman* 41:1–15.
Broad, C. D. 1975. *Leibniz: An Introduction.* Cambridge: Cambridge University Press.
Brook, Richard J. 1973. *Berkeley's Philosophy of Science.* The Hague: Martinus Nijhoff.
Browne, Peter. 1976. *The Procedure, Extent, and Limits of Human Understanding.* New York: Garland.
Brykman, Geneviève. 1987. "Berkeley on 'Archetype.'" In *Essays on the Philosophy of George Berkeley,* ed. Ernest Sosa, 103–12. Boston: D. Reidel.
———. 1997. *Berkeley et le cartésianisme.* Nanterre: University of Paris X.
Chappell, Vere. 1986. "The Theory of Ideas." In *Essays on Descartes' "Meditations,"* ed. A. O. Rorty, 177–98. Berkeley and Los Angeles: University of California Press.
———. 1994. "Locke's Theory of Ideas." In *The Cambridge Companion to Locke,* ed. Vere Chappell, 26–55. New York: Cambridge University Press.
Church, R. W. 1970. *A Study in the Philosophy of Malebranche.* Port Washington, N.Y.: Kennikat Press.
Cook, Monte. 1974. "Arnauld's Alleged Representationalism." *Journal of the History of Philosophy* 12:53–62.
———. 1996. "Descartes and the Dustbin of the Mind." *History of Philosophy Quarterly* 13:17–33.
Craig, E. J. 1968. "Berkeley's Attack on Abstract Ideas." *Philosophical Review* 77:425–37.
Cummins, Phillip. 1975. "Berkeley's Ideas of Sense." *Noûs* 9:55–72.
———. 1996. "Hume on Qualities." *Hume Studies* 22:49–88.
Dancy, Jonathan. 1987. *Berkeley: An Introduction.* New York: Basil Blackwell.
Daniel, Stephen. 2000. "Berkeley, Suárez, and the *Esse-Existere* Distinction." *American Catholic Philosophical Quarterly* 74:621–36.
———. 2001a. "Berkeley's Christian Neoplatonism, Archetypes, and Divine Ideas." *Journal of the History of Philosophy* 39:239–58.
———. 2001b. "Edwards, Berkeley, and Ramist Logic." *Idealistic Studies* 31:55–72.
Descartes, René. 1984–91. *The Philosophical Writings of Descartes.* Trans. and ed. John Cottingham, Robert Stoothoff, and Dugald Murdoch. Vol. 3 also trans. Anthony Kenny. Cambridge: Cambridge University Press.
Doney, Willis. 1983. "Berkeley's Argument Against Abstract Ideas." In *Midwest Studies in Philosophy* 8, ed. Peter French, Theodore Uehling Jr., and Howard Wettsteing, 295–308. Minneapolis: University of Minnesota Press.
Flage, Daniel. 1987. *Berkeley's Doctrine of Notions.* London: Croom Helm.
———. 1990. *David Hume's Theory of Mind.* New York: Routledge.
———. 2001. "Berkeley's Archetypes." *Hermathena* 171:7–31.
———. 2004. "Berkeley's Epistemic Ontology: The *Principles.*" *Canadian Journal of Philosophy* 34:25–60.

———. 2007. "Berkeley's Epistemic Ontology: The *Three Dialogues.*" In *New Interpretations of Berkeley's Thought,* ed. Stephen Daniel, 45–75. Amherst, N.Y.: Humanity Books.
Foucher, Simon. 1995. *Malebranche's First and Last Critics.* Trans. Richard Watson and Marjorie Grene. Carbondale: Southern Illinois University Press.
Frede, Michael. 1987. *Essays in Ancient Philosophy.* Minneapolis: University of Minnesota Press.
Gaukroger, Stephen. 1995. *Descartes: An Intellectual Biography.* New York: Oxford University Press.
Gibson, James. [1917] 1960. *Locke's Theory of Knowledge and Its Historical Relations.* New York: Cambridge University Press.
Gibson, James J. 1976. "Three Kinds of Distance That Can Be Seen, or How Bishop Berkeley Went Wrong." In *Studies in Perception: Festschrift for Fabio Metelli,* ed. Giovanni B. Flores D'Arcais, 83–87. Milan: Martello-Giunti.
Glauser, Richard. 1999. *Berkeley et les philosophes du xiie siècle: Perception et scepticisme.* Sprimont, Belgium: Mardaga.
———. 2002. "Descartes, Suarez, and the Theory of Distinctions." In *The Philosophy of Marjorie Grene,* ed. Randall E. Auxier and Lewis Edwin Hahn, 417–45. La Salle, Ill.: Open Court.
Greenlee, Douglass. 1977. "Locke's Idea of 'Idea.'" In *Locke on Human Understanding,* ed. Ian Tipton, 41–47. New York: Oxford University Press.
Grey, Denis. 1952. "The Solipsism of Bishop Berkeley." *Philosophical Quarterly* 2:338–49.
Hausman, Alan, and David Hausman. 1995. "A New Approach to Berkeley's Ideal Reality." In *Berkeley's Metaphysics: Structural, Interpretive, and Critical Essays,* ed. Robert Muehlmann, 47–66. University Park: Pennsylvania State University Press.
Heil, John. 2003. *From an Ontological Point of View.* Oxford: Oxford University Press.
Hight, Marc. 2001. "Locke's Implicit Ontology of Ideas." *British Journal for the History of Philosophy* 9:17–42.
———. 2002. "Why We Do Not See What We Feel." *Pacific Philosophical Quarterly* 83:148–62.
———. 2005. "Defending Berkeley's Divine Ideas." *Philosophia* 33:97–128.
———. 2007a. "Berkeley and Bodily Resurrection." *Journal of the History of Philosophy* 45:443–58.
———. 2007b. "Why My Chair Is Not Merely a Congeries: Berkeley and the Single Idea Thesis." In *Reexamining Berkeley's Philosophy,* ed. Steve Daniel, 82–107. Toronto: University of Toronto Press.
Hight, Marc, and Walter Ott. 2004. "The New Berkeley." *Canadian Journal of Philosophy* 34:1–24.
Hoffman, Paul. 1996. "Descartes on Misrepresentation." *Journal of the History of Philosophy* 34:357–81.
Hume, David. 1875. *Essays Moral, Political, and Literary.* Vol. 2. Ed. T. H. Green and T. H. Grose. London: Longmans, Green.
———. 1978. *A Treatise of Human Nature.* Ed. L. A. Selby-Bigge. Rev. P. H. Nidditch. New York: Oxford University Press.
———. 1999. *An Enquiry Concerning Human Understanding.* Ed. Tom Beauchamp. New York: Oxford University Press.
———. 2000. *A Treatise of Human Nature.* Ed. David Fate Norton and Mary J. Norton. New York: Oxford University Press.

Jolley, Nicholas. 1984. *Leibniz and Locke.* New York: Oxford University Press.
———. 1990. *The Light of the Soul.* New York: Oxford University Press.
———. 1996. "Berkeley, Malebranche, and Vision in God." *Journal of the History of Philosophy* 34:535–48.
———. 2005. *Leibniz.* New York: Routledge.
Kashap, S. Paul. 1978. "Spinoza's Use of 'Idea.'" In *Spinoza: New Perspectives,* ed. Robert Shahan and John Biro, 57–70. Norman: University of Oklahoma Press.
Kneale, William. 1939. "The Notion of a Substance." *Proceedings of the Aristotelian Society* 40:103–34.
Kulstad, Mark. 1977. "Leibniz's Concept of Expression." *Studia Leibnitiana* 9:55–76.
Lee, Henry. [1702] 1984. *Anti-Scepticism; or, Notes upon Each Chapter of Mr. Lock's "Essay Concerning Human Understanding."* New York: Garland.
Leibniz, G. W. 1875–90. *Die philosophischen Schriften von G. W. Leibniz.* Ed. C. I. Gerhardt. 7 vols. Berlin: Weidmann.
———. 1962. *Samtliche Schriften und Briefen.* Ser. 6. Berlin: Berlin Academy.
———. 1976. *Philosophical Papers and Letters.* Trans. and ed. Leroy Loemker. 2nd ed. Boston: D. Reidel.
———. 1981. *New Essays on Human Understanding.* Trans. and ed. Peter Remnant and Jonathan Bennett. New York: Cambridge University Press.
———. 1989. *Philosophical Essays.* Trans. and ed. Roger Ariew and Daniel Garber. Indianapolis, Ind.: Hackett.
Lennon, Thomas. 1993. *The Battle of the Gods and Giants.* Princeton, N.J.: Princeton University Press.
———. 1998. "Bennett on Ideas and Qualities in Locke's *Essay.*" *Locke Newsletter* 29:13–21.
———. 2001a. "Locke and the Logic of Ideas." *History of Philosophy Quarterly* 18:155–77.
———. 2001b. "Berkeley on the Act-Object Distinction." *Dialogue* 40:651–67.
———. 2004a. "Through a Glass Darkly: More on Locke's Logic of Ideas." *Pacific Philosophical Quarterly* 85:322–37.
———. 2004b. "The Logic of Ideas and the Logic of Things: A Reply to Chappell." *Pacific Philosophical Quarterly* 85:356–60.
Locke, John. 1812. *The Works of John Locke.* 11th ed. 10 vols. London: Otridge and Son.
———. 1894. *The Philosophical Works of John Locke.* 2 vols. Ed. J. A. St. John. London: G. Bell and Sons.
———. 1975. *An Essay Concerning Human Understanding.* Ed. P. H. Nidditch. New York: Oxford University Press.
———. 1976. *The Correspondence of John Locke.* 9 vols. Ed. E. S. De Beer. New York: Oxford University Press.
Lovejoy, A. O. 1923. "'Representative Ideas' in Malebranche and Arnauld." *Mind* 32:449–61.
Luce, Arthur A. 1942. "Berkeley's Doctrine of the Perceivable." *Hermathena* 9:3–15.
———. 1963. *The Dialectic of Immaterialism.* London: Hodder and Stoughton.
———. 1970. "Another Look at Berkeley's Notebooks." *Hermathena* 110:5–23.
Mabbott, J. D. [1931] 1968. "The Place of God in Berkeley's Philosophy." In *Locke and Berkeley: A Collection of Critical Essays,* ed. D._M. Armstrong and C._B. Martin, 364–79. Notre Dame, Ind.: University of Notre Dame Press.
Mackie, J. L. 1972. *Truth, Probability, and Paradox.* New York: Oxford University Press.
Malebranche, Nicolas. 1958. *Oeuvres complètes.* 20 vols. Ed. André Robinet. Paris: J. Vrin.

———. 1997a. *The Search After Truth,* with *Elucidations of the Search After Truth.* Trans. and ed. Thomas M. Lennon and Paul J. Olscamp. New York: Cambridge University Press.

———. 1997b. *Dialogues on Metaphysics and Religion.* Ed. Nicholas Jolley and David Scott. New York: Cambridge University Press.

Mates, Benson. 1986. *The Philosophy of Leibniz: Metaphysics and Language.* New York: Oxford University Press.

McCracken, Charles. 1983. *Malebranche and British Philosophy.* New York: Oxford University Press.

Muehlmann, Robert. 1992. *Berkeley's Ontology.* Indianapolis, Ind.: Hackett.

———. 1995. "The Substance of Berkeley's Philosophy." In *Berkeley's Metaphysics: Structural, Interpretive, and Critical Essays,* ed. Robert Muehlmann, 89–105. University Park: Pennsylvania State University Press.

Nadler, Stephen. 1992. *Malebranche and Ideas.* New York: Oxford University Press.

Nelkin, Norton. 1989. "Reid's View of Sensations Vindicated." In *The Philosophy of Thomas Reid,* ed. Melvin Dalgarno and Eric Matthews, 67–77. Dordrecht: Kluwer.

Norris, John. [1728] 1961. *Cursory Reflections upon a Book Call'd "An Essay Concerning Human Understanding."* Augustan Reprint Society, no. 93. Ed. Gilbert D. McEwen. Los Angeles: William Andrews Clark Memorial Library, University of California.

O'Connor, D. J. 1967. *John Locke.* New York: Dover.

Pappas, George. 2000. *Berkeley's Thought.* Ithaca, N.Y.: Cornell University Press.

Pitcher, George. 1969. "Minds and Ideas in Berkeley." *American Philosophical Quarterly* 6:198–207.

———. 1977. *Berkeley.* Boston: Routledge and Kegan Paul.

———. 1981. "Berkeley on the Mind's Activity." *American Philosophical Quarterly* 18:221–27.

Putnam, Hilary. 2004. *Ethics Without Ontology.* Cambridge, Mass.: Harvard University Press.

Quine, Willard Van Orman. 1980. *From a Logical Point of View.* Cambridge, Mass.: Harvard University Press.

Raynor, David. 1987. "Berkeley's Ontology." *Dialogue* 26:611–20.

Rome, Beatrice. 1963. *The Philosophy of Malebranche.* Chicago: Henry Regnery.

Russell, Bertrand. [1900] 1992. *The Philosophy of Leibniz.* New York: Routledge.

Rutherford, Donald. 1995. *Leibniz and the Rational Order of Nature.* New York: Cambridge University Press.

Ryle, Gilbert. [1933] 1968. "John Locke on the Human Understanding." In *Locke and Berkeley: A Collection of Critical Essays,* ed. D. M. Armstrong and C. B. Martin, 14–39. Notre Dame, Ind.: University of Notre Dame Press.

———. 1984. *The Concept of Mind.* Chicago: University of Chicago Press.

Sergeant, John. 1696. *The Method to Science.* London: Printed by W. Redmayne.

Shoemaker, Sidney. 1990. "Qualities and Qualia: What's in the Mind?" *Philosophy and Phenomenological Research* (fall supplement) 50:109–31.

Simmons, Alison. 1999. "Are Cartesian Sensations Representational?" *Noûs* 33:347–69.

Smith, Norman Kemp. 1964. *The Philosophy of David Hume.* New York: St. Martin's Press.

Spinoza, Baruch. 1985–. *Collected Works of Spinoza.* Trans. and ed. Edwin Curley. 1 vol. to date. Princeton, N.J.: Princeton University Press.

Stack, George J. 1970. *Berkeley's Analysis of Perception*. The Hague: Mouton.
Stillingfleet, Edward. 1697a. *A Discourse in Vindication of the Doctrine of the Trinity*. London: Henry Mortlock.
———. 1697b. *The Bishop of Worcester's Answer to Mr. Locke's Letter, Concerning Some Passages Relating to His Essay of Humane Understanding*. London: Henry Mortlock.
Stoneham, Tom. 2002. *Berkeley's World: An Examination of the Three Dialogues*. New York: Oxford University Press.
Stubenberg, Leopold. 1990. "Divine Ideas: The Cure-all for Berkeley's Immaterialism." *Southern Journal of Philosophy* 27:221–49.
Thomas, George. 1976. "Berkeley's God Does Not Perceive." *Journal of the History of Philosophy* 14:163–68.
Tipton, Ian. 1986. "'Ideas' in Berkeley and Arnauld." *History of European Ideas* 7:575–84.
———. 1988. *Berkeley: The Philosophy of Immaterialism*. New York: Garland.
Warnock, G. J. 1982. *Berkeley*. Notre Dame, Ind.: University of Notre Dame Press.
Watson, Richard. 1987. *The Breakdown of Cartesian Metaphysics*. Atlantic Highlands, N.J.: Humanities Press International.
———. 1991. "Foucher's Mistake and Malebranche's Break: Ideas, Intelligible Extension, and the End of Ontology." In *Nicolas Malebranche: His Philosophical Critics and Successors,* ed. Stuart Brown, 22–33. Maastricht/Assen: Van Gorcum.
Wenz, Peter. 1976. "Berkeley's Christian Neo-Platonism." *Journal of the History of Ideas* 37:537–46.
Wilson, Margaret. 1994. "Descartes on Sense and 'Resemblance.'" In *Reason, Will, and Sensation,* ed. John Cottingham, 10–25. New York: Oxford University Press.
———. 1996. "Spinoza's Theory of Knowledge." In *The Cambridge Companion to Spinoza,* ed. Don Garrett, 89–143. New York: Cambridge University Press.
Winkler, Kenneth. 1989. *Berkeley: An Interpretation*. New York: Oxford University Press.
Wolf-Devine, Celia. 1993. *Descartes on Seeing*. Carbondale: Southern Illinois University Press.
Yandell, David. 1995. "Berkeley on Common Sense and the Privacy of Ideas." *History of Philosophy Quarterly* 12:411–23.
Yolton, John. 1956. *John Locke and the Way of Ideas*. New York: Oxford University Press.
———. 1975. "Ideas and Knowledge in Seventeenth-Century Philosophy." *Journal of the History of Philosophy* 13:145–65.
———. 1983. *Thinking Matter: Materialism in Eighteenth-Century Britain*. Minneapolis: University of Minnesota Press.
———. 1984. *Perceptual Acquaintance from Descartes to Reid*. Minneapolis: University of Minnesota Press.
———. 1985. *Locke: An Introduction*. New York: Basil Blackwell.
———. 1986. "Reply to Mr. Tipton." *History of European Ideas* 7:584.
———. 1996a. *Perception and Reality, A History from Descartes to Kant*. Ithaca, N.Y.: Cornell University Press.
———. 1996b. *Locke and the Way of Ideas*. Bristol, U.K.: Thoemmes.
———. 2000. *Realism and Appearances*. New York: Cambridge University Press.

INDEX

abstraction, 218–33, 235, 243. *See also* ideas, abstract
Anderson, Robert, 254
Aristotle, 9, 11–14, 42, 43, 98, 221
Armstrong, D. M., 234, 238, 239
Arnauld, Antoine, 4, 39, 53, 55, 62, 65–66, 72–78, 80, 82, 114, 116, 118, 119
  critique of Malebranche, 75–78
  as direct realist, 74
  ideas as acts, 73–74
  and mental presence, 75–76
  representation, 41, 72–73, 76
  theory of perception, 74–75
Atherton, Margaret, 239–40
attributes, as distinct from modes, 20–21
Augustine, 19, 59
Ayers, Michael, 86, 165

Beauchamp, Tom, 255
Belfrage, Bertil, 166–67
Bennett, Jonathan, 24–25, 91, 110, 116, 171
Berkeley, George, 4, 8–10, 31, 35, 42, 66, 115, 138–245, 246, 247–48, 250, 257, 266
  and "+" sign, 165–67
  act/object distinction, 143–44, 146–47, 148–52, 154, 195–200
  archetypes, 157, 178–80, 185, 208–9, 210, 213–14
  attributes, 21 n. 10
  and common sense objects, 204, 210
  and continuity of perceived world, 205–6
  esse is *percipi* principle, 141, 154, 171, 175, 181, 194, 195, 199, 224
  God, as preserving the world, 159–60, 206–8, 242
  idea-quality conflation, 155–59, 194–95, 243, 260
  ideas: abstract, 218–33, 235; as acts (*see* Locke, ideas, as acts); adverbial account of, 139–40, 142–55, 241–42; deontologizing, 28, 30, 173; dependence on minds, 25 n. 17, 139, 144, 152, 154, 198, 201; divine, 8, 177–217; as "external" to the mind, 141, 146, 159–60, 182, 186, 188, 240, 241; as fleeting, 209–17, 257–58; as heterogeneous, 9, 218, 233–45 (*see also* heterogeneity); numerically identical to God's, 187–88, 192 n. 17, 206–9; of imagination, 200, 207, 215; as immediate, 154; "in" the mind, 140–41, 158, 181–89, 203–4; as modes, 138, 140, 142–43, 145–46, 148–55, 175, 183, 241–42; as objects, 138, 141–48; as passive, 145, 206–8, 214, 243; as private, 178, 180, 193–205; as quasi substance (*see* substance, quasi); of reflection, 146–47; as relativized qualities, 202–4; as sensations, 151, 194–95; unperceived existence of, 149, 152–53, 159–61
  as identifying content and ontological status, 241–45
  law of saturation, 227
  laws of nature, 168
  likeness principle, 146, 213
  minds (*see* Berkeley, spirits)
  and minimum sensibilia, 157, 239, 253
  mosaic account of creation, 169–71
  notions, 153
  perception, theory of, 157
  and phenomenalism, 161–64, 167–72
  qualities (*see* Berkeley, idea-quality conflation)
  as realist, 156–8, 161, 174–75, 192, 197–98
  and skepticism, 156, 157, 180, 184–85, 192, 193, 198, 203–4
  spirits: as active, 145; no ideas of, 147, 153, 213; as the only substance, 139, 141; passive in perception, 150–51, 156, 197–98
  time, 19, 211 n. 40
  and tulip-smelling argument, 195–98, 201
  and volitional independence, 141, 158, 160, 206, 243
Berman, David, 234 n. 15
Brinkley, John, 123 n. 11
Brykman, Geneviéve, 185 n. 13

causation
  causal reality principle, 48, 50, 63
  as contagion, 47, 49
  among ideas, 50
  mental-mental, 53–54
  mind-body, 46, 52 n. 13
Chappell, Vere, 29, 82, 91
counterfactuals, grounded, 162–63

Craig, E. J., 219
Cummins, Phillip, 247

Daniel, Stephen, 139 n. 2, 167
dependence, ontological and causal, 14–15, 17–18. *See also* Berkeley, ideas, dependence on mind
Descartes, René, 2, 6, 26, 31, 35, 37–54, 55–56, 59, 66, 114, 151, 154, 173, 267
  animal spirits, 45, 51, 53
  causal reality principle (*see* causation)
  concept of mode, 20–21, 67
  concept of substance, 11, 15, 16–17, 19–20
  ideas: adventitious, 47, 54; as corporeal, 6, 38, 44–47; definition of, 38, 43; innate, 47–51; innovative use of, 37
  material/objective distinction, 29, 34, 38–40, 56, 82
  mind-body relation, 46
  pineal gland (gland H), 44–45, 47, 51, 53
  and qualities, 43
  and wax analogy, 42, 45
dispositions, 8, 49, 117–36. *See also* ideas, as dispositions
  grounded, 32–33, 120, 129, 163
  of the soul, 53
distance, not immediately seen, 234
distinctness, strong and weak, 144–45
divine ideas. *See* Berkeley, ideas, divine
Duns Scotus, John, 37

epistemology
  as first philosophy, 266
  as ground for ontology, 174–75
  as "pure," 30–34

Flage, Daniel, 173–75
Foucher, Simon, 39

Gibson, James, 101
God
  as atemporal, 19, 187
  attributes expressed in us, 133–36
  archetypal order of, 177, 179–93, 206, 242
  as enduring, 19
  as independent substance, 15, 17, 59
  as infinite, 68
  as a perceiver, 160–61, 187–88, 194, 199–200, 202
  as *purus actus*, 64, 133–35, 191
  simple nature of, 75, 77, 190, 202

Heil, John, 1
heterogeneity, 9, 218, 233–45. *See also* Berkeley, ideas, as heterogeneous

and abstraction, 235
and adding lines, 238
and distinctness of content, 237–38
and Molyneux thought experiment, 236–37
Hobbes, Thomas, 37
Hume, David, 5, 9–10, 132, 173, 209–11, 246–67
  bundle theory of mind, 247, 253, 259–61, 263, 264
  and conceivability principle, 249–51
  concept of substance, 18, 246, 248–49, 253, 254–58, 262
  and copy thesis, 249
  and difference-existence principle, 250–51
  and immaterial soul, 261–63
  and perceptions: as dependent, 247, 258–65; as determinate, 250–51, 254; distinct from minds, 253; as ideas and impressions, 249; as independent, 248, 251–52, 254, 258, 259, 265; simple and complex, 257–58; as substances, 247, 248–58, 263, 264
  and person, 256
  and powers of the mind, 260, 264
  as skeptic about substance, 247, 255, 262–63, 267

ideas
  abstract, 9, 58; as determinate, 223–24, 228–31, 233; as impossible entities, 224–26, 231; as particular, 220–23, 228. *See also* abstraction; Locke, ideas, abstract
  as corporeal, 6, 38, 92–93
  deontologized, 4, 10, 28–34, 81–83, 173, 267
  as dispositions, 8, 32–33, 49, 117–24, 129–36
  "external" to the mind, 9, 108, 112, 141, 146, 159–60, 180
  general, 224, 231–33
  as heterogeneous (*see* Berkeley, ideas, as heterogeneous)
  as images, 39, 46, 96–98, 109
  innate (*see* Descartes, ideas, as innate; Leibniz, ideas, as innate)
  as intentional objects, 29, 31–34 (*see also* Locke, ideas, as intentional objects)
  material and objective (*see* Descartes, material/objective distinction)
  as objects, 23, 31, 31–33, 64, 90–92, 102, 138, 141–48
  reified, 5, 23–27, 30, 31, 93
  as signs, 40–41
  as things, 22, 24, 90, 93, 153, 157, 228, 233, 243
  as veridical, 39–40
  as volitionally independent, 35, 102 (*see also* Berkeley, and volitional independence)

Jesseph, Douglas, 123 n. 11
Johnson, Samuel, 179, 185–86
Jolley, S. Nicholas, 8, 37, 63, 116–19, 121 nn. 8 and 9, 124, 134, 136, 191

Kneale, William, 13
Knox, Ronald, 159

Lee, Henry, 96–98
Leibniz, G. W., 4–5, 7, 24 n. 14, 115, 116–37, 138, 209, 212
  and God and simple ideas, 130, 133–34
  and expression 119, 129–30, 132
  ideas: definition of, 116, 118–19; as dispositions, 117–36; having vs. being, 124–26, 136; as innate, 121, 126–28; as modes, 117, 118, 123, 124, 128, 136–37; occurrent, 125–26; as qualities, 122; simple and complex, 130–31
  and image of God doctrine, 134
  and *petites perceptions*, 120–21, 127, 129, 131
  and powers, 118–19, 131–32, 135
  and substance, 13, 14, 16, 17–18
Lennon, Thomas, 7, 23 n. 12, 81, 88–94, 110, 114, 150 n. 15
Locke, John, 3, 4, 6–7, 9, 31, 32, 33, 42, 62, 78, 79–115, 116, 127, 130, 131, 138, 143, 154, 155–56, 178–80, 191, 200, 203, 209, 212, 215, 265, 266
  ambiguity of perception, 83–84
  as bracketing ontology, 79–80, 113
  and concept of substance, 15
  as deontologizing ideas, 28–30, 81
  ideas: abstract, 219–31, 232; conflation with qualities, 106, 109–13; definition of, 84, 94, 99–100, 106–7; as images, 92; as intentional objects, 84–87; as intrinsically representational, 87; as material, 114; as modes, 97–99, 102–6, 108, 112, 114; as objects, 90–92, 100; as particular 85; as signs, 85–87; simple and complex, 89–90, 130; as substances, 102, 104, 107–14
  and knowledge, 84–85
  and material genitive, 93–94
  memory, 98, 102–3, 110
  pain, idea of, 107–8
  and presence to the mind, 86, 87, 88, 100
  and the soul, 101
  and transparency of the mind, 103, 111
  time, theory of, 212
Luce, A. A., 157, 165

Mabbott, J. D., 177, 206–07
Malebranche, Nicolas, 4, 19, 31, 32, 53, 55–78, 80, 94, 98, 100, 104–7, 113, 114, 116, 118, 119, 143, 151, 178–80, 189–91, 208, 212, 244, 246
  archetypes, 60
  dispute with Arnauld, nature of, 6, 72
  ideas: concept of, 55, 58–66, 69; as efficacious, 63–64, 65; of the infinite, 68; as modes, critique of, 55–56, 61, 66–69; similar to substances, 59, 61–66, 70–71
  and imagination, 57
  and mental presence, 62–63, 66, 75–76, 86
  and perception, 61
  and representation, 41
  and sensations (*sentiment*), 56, 57, 64, 100, 104, 106, 151
  vision in God doctrine, 60, 75, 107, 179, 189
Mates, Benson, 7, 117, 119, 136
mind, transparency of. *See* soul, transparency of
mode, 11, 105. *See also* Berkeley, ideas, as modes
  distinct from attributes, 20–21
  as things, 20–22, 24
Molyneux, William, 236
Muehlmann, Robert, 108 n. 23, 139 n. 2, 188, 194–202, 242–44

Nadler, Steven, 58, 63, 106 n. 21
Nelkin, Norton, 108 n. 23
Nicole, Pierre, 41
Norris, John, 7, 98, 113, 190–91

O'Connor, D. J., 4
occasionalism, Cartesian, 52–54
Ockham, William, 37
ontology
  abandonment of, 2, 5, 7, 70–72, 244, 247, 263
  breakdown of, 5, 11
  exhaustive nature of, 3, 11, 20, 22, 98, 141
  traditional, 2 n. 2, 5, 8, 11, 70–72, 95, 99, 101, 115, 139–40, 231, 244–45, 247–48, 254, 257, 259, 263–64

Pappas, George, 219
perception
  and act/object distinction, 31–32, 74, 103–4, 143–4, 146–47, 148–52, 154, 195–200
  always takes an object, 32, 65, 83
  as broad umbrella term, 58, 160
  camera obscura model of, 27
  and error, 206–7
  at a mental distance, 41
  as requiring mental presence, 30, 62
  and nature of ideas, 22
Pessin, Andrew, 122 n. 10

Pitcher, George, 142, 144, 149–50, 154–55, 227–28, 237
Plato, 26, 96, 211–12
privacy. *See* Berkeley, ideas, as private
Putnam, Hillary, 1

Quine, W. V. O., 23, 26
quasi substance. *See* substance, quasi

reification. *See* ideas, as reified
relations, 33, 102, 107
representation, 30, 31, 34, 38–41, 223, 240
  by "calling attention to," 92
  of the infinite, 68
  and Malebranche-Arnauld dispute, 72, 76–77
Ryle, Gilbert, 99

Sergeant, John, 100
soul, transparency of, 56, 103, 111, 236
Spinoza, Baruch, 7, 12, 21, 209, 261–62
Stillingfleet, Edward (Bishop of Worcester), 95–96
Stoneham, Tom, 152 n. 19, 202–4, 207 n. 33
Stubenberg, Leopold, 177, 205–6
substance, 11–20, 254–58
  as atemporal, 19
  breakdown of (*see* ontology, breakdown of)
  as conceptually thin, 10, 254–57, 261–63
  core conception of, 11–20, 35–36, 102 (*see also* ontology, traditional)
  created, 16, 19
  and endurance criterion, 12–14, 18–19, 26, 257–58
  and epistemic priority, 19
  and independence criterion, 14–18, 26, 102
  and mode, 5
  primary and secondary, 13–14, 26, 221, 231
  quasi, 8, 35, 141, 158, 162, 175, 189, 218, 219, 228, 231, 233, 240, 242–45, 248, 258, 265
  as "thing thought," 13–16, 257
  traditional conception of (*see* ontology, traditional)

tale, the early modern, 35, 265–67
  and Berkeley, 139, 147, 172–76, 177, 193, 233, 244–45
  defined, 2–10
  and Descartes, 37
  and Hume, 173, 246–47
  and Leibniz, 117
  and Locke, 87–88
Tipton, I. C., 27, 28, 142

Watson, Richard, 3, 27–28, 30, 70–71, 140, 172–73, 246, 252
Wenz, Peter, 181 n. 8
Willis, Doney, 224–26
Winkler, Ken, 31 n. 23, 32 n. 24, 141–42, 144–45, 147–48, 161–63, 165, 171–72, 197

Yandell, David, 187, 207
Yolton, John, 3, 7, 27–30, 81–87, 88, 93, 104, 173, 248

www.ingramcontent.com/pod-product-compliance
Lightning Source LLC
Chambersburg PA
CBHW021938290426
44108CB00012B/877